ARCHAEOLOGICAL INSTITUTE *of* AMERICA

117TH ANNUAL MEETING
ABSTRACTS

VOLUME 39

■ January 6–9, 2016 ■ San Francisco, California ■

Published by the Archaeological Institute of America
Located at Boston University
656 Beacon Street
Boston, Massachusetts 02215-2006
www.archaeological.org

Cover Illustration: A California Street cable car pauses before continuing its journey to the end of the line near Market and Drumm streets. Image courtesy of San Francisco Travel Association/Scott Chernis

Printed in The United States of America
ISBN-10: 1-931909-33-4
ISBN-13: 978-1-931909-33-4

Abstracts appear in the order of presentation and represent papers accepted by the Program Committee during its review process in the months of April and September 2015. Adjustments to the program or to individual abstracts made after November 30, 2015 are not reflected in this publication.

CONTENTS

Session 7

SESSION 1A
Coastal and Maritime Contacts in the Eastern Mediterranean

CHAIR: *Dan Davis*, Luther College

Discovery of a New Nilometer from Graeco-Roman Thmuis, Egypt
Robert J. Littman, University of Hawaii at Manoa

Beginning in the fifth century B.C.E. and accelerating through the Ptolemaic period, power and wealth shifted from Mendes to Thmuis, 500 m to the south. Mendes dominated its nome politically and religiously for 2,000 years. Mendes led the resistance against Persian rule and was the capital of Egypt during the 29th Dynasty. Two factors dominate discussion of this transition of power between Mendes and Thmuis: (1) the meandering of the Mendesian branch of the Nile, and (2) the influence of Hellenization on the organization of Egypt. The transition of power has been attributed to shifting Nile watercourses and the transition of the harbor from Mendes to Thmuis, in conjunction with the economic development and demographic growth of Thmuis under Hellenism. Excavations at Mendes showed that in the fourth century B.C.E. the harbor on the eastern side of Mendes silted up and commerce moved to Thmuis. It had been suggested from the paleochannels that the Nile shifted from the eastern side of Mendes and Thmuis to the western during this period. We now have proof of the shifting of the Nile to the western side of the city. In 2014, a largely intact Nilometer was discovered on the western side of Thmuis. This is one of only three surviving Nilometers in the Nile Delta. Found as part of the Nilometer was a reused Greek dedicatory inscription from the third century B.C.E.

Tel Akko Total Archaeology Project: The 2014 and 2015 Seasons of Excavation
Ann E. Killebrew, Pennsylvania State University

The 22 ha maritime harbor settlement of Tel Akko, Israel, has dominated the Plain of Akko's ancient landscape for millennia. First inhabited in the Early Bronze Age, Tel Akko served as a major urban center for most of the second and first millennia B.C.E. During the Hellenistic period, the population of Akko migrated westward off the tell to an area now under the modern city and its historic walled Old City, probably as a result of the changing coastline. First excavated by Moshe Dothan (1973–1989), the renewed excavations at Tel Akko (2010–2015) are currently under the directorship of Ann E. Killebrew (Pennsylvania State University) and Michal Artzy (University of Haifa) and incorporate a holistic approach to the region's past, present, and future, an approach we term "total archaeology." Our goals and research questions at Tel Akko include (1) the investigation of Bronze and Iron Age Akko in its role as the major Canaanite and Phoenician maritime industrial urban center in the Plain of Akko; (2) the development of Akko/Ptolemais during the Persian and Hellenistic periods, and especially the significance of the large scale iron industry recently excavated on the mound; (3) the integration of our excavation results with Dothan's earlier extensive excavations on Tel Akko, which remain unpublished; and (4) a comprehensive archaeological field school that incorporates excavation, survey, GIS, three-dimensional documentation and new technologies, archaeological sciences, on-site conservation, and a robust public archaeology program. This paper presents the results of the 2014 and 2015 excavation seasons with a focus on recent discoveries relating to the Phoenician occupation at Tel Akko, including the region's first large-scale industrial iron-working area dating to the seventh to fifth centuries B.C.E., and our community outreach program to Akko's diverse populations.

Navigation and Trade in the Eastern Aegean: Research in the Fourni Archipelago

Peter Campbell, University of Southampton, *Jeffrey Royal*, RPM Nautical Foundation, and *George Koutsouflakis*, Ephorate of Underwater Antiquities

The Fourni Archipelago is a collection of 13 islands and islets located between Samos and Ikaria. Rarely mentioned by ancient or modern authors, the islands have maritime significance. Positioned between harborless Ikaria and the major Ionian cities of Asia Minor, it is Fourni that provided safe anchorages and harbors for vessels en route to the Cyclades or Greek mainland, or up to the Hellespont and Black Sea. While the archipelago was never a major settlement, its many bays were important anchorages and roadsteads in the shifting winds of the eastern Aegean.

In 2015, a field survey was undertaken by the Ephorate of Underwater Antiquities in collaboration with RPM Nautical Foundation with the aim of identifying and recording the underwater cultural heritage of the Fourni Archipelago. While Fourni's terrestrial settlements were minor, the island's significance lies within its maritime cultural landscape. This paper examines the maritime significance of the Fourni archipelago and its use by mariners and pirates from the Archaic through Roman periods. The maritime cultural landscape is presented, as well as archaeological findings from the 2015 field season.

Between the City and the Sea: 2015 Fieldwork in the Harbors of Burgaz, Turkey

Elizabeth S. Greene, Brock University, *Justin Leidwanger*, Stanford University, *Lana Radloff*, University at Buffalo, SUNY, *Numan Tuna*, Middle East Technical University, and *Nadire Atıcı*, Middle East Technical University

Archaeological investigations at the Archaic through Late Roman harbors associated with Burgaz ("Old Knidos") on Turkey's Datça Peninsula have been conducted since 2011, with the aim of exploring the long-term development of the ports and their integration within the urban settlement. As a collaboration between Brock University, Stanford University, and Middle East Technical University, the Burgaz Harbors Project focuses on the changing maritime and economic landscape of the site, before and after the Late Classical expansion of New Knidos at the tip of the peninsula; around this time, activity at Burgaz shifted toward large-scale industry. In 2015, fieldwork and analysis focused on research related to the earliest phases of harbor use. Ongoing excavation in Harbor 1 is providing evidence for the development of Burgaz's initial maritime facility: an enclosed but now largely silted basin adjacent to the city center. The expansion of an excavation area opened in 2014 has revealed well-preserved ceramics and organics.

Within the context of these recent finds, we explore the relationship between harbor and settlement at Burgaz. As the residents' needs and the city's political, social, and economic circumstances changed, so did the urban-harbor matrix. In the settlement's early stage as a center of regional agricultural activity, a single harbor with minimal architectural embellishment may have served as a multifunctional space. During the Late Classical period, however, Burgaz dedicated significant resources to the construction of a fortified port south of the acropolis, which divided the functional attributes of the harbors between military to the south and communication and commercial activities farther north, while retaining physical connectivity to the settlement core. Even after the decline of Burgaz as a primary regional cultural center after the fourth century, the site's maritime connections appear to have expanded again, with an emphasis on industrial and commercial activity that shifted focus back toward the north. While investigations in 2015 revealed clues to the settlement's early maritime connections, that maritime exchange and investment continues at Hellenistic Burgaz even after its presumed "abandonment" should be no surprise. Evidence from the harbors suggests long-term socioeconomic activity along the peninsula in which different small ports and production centers play complementary roles in overlapping local, regional, and interregional maritime networks.

Sinop Kale Excavations, 2015 Report
Owen Doonan, California State University Northridge, *Andrew L. Goldman*, Gonzaga University, *Alexander Bauer*, Queens College, CUNY, *Jane Rempel*, Sheffield University, *Krzysztof Domzalski*, Institute of Archaeology, Warsaw, and *Anna Smokotina*, Krymsky Institute of Oriental Studies

The Sinop Regional Archaeological Project conducted its first season of excavations at the site of Sinop Kale in July to August 2015. The excavation builds on more than a decade of survey and environmental research in Sinop and ties in with the longer-term regional project through ongoing environmental studies, ceramic analyses, and regional-scale archaeological research. Excavations at the Sinop Kale site are expected to continue for at least 10 years and will include excavation of a large precolonial settlement, the ancient urban center, and the history of the remarkable city wall.

The purposes of the excavation at Sinop Kale in the 2015 season included the following:

1) to test the hypothesis that precolonial maritime culture in the Black Sea laid the foundations for cultural and economic developments during Ionian and subsequent colonial systems;

2) to examine the stratigraphy of the city wall and its relation to and impact on earlier occupation phases; and

3) to establish of the first stratified sequence of ceramics spanning the protohistoric to Medieval periods along the north coast of Anatolia.

Remarkable results were obtained relating to all these goals despite an abbreviated field season. Excavations found the first evidence of an Early Bronze

Age settlement in the main town of Sinop, a remarkably diverse assemblage of Iron Age ceramics and architecture. In addition, the stratigraphy related to the city wall was clarified. In our main 5 x 10 m trench, two protohistoric houses of different types, a destruction layer and a Byzantine wall, were excavated. The first was an ovoid pit house with seven courses of river pebbles and a series of ephemeral surfaces and fills with a diverse assemblage of Bronze Age and Iron Age ceramics typical of the north and west coasts of the Black Sea. The second house has a rectangular plan and is associated with Middle Iron Age ceramics from the Bafra Plain and the Anatolian interior. A Late Hellenistic destruction phase was filled with large roof tile, pithos, charred wood, and at least seven ballista balls. A Byzantine outer wall cut the trench in half and isolated these remains.

Two smaller-scale stratigraphic investigations established some initial results relating to the building of the city wall and to an uninterrupted superimposed sequence from the mid first millennium B.C.E. to the late first millennium C.E. These results are highly significant for our understanding of the early Black Sea and demonstrate the outstanding promise the Sinop Kale excavations hold for future research.

Holding Resistance of Ancient Anchor Reconstructions on the Mediterranean Seafloor
Gregory Votruba, University of Oxford, and *Osman Erkurt*, 360° Research Group

The authors have commenced the World Anchors Reconstruction and Experimentation Project (WAREP) in Izmir, Turkey. The aim of WAREP is to test hypotheses for the construction and function of ancient and ethnographically recorded anchors by experimenting with full-scale reconstructions employing the correct materials and construction principles.

Several forms of testing have been completed in the sea, including cast and canting experimentation. This paper reports, specifically, the holding resistance results of 27 different anchor designs, measured on both sand and sea grass (*Posidonia oceanica*) seafloors, the most common types of the Mediterranean littoral. This holding resistance data was objectively measured with a dynamometer, with the anchors being pulled by a winch situated on the shore. Questions investigated include how single-holed stone "weight" anchors compare in efficiency with those with inserted wooden arms, stone anchors vs. stock anchors vs. grapnel designs, wooden and lead stock anchors vs. iron, etc. This experimentation also provides information regarding the distinctions in design of ancient anchors—for example, comparing the holding efficiency of those with or without palms and different forms of the arms, including the V and U of the Roman period with the ubiquitous T and Y forms characteristic of Byzantine times.

The results prove informative regarding the changing efficiency of anchoring over time. Finally, the data can be applied to shipwreck assemblages themselves to clarify debated issues, such as the practicality of the 24 anchors found with the Uluburun wreck assemblage, as well as to further discussion about the nature of ancient seafaring generally.

SESSION 1B
Mycenaean Architecture

CHAIR: *Daniel J. Pullen*, Florida State University

Malthi Mapping Project Preliminary Results
Rebecca Worsham, University of North Carolina at Chapel Hill, *Michael Lindblom*, Uppsala University, and *Rachel Opitz*, University of Arkansas

The Middle Helladic to early Late Helladic site of Malthi in the southwestern Peloponnese is a critical source of information for social organization in Early Mycenaean Greece. Though Malthi represents one of the most completely excavated settlements of this period, its 1938 publication by Natan Valmin is problematic for a number of reasons, including contentious dating of the ceramic sequence and abundant errors in the plan itself. These issues have complicated the integration of this valuable data into contemporary models of aggregation and state formation, which are of particular concern for the Early Mycenaean period and for the question of the development of the palatial center at Pylos and its broader "kingdom," especially.

Toward a reevaluation of this site, a new study of the excavated architecture and topography was undertaken in the summer of 2015 in cooperation with the Swedish Institute at Athens and the 38th Ephorate of Prehistoric and Classical Antiquities. This work included the reinterpretive mapping of all visible architecture using a DGPS and terrestrial laser scanner. Some initial interpretive remarks can be made. First, the settlement was well-integrated into the natural landscape and made extensive use of the natural bedrock, both for building material and to frame entrances and direct movement across the site. Second, movement was fairly tightly controlled and perhaps increasingly restricted, with particular attention toward entrances and routes of approach. Third, it is likely that Valmin was correct in arguing for the planned construction of the settlement as a part of a single, unified project, though the date of this construction is still in question.

The third point is particularly important for the identification of this settlement as the probable product of a hierarchically organized polity similar to the later Mycenaean citadels. The investment of labor and capital necessary for the creation of the substantial settlement wall—more than 3 m in width where both interior and exterior faces are preserved—represents a major undertaking. Several walls of the interior "magazines" are bonded with the fortification and are likely to have been constructed contemporaneously, possibly in sections, suggesting a high level of planning and a preconceived vision of what a settlement should be. Similarly planned settlements may have arisen at the same time elsewhere in the valley, perhaps indicating early peer-polity interaction in this area. Though preliminary, this work has much to contribute to models of state formation during the Early Mycenaean period.

Spatial Analysis and the Study of Mycenaean Architecture
Donna M. Nagle, Florida State University

When dealing with ancient architecture, challenges surrounding the fragmentary nature of the evidence are common. An incomplete understanding of the use of spaces can also complicate interpretations. Two houses from within the citadel of Mycenae, the House of the Warrior Vase and the Room with the Fresco Complex, provide opportunities to test the applicability of spatial analysis techniques. The results of spatial analysis allow interpretations of use patterns and suggest new reconstructions of the buildings.

The ground-floor plan of the House of the Warrior Vase has long been known. The remains of the building as it appears today, however, suggests a different arrangement that contradicts scholarship concerning Mycenaean architecture. The addition of one door into a room previously thought to have been accessed only through a trap door from the floor above produces an axial map that appears to be a more reasonable representation of movement patterns, more so than the original reconstruction. Thus, an alternative reconstruction of the House of the Warrior Vase may be in order.

The spatial arrangement of the last phase of use of the Room with the Fresco Complex has been presented as two units: the ritual core of the interior and three external rooms adjacent to the central court of the Cult Center. Initial attempts to apply spatial analysis to this building used an arbitrarily drawn boundary that enclosed the area of the three exterior rooms. The arbitrary boundary may produce a less accurate result with implications for the interpretation of the use of this area. The proximity of the exterior rooms does not necessarily mean that the rooms functioned as a unit. The Room with the Fresco Complex could best be understood as three distinct units that functioned independently. Axial analysis does not connect the interior ritual space with any of the exterior rooms adjacent to the central court of the Cult Center. In fact, no connection is drawn between the rooms on either side of the round altar. The attempts to analyze the complex demonstrate the importance of the researcher's assumptions and the impact this could have on the analytical results. The results of spatial analysis elucidate patterns of activity and behavior not visible from the plan alone.

Reinterpreting Glas and Mycenaean Regional Political Geography in the Light of Recent Field Discoveries
Christofilis Maggidis, Dickinson College, and *Antonia Stamos*, American University of Kuwait

In the closing years of the 14th century B.C.E., an engineering project of gigantic proportions was realized in Boeotia, which effectively transformed the Kopais Basin (ca. 20,000 ha) into the most fertile plain on mainland Greece. The submerged marshland was artificially drained by means of an ingeniously complex and massive drainage-control system. The Kopais drainage project was colossal by both ancient and modern standards. The area once named "Arne" was still remembered as "multi-vined" in the Iliad (2.507), and Orchomenos as one of the richest kingdoms of the heroic past (*Il. 1.381–82*), whose wealth and power were associated in the ancient literary sources with the cultivation of the drained lake (Strabo 9.2.40; Pausanias 9.17.2; Diodorus 4.18.7).

A vast citadel, today known as "Gla(s)" or "Kastro" (castle) was built on top of an island-like, flat-topped bedrock outcrop encompassing an area of 50 acres (ten times the size of Tiryns and seven times that of Mycenae) at the northeastern edge of the Kopais Basin. Glas has long been viewed as a fortified regional administrative and storage center, maintaining the complex draining system of Kopais and regulating the agricultural production. The citadel was fortified by a massive cyclopean wall with four gates, but only one-third of the total fortified area was occupied, by a cluster of three adjacent and intercommunicating central enclosures. These central enclosures demarcated different groups of buildings (storage facilities/workshop areas, residential quarters, and administrative complexes), delineated their symmetrical spatial arrangement, and isolated these sectors from the remaining vast fortified area, which oddly appeared to be vacant—until now.

This long-established archaeological picture of Glas as a fort was recently challenged. The systematic geophysical survey of Glas (funded and conducted by Dickinson College, INSTAP, and the Exploration Geophysics Laboratory, University of Thessaloniki, under the auspices of the Athens Archaeological Society) established that the citadel of Glas was not left void of structures outside the central enclosures after all but was apparently covered with many buildings of various uses, including at least five large and well-built complexes, extensive residential quarters and clusters of buildings, silos, cisterns, staircases, retaining walls, and terraces. There is a whole town within the walls, whose identification raises interesting questions about Mycenaean regional political geography, the dynamics between this regional center and satellite peripheral settlements in the Kopais Basin, and the geopolitical relations between the palatial centers of Glas, Orchomenos, and Thebes.

The Mycenaean Pendulum Saw: Application, Adaptation, and Reconstruction
Nicholas G. Blackwell, North Carolina State University

Tool cuttings preserved on Mycenaean architecture indicate the use of a sophisticated stone-cutting machine known in modern scholarship as the pendulum saw. No trace of this device exists in the archaeological record except for the physical marks left on worked stones. This paper presents examples of elongated, curved saw cuts on anta blocks, thresholds, posts and lintels, tomb facades, and monumental sculpture while illustrating that the pendulum-saw technique was restricted to two regions in Greece. Presently, only stones from Tiryns, Mycenae, Gla, and Orchomenos bear traces of curved saw cuts, suggesting that the palaces controlled the technology. Although scholars understand the pendulum saw as a suspended blade that swung back and forth to cut hard stones, many practical questions about the device remain. For instance, the blade shape and the design/size of the structure that supported the suspended saw differ from reconstruction to reconstruction. To address these technical issues, I built a functional pendulum saw and tested the different designs. From these experimental efforts, I offer a conclusive picture for how the Mycenaeans operated the stone-cutting machine.

An unexpected observation stemming from my analysis of ancient and experimental saw cuts is that the pendulum saw's design and functionality were altered by masons at Mycenae and Orchomenos. Long, curved saw marks are found along the stomion facades of three famous tholos tombs—the Treasury of Atreus at Mycenae, the Treasury of Klytemnestra at Mycenae, and the Treasury of Minyas at Orchomenos. These cuttings are vertical and were made after the facade blocks were in place (judging by the different block sizes of the stomion), thus eliminating the possibility that a pendulum saw cut them. Rather, masons sawed large swaths of the facade in an up-and-down fashion by adopting and modifying the concept of the swinging pendulum saw. Experimental work tested the cutting ability of this fulcrum-based sawing device. The implications of this study go beyond the revelation of the adapted device and the technical workings of the original pendulum saw. A distinct picture of shared technology and stone-working techniques emerges between Mycenaean centers in the Argolid (Mycenae and Tiryns) and Boeotia (Gla and Orchomenos). Whether the same craftspersons worked at these sites is debatable, but the stone-working links among them are undeniable.

A New Reconstruction of the Upper Story of the Palace of Nestor
Shannon L. Hogue, Xavier University

In this paper, I present a new reconstruction of the upper story of the Palace of Nestor's Main Building. Although the architecture of the ground floor has been extensively studied since Carl Blegen's excavations in the mid 20th century, the upper story remains poorly understood. To evaluate previous reconstructions, I undertook a more methodical examination of evidence for the location of upper-story rooms. By examining the collapse patterns of floor plaster fallen from upper-story rooms together with artifacts fallen from above and architectural features—namely, thickness of walls and locations of staircases—I identify the locations of upper-story rooms throughout the palace, as well as spaces that lacked an upper floor, most notably the Megaron. My analysis allows for the most complete reconstruction of the palace's upper story to date.

Clear evidence of an upper story is identified for 32 of the 57 numbered spaces in the Main Building. Each of these areas had floor plaster fallen from above and walls of a standard thickness, >1.0 m, for the Main Building. Many of these rooms (Rooms 12–24, 29–41, and 43) also had artifacts and wall plaster fallen from above, which I conclude based on their stratigraphical position above fallen floor plaster. Some areas of the Main Building bear clear evidence for the lack of an upper story. These areas include several open-air courtyards and two late additions to the building's northern corner.

In addition, I demonstrate that the Megaron, including the Throne Room, did not have an upper floor, based on the lack of fallen floor plaster or burned debris indicative of a wooden balcony. I do, however, reconstruct the Throne Room as a lofty, two-storied hall. To arrive at a reconstruction of the Throne Room, I pay special consideration to the archaeological remains as well as the logistics of ventilating a room with a large open hearth. This new reconstruction provides a more accurate vision of the Throne Room and a better understanding of the available space when considering its functions. Likewise, a more secure reconstruction of the upper story as a whole creates a framework to contextualize artifacts, thereby enabling future studies to interpret space functions within the palace more accurately.

SESSION 1C
Neolithic Diros

CHAIR: *William A. Parkinson*, Field Museum of Natural History

The Diros Project: Multidisciplinary Investigations at Alepotrypa Cave and Ksagounaki Promontory, 2010–2015

William A. Parkinson, Field Museum of Natural History, *Anastasia Papathanasiou*, Ephorate of Speleology and Paleoanthropology, *Daniel J. Pullen*, Florida State University, *Panagiotis Karkanas*, Weiner Laboratory, American School of Classical Studies at Athens, *Michael L. Galaty*, Mississippi State University, and *Giorgos Papathanassopoulos*, Honorary Ephor of Antiquities, Hellenic Ministry of Culture

This paper summarizes the results of multidisciplinary research conducted by the Diros Project in Diros Bay on the western Mani Peninsula of the southern Peloponnesos. The project centers around Alepotrypa Cave, a massive cave that was used for burials and other ritual and domestic activities throughout the entire Neolithic period (ca. 6000–4000 B.C.E.). Under the direction of Giorgos Papathanassopoulos (Honorary Ephor of Antiquities), the Diros Project was established by a team of international researchers in 2010 to catalogue and publish the materials that had been excavated from Alepotrypa Cave and to survey Diros Bay in an attempt to place the cave site into a regional context. Excavations also were conducted at the open-air settlement of Ksagounaki Promontory, located adjacent to Alepotrypa Cave, where the team discovered evidence of an extensive settlement and burials that date exclusively to the Final Neolithic period. A rock-built Mycenaean ossuary also was discovered on the promontory, suggesting the locale had retained a special importance into the Bronze Age.

Neolithic Alepotrypa Cave: 6000–3200 B.C.E.

Anastasia Papathanasiou, Ephorate of Palaeoanthropology and Speleology

Alepotrypa Cave is located at Diros, Lakonia, at the southernmost tip of Greece and has been excavated since 1970. It is a massive karstic formation of several chambers ending at a freshwater lake. The thick cultural deposits have been radiocarbon dated from 6000 B.C. E. to 3200 B.C.E. corresponding to the periods from the Early to the Final Neolithic. Its use was more extensive during the Late and Final Neolithic periods.

The site was used repeatedly over time for purposes related to a variety of human activities (domestic, funerary, ceremonial) resulting in thick stratified deposits and significant horizontal exposure as well as extremely good preservation of the massive quantity of artifacts and features, such as hearths, clay floors, primary and secondary burials, domesticated and wild animal remains, fish bones, marine shells, botanical material, a concentration of cores and painted pottery, chipped and ground stone tools, bone tools, weaving equipment, figurines, copper artifacts, and ornaments.

This paper attempts an interpretation of the excavated cultural material in light of the last five years of chemical, microscopic, and macroscopic analyses and the research on the surrounding area. The aim is to present the dated stratified deposits and their cultural sequence and, therefore, to provide evidence that will shed more light on the nature of human activities in Alepotrypa Cave during the Neolithic period.

Trial Trench B1 in Alepotrypa Cave in Diros Laconia: Structures, Stratigraphic and Pottery Sequence

Barbara Katsipanou, Ephorate of Antiquities of Messenia, Hellenic Ministry of Culture, Education and Religious Affairs

Trial trench B1 is the oldest trench in Alepotrypa Diros Cave and is so far unique. It was opened in the second-largest room of the cave (Room B), and specifically in the periphery of a large, in extent and depth, tumulus, which contained undisturbed human deposits.

The greatest depth of the trench is today 4.80 m, and its dimensions are 1.80 x 1.55 m. During the long and often interrupted period of the excavation (1970–2013), 15 layers of fill were excavated, which yielded an abundance of human remains, ancient artifacts, and pottery, elements that are dated from the Middle Neolithic to the Final Neolithic. The elements of use of the area, strongly varying in density and importance according to the period, consist of hearths, pyres, coated surfaces and space leveling, special stone structures, pits (Vothros 1), and primary, single and multiple, burials.

The Middle Neolithic in trench B1 is short, with breaks in use but also disruption by pit form formations, with a limited amount of pottery. The NN Ia and NN Ib periods make a dynamic appearance, although at points elements of uneven use of the area appear. In NN II, the layers follow a greater consistency in sequence with a dominating presence of coarse ware, but NN IIb seems more limited, in quantity, regarding pottery production, compared with preceding layers in other spots of the cave.

The total number of pottery sherds from the trench reaches 26,847. Of these, 17.5% are fine pottery and 82.5% are semicoarse and coarse wares. The categories of pottery on the one hand follow the main "common" pottery categories of the southern Helladic area, in both their class of appearance and their main typological features, such as Urfirnis, Black Burnished, Gray Burnished, Matt Painted (with three subcategories), Polychrome, Monochrome Burnished, coarse and semicoarse ware, but on the other hand they are differentiated through the absence of other basic categories, such as Crusted and Pattern Burnished Ware.

The fragmentary preservation of pottery in trench B1 and the advanced wear of the material, raise, at least concerning some particular deposit layers, critical questions regarding the frequency of use and the "functionality" of the area. The pottery from trench B1, with its large quantity and variety of types, styles, and shapes, on the one hand testifies to contacts with important Neolithic sites of the period and on the other hand features an interesting "locality" in pottery production.

The Diros Cave Alepotrypa, Greece, Ossuaries: Performances of Memory in Front of the Dead

Styliani Katsarou, Ephorate of Palaeoanthropology and Speleology, Greece

The aim of this paper is to discuss funerary rituals in Cave Alepotrypa Ossuaries I and II, two of the most prominent sites for post-burial mortuary inside the cave. The ossuaries have so far been studied in terms of the anatomical details of the deceased and their ^{14}C chronology from the earliest Neolithic to the Final Neolithic, which testifies to a long span of burial tradition in the cave. My focus here is on the archaeological context of the mortuary, as can be assessed based on the range of the fragmented vessels and other offerings, and in particular their stratigraphic associations with the disassociated skulls. The overview of the data from the two funerary deposits introduces Alepotrypa to one of the major traditions discussed in the European and the eastern Mediterranean Neolithic, which has involved the establishment of staged mortuary in Diros Cave as part of a transgenerational practice by the living. The rituals culminated by the very end of the period, when the communities inhabiting Alepotrypa were likely to find themselves in competition for the cave space. The mortuary behavior may indicate the deployment of politics of memory by kin groups who raised certain territorial claims.

The Dark Side: Acts of Deposition in Chamber Z of Alepotrypa Cave During the Neolithic Period (Sixth to Fourth Millennia B.C.E.)

Aikaterini Psimogiannou, University of Illinois at Chicago

The Neolithic period in the Balkans and the wider Mediterranean region witnessed the use of caves for several human activities. Of special interest are the burial practices, such as complex ritual and funerary treatment of dead bodies (inhumations, secondary burials, ossuaries, defleshing); in many cases, the skeletal and cultural material was brought into the caves from sites farther away. In the southern Greek mainland, Alepotrypa Cave in Laconia served as such a locus for human burial deposition, possibly among other activities, for almost 3,000 years. In Chamber Z, the innermost and darkest part of the cave, a thick, burned layer of a large quantity of fragmented pottery spanning the time from the Early to the Final Neolithic period (sixth to fourth millennia B.C.E.) has been excavated. The same layer has yielded two human secondary burials, human bone scatter, animal bone fragments, stone tools, and other kinds of material culture. This paper examines the deposit of Chamber Z as the result of mortuary and ceremonial activities involving repeated episodes of fragmentation, dispersal, and selective deposition of broken pottery and disarticulated human remains, in which the Neolithic people were engaged for thousands of years.

Use of Plants and Use of Space in Alepotrypa Cave: A Microscopic Approach

Georgia Tsartsidou, Ephorate of Palaeoanthropology and Speleology, Greece

The study presents the results of phytolith analysis at Alepotrypa Cave, southern Peloponnese, Greece. The assemblages come from two distinct areas of the cave, the anterior (chamber close to the entrance of the cave) and the interior (deepest part of the cave with a lake). The archaeological finds suggest two different modes of space use: a domestic use for the anterior and a ritualistic setting for the interior. The aims of this study are twofold: (1) to investigate the use of plants and the use of space along the habitation history of the cave from the Early Neolithic to the Final Neolithic and (2) to shed some light on the twofold usage of the two areas of the cave.

The results show that the Neolithic inhabitants of the cave fed their hearths with different fuel either based on seasonal vegetation availability, which would point to a year-round habitation of the cave, or because of a need to serve specific purposes. The two areas of the cave show dramatically different use of plant material: leafy wood branches were used for the hearths of the anterior, and sporadic plant remains are preserved in its sediments, as opposed to composted burned dung, together with wood-fed small hearths preserved in the interior, which is rich in organic remains. The activities that took place in the interior of the cave involved the use of dung for fuel parallel to small-diameter wood branches. The excellent burning qualities of dense sheep dung and the ease of transportation of such material as well as of the small-sized firewood to serve for kindling would explain their preferential use in the interior chambers, where access was exceptionally difficult. On the symbolic side, the powerfully evocative atmosphere of the interior chambers would have been further enhanced by the slow-burning glow and smell of dung.

Firewood Use at Alepotrypa Cave: Domestic Hearths and Ritual Fires

Maria Ntinou, M.H. Wiener Laboratory for Archaeological Science, American School of Classical Studies at Athens

Wood charcoal macroremains are a very characteristic feature of the sediments at Alepotrypa Cave, both in the anterior Chamber B close to the entrance and in the interior Chambers D and Z and the chamber of the lakes. The study of wood charcoal assemblages aims (1) to investigate the local vegetation setting at different periods along the habitation history of the cave and (2) to shed some light on the activities that took place in the interior chambers. The results, in agreement with the analysis of other categories of the material culture, support a differentiated use, domestic in Chamber B and ritualistic in the interior chambers. From the late Early Neolithic to the Final Neolithic, the group(s) that used the cave as a short-term habitation space collected firewood for domestic purposes from the local vegetation. The open vegetation growing on the rocky slopes was systematically used for fuel, but through time firewood procurement expanded to the evergreen woodland and the deciduous thickets, probably as a response to higher demand. The rituals in the interior of the cave involved the use of fire. The main fuels were dung and twigs of scrub vegetation (Fabaceae, Labiatae, *Cistus*, and

Phillyrea / Rhamnus alaternus). The use of these light and easy-to-carry fuel types was dictated by the difficult access to the interior chambers. The selection of an impressive setting such as the interior chambers for the performance of rituals was a purposeful act in all its aspects, including the selection of specific fuel types and black pine torchwood brought from quite a distance.

SESSION 1D
Photogrammetric and Three-Dimensional Approaches in Archaeological Fieldwork

CHAIR: *John Wallrodt*, University of Cincinnati

Establishing Best Practices for Archaeological Photogrammetry
Philip Sapirstein, University of Nebraska–Lincoln, and *Sarah Murray*, University of Nebraska–Lincoln

Photogrammetry has become a popular method for documenting archaeological excavations, artifacts, and architecture. Having eliminated the formidable cost and technical expertise required to operate proprietary three-dimensional recording hardware—notably terrestrial laser scanners—photogrammetry has enabled many projects to produce detailed, geometrically clean three-dimensional models of objects, trenches, and monuments. The technique makes three-dimensional scanning affordable and fast enough for daily recording during fieldwork.

Despite the growing popularity of photogrammetry in archaeological projects, practitioners have yet to establish standard protocols for the implementation of this technique. However, there are many potential pitfalls. Most importantly, modern photogrammetry software relies on SIFT/SfM/MVS algorithms that automate most stages of the process. The automation is key to the technique's efficiency and success, but it also leaves the unpracticed user little idea of what the software is actually doing, making it difficult to assess the accuracy of the resulting three-dimensional measurements. Catastrophic failures are obvious, but when photogrammetry "works" we have only a vague notion of the actual fidelity of the models to reality.

In this paper, we discuss recent implementations of photogrammetry for epigraphical, architectural, and survey recording and analysis. Over the past several years, we have developed approaches and protocols for both calculating and controlling measurement error. Critical elements include the use of coded targets in the scene to be modeled and a judicious (but not necessarily expensive) selection of camera equipment. The approach not only accelerates the normal workflow but also reliably achieves an accuracy of at least one part in 50,000—approximately equivalent to a 1 mm error over a 50 m area. This means that photogrammetry can also be used as a powerful new tool for field survey, which can significantly outperform the total station. We discuss the hardware, software techniques, and subsequent analyses that can be done with models surveyed at such high accuracy, focusing primarily on two sites: the Temple of Hera at Olympia (for the Digital Architecture Project) and the fortress at Eleutherai (for the Mazi

Archaeological Project). We advocate for the use of coded targets, carefully selected camera equipment, and a workflow designed to maximize survey accuracy. We believe this system is a step toward establishing "best practices" for rigorously controlled and efficient archaeological photogrammetry in even the most difficult field conditions. We close with a discussion of the new potential for the analysis of monuments and inscriptions through accurate photogrammetry.

Total Paperless Recording of the *Legio VI Ferrata* Camp in the Jezreel Valley, Israel

Michael Ashley, Center for Digital Archaeology, and *Matthew Adams*, W.F. Albright Institute of Archaeological Research

In partnership with the Jezreel Valley Regional Project, the Center for Digital Archaeology developed a fully paperless recording system, successfully deployed for the 2015 excavations of the *Legio VI Ferrata* camp in the Jezreel Valley. All aspects of the recording process were "born digital," harmonized into a single database we call Codifi. All told, more than 10,000 images, 4,000 bagged artifacts and samples, thousands of total station points, hundreds of loci, and 50+ field school students were managed digitally, in real time, by six field archaeologists and supervisors with Codifi.

The poster visually presents the Codifi workflow, tuned through real-time user experiences and priorities. We explore the new touch interface for materials management, including two-click bag-label generation and QR codes, integrated photographs, video, and documents per locus, and automated reporting. Codifi eliminated hundreds of hours of "paperwork" in the field, allowing the field team to focus on field recording, materials analysis, and planning for future seasons.

The results of the 2015 season demonstrate the substantive benefits of paperless recording while putting to rest the reasonable fears to commit to digital what has been traditionally a paper-based discipline by emphasizing a philosophy that assures content is digitally safe, archival, accessible, and sustainable.

Three-Dimensional Modeling and GIS for Temporal Visualizations of Multiphased Ancient Sites

Elaine Sullivan, University of California, Santa Cruz

Scholars of the ancient world seeking to understand complex ancient landscapes (both natural and built) commonly use Geographic Information Systems (GIS) to organize and analyze surveyed or excavated cultural data. GIS places archaeological information within a two-dimensional geospatial framework linked to real locations on the Earth's surface. Human lives are not lived, however, on a flat surface or plane but are embedded within a three-dimensional world. Archaeologists seeking a more contextualized framework for their data must add a third coordinate, elevation or height, to their analysis. Additionally, change over time (the fourth dimension) is a fundamental aspect of human life and necessary for any study that aims to understand human experience in the past. These elements—height and time—are often neglected in archaeological GIS projects. The project 3D Saqqara attempts to create a truly four-dimensional visualization of an ancient Egyptian site. The project presents a workflow for how two-dimensional archaeological data can be transformed into three-dimensional representations of ancient built and natural environments, maintaining the geospatial coordinate system of GIS and allowing for both quantitative and qualitative visual analysis. While the project focuses on Egyptian material, such techniques can be applied by scholars of the ancient world interested in landscape and human perception in general.

Mapping Notion: Noninvasive Survey Using Aerial Photogrammetry, Personal Autopsy, Thermal Sensing, and Geophysical Prospection

Matthew Naglak, University of Michigan, and *Gregory S. Tucker*, University of Michigan

One of the principal objectives of the Notion Archaeological Survey (University of Michigan and Brown University) is to create a detailed state plan of the site. In 2014 and 2015, we pursued this goal using an integrated, non invasive approach that has allowed us to map the urban center of the city in the absence of any excavation. This paper describes our methods and our preliminary results, focusing on how multimethod investigation has contributed to documenting both the standing and buried remains at Notion.

The basic outline of the city plan is clearly visible in publicly available satellite imagery. We have, however, produced much higher-resolution imagery using two unmanned aerial vehicles: a tethered balloon and lightweight drones. The drone photography was used to generate a detailed digital surface model (DSM) and high-resolution orthorectified images of Notion and its immediate environs. Identifiable features were recorded digitally, and documentation at ground level of architectural details, such as material and masonry type, was undertaken with the aid of GPS-equipped tablet computers. In addition to this photography in visible spectra, we surveyed select parts of the site using thermal sensors mounted on the lightweight drones. Due to differential heat dissipation by various materials, this technique proved an effective way of quickly mapping stone structures as well as revealing the presence of cut features, both ancient and modern.

We have concurrently carried out an extensive program of geophysical prospection, which, to date, has mapped one-third of the intramural area of the site with magnetic gradiometry. Where the surveyed area has overlapped with the aerial imagery, the results have provided more detailed plans of subsurface features and have illuminated areas obscured from the air by vegetation. Some results that appear to be of special interest include the extended grid plan of the site and subterranean features cut in the bedrock, including an anomaly, potentially a drainage channel, running through the agora.

In the first two seasons of our multimethod survey, we have revealed features that, when considered together, have given us a better understanding of the city plan. In addition to producing a detailed map of the site, the results of our survey will help determine what areas are most promising for future intensive exploration, including excavation. In this paper, we present the technical results and interpretive conclusions from our integrated approach to surveying at Notion.

Experimental Photogrammetry Methods for Submerged Sites
Douglas Inglis, Texas A&M University, and *Kotaro Yamafune*, Texas A&M University

This paper describes how experimental photogrammetry techniques were used to create a 1:1 scale-constrained three-dimensional model of a submerged shipwreck site in Rockley Bay, Tobago. The authors discuss how the resulting site and artifact models were used for scientific analysis, digital heritage preservation, and as part of an outreach and education program designed to energize future generations of Tobagonian scientists and historians.

Shipwreck site TRB-5 consists of a ballast pile and at least seven cannon dispersed over a distance of 40 m. The Rockley Bay Research Project (RBRP) team identified the site in the spring of 2014 during magnetometer survey and excavated a test trench near a pair of cannon. Preliminary analysis of the artifacts suggests TRB-5 may represent the remains of a warship lost during the 1677 Franco-Dutch Battle of Rockley Bay, though additional investigation is required. The 2014 RBRP team recorded the site using the direct survey method (DSM) and used photogrammetry to individually document the exploratory trench and cannon. However, a complete three-dimensional model of the site was not created.

In 2015, the authors applied an experimental methodology to create a three-dimensional model of the entire 40 m long shipwreck site. The site has a complex surface topography consisting of undulating coral heads, scattered ballast, encrusted cannon, and concreted ferrous objects. To combat limited visibility and the complicated topography, the team combined video photogrammetry of the entire site with concentrated high-resolution photographs to capture areas of interest.

The resulting models were 1:1 scale-constrained using the DSM results from the previous season. Therefore, the site model can be used for precise archaeological analysis, including plotting the positions of artifacts and cannon, directly taking measurements missed in the field, incorporating three-dimensional models from both previous and future seasons, and accurately producing elevation plans.

The 2015 team also created three-dimensional models of the artifacts found in Rockley Bay. Archaeologists used either structured light scanning or photogrammetry with automated masking to capture submillimeter details of the objects. We exported high-resolution three-dimensional models for meticulous archaeological analysis, and artifact orthophotographss to facilitate the creation of precise, digitally inked artifact illustrations. We also created low-resolution, web-friendly models for public outreach and education. Our programming team developed both an interactive website and a new iPad app that allows students, educators, and people everywhere to physically interact with the three-dimensional artifacts and site.

UAV's Prospects for Mapping Archaeological Sites: Çatalhöyük and Isaura Vetus (Turkey)
Maurizio Forte, Duke University, and *Nevio Danelon*, Duke University

Unmanned aerial vehicles (UAVs) are increasingly popular in archaeology because they are user friendly and extremely powerful in the field of remote sensing, GIS, mapping, and digital photogrammetry. This paper is focused on the use of drones for site mapping and remote-sensing classification in two archaeological sites in Turkey: the Neolithic site of Çatalhöyük and the Hellenistic and Roman city of Isaura Vetus. In the first case, the main goal was the study and reconstruction of the Neolithic and Chalcolithic landscape; in the second case, it was the digital documentation and mapping of the site.

The system involves the drone DJI S-900 with six propellers and an 18 mp camera in conjunction with the software PhotoScan and ER Mapper for digital photogrammetry, three-dimensional modeling, and image classification. The aerial photographs are then georeferenced and corrected by a differential global position system (DGPS) with OmniSTAR real-time satellite correction.

Çatalhöyük (Turkey, 7400–6000 B.C.E.), a World Heritage site since 2012, is one of the most famous archaeological sites worldwide and known as "the first city of the world." It is famous because of the rituals, the figurative wall paintings, and the preurban organization of the site as well as the domestication of plants and animals, which is widely known as the first agricultural revolution.

The ancient city of Isauria (Isaura Vetus, 330 B.C.E.–640 C.E.) is a fortified site 10 km east of Boskir in Turkey. The defense walls, still preserved, 3.8 km long, include two fortified gates and 14 polygonal towers. Part of the site is well preserved, but apart from very limited archaeological investigations in the early 1990s, it is still unmapped and undocumented.

The digital post-processing of all these data produced a very detailed digital elevation model, a three-dimensional model of the landscape, classified imagery, and a high-resolution orthophotograph (2 cm of accuracy) of the sites. The aerial survey was able to identify several crop marks, soil marks, and archaeological features not visible on the ground.

Photogrammetry and Aerial Photography in the 21st Century: The View from Methone, Greece

Michael Rocchio, University of California, Los Angeles, and *Hugh P. Thomas*, University of Sydney, Australia

Bridging the gap between academic and popular archaeological reporting has in the past been a difficult and complex process. This involves ensuring that the academic quality of the research is not compromised yet retains the ability to capture the public's interest. Currently, promoting the importance of archaeological sites often comes from static, two-dimensional imagery that fails to demonstrate the environmental and topographic intricacies of the site and its larger geographic and cultural hinterland. Furthermore, emphasizing significant finds that do not match popular preconceived ideas of "important objects," commonly highlighted by museums and projects, can be a challenge.

This paper explores the different ways and mechanisms of using new digital and technological methods, such as unmanned aerial vehicles (UAVs) and photogrammetry, as a mechanism for providing new academic insight as well as maintaining the wider public's interest. Through a combination of aerial photographs, along with terrestrial-based photography, both small- and large-scale photogrammetric models can be produced that provide a new medium in which to present the results of archaeological field-work. Unlike conventional photography or videography, these three-dimensional models are manipulated by both novices and experts alike. Furthermore, simple three-dimensional models can be produced in the field during the course of excavation or as part of subsequent post-excavation analysis. These models can also be uploaded onto the Internet, allowing for instantaneous and widespread distribution in the wider public sphere.

The focus of this paper revolves around the digital recording of the archaeological site of Methone in northern Greece. The site, famously besieged and destroyed by Phillip II of Macedon, who lost his eye in the process, is the current focus of excavations from a *synergasia* between the University of California, Los Anglees and the Greek 27th Ephorate of Prehistoric and Classical Antiquities (Pieria). During the course of the 2014 season, a methodology for the use of this technology was developed, and these techniques were extensively employed in the creation of models, not only of important objects, but also of entire buildings, complexes, and the site itself. In total, 80,000 m^2 were photographed using drones, producing a full site model of the area to an accuracy of 10 mm. The models, along with traditional plans and photographs, add a new method of recording that has the potential to change the way we document and present archaeological information in the digital age.

SESSION 1E: Joint AIA/SCS Colloquium
Globalizing the Field: Preserving and Creating Access to Archaeological Collections

ORGANIZERS: *Sarah Lepinski*, National Endowment for the Humanities, and *Mary Downs*, National Endowment for the Humanities

Colloquium Overview Statement

The National Endowment for the Humanities (NEH) has been a leader in creating access to primary source materials and developing new tools and technologies for the study of the ancient world. Global access to museum collections, libraries and archives, archaeological field data, and scientific imaging is changing the way that scholarly work is done and is providing opportunities to build and integrate new and existing technologies for research, teaching, and public programs.

This session assembles scholars associated with NEH-supported projects with the primary aim of providing a forum for discussion of issues surrounding access to archaeological collections and fieldwork data. Project directors will share their project goals, methodologies, and results with the wider AIA/SCS community. The projects, as a group, engage with collections of field data and legacy materials, objects, and artifacts, as well as archives, libraries, and web resources, and they range geographically and chronologically, encompassing collections from both the ancient and Late Antique Mediterranean and prehistoric North America. Collectively, in terms of methodologies, the projects combine traditional approaches, such as cataloguing and archival work, with the use of advanced technologies for managing, preserving, and presenting data, and they cultivate both academic and public audiences.

Short presentations by project directors will be followed by a panel commentary designed to open up discussion and foster discourse among the presenters, panelists, and audience. Questions and issues to be addressed include the documentation of cultural heritage, information ethics, data sharing, current standards, emerging technologies and platforms, open access, and long-term sustainability of archaeological collections and resources. For scholarly communication in the humanities to keep pace with the sciences and social sciences, it must develop a robust technical infrastructure that is accessible as a public good, that is sustainable and interoperable, and that facilitates collaboration and supports experimentation. Wider access to data about the past can help ensure a higher level of sustainability both for the data and for the field of classical archaeology as a whole.

DISCUSSANTS: *Hugh Cayless*, Duke Collaboratory for Classics Computing, *Jillian E. Galle*, Digital Archaeological Archive of Comparative Slavery (DAACS), Thomas Jefferson Foundation (Monticello), *Sebastian Heath*, Institute for the Study of the Ancient World, NYU, and *Sarah Kansa*, Alexandria Archive Institute

The Giza Project at Harvard: Consolidated Access to the Pyramids
Peter Der Manuelian, Harvard University

The Giza Project, a collaborative international initiative based at Harvard University, has as its ultimate goals the collection, electronic preservation, study, and presentation of all records from the world's most famous archaeological site: the Giza Pyramids and their surrounding cemeteries and settlements (third millennium B.C.E. to present). Giza's archaeological and historical contexts, including an artifactual record of tens of thousands of objects and the decorated, inscribed walls of Giza tombs, provide glimpses into every aspect of Egyptian culture. They offer primary source starting points for almost any conceivable kind of inquiry into life during the first flowering of the long-lived Egyptian civilization. The Giza Project will provide unprecedented access to the site's record across time and space through an innovative blend of old and new approaches to digital archaeology and data management. We unite intensive parsing of diverse, primary documentation with advanced three-dimensional visualization to produce powerful online research tools and new teaching technologies for the world community at all levels of expertise.

Some projects digitize archival collections; others visualize ancient monuments in computer renderings. The Giza Project is one of extremely few to combine both approaches with the aim of comprehensive access to a site, its artifacts, and centuries of documentation from almost any starting point of inquiry—visual or textual in nature, amateur or expert in scope. The innovative facets of the Giza Project are realized through two coordinated offices with distinct production tracks: Data/Informatics (Track 1) and Modeling/Visualization (Track 2). The work of Track 1 (Giza Consolidated Archaeological Research Database, or GizaCARD) consists of the assembly, processing, and cross-referencing of digitized documents and media related to Giza's archaeological record—currently housed in physical archives scattered across the globe in a relational database framework that is logically structured specifically for site-oriented archaeological data. We have assembled archival collections from 10 major collaborating international institutions and continue to build holdings at a scale not previously achievable, all with the aim of producing the most comprehensive repository for Giza's record, past, present, and future. These diverse data types include photographs, excavation diaries, expedition find logs, museum object metadata, architectural maps and plans, epigraphic facsimile drawings of tomb wall scenes and hieroglyphic inscriptions, and (un) published scholarly works.

Our Track 2 (three-dimensional model production) relates directly and operates in parallel with Track 1. We have already made progress in the construction of an archaeologically accurate, real-time interactive three-dimensional model of the Giza Plateau and all its monuments, which is currently available as a pilot outreach website (http://giza.3ds.com). Our plan is to merge the traditional archival legacy content (Track 1) with three-dimensional visualization technology (Track 2), in order to create a free online public resource. This website will include a new form of visual database, a freely navigable, real-time "virtual Giza" that is dynamically and seamlessly integrated with the archaeological database. As a visual and contextual access point to the Giza database, this new interface will act as a front-end three-dimensional graphic "information environment" that embeds rich Giza data sources into their appropriate geographical and spatial contexts.

The collection, organization, and presentation of Giza's archaeological source material via an archaeological framework make up the backbone of this next-generation paradigm for archaeological information management and interactive appreciation. It is applicable to other archaeological sites and indeed to any spatially oriented or site-based data sets beyond archaeology as well.

Who Owns the Past? Evidence, Interpretation, and the Use of Digital Archaeological Data
Jon Frey, Michigan State University

While the move to digital collection and storage of archaeological evidence is generally seen as a positive development, the transformation of predigital records into an electronic format has raised a number of significant issues for many traditional projects. The question of open access is particularly problematic. In this paper, I discuss three specific areas of concern that have been raised in conjunction with the development of the Archaeological Resource Cataloging System (ARCS), an open source digital asset management system for archaeological legacy data. First, there is the question of who should have access to the evidence generated at archaeological projects. Here, the sentiment that information about the past should be universally shared comes into conflict with the fear that the misuse of evidence may lead to widely circulated yet erroneous conclusions. Second, providing open access to archaeological information raises important issues related to the cultural heritage of the nations and groups to whom the artifacts and monuments legally belong. In this case, the digital divide that often separates archaeologists from the regulatory bodies that oversee their work holds the potential to amplify debates over the use of cultural capital. Third, there is the question of how much effort should be directed toward standardizing archaeological evidence to support a "big data" approach to the study of the material past. Because older archaeological projects have often developed their own unique recording systems over the course of decades, there is little interest in expending limited resources on the adoption of uniform naming conventions. Yet without the use of common vocabularies, digital information remains no more "discoverable" than its analog counterpart. While there are no easy answers to these questions, I suggest that we may chart a way forward by addressing in a serious way one of the long-standing critiques of classical archaeology. For if we recognize that cataloguing and classifying ancient objects is merely the first step in the far more difficult process of interpreting the past, we may find ourselves more willing to adopt the open research practices that are inevitably required to deal with the immense complexities of our evidence.

Online Coins of the Roman Empire: An Open Resource for Roman Numismatics

Andrew Robert Meadows, American Numismatic Society

This paper presents the Online Coinage of the Roman Empire (OCRE) project based at the American Numismatic Society, funded under a three-year National Endowment for the Humanities Preservation and Access grant awarded in 2014. The project aims, using principles of Linked Open Data, to provide a multilingual reference and cataloguing tool aimed at curators and archaeologists, while at the same time providing the framework for amalgamation of specimens of Roman coinage from a distributed set of numismatic collections. The presentation will briefly demonstrate aspects of OCRE's functionality, outline the nature and extent of the collaboration, note the way in which this resource has been in technical and practical terms, and offer the audience guidance in how they and others may participate in the project.

Expanding the Archive: The Creation of the Salmon Pueblo Archaeological Research Collection (SPARC)

Carolyn Heitman, University of Nebraska, and *Paul F. Reed*, Archaeology Southwest

In this paper, we discuss the goals, collaborations, and methods associated with the creation of the Salmon Pueblo Archaeological Research Collection (SPARC). The primary motivation for this project is to preserve and make accessible incomparable legacy data from the important excavations of Salmon Pueblo. Built ca. 1090 C.E., this ancestral Pueblo site was the first major colony outside of Chaco Canyon, New Mexico, and was a cultural center on the north bank of the San Juan River 45 miles north of Chaco. The site of Salmon Pueblo is important both for its place in the larger Chacoan world of the 12th century and for its unique archaeological history.

SPARC brings together four institutions dedicated to the preservation of Pueblo cultural heritage: the Salmon Ruins Museum, Archaeology Southwest, the Center for Digital Research in the Humanities at the University of Nebraska–Lincoln, and the Institute for Advanced Technology in the Humanities at the University of Virginia. Through this implementation project, these institutions are expanding the

Chaco Research Archive (CRA) by digitizing archival collections, preserving and improving access to born-digital resources, and developing a relational database to provide integrated access to these materials. This partnership will allow the entire Salmon Pueblo archive to become freely and openly available through their online research portal.

When integrated within the existing information architecture of the CRA, SPARC resources will be distributed to diverse audiences interested in issues ranging from material culture studies, indigenous religions, identity and ethnicity, and the transformation of human communities over time. Once completed, SPARC promises to enhance our understanding of ancient Pueblo culture. Access to these cultural resources will essentially characterize the relationships among the various Puebloan villages that made up the Chacoan world for more than 200 years of human history. Enhanced access to this collection will launch more comprehensive comparisons of cultural practices and forms of interaction across the Chacoan World and facilitate comprehensive research by a much more diverse group of scholars, students, descendent communities, and the interested public.

SESSION 1F
Cultural Encounters and Frontier Interactions: Part 1

CHAIR: To be announced

Building Blocks of a Punic and Roman Community: Excavations at the Lago di Venere Site, Pantelleria, Italy
Carrie Ann Murray, Brock University, and *Clive Vella*, Joukowsky Institute for Archaeology and the Ancient World, Brown University

This field report provides the latest insights into the Punic and Roman phases of life on the island of Pantelleria. Excavations were conducted by the Brock University Archaeological Project at Pantelleria (BUAPP). The results of the BUAPP 2014 ground penetrating radar survey season, as presented at the 2015 AIA Annual Meeting, indicated the presence of a large architectural complex at the northeastern section of the Lago di Venere volcanic crater lake. The 2015 season, during May and June, commenced with the first season of excavation at the *lago*. The initial lines of inquiry focus on understanding the effects on the population during and after the Roman attack of 255 B.C.E. and later Roman conquest of the island in 217 B.C.E.; investigating the supposition that this area contains a Punic and Roman sanctuary; and questioning the role of the volcanic landscape in the development of the area.

The preliminary results of the excavations at the Lago di Venere reveal a complex set of structures dating to the earliest periods of interaction between the Punic and Roman populations on the island. The stratified material dates the contexts from the late third to mid/late second century B.C.E., and the unstratified material shows a broader chronology through the first century C.E. In particular, the ceramics indicate that the Lago di Venere site existed within a central Mediterranean network including peninsular Italy, western Sicily, North Africa, and Malta.

Of central interest are the forms of architecture present, which appear to represent a fusion of Roman and local architectural practices. In particular, nontraditional forms of *opus incertum* and the reuse of building materials suggest a combination of traditional Roman architectural techniques grounded in the use of volcanic materials in central Italy and innovative techniques for dealing with the resources available on this small island.

While the existence of a sanctuary is posited in the neighboring field, evidence from the BUAPP research area suggests activities of a nonsacred character. The excavations have only begun to shed light on functions of this site and its relationship to the other Punic and Roman areas of Pantelleria. This forms the first of three planned seasons of excavations in the area. The Lago di Venere site holds the potential for illuminating the relationship between Punic and Roman communities during and after the Punic Wars through evidence of cultural interaction or isolation. Permission for this research is granted by the Soprintendenze di Beni Culturali ed Ambientali, Trapani, Sicilia.

The S'Urachi Project: Cultural Encounters and Everyday Life Around a *Nuraghe* in Phoenician and Punic Sardinia

Peter van Dommelen, Joukowsky Institute for Archaeology and the Ancient World, Brown University, and *Alfonso Stiglitz*, Museo Civico, San Vero Milis, Italy

Nuraghi, the famous dry-stone walled towers of Sardinia, are usually regarded as prehistoric monuments, because they were first built in the Bronze Age. They continued to be inhabited long after, however, and survived as often substantial settlements into later periods. Even if the later occupation phases of these monuments are routinely acknowledged, they have rarely been investigated in their own right—which is precisely what the S'Urachi Project has been set up to do, as it endeavors to investigate the "afterlife" of one major *nuraghe* from late prehistory through to Classical and Hellenistic times. The Sardinian *nuraghi* are moreover key sites for the investigation of the colonial encounters and cultural interactions between local Sardinians, Phoenician traders, and Punic settlers, because they are the only places that were continuously inhabited before and during the colonial presence of Phoenicians and Carthaginians in Sardinia.

The *nuraghe* under investigation is that of S'Urachi, situated in the Upper Campidano and Gulf of Oristano regions of west-central Sardinia. Standing halfway between the rapidly rising slopes of the Monti Ferru to the north and the extensive salt marshes and lagoons of Cabras to the south, its inhabitants enjoyed easy access to a wide range of environmental zones. S'Urachi is one of the largest *nuraghi* in the region; it is also just 15 miles away from the Phoenician colonial settlement of Tharros, and a rich variety of imported objects suggests that the site has long been a key place of colonial encounters.

The S'Urachi Project was set up in 2013 as a joint project between the Joukowsky Institute for Archaeology and the Ancient World at Brown University and the Museo Civico of San Vero Milis to investigate domestic and public contexts of the first millennium B.C.E. at S'Urachi and to gauge colonial and cultural interactions in the region. The main, though not only, activity of the project is accordingly the excavation of two large areas outside the surrounding defensive wall. Despite their proximity, they are revealing two very different situations that both shed interesting light on domestic life and production at S'Urachi throughout the first millennium B.C.E.

In this paper, we outline the aims and relevance of the S'Urachi Project in both Sardinia and beyond and discuss in some detail the various activities undertaken as part of the project. We focus in particular on the results of the excavations carried out so far.

The Space Between: Location Analysis and Relations Between Military and Local Communities on Rome's Northern Frontier
Eli J.S. Weaverdyck, University of California, Berkeley

I propose a new method for investigating economic relationships between military communities and locals on Rome's northern frontier based on settlement patterns and the settlement systems behind them. This method focuses directly on the activities of rural people and their interactions with military communities rather than on the activities of the army and soldiers. Only recently have the people living in the frontier zone become an object of investigation. Intensive study of rural settlements in the Lower Rhine region has revealed changes in economic strategies but has not been able to link these to the influence of the army. Using locational analysis, I reconstruct the suite of factors influencing the locations of rural settlements and pay special attention to military bases. The spatial relationship between military centers and rural settlements is a fundamental determinant of the potential for interaction between military and rural communities. By focusing on this, I make the relationship itself the object of investigation rather than relying on scarce and context-specific documentary evidence or proxy indicators.

This method also allows me to posit and test competing hypotheses about the army's economic impact. I create "predictive" models using different variables and compare their performance in explaining the known distribution of rural settlements to determine which model most closely approximates historical reality. The key variable that is manipulated in these different models is "market potential," which describes the accessibility of potential customers from any given location. This is calculated in three different ways corresponding to three hypothesized relationships: the military communities could have acquired local produce through market mechanisms stimulating the local economy; they could have acquired what they needed through long-distance supply chains and had little effect on the local economy; or they could have acquired local goods through exploitative means and depressed the local economy. Locational analysis allows these hypotheses to be quantitatively compared, providing powerful empirical evidence for the local impact of the Roman army.

Hoarding Practices and Entangled Interactions Beyond the Roman Frontier
Kathryn McBride, Brown University

[O]bjects are not what they were made to be but what they have become.—Nicholas Thomas, *Entangled Objects*

The socially and politically decentralized nature of the northern frontier of Roman Britain was one of the major factors related to the periodic subjugation, and subsequent abandonment, of the region north of Hadrian's Wall. Although Roman political control was never fully enforced over this area, the material culture remains clearly show that a significant degree of interaction occurred between the native population and the southern occupiers. The ways that Roman objects were treated by indigenous peoples reflects the social values, relationships, and power dynamics between the local populations and Romans, particularly the Roman military presence, within this frontier zone.

This paper explores the entangled nature of material culture at and beyond the frontiers of the Roman empire, through a close examination of the use of coins, particularly of local hoarding practices, in Roman Scotland. The precise nature of coin hoarding within this region during the second and third centuries C.E. illustrates the unusual and interesting reactions of the local population to Roman goods and through them highlights the relationship between the inhabitants of northern Britain and the resident representatives of Rome. I argue that coin hoards, likely entering the region through a consistent and continuous practice of gifts (or bribes) made to tribes in the north, were used within a region with a pre-monetized economy as layered expressions of social status. The social meaning of hoarding in this example serves as a manifestation of a complicated and varied relationship with the Romans living mainly to the south of Hadrian's Wall.

One of the main goals of this project is to reintegrate coins (as a category of material culture) into a broader archaeological discussion. Often coins are used in more traditional numismatic studies, and I hope to instead use this material as a lens through which to view larger social issues and relationships that tend to play out on a material level. I argue as well that coins are a particularly useful medium through which to understand power relationships, systems of value (whether economic, political, or symbolic), and dynamic social interactions, such as those that occurred in Roman Scotland.

Tradition or Innovation? A Perspective from the Mansions of Judaea-Palestine
Shulamit Miller, Hebrew University of Jerusalem

Archaeological research of ancient Judaea-Palestine during the Roman and Late Antique periods has focused mainly on urban planning and monumental architecture. A unique architectural group often neglected is the mansions, whether urban or rural, belonging to the upper echelons of society.

As is common elsewhere in the empire, the society of the Roman East was hierarchical, headed by imperial officials. To propagandize their status, members of the social elite emulated the imperial circle, mimicking their behavior and lifestyle and competing with one another for power and esteem. The homes of the wealthy are excessively large, elaborate, and lavishly decorated, effectually creating a common visual language distinguishing the elites from their surrounding society.

In the current state of research, the evidence from Judaea-Palestine is often left out of the academic debate on elite domesticity, despite the abundance of both archaeological and literary sources pertaining to this region. In the Levant, mansions displaying the attributes of the elite domestic architecture first appear in the first century B.C.E. and continue throughout late antiquity. They are primarily located in urban centers, but extant examples are also located along the rural margins. Similar to their western counterparts, these are opulent complexes decorated according to the latest fashionable trends. Both private and public wings are centered around a peristyle courtyard. Among the various units found within the mansions are reception and dining halls, bathhouses, shops, and storage units, all attesting to the wealth and social standing of their resident patrons.

In an endeavor to reconstruct daily life within these mansions, my paper addresses such questions as, What were the main characteristics identifying the homes? To what extent do local building traditions shape the houses vs. external influences, and from where? How was the internal space organized? Is there a division between "public" and "private" space, and how does it manifest itself? Can a hierarchy be noted by an analysis of the decorative components and their location, style, and complexity? Who used the homes, and how did these dwellings routinely function? Who were the home owners? How did they perceive themselves, and how were they perceived by their society? What may be learned of the daily life of the various ethnic groups, and what was their social standing in relation to one another? How (if at all) do the mansions of this region differ from others throughout the empire, and why?

SESSION 1G
People in the Greek Landscape

CHAIR: *David Gilman Romano*, University of Arizona

When the Streets Had No Names: Shrines and Navigation in Attica
Johanna Best, University of Pennsylvania Museum of Archaeology and Anthropology

Roads served as a primary means for the movement of people and goods in the ancient Greek world, and they also were dynamic, social, and religious spaces. Roadside shrines were convenient locations for sacrifice, libation, offerings, prayer, and protection, and individuals in all walks of life used roadside religious spaces for both incidental and organized worship. Additionally, in a landscape with few street signs, the presence of roadside shrines may have informed individuals of natural resources—such as water or shade—and could have helped travelers with orientation and navigation to a destination.

As part of a larger study focusing on the literary, epigraphical, and archaeological evidence of roadside religious spaces in Attica between the Archaic and the Early Roman periods, this paper examines how roadside shrines may have provided information about location and direction to travelers. Several literary sources indicate that some gods associated specifically with roads were thought to provide directions, that travelers were welcome at roadside shrines, and that some shrines served as well-known landmarks (e.g., the Altar of the Twelve Gods in the Athenian Agora). More than 50 roadside shrines can be identified in the region, and mapping their placement suggests that many sites were located at crossroads and gateways where they would have been highly visible. In addition, examples from the epigraphical evidence support the idea that roadside shrines were landmarks. Some lease and sale records used religious spaces as topographical markers in official documents, likely because many shrines were known and visible for centuries.

The study of roadside religious spaces not only offers a more complete view of the Attic religious landscape, but it also provides an opportunity to examine the concurrent practical uses of shrines as landmarks or "rest areas" that mitigated some of the significant risks of ancient travel.

"Who Goes There?": Discerning Local Identity in the Diros Region of the Mani Peninsula in Classical Antiquity

Chelsea A.M. Gardner, University of British Columbia

This paper presents a new approach to studying ancient identity in regions with sparse historical records, using the Mani Peninsula in southern Lakonia as a case study. The majority of inquiries into ancient Greek identity focus on societies that are situated, chronologically, either firmly within the historical period or, alternatively, within the realm of prehistory. Therefore, there has been an overwhelming separation between the investigation of (1) prehistoric identity through examinations of geography and archaeology and (2) historic cultural identity through examinations of written records and literature. The result of this divide is that investigations of ancient ethnic and cultural identity tend to center on areas with either an abundance or a complete absence of written history.

Regions that have archaeological and even epigraphic evidence of human activity during the Archaic through Roman periods but that lack a proportionate number of written sources are left in the dark. Mani is one such area and can be classified as an "ahistorical historical" region—one that is inhabited within the historical period but that does not itself produce emic written evidence. With this new classification in mind, this paper presents the theoretical methodology applied to understand ancient identity in this remote peninsula and the way in which regions like Mani (those that are occupied within the historical period but that lack historical sources) are still able to contribute to the discussion of ancient identity. Specifically, this paper uses the results of a pedestrian survey in the Diros Bay region to illustrate this "ahistorical-historical" approach to identity on a hyperlocal level.

The Mani Peninsula is in no way unique in that it defies and straddles both historic and pre- (or a-)historic classification. However, the impetus for applying a new theoretical framework for elucidating identity to this particular region lies in the goal of developing an appropriate methodology that is able to be replicated for the myriad regions that elude strict historical categorizations, both within Greece and elsewhere in the Mediterranean.

Size Matters? A Case Study of Population Estimations from the Mani Peninsula in Greece

William P. Ridge, University of Illinois at Chicago, and *Rebecca M. Seifried*, University of Illinois at Chicago

In this paper, we examine the relationship between population and settlement size and how this is used to infer the population density of archaeological sites. In prehistoric contexts especially, the physical extent of a site may be used to estimate its past population. The numbers used in these calculations—"population multipliers" or "density coefficients," for example—are typically derived from ethnographic studies of modern or historic populations. However, these numbers can vary widely depending on the context of the settlement, such as its location in the landscape. In turn, the resulting range in population estimates can produce different pictures of the past, as settlement size is often used as a basis for modeling social organization and cultural change.

Our case study is the Mani Peninsula in southern Greece during the Late Medieval and Early Modern periods (13th–17th centuries C.E.). These periods are characterized by a relatively dense pattern of small villages in a marginal area of the Byzantine and then Ottoman empire that used the diverse landscape of the region. While the settlements were similar in construction style and appearance, they vary in their layout according to their specific location in the landscape. Some sites are spread across the flat plains along the coast, while others are perched atop hills or along mountainsides. Using historic demographic records—namely, Ottoman tax registers and European settlements lists—we examine the range of population densities for a number of settlements from the Late Byzantine and Early Ottoman periods. These data were collected through archival research, field reconnaissance, and remote-sensing analysis of the region as part of Seifried's dissertation research. With this study we hope to contribute to the discussion of demographic analysis in archaeology and thereby add to our understanding of the range and structure of ancient populations in a diverse region like southern Greece.

The Palaea Zichni: The Ethnoarchaeology and Multicultural History of a Northern Greek Town

Stephen McPhillips, University of Copenhagen, *Aris Anagnostopoulos*, University of Kent, *Evangelos Katafylis*, University of Cambridge, *Stefan Lund*, University of Lund, and *Giacomo Landeschi*, University of Lund

The history of northeastern Greece has followed a distinctive trajectory, notably having a longer period of Ottoman rule (1383–1913) commensurate with the empire's first expansion into Europe here in the late 14th century and ending only in the early 20th century, with the events of the Balkan Wars and World War I. Zichni (Ottoman Zihne) had thrived as a market town under Byzantine rule and under the Ottomans saw its economy reinvigorated by investment in new crops: silk and cotton, remaining throughout an area of important Orthodox monastic landholdings and a major pottery-making center. Zichni was a multicultural place with Christian, Muslim, and Jewish neighborhoods, and is mentioned in a great number of Greek and Ottoman Turkish sources. Situated near a spur of the Rhodope

Mountains, supporting seasonal pastoralism, it lies in the intensively farmed foot-hills of the same ranges and adjacent to the irrigated plains of the Strimonas River, all of which preserve many archaeological features and traces of premodern land organization.

Now the site of Palaea Zichni is a rarity in Greece: an important medieval and early modern rural town that is completely abandoned, permitting new archaeo-logical, ethnographic, and historical work to investigate the society and economy of the town and its landscapes over the past 800 years. Its region is still a lived landscape whose population preserves memories of the town, its ways of life, and its death. This presentation outlines the preliminary results of the first re-connaissance work in the summer of 2015, highlighting the significant potential that cross-disciplinary historic landscape characterizations have in providing new perspectives on Byzantine and Ottoman rural history in northeastern Greece. In the context of 21st-century fault lines that can see diversity as a cause of conflict, Zichni highlights a multi-cultural past, when diversity produced a dynamic ru-ral economy and a tolerant urban community characterized largely by peaceful coexistence.

From Kopai to Halai: Towns on Pausanias' Route Through North Boeotia and East Lokris
John E. Coleman, Cornell University

The locations of ancient towns in east Lokris and north Boeotia have interested travelers and scholars since the 19th century. Inscriptions found at particular sites and mentions in ancient literature are conclusive for some towns, such as Kopai, Hyettos, and Halai. However, attempts to assign the names Olmones, Kyrtones, and Korseia to particular archaeological sites have not won general consensus. These three towns are mentioned only by Pausanias (9.24.1–5) on his trip from Kopai in Boeotia to Halai on the coast of east Lokris. I here put forward candidates for Olmones and Korseia that have yet to be suggested and that make good sense of Pausanias' account.

Olmones can be identified with Monachou-Paliochori, a site that has not been systematically excavated about 4.3 km east of Hyettos. Pausanias calls both Hyet-tos and Olmones villages (*komai*) rather than towns (*poleis* or *polismata*). He was clearly mistaken about Hyettos, which was surely a town throughout its existence, but probably correct about Olmones.

Korseia can be identified with remains around the modern town of Kyparissi at the southeast corner of the Opountian Plain, including the acropolis of Kok-kinokastro. Although this site has often been identified as Opus, the metropolis of east Lokris, recent finds show that Opus was in the modern town of Atalanti. Carl Blegen conducted a brief campaign of excavations at Kokkinovrachos and vicinity in 1911, and Phanouria Dakoronia excavated a stoa at the foot of the acropolis in 1978–1979. Pausanias is key to this identification of Korseia, since he places Halai immediately to the east, a detail that earlier scholars failed to appreciate. The ap-proximate boundaries of the Korseia's territory can be traced out as a result of surface survey by the Cornell Halai and East Lokris Project and salvage excava-tions by the 14th Ephoreia of Prehistoric and Classical Antiquities. A fragmentary inscription from Kyparissi (*IG* 9.12.5, no. 1922) likely records a boundary dispute between towns and tends to confirm Pausanias' statement that Korseia was a town (*polisma*).

Kyrtones bordered Korseia, according to Pausanias. The identification of its acropolis as the site of Neochori, 2.8 km southwest of Korseia-Kyparissi and 3.4 km northeast of the modern town of Kolaka, conforms reasonably well to Pausanias' statement that Kyrtones was located on a high mountain that one passes over in traveling to Korseia, and there is ample area in the Kolaka highlands for its territory.

SESSION 1H
Craftsmen and Patrons in the Roman World

CHAIR: To be announced

Cognitive Dissonance in Roman Attitudes Toward Craftsmen
Jared T. Benton, University of Victoria

In recent years, scholars of the Roman world have struggled with a seeming incongruity between how craftsmen were perceived and how they presented themselves. In Latin literature, craftsmen and participation in a craft are presented in a very negative way. This is seemingly contradicted by craftsmen's self-promotion through association with their craft in epigraphy and iconography. Some have suggested that the craftsmen were emulating elite practices or even mocking them with their own brand of self-promotion. More recently, Mouritsen has proposed that epigraphy of this sort was private, hidden in columbaria, and intended solely for the immediate family. But the visual evidence, shop signs and decoration on street-side tombs, would suggest that association with one's craft was also an outward display. I argue that—in a world where social relationships defined commercial transactions—craftsmen were probably unaware of elite attitudes toward them, or at least believed that they were the exception to the rule.

A 2013 Gallup poll showed that, although the overall approval of the U.S. Congress was very low, constituents held generally favorable views of their individual representatives. Similarly, when Latin writers describe craftsmen in general or an abstracted individual craftsman, the characterization is almost always bad. But when a specific craftsman is discussed, a baker or fuller with whom the author has had contact, the characterization is more commonly positive. Moreover, recent archaeological research suggests a close relationship between craftsmen and their customers. Most workshops were small and often integrated into modest domestic spaces. The atmosphere in such workshops was intimate, and the lack of shops or counters in many workshops—other than bars—suggests that customers were also familiar faces.

Roman attitudes toward craftsmen, particularly among elites, were characterized by a type of cognitive dissonance. The idea of craftsmanship and of the uppity craftsman was offensive. But a specific craftsman, a friend or client, may not have incurred such vehemence, at least not directly. Most craftsmen probably had contact with only those elites with whom they had a preexisting relationship. If the literature is any indication, such elites probably held a more positive view of specific craftsmen than they did of craftsmen in general. As such, craftsmen may have remained blissfully unaware of the elite distaste for them, or they somehow believed themselves exempt, possibly assured by their few elite associates. Freed from such stigma, craftsmen could promote themselves through their trade without shame.

Aphrodisian Sarcophagus Sculptors Abroad?

Sarah Madole, CUNY–BMCC

This paper questions the association between an elaborate Roman sarcophagus found in Italy and sculptors from the East Greek city of Aphrodisias. This connection presents a unique case for two reasons: Aphrodisian sculptors famously are known to have participated in the decoration of Hadrian's villa at Tivoli and elsewhere abroad. However, the extensive Aphrodisian sarcophagus corpus pertains to an exclusively local context. In other words, the craftsmen of Aphrodisias traveled; its sarcophagi did not.

This topic is problematic despite its extraordinary potential for helping scholars to better understand the complex nexus of the marble industry around the ancient Mediterranean. Sweeping scholarship has conflated documented second-century examples of Aphrodisian sculptors abroad with mid third-century material. More careful analysis is required to make a convincingly grounded study. To date, three sarcophagi found in Italy have been associated with Aphrodisias, yet only one case, the richly ornamented columnar muse sarcophagus in Pisa, convincingly furthers this claim. The marble of the sarcophagus appears to have been imported from Proconnesus and carved by the hands of Aphrodisian sculptors.

Marble analysis only helps clarify likely quarry sites, yet as scholars increasingly recognize the likelihood of on-site (or geographically proximate) completion of such cumbersome marble objects, it must be that recognizable relief styles bear some relationship with regional craft and reflect the work of traveling sculptors when found abroad. The inherent problems of using exclusively stylistic or typological evidence are considered along with recent studies that explore, for example, the procedural operations of ancient marble workshops. Two other examples, one from Subiaco in Latium, the other now in Lucca, are considered, as is a fourth example found in Thessaloniki.

Elite Competition and the Religious Uses of Statuary in Imperial Italy

Zsuzsanna Varhelyi, Boston University

The abundance of statues in the public spaces in the municipia of imperial Italy has primarily been interpreted within a framework of local competition that followed an imperial example and was also key to the intensive development of physical spaces in these cities. In this paper, I propose that a number of ritual practices engaging statues, depicting members of both the imperial family and the local elite, complicate this picture.

Recent work on statuary in municipal sanctuaries in Pompeii confirms a general sense that statues were often presented in complexes, potentially also including emperors. Thus, the cella in the Pompeian temple of Fortuna Augusta, built in the last decade of the first century B.C.E., included the central image of the goddess flanked by a statue of the ruling Augustus as *parens patriae*; it also housed the statue of the local benefactor, M. Tullius, who financed the building. The placement of this benefactor statue in this most sacred area may be conceptually challenging to us when we consider it as a matter of competitive representation: should we see the individual "divinized" and competing with the emperor or even the goddess? Looking at the placement from the perspective of ritual practice, however, suggests something similar to the apparent comfort with statues of imperial family members even in the temples of traditional divinities: the placement of benefactor statues in sanctuaries represented political power but also religious piety and thereby could enhance any ritual celebrations taking place therein.

Further, I argue that the same complex perspective allowed for the development of ritual engagement with statues in public spaces as well. In parallel with the evolving calendar celebrations for members of the imperial family on their birthdays in this period, almost 20 examples in the epigraphic evidence confirm annual celebrations around statues depicting members of the local elite specifically on their birthdays. A number of these inscriptions also mention the crowning and other decoration of the statues for these occasions, an arrangement in parallel with gods and emperors. While elite competition is an obvious motivation for establishing such celebrations, the interaction with the statuary in these ritualized ways confirms a more complex rationale, one that allows the statues to be engaged as standing in not only for a competitive individual but also for a much desired religious attitude.

Who Bought Bucolic? Sheep, Cows, and Villas on Roman Sarcophagi
Mont Allen, Southern Illinois University

What was the allure of the so-called bucolic sarcophagi that so dominated Roman funerary output of the later third century? Of those many thousands of coffins with figural scenes carved between 250 and 310 C.E., roughly every fourth one featured bucolic imagery; metropolitan workshops, it seems, could hardly crank them out quickly enough, and their scenes of rustic life amid tranquil surrounds went on to define the Roman visual imagination of the late empire. Yet their popularity remains opaque. What resonance would they have had? What, actually, did these pieces show? And who bought them?

Statistical analysis of the roughly 400 extant bucolic sarcophagi reveals definite patterns in the imagery, with a marked preference for depicting certain types of animals, landscapes, and activities over others: purely pastoral scenes heavily outweigh the small number that incorporate agricultural activities; among the former, sheep and, to a lesser extent, goats are far more commonly depicted than cattle or horses. Gaining critical leverage on these patterns requires reconstructing the set of associations and assumptions that Roman viewers would have brought to bear on these pieces. Here I marshal a variety of evidence, both literary (the writings of Livy and Cato on the tension between farming and herding, Varro's treatise on agricultural practices, the rural social hierarchies related in the *Vita Donati*) and archaeological (the booming construction of great *horrea* in major cities during the second century, the ongoing shift in Italy's rural economy toward agricultural over pastoral yield, bucolic motifs on Roman coinage). The resulting picture makes it clear that—contrary to the most commonly accepted theory for their popularity— the scenes on bucolic sarcophagi were pointedly not intended to evoke the rural estates dotting the Roman countryside, nor did they mean to index the villas of Rome's senatorial class. They strove, rather, to conjure up the romantic, hazy, and exoticized landscape of the Arcadian pastoral idyll, an atmosphere thickly Greek. In abstract terms, these findings force us to rethink the third-century disappearance of mythological imagery from metropolitan sarcophagi. They also, however, provide concrete traction in the ongoing debate over sarcophagi's clientele, allowing us to specify which classes and social groups were indeed the intended market for these elaborate coffins.

Bread and Circuses and Basilicas? Reassessing the Basilica of Junius Bassus
Stephanie A. Hagan, University of Pennsylvania

The so-called Basilica of Junius Bassus in Rome, known for its splendid examples of figural *opus sectile* (marble inlay) wall decoration, was a single-naved apsidal hall built on the Esquiline in the fourth century C.E. The basilica has been identified as the domus of the eponymous consul, yet the evidence to support this conjecture is lacking. In fact, the domus hypothesis is just the latest in a number of interpretive proposals that have been put forth to explain the function of the hall. Its extant decoration, with animal combats, Egyptianizing drapery, the rape of Hylas, and a consular inauguration procession, led its Renaissance-period observers to believe that the hall had been an ancient temple to Isis Patricia or the goddess Diana. Later the hall would be identified as a funerary basilica, a library, a neo-Pythagorean *schola domestica*, and a triumphal monument celebrating Constantine's victory over Maxentius, and thus the triumph of Christianity over paganism.

None of these interpretations takes into account the epigraphic evidence associated with the basilica. A well-attested dedication inscription known to us through multiple Renaissance manuscripts (*Codex Senensis* K, X, 35; *Veneto Marciano Latino* X, 195; *Barb. Lat.* 1994) declares that the patron built the hall with his own money and dedicated it auspiciously: "propria impensa a solo fecit et dedicavit feliciter" (*CIL* 1737).

Such an inscription is radically out of place in a domestic context. The verb *dedico* was rarely used with the object *domus* in Latin texts and inscriptions and more typically indicated the setting up and devotion of something (if not for a deity) for public enjoyment or spectacle. Moreover, a patron hardly needed to remark that his house was built by himself with his own funds, since any visitor would have regarded the house as an extension of its proprietor. Emphasis on self-funding is, however, common in inscriptions by Roman magistrates who wished to distinguish between their personal donations and the improvements they made in their capacity as city officials.

Through such inscriptions, we have evidence for five privately-funded forums in Late Antique Rome. This basilica was likely a similar public or semipublic donation, which would have stood apart from the imperial *horti* and elite residences that surrounded it. Emerging from a long period of imperial restriction on public building projects, Bassus' benefaction adhered to a long tradition of civic euergetism with its roots in republican Rome.

Defining Collection: The Villa of Chiragan, Statuary Assemblages, and "Collection" in Scholarship of the Ancient World

Sarah E. Beckmann, University of Pennsylvania

New excavations and recent scholarly analyses have brought attention to the collection and display of both antique heirloom and contemporary statuary in Late Antique villas of the western Roman empire. In highlighting sculptural assemblages found in private contexts, however, archaeologists have failed to provide a methodological definition for how we recognize a "collection" of statuary in an archaeological context. This paper examines scholarly approaches to "collection" in the ancient world, scrutinizing the villa of Chiragan and its statuary as a case study.

Our understanding of collection in the ancient world is based largely on traditions and practices of art acquisition originating in Hellenistic court circles, which, to judge from Cicero's writings and Pliny's letters, subsequently influenced wealthy Romans in the late republic and early empire. Thus, texts on collecting practices are regularly used to interpret archaeological assemblages of sculpture as material evidence of elite status assertions and power maneuvers within a highly social world. Yet the link between texts and extant material culture is tenuous, and archaeological interpretations must stem from analysis of the objects themselves. With this in mind, I ask how we define "collection" in archaeology, since extant assemblages of sculpture vary greatly in both quantity and quality, and the demarcation between "assemblage" and "collection" is rarely clear.

To test whether it is possible to establish guidelines for identifying antique collections of art, I examine the sculptures from the villa of Chiragan in southwestern France, where more than 200 pieces were excavated in the late 19th century. The assemblage includes sculptures from the first to fourth/fifth centuries C.E.: freestanding statues and statuettes, reliefs, and imperial and private portrait busts. Though recent studies have reexamined the villa's imperial busts and Late Antique mythological statuettes, the extant assemblage has not yet been fully synthesized. I present the villa's statuary and ask whether the discovery of sculptures at a single, residential site is sufficient proof to term them the vestiges of a larger collection of art. I further ask whether the existence of sets and groups of sculptural types within a larger assemblage adds or detracts from our understanding of ancient art collection and how we might move forward archaeological interpretations of Late Roman villas and their decor.

SESSION 1I
The Archaeology of Greece in Late Antiquity

CHAIR: *William Caraher*, University of North Dakota

House Size and Elite Inequality in Roman Greece
Kilian P. Mallon, Stanford University

This paper aims to speak to the debate about the nature of the economy in Roman Greece. Since the 1970s, the discovery of vast quantities of Roman ceramics traveling all across the eastern Mediterranean has confounded earlier notions of impoverished fifth and sixth centuries. Historians and archaeologists have worked to understand and explain this efflorescence in the Late Roman economy. However, the economics of Roman private housing and its development from the first to sixth centuries in Greece has remained neglected by comparison. My argument in this paper is that the elite across Roman Greece took advantage of the general growth in the economy to marshal resources for building enormous houses. A large data set of known house sizes throughout the period shows that, although excavation in Greece has disproportionately recorded enormous urban houses instead of smaller impoverished dwellings and rural settlements of the Roman era, the overall number of large houses and the level of inequality among the largest houses both rose markedly from the third century onward. Stagnation in the first and third centuries gave way to significant growth in the Greek economy of the fourth through sixth centuries. Additionally, the largest houses often became palace-like. They took on nonresidential functions normally reserved for temples, churches, or the forum. After the emergence of the Dominate, the elite turned their public spending from the city to their homes by moving political, social, and religious functions into their own domestic sphere. This pattern appears different from that seen in Syria and other parts of the eastern Mediterranean in the same period, where house sizes are more equal. While there remains debate about the exact causes of the Late Roman efflorescence and their relative weight, importance, and sequence, it is clear that Late Roman economic success in Greece benefited the wealthy most by the concentration of wealth and power in enormous private houses. This centralized Late Roman economic power allowed the elite to exponentially outstrip the rest of society in ways not possible in the Early Roman, Hellenistic, or Classical periods.

Keeping an Even Temper in Times of Trouble: Continuity and the Maintenance of Ceramic Traditions in Late Roman Corinth
Mark D. Hammond, AIA Member at Large, and *Heather Graybehl*, AIA Member at Large

Throughout the seventh century, the eastern Roman empire fell victim to numerous catastrophes, with much of southern Greece commonly understood to have succumbed to desolation by the end of the sixth century. While the results of archaeological excavations by the American School of Classical Studies at Corinth have recorded decreases in imported pottery and coins and revealed that the urban fabric of the Roman city was no longer maintained by the later sixth and seventh centuries, research in recent decades has advanced the identification of seventh-century pottery and offered new evidence and interpretative methods that are slowly pulling Corinth's later settlement from obscurity. This paper is based on the study of Late Roman (late fourth- to seventh-century) ceramics recovered from the excavations of the Panayia Field in Corinth. Employing typological and fabric analyses, supplemented by petrographic analysis, we identify and characterize not only the long-distance imports but also the numerous ceramic products from regional (southern Argolid fabric, Boeotian fabric) and local (northeast Peloponnesian cooking fabric, Late Roman Corinthian lamp fabric) sources. These regional and local potters continued to manufacture standardized and high-quality ceramics in a variety of classes and shapes into, and in the majority of cases throughout, the seventh century. Thus, access to regional and local ceramics, and the manufacturing traditions practiced within each workshop, remained unbroken, contributing to the argument for Corinth's continuity throughout this troubled century.

Manufacture of high-quality ceramics represents no small feat: as these potters likely operated at a level characterized by D.P.S. Peacock's model of a nucleated workshop (*Pottery in the Roman World: An Ethnographic Approach* [London 1982] 9, 38–43), various logistical considerations (such as raw-material procurement, labor, and transportation of finished products) would have necessitated substantial investment in organization and infrastructure. In the case of the workshop using northeast Peloponnesian cooking fabric, its production was not only maintained but also significantly expanded throughout the late sixth and the seventh century to account for increasingly more forms among its output. The presence of imports is typically taken to represent a thriving economy and their absence a crisis and gap in supply that a desperate population fills by resorting to local production; taking the opposite approach, this paper furthers the argument against the "decline and fall" of Late Roman Corinth by emphasizing the considerable financial and administrative resources that were required to maintain the city's sources of regional and local ceramics.

Local Prosperity and Regional Economy in Roman to Early Byzantine Greece: The American Excavations at Kenchreai, 2014–2015

Joseph L. Rife, Vanderbilt University, *Jorge J. Bravo III*, University of Maryland, College Park, and *Sebastian Heath*, Institute for the Study of the Ancient World, New York University

The American Excavations at Kenchreai have begun a new phase of exploration at the eastern port of Corinth that is uncovering important evidence for the vitality of regional commerce and local prosperity in Roman to Early Byzantine Greece. Working under the auspices of the American School of Classical Studies and with the permission and oversight of the Greek Ministry of Culture and Corinthian Ephoreia in 2014 and 2015, our team is studying an expansive building found during salvage excavations by the Archaeological Service in 1976.

The Threpsiades site is located ca. 25 m west from the modern shoreline and the middle Roman quay. In 2014, we cleared the site, and in 2015 we exposed architecture for recording by three-dimensional photogrammetry, digital model-ing, and GIS integration. Although not fully excavated, the building has an im-pressive two-story plan with an ornate central peristyle bounded by wide halls opening into spacious rooms and a massive stairwell. In addition to conducting fieldwork our team is examining more than 100,000 objects saved from the site in 1976. This rich assemblage chiefly represents activity during the early seventh cen-tury. Among the pottery, we have identified imported and regional table and cook-ing wares; hundreds of amphoras from Palestine, North Africa, and the Argolid, including both big and small versions of Late Roman Amphora 2; and numerous stoppers and funnels. Lamps include North African imports, regional imitations, and a conical-stepped lamp from the Middle East that is unparalleled in Greece. The abundant glass includes cylinder-blown window panes and eastern spherical flasks.

Our study of these remains offers new perspectives on the history of Kenchreai and its region. The building's design and decoration enrich our impression of a busy port town characterized by monumental wealth during the Middle to Late Roman periods. The pottery and glass point not only to thriving exchange be-tween the Aegean port and North Africa, Asia Minor, and Syria-Palestine into the seventh century C.E. but also to dynamic communication within the northeastern Peloponnese. The complex seems to have served as a distribution center for com-modities, whether as an independent facility or as an annex to a productive villa, perhaps like one found south of the basilica at Lechaion. Our future plans include integrating these discoveries on the Threpsiades property into the history of the port as a whole, final publication of architecture and artifacts, and conservation to prepare the site for public display.

Market Access in Late Antique Thrace: The Ceramic Perspective from Molyvoti

Alistair Mowat, University of Manitoba, *Nicholas Hudson*, University of North Carolina–Wilmington, and *Thomas F. Tartaron*, University of Pennsylvania

The intensive archaeological survey of the Molyvoti Peninsula (2014–present), 25 km southwest of Komotini, has revealed multiple discrete concentrations of pottery dating to the Late Roman and Early Byzantine periods (fourth to seventh centuries C.E.). The pottery collected from these concentrations was consistently domestic in nature and may represent small settlements or farmsteads. One of the largest settlements, covering approximately 6 ha, yielded a dense concentration of pottery with a limited date range of the mid sixth to early seventh century C.E. The size, location, and topography of the site, including a promontory overlooking two sheltered beaches, may suggest that it served as a centralized port. The collect-ed pottery included enough imported amphoras and fine wares to allow for some initial observations to be made on the nature of access the site and its environs had to regional markets. Of particular note is the regular presence of North African im-ports from the Late Roman and Early Byzantine settlement. While North African products, amphoras, and African Red Slip fine ware do not make up a major com-ponent of the imported ceramic evidence, they do constitute a constant presence, approximately 10% of the imported amphoras or fine wares in the assemblage. By contrast, the most common imported fine ware at the site is Phocaean Red

Slip from Asia Minor, along with the second-most common amphora, Late Roman Amphora 1 from Cilicia and the eastern Aegean. The most common amphora type, Late Roman Amphora 2, was produced across the Aegean, including sites in mainland Greece, an area not represented in the fine wares.

Our initial analysis of the imported amphoras and fine ware imports addresses the character of regional markets' access to imported goods, including both agricultural products (wine and oil) and nonagricultural consumables (pottery). This flow of goods to the site contributes to our economic and social understanding of the Thracian regional market, which was part of an important agricultural zone for Late Antique Constantinople. The question of directional flow of goods in relation to Constantinople is raised in light of historical documentation that Thrace was a conscripted source of grain for the city under Justinian (Procopius, *Secret History* 22). Did such conscription result in an open flow of goods to and from Constantinople, or was it unidirectional? Similarly, to what extent did this role in the imperial economy benefit supplier regions like Thrace, and the Molyvoti area in particular?

Excavation in the Late Antique City at Golemo Gradište, Konjuh, 2014–2015

Carolyn S. Snively, Gettysburg College, and *Goran Sanev*, Archaeological Museum, Skopje

The international project under the auspices of Gettysburg College and the Archaeological Museum in Skopje, Republic of Macedonia, continued work in the anonymous Late Antique city at Golemo Gradište, village of Konjuh, in the 2014 and 2015 seasons. In keeping with long-term goals of investigation of ecclesiastical architecture and the urban plan, excavations were conducted mainly in a Christian basilica and a large residence in the lower city on the northern terrace of the site.

The L-shaped Northern Residence stood only a few meters north of the basilica. In 2014, a new wall came to light, running north from the north wall of the basilica and forming the west wall of the residential complex. But several meters south of the north wall of the residence the wall turned a corner and ran west. Investigation in 2015 showed that that this wall and others continued to the west but provided no evidence for the function of this northwestern extension of the building. In the space between the west wall and the southeast wing, several pits were discovered. Two skeletons had apparently been thrown into one pit; a cist grave had been placed partly above and partly beside a second pit. A colonnade marks the north edge of a roughly paved street running along the north wall of the residence.

In the basilica, now identified as an episcopal church, investigation continued in the southern and western annexes. Two rooms with benches occupy the southwestern part of the structure. North of the second room is an exo-narthex; walls running west from it raise the possibility of an atrium located to the north of the main axis of the church. Along the south side of the basilica, excavation of the baptismal complex discovered in 2013 was completed. It consisted of an entrance corridor and two rooms that communicated through a doorway, whose position explains the off-center location of the piscina within the eastern apsidal room.

Recent discoveries in both church and residence add new details to our understanding of both the urban arrangement and the brief history of this unusual Late Antique Balkan city.

SESSION 1J
Histories of Classical Collecting

CHAIR: *Giovanna Ceserani*, Stanford University

A Fifth-Century (hypen) Grave Stele of a Greek Athlete in the Vatican Museums and Its Afterlife in the City of Rome
Gabriella Cirucci, Scuola Normale Superiore, Pisa

This paper focuses on a marble funerary stele showing an athlete with a younger attendant in the Museo Gregoriano Profano. The discussion aims to enlighten the several transformations it underwent as it transitioned from its original setting over the centuries by addressing aspects of its complex history that are still controversial. Typology, style, and iconography allow us to consider the stele as a product of a Greek workshop dating around the middle of the fifth century B.C.E., although its geographical frame is still debated. Its precise findspot is not recorded, but there is sufficient evidence to support that it was discovered in Rome, where it had been moved in antiquity. Originally meant to represent and praise a deceased, this image of a nude athlete embodied values, rituals, and beliefs that were related to the identity of the Greek polis community. Since the same image was inappropriate for a Roman deceased, however, it is improbable that the relief maintained the same function in Rome. In this vein, M. Bell (in *Horti Romani*, edited by M. Cima and E. La Rocca [Roma 1998] 295–314) has assigned the stele to the decoration of the Esquiline *horti*, where other Greek funerary reliefs of the fifth century B.C.E. were unearthed in different times. His suggestion, increasingly accepted by scholars, is that the gravestones were purchased by Maecenas to recreate a refined evocation of the Athenian Kerameikos Cemetery in his gardens. This paper revises this interpretation by further investigating the provenance of the Vatican stele and its alleged belonging to a sculptural ensemble set up in the gardens of Maecenas. By questioning the identification of a specific decorative program in the *horti Maecenatis*, the research offers deeper insight into the mobility and transformation of the sculptural decoration of the Esquiline gardens over time. The function and meaning of the athlete relief in Rome is also considered in light of the popularity of Greek athletic images in Roman villas, recently addressed by Z. Newby, *Greek Athletics in the Roman World* (Oxford 2005). By revising the current interpretation of the Vatican stele, this paper intends to achieve a better understanding of how meaning was added to (or subtracted from) this object and how many transitions it underwent until our times. This new perspective also helps illuminate overlooked aspects of the circulation of artifacts looted from Greek cemeteries in the ancient Roman art market.

The House of Sallust in 1840: The Aschaffenburg Model in the Pompeianum of King Ludwig I
Anne Laidlaw, Johns Hopkins University

In 2012 at the Gold Medal Symposium for Lawrence Richardson, I gave a preliminary report on the excavations in the House of Sallust in Pompeii. John

Humphrey has now published our final study as *JRA* Supplement 98 (Portsmouth, R.I. [2014]). This was intended to be the definitive publication, the result of more than fifty years of research.

However, almost as soon as our book was distributed, Valentin Kockel of the University of Augsburg informed me of a remarkably complete model of the house, made for King Ludwig I in 1840, which is presently on display at the Pompeianum Museum in Aschaffenburg near Frankfort. Here I present the new information from this model, with comparisons from the extant remains.

The model was made by Agostino Padiglione, and the decorations were painted by Giuseppe Abbate. Their work was based on observations and detailed measurements made in Pompeii and was intended as a precise archaeological record of the actual state of the building at that time. At a scale of 1:50, it is double the scale of the well-known model now in the Naples Museum. Thus, it depicts the house as it was some 30 years earlier, when it was in a far better state of preservation.

What the Aschaffenburg model shows us is basically the Augustan reconstruction, as modified up to 79 C.E. Abbate's meticulous copies of the First and Third Style paintings and the patterns of the pavements are a precise and accurate record of what was still extant in the 1840s. Padiglione's model also provides us with a complete three-dimensional view of the southeast corner, the peristyle and kitchen and back rooms that were totally destroyed in World War II. His careful reproduction of details of the second story, eliminated in the reconstruction of 1970, also confirms or, in a few instances, modifies hypotheses that we have proposed about these lost structures.

The Metropolitan Museum of Art's Classical Collection in Its Early Years
Elizabeth Bartman, AIA-New York Society

Classical art was central to the vision and mission of the Metropolitan Museum of Art from its founding in 1870 through the 1940s. Indeed, the active stewardship of two early directors, Luigi Palma di Cesnola (1879–1904) and Edward Robinson (1910–1931), propelled the collection of what came to be called the Greek and Roman Department to the preeminence among American institutions that it has still today.

But how was "classical" defined? To a large extent, the Metropolitan's collection embodied the aesthetic values of Enlightenment Europe in the 18th century, when Johann Winckelmann espoused Greek art as the pinnacle of aesthetic taste. In the Enlightenment hierarchy, all other ancient cultures produced inferior art. This paper examines how that mentality played out in the collection's formative years: from accession to display to publication, Etruscan, Roman, and Cypriot art all were marginalized in relation to Greek. Curator Gisela Marie Augusta Richter was Greek art's most vocal champion.

Supplemented by plaster casts of important antiquities belonging to other museums, the Classical Collection anchored the museum's narrative of human artistic achievement. In the context of a universal art museum like the Metropolitan, however, the collection inevitably skewed toward the aesthetic and away from the social and historical dimensions that archaeology had been illuminating so brilliantly since the 19th century. Although the department briefly displayed objects of "daily life" in a discrete gallery, it did not itself undertake excavations such as those that brought wax tablets from Karanis to Ann Arbor or mosaics from Antioch to Princeton and Worcester. Historically, this divide between aesthetic and archaeological—often disparagingly called "antiquarian"—has riven museums with collections of antiquities, leaving a legacy that continues today.

Classical Sculpture and Eugenics at the 1915 Panama-Pacific International Exhibition in San Francisco

Mireille M. Lee, Vanderbilt University

The role of ancient sculpture in the modern eugenics movement has not received the scholarly attention it deserves. Certainly the influence of classical forms on Nazi artists is well attested, from the idealized figural sculptures of Arno Breker to Leni Riefenstahl's famed propaganda film *Olympia*. But such imagery was not pure invention by the Third Reich. In the early 20th century, the progressive eugenics movement embraced classical sculpture as an illustration of the benefits of proper human breeding. This paper analyzes the use of classical sculpture and classicizing imagery in the display of the Race Betterment Foundation at the 1915 Panama-Pacific International Exhibition in San Francisco, which is celebrating its centenary this year.

The Race Betterment Foundation was established by John H. Kellogg, the inventor of Corn Flakes cereal and chief medical officer of the Battle Creek Sanitarium. Its membership included physicians, scientists, church leaders, and intellectuals. The Second Conference of the Foundation coincided with the Panama-Pacific Exhibition, and the leaders of the group took full advantage of the large numbers of visitors to the fair to disseminate their ideas. The Race Betterment booth, installed in a prominent location in the Education and Social Economy building, was among the most popular of the exhibition. The exterior of the display was adorned with photographic reproductions of Greek and Roman sculptures, including the Nike of Samothrace and the so-called Diana of Versailles, interspersed with images of classicizing sculptures of mothers with their babies and vigorous, healthy youths. The interior featured more photographs with didactic texts, as well as plaster casts of the Knidian Aphrodite, Apollo Belvedere, and the Farnese Atlas. Advertising itself as "a popular non-sectarian movement to advance life saving knowledge," the Race Betterment Foundation established a "Eugenics Registry" to create an "aristocracy of health" and, ultimately, racial perfection. The profusion of classicizing imagery in the display clearly illustrated the goals of eugenics.

Elsewhere in the exhibition, the imagery of the classical past was consciously employed to create a vision of a new, utopian, future. Classicizing buildings and sculptures permeated the fairgrounds. The official fair poster featured Hercules excavating the Panama Canal as his "thirteenth labor." All these images were intended to create a beautiful, idyllic past, present, and future for the still-young state of California—and to hide the ugly realities of racism and forced sterilization that were suffered by many.

Soldiers in "A Country Rich in Monuments": Allied Military Personnel as Tourists at Pompeii, 1943–1945

Nigel D. Pollard, Swansea University

This paper examines the experience of visiting the ancient site of Pompeii in 1943–1945 through materials produced to guide visitors and through memoirs and diaries of Allied service personnel. It considers how rank, socioeconomic and educational background, gender, and nationality both affected and reflect this experience and the visitors' responses to the remains of Roman antiquity.

In Italy during World War II, Allied military personnel were actively encouraged to visit cultural sites, including remains of Greek and Roman antiquity in Sicily, Campania, and Latium. Transport and official tours were provided, and many troops visited such sites on individual initiative or in small informal groups organized by their units. An extraordinary range of guidebooks and other materials were produced, many by the military authorities (the Monuments, Fine Arts and Archives Sub-Commission "Monuments Men," the British Army Educational Service, and Base, Corps and Army Headquarters). Others, particularly for Pompeii, were written, translated, and published by Italian civilians for commercial purposes.

The reasons for these official efforts and encouragement were twofold. One was the perception by many Allied politicians and senior commanders that the citizens of liberal democracies such as the United Kingdom and the United States made better soldiers when educated about the reasons for fighting and about the wider historical and cultural contexts of the war. The second was the Allies' attempt to secure moral high ground by explicit respect for the remains of the past, exemplified by Eisenhower's Allied General Order on the protection of monuments (29th December 1944) in which he described Italy as "a country which has contributed a great deal to our cultural inheritance, a country rich in monuments which . . . helped and now . . . illustrate the growth of the civilization that is ours." These motives enabled many men (and some women) to visit ancient sites that they would never have had the opportunity to see but for the war, in a democratic "Grand Tour" unrivaled until the advent of mass tourism.

Protection of heritage sites in conflict zones is of particular current interest and importance, and the experiences of World War II "Monuments Men" inform contemporary policy and practice in cultural property protection. Given the damage done to heritage sites in recent conflicts by occupying military personnel, a comparative historical study of troops' attitudes to such sites is of considerable value, and these materials from World War II provide an important and unique body of evidence for such research.

SESSION 2A
Current Issues in Heritage Management

CHAIR: *Elizabeth S. Greene*, Brock University

Integrating Conservation Data to Improve Access and Preservation: Case Studies from Open Context
Eric Kansa, Open Context

Information about the conservation status of an archaeological site is critical to developing a successful conservation plan. Though this information exists for many sites, the inability to access, manage, and manipulate it puts sites at risk. This paper presents data-sharing methods and practices that facilitate discovery and understanding of archaeological conservation data. This work builds on Open Context's (http://opencontext.org) archaeological data publication services to attempt to meet the professional needs of cultural heritage conservation. Relating conservation data to other critical information (archaeological documentation, museum collections) provides a more accurate, detailed, and accessible record of the entire history of an archaeological site. Incorporating conservation data sets into larger bodies of archaeological documentation will help ensure that critical relevant information will not be left in isolation.

The paper presents case studies from artifact conservation at Poggio Civitate and examples of architectural conservation from urban sites in the Near East and eastern Mediterranean. Because of the archaeological, historical, political, diplomatic, and economic issues surrounding heritage conservation, treatment of conservation information needs to be considered in light of larger "Open Government" and "Open Data" initiatives. Thus, this paper highlights licensing issues, international data standards, and the larger policy concerns that arise from including conservation information with data access and preservation. With support from the J.M. Kaplan Fund, this work helps conservation documentation to be recognized as an integral part of understanding and preserving the past.

Volunteer Site Stewardship in California
Beth Padon, Discovery Works, Inc.

Since 1999, the California Archaeological Site Stewardship Program (CASSP) has trained members of the public to become volunteer site stewards, who help protect archaeological sites on public lands by visiting assigned sites and reporting on their conditions.

More and more archaeological sites on public lands are suffering damage from visitor impacts. The Internet provides multiple sources of information about sites, even in isolated locations, and it's easier to get to sites with high-clearance vehicles and GPS guidance.

The effects of climate change also damage archaeological sites through increased wind and water erosion, lake and reservoir fluctuations, rising sea level, wildfires, and other changes in natural conditions.

Volunteer site stewards help deter vandalism through their presence and by telling other visitors how to behave at archaeological sites. They help identify problems before greater damage is done. Volunteers also present challenges. Because volunteers are not paid, organizations typically spend less time and money to supervise and train them, which can diminish their effectiveness and retention. And volunteers require an up-front investment in training, which will not be recovered if they do not stay.

At the 2015 annual meetings of both the Society for California Archaeology and the Society for American Archaeology, symposiums were held on volunteer site stewardship. The symposium panels raised important questions. Why do people volunteer as site stewards? Do site stewards make a difference? Have they contributed to greater protection? Have they helped the agency reach its goals? How are volunteers selected, and trained, and kept motivated? How is confidentiality of site locations maintained? Where do we find stable funding for site stewardship programs?

From recent conversations about these questions with CASSP volunteers and the agency archaeologists who work with them, and from 16 years of experience in coordinating CASSP, we offer some conclusions about ways that site stewardship can be improved, in California and beyond the state's borders. We present goals for future efforts and describe steps that have already been taken towards them.

Única al Món: Heritage Management in Menorca, Spain
Zoe P. Strassfield, New York University

In January 2013, the Spanish Ministry of Education, Culture, and Sport submitted an application to UNESCO to have 25 sites on the Mediterranean island of Menorca associated with the pre-Roman Talayotic culture added to the World Heritage List. If approved, this status would come in addition to the designation as a UNESCO Biosphere Reserve that Menorca has possessed since 1993. Menorca, sometimes spelled in English as "Minorca," is the easternmost of the Balearic Islands.

The Talayotic culture is named for the Iron Age stone towers found across Menorca and nearby Mallorca that later settlers referred to with the Arabic word for "watchtower," *atalaya*. The true purpose of these *talayots* remains a subject of debate among archaeologists. On Menorca, unlike Mallorca, *talayots* are commonly located near *taulas*, stone enclosures constructed slightly later surrounding a large upright stone atop which another stone lies in a "T" form. This form has given the enclosures the name *taula*, Catalan for "table." The upright stones of the *taula*, with no known analogue anywhere else in the Mediterranean, have become an emblem of Menorca's cultural heritage, appearing in silhouette on the logo of the Menorca Talayotica campaign supporting the UNESCO application with the Catalan slogan Única al Món—"unique in the world."

However, not all of Menorca's historic sites are Talayotic—even the UNESCO application, despite its name, includes several *navetas*, stone houses and tombs that predate the construction of the *talayots*. Archaeological remnants also reflect Menorca's Roman, Islamic, and Medieval Christian periods and the tumultuous 18th and 19th centuries when the British, Spanish, and French all sought to control the strategic port of Maó-Mahón. Many of these structures were reused long after their construction, most notably the British-built naval hospital on Maó-Mahón Harbor's Isla del Rey, which remained in use until the 1960s.

Contemporary Menorcan heritage management thus must face the question of which era(s) in a site's history to represent. Additionally, the island's position as a Catalan-speaking region within Spain, the home of a large British expatriate population and a popular vacation destination with tourists from mainland Europe, gives any site a variety of potential audiences. Which era is a site presenting, and for whom?

In this paper, I describe how these concerns are managed at several historic sites across Menorca, drawing on my own experiences at a Boston University–Universitat de les Illes Balears field school in the summer of 2014.

The Impact of Media on Archaeology: The Northern Cape as a Case Study
Michael Chazan, University of Toronto

Recent developments in web-based media enable the rapid spread of news of major discoveries, providing an exciting opportunity for archaeologists to share the advances in our understanding of the past and to strengthen an understanding of the importance, and fragility, of cultural heritage. The importance of engaging with media is clear, particularly in an environment where there are many highly vocal dubious claims about the archaeological past, but the implications of this engagement must also be considered. The research team I codirect in the Northern Cape Province of South Africa has drawn wide media coverage for discoveries relevant to major themes in human evolution. This paper examines how this coverage has contributed to the protection of heritage in the region and also considers how the structure of media stories shapes the structure of the archaeological debate. The case study suggests that the impact of media and public interest should be considered as an integral element of the process of archaeological research and not treated as a "sideshow."

Cultural Racketeering in Egypt: Predicting Patterns in Illicit Activity: Quantitative Tools of the 21st-Century Archaeologist
Katie A. Paul, The Antiquities Coalition

The modern era of globalization has made the world more heavily connected than ever before, technologically, politically—and criminally. The Arab Spring uprisings of 2011 facilitated social movements that redefined the modern world. They also served as the catalyst for cultural racketeering—the systematic theft of art and antiquities by organized criminal syndicates.

This study presents an examination of the patterns and trends of cultural racketeering in Egypt. Data was gathered from research and analysis of social media and media within Egypt and around the world. The various aspects of media examined reported on the threats and damage to cultural heritage in Egypt. Social media has proven to be a major means of information sharing in Egypt and the Middle East and North African region. The Egyptian population's extensive engagement in social media was first displayed during the January 2011 revolution and has only increased in popularity since. This study breaks down the individual reports of looting and/or trafficking into demographic data, site classifications, and illicit activities taxonomies on a month-by-month basis in the years following the 2011 revolution. Graphing the quantitative data collected from the analysis of these on-the-ground reports provides a glimpse into the patterns that have emerged and the methods of operation for various types of looting and smuggling networks within Egypt. This quantitative examination reveals the patterns of cultural heritage crimes taking place in Egypt—and more importantly, identifies cyclical activities that can help predict the activities that lie ahead.

The post–Arab Spring expansion of criminal networks in the Middle East antiquities trade has created a new atmosphere where archaeologists must be investigators of the present as well as the past—navigating technology, politics, security, and economy to protect and preserve heritage and keep up with the criminals involved.

There is an increasing need for experts in the field to not just grasp the science of archaeology but also understand the dynamics affecting cultural heritage within political and economic sectors. Coordinating with the efforts of experts beyond the archaeological arena creates immense opportunity for archaeologists to undertake solutions to combatting cultural racketeering that are practical, workable, and flexible.

The Egyptian government is faced with the crisis of too many crimes and too few resources. By understanding established patterns in the illicit trafficking of antiquities, we can help governments allocate their already scant resources in the most effective manner to combat looting. Researching beyond the scope of the archaeological material affected and engaging in this quantitative ethnography of social media and media helps provide archaeologists and heritage experts with the tools to create a targeted approach to thwarting looting networks and their patterns of activity. This study has identified new tools, techniques, routes of research, and potential for cross-disciplinary cooperation to glean credible information pointing to activity cycles and overall trends of cultural racketeering in Egypt. The practical applications of this research toward streamlining government activities in the fight against looting can serve as a model for examining patterns and solutions in other tech-oriented nations facing challenges of high heritage crime coupled with low heritage resources.

SESSION 2B
Asia Minor

CHAIR: *C. Brian Rose*, University of Pennsylvania

Recent Fieldwork at Sardis, Turkey
Nicholas Cahill, University of Wisconsin–Madison

Field research at Sardis between 2010 and 2015 has produced important and unexpected results. Two natural spurs on the slopes of the acropolis were terraced in the Lydian period and may be the site of the Lydian palace. Excavation has recovered terrace walls and artifacts consistent with this interpretation, with a probable destruction in the mid sixth century and a subsequent gap in occupation. Important later features on these hills include many phases of Hellenistic and Roman occupation, an Early Byzantine cemetery, and artifacts including a bronze triangle incised with figures of Hekate and perhaps used for divination, similar to examples from Pergamon and Apamea.

A lower terrace was part of an Early Roman sanctuary of the imperial cult (the "Wadi B Temple"). This was dismantled during the Roman period, and its architectural fragments, inscriptions, and sculptures were reused in a later monumental building. This later building was then destroyed by an earthquake in the sixth century C.E. Excavation here has produced new evidence for the Early Roman temple, which seems to have had figural capitals, one or more friezes, and perhaps pedimental sculpture; associated finds including an unusual number of honorific inscriptions; and an important Late Roman destruction horizon.

A third excavation area of a Late Roman colonnaded avenue near the Lydian city gate revealed a previously unsuspected monumental arch composed of eight piers and with a 13 m central span, perhaps the largest such arch in the Roman world. This arch will be discussed in more detail in a separate presentation.

Excavation in the Temple of Artemis focused on problems of phasing and chronology and will be published in a forthcoming issue of the *AJA*. A new project using a gentle biocide to remove colonies of lichen and cyanobacteria from the marble is returning the building to its original, unblemished state.

Modeling the Appearance and Experience of the Pseudodipteral Temple of Artemis at Magnesia
Samuel Holzman, University of Pennsylvania

The scarcity of illustrations of the Temple of Artemis Leukophryene at Magnesia has limited a full understanding of the appearance and experience of this monument's audacious spaciousness. Designed by Hermogenes ca. 200 B.C.E., the Temple of Artemis is not the first pseudodipteral temple (*Vitr.* 3.3.8–9), but it is the prototype for the popular plan frequently repurposed in the Roman period. In a pseudodipteral design, an open interior is screened by a deceptive outer colonnade simulating a double row of columns. The widened porticoes of the temple must be visualized to understand this building's pivotal role in the changing visuality of the Hellenistic period. The *Ringhalle*—the space encircling the cella—can now be analyzed in a three-dimensional model developed by the Modeling Hermogenes project at the University of Pennsylvania. This model is based on new measurements of the column heights, a new conjectural reconstruction of the ceiling design, and geolocated shadow modeling. In this project, the boundaries of digital visualization are explored to create abstract fish-eye lens images that better simulate the neck-craning experience of entering an immense, enveloping interior. This application of new digital visualization has broad ramifications for understanding developments in space-positive architecture in antiquity.

That This Water Is Prophetic Is Hence Manifest: Groundwater Geochemistry at Delphi, Didyma, and Claros

Jonathan M. Flood, University of Texas at Austin

According to ancient sources, groundwater played a paramount role in the divination process at these three most influential oracular centers in the Graeco-Roman world, the Temples of Apollo at Delphi, Didyma, and Claros. At each sanctuary, the individual designated to convey divine responses to worldly quandaries would bathe in and/or drink from one or several hallowed groundwater sources shortly before delivering an oracle. So, what's so special about the groundwater at these three locations? From a geochemical perspective, quite a lot! This paper presents new discoveries from a multiyear geochemical study of the sacred springs at Delphi, Didyma, and Claros. The major ion and trace elemental chemistry of groundwater from these sites is linked to: (1) the underlying geology that instills the observed aqueous geochemistry; (2) the peculiar ritual phenomenon at each site recorded by authors in antiquity; and (3) the general settlement and water-use history in the landscapes containing these renowned sanctuaries. This study uses methods and tools from hydrogeology and environmental chemistry to further our understanding of past cultural phenomena and land-use systems. The discussion is structured to emphasize the importance of an often forgotten yet salient structural feature in many natural and human ecosystems, groundwater and its geochemical composition. All three case studies presented in this paper illustrate the interlocking of social/cultural systems with hydrologic systems and in two cases demonstrate novel adaptive responses to naturally toxic groundwater regions.

Archaeological Research at Notion

Christopher Ratté, University of Michigan, and *Felipe Rojas*, Brown University

Notion is a well-preserved and almost completely unexcavated ancient city on the Aegean coast of Turkey near several other major archaeological sites, including Klaros, Kolophon, and Ephesos. Notion was occupied from the early first millennium B.C.E. until the Middle Ages, and textual evidence suggests it played a significant role in the history of the surrounding region in all periods. In 2014, work began on a new archaeological survey project at Notion, focused on mapping and documentation of visible remains (paying particular attention to the fortifications, cisterns, and stone quarries), remote sensing (aerial photogrammetry and thermal sensing using a tethered balloon and lightweight drones), geophysical prospection (magnetic survey of one-third of the site to date), collection and study of surface finds, and the development of a long-term conservation/management plan. This paper presents a summary of the results of work to date.

The earliest well-preserved remains on the site are the fortifications, datable on grounds of technique and style to the Late Classical or Early Hellenistic period. The orthogonal grid plan is probably contemporary. Incorporated into this plan are two major sanctuaries in the western portion of the city (the Temple of Athena, identified by inscriptions, and the "Heroon," a sanctuary of uncertain identification) and two major open areas, the agora in the center of the city and the so-called

East Agora. The dates of the buildings in these sacred and civic areas are uncertain, but all or almost all of the surface pottery collected so far belongs to the Late Hellenistic and Augustan periods, raising the possibility that the city was largely abandoned in the Roman era. It is possible that some of these buildings, such as the stoas enclosing the agora (preserved only in their foundations), were never completed. Later occupation is attested by a small number of dedicatory inscriptions, dated on letterforms to the Imperial period, and at least one church, which may have both Late Roman and Middle Byzantine phases.

Research at Notion has already begun to shed new light on the history of this and other Ionian cities, especially in the Late Hellenistic and Augustan periods. Continued fieldwork will contribute new information on major issues of contemporary west Anatolian archaeology and help secure the future of an invaluable cultural resource.

The Cisterns of Notion
Angela Commito, University at Albany

The seaside city of Notion in ancient Ionia suffered from a lack of freshwater. The Notion Archaeological Survey has identified a network of at least a dozen cisterns, along with a number of stone pipe blocks, that reveal how the city's inhabitants responded to this challenge. This paper introduces the cisterns of Notion and examines them in the broader context of civic water supply in Hellenistic and Roman Turkey. The cisterns are generally carafe shaped in section and range in capacity from about 6 to 60 cubic m. They are located across the site, both in public areas, such as around the agora and theater, and in residential quarters. Though carafe-shaped cisterns are found throughout the Mediterranean from the fifth century B.C.E. through the later Roman era, they are most common in the Hellenistic period, especially the second and first centuries B.C.E. The construction of the cisterns at Notion may therefore correspond with the period of greatest activity in the city as suggested by the surface pottery collected thus far, which dates to the Late Hellenistic and Early Augustan periods. If so, the cisterns may indicate that the population of Notion was never very large and that the city was mostly abandoned in the Roman period. However, it is also possible that an as yet undiscovered aqueduct provided the city with a more-abundant and higher-quality water supply. This paper discusses both possibilities and explores how research on the civic water supply of Notion offers clues about the lifespan of the ancient city.

Quarrying at Notion: Urban Settlement and the Natural Environment
Catherine Steidl, Brown University

Visible remains at Notion demonstrate the variety and quantity of stone once employed in the city's architecture. Located on a rocky promontory, the site sits on—and is surrounded by—a variety of potential building material. Furthermore, Notion's topography, with several broad, flattened areas and craggy chunks missing from the landscape, suggests that its builders took full advantage of this natural resource. As part of a larger effort to investigate the interaction between human settlement and the natural environment, we began a program of identification and documentation of quarries on the site during the 2015 season of the Notion Archaeological Survey. This paper presents the early results of our study of the quarries onsite and outlines future plans to integrate our understanding of them into the broader study of resource acquisition and its social implications in the city, as well as landscape modification and change at the site.

We began with extensive survey, locating as many quarried areas as possible. We recorded these using a combination of qualitative description, photography, and GPS coordinates. Quarry identification was based on a number of factors, including the appearance of outcroppings and surrounding ground level. We noted locations with obvious terracing, vertical rock faces, and conspicuously absent chunks of earth and rock; weathering has obliterated many tool marks, but in rare cases preserved marks have been uncovered by looters' trenches. Thus far we have mapped a scatter of approximately 20 quarries all over the site, which vary in size from approximately 5 to 500,000 m². Quarried rocks include gray, white, and tan carbonates, the former being the two most prevalent at Notion. Schist and fault breccia are also found around the site as part of the geological landscape, but one type of stone seen in architectural blocks—a conglomerate—appears in a single possible quarry and in a quantity too small to have produced what we see in the fortification wall.

Preliminary results suggest that much of the stone used for construction in the city may have come from the site, but certainly not all. In particular, we are working to identify where the conglomerate stone may have been sourced. Why might materials have been transported up the steep slopes to the city when other rock was available there? How did Notion's builders exploit the site's natural resources? These are some of the questions we can begin to consider in our future work.

SESSION 2C
Landscapes and Households in the Aegean World

CHAIR: To be announced

From "Good Condition" to "Dry and Barren": The Geoarchaeology of Climate and Post-Palatial Landscape Change at Mycenae, Greece
Daniel J. Fallu, Boston University

Despite decades of research into the events of the late second millennium B.C.E., the causes of the Mycenaean palatial collapse are not yet fully understood. Aristotle, in 350 B.C.E., was perhaps the first to blame this "catastrophe" on changes in climate and environment, taking Mycenae from being in "good condition" to being "dry and barren," and drying out Argos sufficiently enough to permit agriculture (*Mete.* 14.325). In recent research, multiple methods of environmental reconstruction, including palynology, isotope archives, archaeoseismology, and sedimentary history, have yet to produce sufficient evidence of any ubiquitous environmental event in the Aegean during the final decades of the palaces. Where "disasters" are detected, they are limited in scale and they do not prove a permanent obstacle to continued occupation. The author here presents the results from targeted sedimentological and elemental study of rapidly deposited sediments dating from the Late Bronze Age and the Early Iron Age at Mycenae in the Argolid in an effort to place these changes in a greater climatic and environmental context.

Excavation from 2007 to 2011 by the Dickinson Excavation Project and Archaeological Survey at the Lower Town of Mycenae has uncovered a sequence of debris flows that occurred in the three centuries immediately following the palatial collapse. A combination of X-ray fluorescence (XRF) analysis of sediments and micromorphological analysis of calcite cements deposited on rock fragments provide environmental data in this higher-elevation, semiarid region where little traditional environmental evidence is preserved. A total of 38 bulk samples and 75 micromorphological slides were analyzed, allowing the deposits to be divided into two periods of instability. Preliminary results suggest a semiarid environment with little to no retaining vegetation that left slope soils unprotected and prone to disruption by sudden storms and seismic disturbance. It is hoped that continuing investigation of microenvironments via geoarchaeological investigation will explain the evolution of the Greek landscape and the impacts of Mycenaean occupation and agricultural expansion.

Settlement Ecology in Bronze Age Messenia

Christopher S. Jazwa, Pennsylvania State University, and *Kyle A. Jazwa*, Florida State University

In this paper, we attempt to understand patterns of expansion and contraction of settlement sites in Bronze Age Messenia (ca. 3000–1050 B.C.E.) using the ideal free (IFD) and ideal despotic (IDD) distribution models. We have ranked potential settlement locations on the landscape using environmental and cultural variables, including freshwater availability, net primary productivity, distance to a viable harbor, and distance to tholos tombs and central sites of cultural or political importance. The models predict that the highest-ranked habitats will be settled first and there will be an expansion to progressively lower-ranked habitats as population density increases. The IFD and IDD have been applied successfully at a variety of geographic scales to both hunter-gatherers and more complex societies. The IDD in particular has been used to understand developing complexity in California, Belize, and the Pacific Islands.

Messenia, in the western Peloponnese, is a prime candidate for the application of this model in Greece. Messenia offers a long history of archaeological survey, excavation, and environmental analyses, which provide sufficient data with which to apply these models. Additionally, the Linear B evidence and long history of fieldwork in the region provide a well-studied historical narrative, particularly in the Late Bronze Age (ca. 1600–1100 B.C.E.). We use this to understand the settlement distribution and discrepancies from the results of the model. Our results demonstrate general agreement of the available data from the Minnesota Messenia Project and Pylos Regional Archaeological Project (PRAP) surveys with the predictions of the IFD/IDD. We comment on the settlement disruption that occurred with the rise of the palace of Pylos in LH IIIA–B to demonstrate the impact of the palatial centers on the surrounding region. We reveal how the unique environmental and the geological and cultural landscape of the region affected settlement prior to the rise of the major Mycenaean centers in mainland Greece.

Crisis Building: Social Implications for Domestic Architectural Change in Mainland Greece During Late Helladic IIIC and the Protogeometric Period
Kyle A. Jazwa, Florida State University

In this paper, I consider domestic architecture for evidence of social integration and interaction among the mainland Greek population following the collapse of the Mycenaean palatial administration (Late Helladic [LH] IIIC to Protogeometric periods). To this end, I analyze each excavated and published LH IIIC to Protogeometric building for 200+ aspects of architectural construction and spatial organization. Because domestic structures are built and lived in by the local population, significant changes in human practice associated with these buildings suggest alterations to the social network of the inhabitants. With a statistical analysis of the correspondence of these aspects between contemporary buildings, I comment on the implications of the changes to the dynamic social network(s) following the collapse of the Mycenaean palatial system.

The results of this study demonstrate substantial alterations to long-held construction traditions and organizing principles in LH IIIC and the Protogeometric period. A closer examination of the nature of the changes, however, reveals a fundamental difference between the two periods. Whereas the LH IIIC period demonstrates substantial and pervasive changes in the scale of buildings and their constituent parts, Protogeometric architecture indicates a fundamental reorganization of the spatial layout of domestic structures. In other words, architecture in the Protogeometric period suggests an essentially different way of living and use of domestic space relative to LH IIIC and earlier periods. By examining these architectural changes and the reconstructed networks of correspondence of sites, it is clear that the LH IIIC to Protogeometric transition is far more significant than LH IIIB–C. I argue that the cause of the changes in the Protogeometric period can be attributed to the influx of several small groups of individuals during the preceding decades (possibly centuries) who engaged in daily practices distinct from the native Mycenaeans but who remained a minority within society. During the Postpalatial crisis and depopulation, some of these individuals or groups increasingly held more influential positions in society. With their greater social role and visibility in the Protogeometric period, members of these social groups came to hybridize and reform daily interaction with domestic built space in mainland Greece.

Burning Down the House: Arson, Accident, or Natural Disaster?
Julie Hruby, Dartmouth College

The original excavators suggested that the Palace of Nestor was destroyed when Dorians invaded and burned it. For a number of reasons, this hypothesis no longer seems likely. A current favorite approach to the question of palatial collapse shifts the question from why the system collapsed to why it was weakened or why structures were never rebuilt, or treats the collapse as the inevitable result of a multitude of factors.

Klaus Kilian repeatedly proposed that earthquakes were responsible for the fall of the Mycenaean palaces. His hypothesis has not been universally accepted, in part because his claim that the Palace of Nestor at Pylos fell in an earthquake has not been widely accepted, even by those who would otherwise accept earthquakes as causative. The basis for his assertion was that Pylos had walls that deviated from a straight line and that the corners of the foundations of the northeastern building had opened by more than a meter. I argue, on the basis of additional evidence, that Kilian was correct.

The primary evidence for this consists of indications that the palace collapsed before, not after, it burned, with walls and shelves generally falling in a southwest to northeast direction. Evidence for heat damage along the northeast wall suggests that the collapse preceded the fire. Furthermore, the frequency with which ceramic vessels, including chimney pots, were broken shortly before they burned also suggests that an earthquake was the most plausible immediate cause of the palace's demise.

SESSION 2D
The Mycenaean Coast

CHAIR: *Aleydis Van de Moortel*, University of Tennessee, Knoxville

Alternative Worlds: Mariner Networks in Ports Across the Late Bronze Age Aegean

Senta C. German, Montclair State University, and *Linda Hulin*, University of Oxford

The Late Bronze Age in the Mediterranean was the first truly international age as evidenced through textual, iconographic, and archaeological records. Numerous active ports of the era have been identified and framed as entrepôts, hubs around which moved people, goods, texts, and ideas in the wider terrestrial landscape. In our paper, we shift away from these far-flung networks and instead focus on mariners' perspectives. Mariners, key players in this newly technologically advanced and cross-cultural age, have yet to be examined on land, and we believe their experience and aspect, as manifest archaeologically onshore, offers an important view of a unique society within mobile and changeable maritime landscapes.

As historical and anthropological research of ports document, sailors congregate in limited zones, often by the shore, and exhibit uniquely self-defined social practice associated with rest, socialization, and cultural intercourse. Mariners also have access to and are inventors of cutting-edge engineering, communication, and administrative technologies. These men and women inhabit the rich margins where economies, technologies, faiths, and social practice overlap and act as primary agents of cosmopolitism.

We argue that mariners' quarters can be identified in the archaeological record, both architecturally (modest dwellings close to the shore) and through unique artifact groupings (diverse ceramic wares, small-scale imported items, evidence of technical sophistication and varied cultic paraphernalia). In our paper, we first outline our criteria for the identification of these quarters and illustrate the type using examples from the eastern Mediterranean and Aegean (Enkomi, Kition, Hala Sultan Tekke, Kommos, Phylakopi, Amnisos). We then turn toward a discussion of the importance of these alternative worlds in our understanding of the history of the Late Bronze Age Mediterranean.

Korakou, the Port City of Mycenaean Corinth
Ioulia Tzonou-Herbst, American School of Classical Studies at Athens

Korakou, a hill overlooking the Corinthian Gulf and Lechaion Harbor, has played a significant role in Aegean Bronze Age studies since Carl Blegen's groundbreaking excavations in 1915 and 1916. After a conference on the centenary of the excavations and the purchase of the land thanks to a grant from the Institute of Aegean Prehistory, there is renewed interest in the site, its legacy data, and its future.

Blegen's excavation journals and the site's artifacts continue to provide evidence on diverse aspects of the Bronze Age. In the 1970s, these data were used to refine the ceramic chronology of the Late Bronze Age on the mainland. Current scholarship focuses on ceramic technology, production and consumption of pots, provenance studies, and relations with sites in the Corinthia, Argolid, Achaia, and the Saronic Gulf. Tools for abrasion, textile production, and weighing are another area of recent work.

In addition to the legacy data, new information is generated by digital technologies and geophysical survey. The former advance our understanding of the topography of the site. It is argued that Korakou was the port city of the thriving settlement at Corinth in Mycenaean times. Recent excavations have shown an extensive habitation on the plain to the south of Korakou and north of the later city, continuing the settlement that must have existed on the upper terrace. A wealth of imports at both sites throughout the Bronze Age and the position of Corinth and Korakou along trade routes used for transporting goods and connecting people lead to the hypothesis that a center of power existed here. The site of Korakou must have played this crucial role in the development of Corinth already from the Late Neolithic/Early Helladic times and continued to do so into the Early Iron Age and Archaic times, when the harbor was located to the west of the hill. The promontory of Korakou with its advantageous position as a lookout overlooking the harbor was used at least into the sixth century B.C.E.

The Late Helladic I Ceramic Sequence at Mitrou, East Lokris: Chronology and Wider Cultural Implications

Christopher Mark Hale, Australian Archaeological Institute at Athens, *Salvatore Vitale*, Università degli studi di Pisa, and *Aleydis Van de Moortel*, University of Tennessee, Knoxville

Late Helladic (LH) I (ca. 1675–1600 B.C.E.) is considered a crucial phase in Greek prehistory because of its association with the rise of sociopolitical complexity and the beginning of Mycenaean civilization. The majority of studies, however, have focused on the Argolid and Messenia, while other regions have remained relatively poorly known. The aim of this paper is to provide for the first time a detailed presentation of the LH I ceramic sequence from Mitrou, East Lokris, and to establish a solid chronological framework for the comprehension of wider cultural developments in the central Greek mainland during this initial phase of the Prepalatial period.

The 2004 to 2008 excavations at Mitrou by the University of Tennessee and the Ephorate of Phtiotida and Eurytania have revealed an impressive number of finely stratified LH I settlement levels, as well as 17 LH I graves. The settlement deposits were recovered from sealed superimposed fills located between various occupation surfaces and floors connected to multiple architectural phases. These finds represent the richest and most complete LH I pottery sequence discovered thus far in central Greece.

Quantitative analysis of these materials has enabled the identification of four LH I ceramic subphases, each of which is characterized by clearly defined typological features along with shifting patterns within the proportion of diagnostic classes in the overall assemblage. The latter include central Greek pottery productions, as well as imports from Kea, Aegina, the Argolid, and a variety of other regions.

A major divide during LH I at Mitrou falls between subphases 1 and 2 on one side and subphases 3 and 4 on the other. Subphase 3 is characterized by the appearance of Mycenaean lustrous-decorated pottery, the significant increase of Fine Pale Unpainted pottery at the expense of Fine Gray Burnished and Fine Dark Burnished pottery, the rise of Aeginetan imports, and the drop in the presence of Kean vessels. These characteristics have been confirmed across four separate areas of the site. With this new LH I pottery chronology, we can more accurately date architectural developments and changes in Mitrou's society, particularly the initial adoption of Mycenaean ceramics and elite practices. Beyond Mitrou, this paper contributes to an understanding of LH I central Greek ceramic and cultural developments with a far greater resolution than previously possible.

Toward an Explanation for the Primacy of the Euboean Gulf Coasts During the Bronze Age to Early Iron Age Transition

Margaretha Kramer-Hajos, Indiana University

Sites along the Euboean Gulf coasts of central Greece, especially Kynos and Lefkandi, are well known for their prominence at the end of the Bronze Age and in the Early Iron Age: whereas much of Mycenaean Greece, including the interior of central Greece, fell into decline after the collapse of the palatial system ca. 1200

B.C.E., a number of sites along the Euboean Gulf coasts boast impressive remains dating to Late Helladic (LH) IIIC and the Protogeometric period. Combining network analysis with iconographic analysis, this paper ascribes the prominence of these sites to their highly successful exploitation of maritime routes and networks, facilitated by their use of an innovative warrior package consisting of ships and armor that had much in common with that used elsewhere in the contemporary eastern Mediterranean but owed relatively little to the palatial Mycenaean period.

Pottery analysis suggests that after the collapse of palatial networks, sites on the Euboean Gulf created a coastal network; the presence of exotica from the Levant, Cyprus, and Egypt at central Greek coastal sites shows the extent of the links of this network and suggests that these sites capitalized on the collapse of the organized palatial trade system by taking over the preexisting trade routes. Since ships were the means allowing the coastal settlements to do so, it is perhaps unsurprising to see them play a prominent role on LH IIIC pottery from, for example, Kynos and Lefkandi. They represent a relatively new type: a rowed galley with a sleek hull, reinforced at the bow, and an improved steering mechanism. Similarities with ships of the "Sea Peoples" as depicted on Egyptian reliefs suggest intensive exchange of maritime technology in the southeast Mediterranean. These ships excelled at executing quick raids; that they were indeed used in hostile naval encounters is borne out by pictorial pottery from Kynos, which shows warriors fighting on and from the decks of such galleys.

Some of these warriors are equipped with "proto-Dipylon" shields: small incurved shields that also occur on pottery from nearby Volos and seem inspired by earlier Hittite shields, suggesting exchange of military technology. When the first Dipylon Shields occur in Attic Middle Geometric depictions, they are likewise combined with galleys. This suggests that galley and shield formed a successful warrior package that survived the end of the Bronze Age and propelled sites to prominence during the chaotic years following the collapse of palatial civilization.

SESSION 2E
Athens: The Acropolis and the Agora

CHAIR: *Kathleen M. Lynch*, University of Cincinnati

The Parthenon: One Gap or Two?
John G. Younger, University of Kansas

Building accounts make it clear that temples were built in five phases from the outside in: colonnade first, then cella, then ceiling and roof. A gap in the colonnade would have allowed workers inside to build the cella (cf. the three nonmonolithic columns of the north colonnade in the Aphaia temple).

For the Parthenon, the west frieze was carved on the ground since each slab carries an integral scene; most of the rest of the frieze carries scenes that overlap joins. If the Parthenon also had a gap in the colonnade, it could have been at the west end, where, when it came time to close the gap (440–438 B.C.E.), the west frieze, finished and stored in Pheidias' workshop, could be swiftly installed. This could explain the jumbled nature of the overall composition.

In the south side of the Parthenon, frieze slabs 16, 19, and 22 (behind columns 7–10) have blank spaces that may once have separated work sections but were never filled in (contrast the filler figures in the north frieze—e.g., XI/11.44 and XVII/23.65).

Most of the south metopes carry single combat scenes between a centaur and a Greek, but metopes 13–21 (above columns 7–11) contain no centaurs at all; instead, the scenes seem unrelated to each other and to a centauromachy. Scholars have tried to explain these scenes on iconographic grounds, but most attempts are unconvincing.

Pheidias' workshop lies just to the south of the Parthenon. The building was slightly smaller than the entire east and west cella (ca. 10 x 29 m), but the plan is similar. Both his acropolis workshop and his Olympia workshop were built, therefore, to construct their respective chryselephantine statues and to convey their eventual appearance prior to installation.

The anomalies in the south frieze and metopes align, and both span the area behind/above columns 7–10/11. This area corresponds to the Parthenon's eastern cella from the partition wall to immediately in front of the statue.

Different iconographic considerations might explain the anomalies in the frieze and metopes, but one processual explanation would explain them all: that there was a second gap in the wall just south of the Parthenos statue to allow workers to install it easily. Evidence for this gap would have been destroyed by the 1687 explosion.

The Martial Context of the Archaic Athenian Rider Statues
Alexander E. Skufca, Florida State University

This paper suggests that several archaic rider statues found on the Athenian acropolis as well as in local cemeteries are related to a small, aristocratic cavalry service indicated by literary and ceramic evidence. Scholarly consensus about the context of these unique marble horsemen remains elusive, even after the publication of Mary Ann Eaverly's seminal study in 1995. While their monumentality places them within an aristocratic framework, their fragmentary survival makes it hard to identify the riders within a mythological or historical fabric. Certain statues, however, provide enough detail to connect them with other evidence that, I argue, places them within a sketch of the archaic Athenian cavalry outlined by Glen Bugh. The literary record suggests that this corps was much smaller than its classical successor, and the troopers seem to have been selected from the young men of only a few wealthy, hippotrophic families of Attica. Previously, scholars have attempted to identify the riders either as mythological figures or as monuments celebrating distinct historical events, but it may be better to associate them with the upper echelons of the Attic aristocracy seeking to commemorate their sons' entrance or service in the small cavalry squad. The nude riders found on the acropolis need not, then, represent an ancient hero or contemporary politician but rather may represent an abstract ideal of a young, aristocratic male, thereby providing a link between the commemorated Athenian *kalos k'agathos* and a panoply of heroic ancestors. Classical sources highlight the importance of a young man's initial *dokimasia*, or enlistment review (*Const. Ath.* 49.2; see also Xen., *Eq.*

mag. 1.9–12), and the statues on the acropolis may be associated with an archaic antecedent. The riders found in the Kerameikos and the cemetery at Vari are, conversely, fully clothed and appear to carry military equipment. In this context, they seem to highlight the actual service of a deceased young cavalryman, which corresponds to the relief representations of young horsemen on archaic grave stelai. By viewing the riders within an Athenian military establishment, certain statues can be better contextualized, and a link emerges between the diverse locations in which they were discovered.

Feeding the Prytaneis with Standard Measures at the Tholos in Athens
Ann Steiner, Franklin & Marshall College

This paper presents results of a new study of the ceramics from the tholos in the Athenian Agora using an innovative technology, an online tool for measuring vessel capacity. The study demonstrates that (1) the capacity of some shapes of black-gloss tableware used in the tholos replicates that of the official standard measures adopted by the demos; and (2) that the delta/epsilon ligature, short for *demosion* or "property of the demos," could indicate both public ownership and a capacity that matches a standard measure.

Ancient sources tell us the tholos was the dining room for the prytaneis and that it held one set of the official weights and measures that governed commercial activity in the Agora. Tholos pottery in Deposit G 12:22 (475–450 B.C.E.) includes several examples of black-gloss eating and drinking shapes preserving the incised ligature delta/epsilon. Work to date has discovered a relationship between the capacities of standard measures and those of certain black-gloss shapes selected for the common meals of the prytaneis—for example, the capacity of the most common drinking shape, the black-gloss Type C Vicup, matches that of the standard olpe, a pouring vessel that holds the standard measure of one kotyle ("Measure for Measure: 5th Century Public Dining at the Tholos in Athens," in *Feasts and Polis Institutions*, ed. J. Blok et al. [Utrecht, forthcoming]).

New evidence presented here tests the capacity of echinus salt cellars using an online program developed at the Université de Bruxelles Centre de Recherches en Archéologie et Patrimoine and finds a correspondence to the standard measure of one kyathos, or about 40 cc. Including more than 100 unpublished examples, the study concludes that there is in fact deviation from this capacity within the sample. Closely related shapes of similar small bowls, however, demonstrate much less consistency. While only a small number of salt cellars preserve the delta/epsilon ligature, it appears that the standard measure was only a general benchmark for potters in creating this shape. The relatively large proportion of such vessels in the deposit helps confirm a hypothesis that the prytaneis, paid an obol a day by the state as a food allowance, received approximately similar portions of drink, spices, and perhaps food in return. The general reliance on similarity in capacity for the size of these small containers for spices allowed for only roughly consistent implementation of this principle of equality.

The *Chaîne-Opératoire* of Professional Butchery in the Archaic to Classical Athenian Agora: Changing Foodways in an Urban Context

W. Flint Dibble, University of Cincinnati

The zooarchaeological evidence from the Athenian Agora presents a rich record of ancient activity relating to animals, their carcasses, and their extant remains. Previous analyses of the material from the Athenian Agora have focused on questions of animal husbandry and sacrificial ritual. However, 1,000+ zooarchaeological remains contain cut marks, which provide evidence for diachronic changes in the craft of butchery. Conclusions are drawn from a detailed analysis of cut marks: spatial analysis (precise anatomical location of cut marks, recorded in GIS), tool-type analysis (small knife, heavy knife, saw, or cleaver), and cut mark types (skinning, dismembering, filleting, marrow extraction, or bone working). Butchered animal remains provide evidence for increasing standardization in urban Athenian butchery techniques beginning in the Late Archaic period, which produced standard cuts of meat for both festival and commercial contexts.

It is possible to identify a switch from smaller knives to larger cleavers in Athenian butchery activities, with the exception of animal skinning and bone working. The use of cleavers led to an increasing efficiency in butchery practice. An analysis of the *chaîne-opératoire* of animal butchery, evident from cut mark location and directionality of chops, indicates that most carcasses were suspended during butchery activities. After skinning and removal of the head, the carcass was subsequently split longitudinally, after which the limbs were dismembered and processed into smaller portions. A detailed anatomical plot of cleaver butchery marks suggests a standard operation for all steps within. Redundant chop marks indicate redundant actions were used to dismember the fore and hind legs from a hanging carcass or to remove the kneecap from a hanging joint. Oftentimes, these cleaver marks are redundant regardless of context (evident in both consumption refuse and bone-working waste) or species (standard chop marks are evident on cattle and dogs).

The growing standardization in Athenian cleaver butchery, in contrast to earlier Late Bronze Age and Geometric-period remains, suggests a transition from ad hoc domestic butchery activity to professional butchery, likely associated with both public feasts and commercial meat distribution. This change in butchery practice signifies important changes in the distribution of urban foodstuffs and changes in cuts of meat. New cuts of meat would have had an important effect on both Athenian food preparation and diet in public and private meals. These changes also relate to other contemporary social changes: the increasing scale of Athenian public feasts in the Agora, the growth of the commercial Agora, and changing foodways affecting the diet and lifestyle of the urban population.

Chasing Ghosts in the Athenian Agora: The So-Called Hadrianic Basilica

Valentina Di Napoli, Swiss School of Archaeology in Greece, and *Gilberto Montali*, University of Macerata

Excavations in the Athenian Agora in the early 1970s brought to light an apparently huge building of the Imperial period, located at the northeastern corner of the area, to the north of the Stoa of Attalos. According to the reports by S.G. Miller, supervisor of the trenches, and T.L. Shear, then-director of the Agora excavations, the building consisted of a colonnaded portico dating to the Augustan period that in the Hadrianic age was transformed into a large basilica provided with sculptural decoration. Late Antique interventions blurred further the topography of the area, while modern works for the construction of the railway cut the building into two. It is now partially buried under a modern road.

This paper presents the first results of new research on the monument, utilizing thorough study of the excavation notebooks, the finds in situ, and the relevant sculptural fragments. In particular, the architecture of the building is critically reassessed, and the building is set in its wider context within the topography of second-century Athens. Consequently, its architectural and sculptural decoration is reconsidered, and unpublished pieces are also taken into account.

SESSION 2F
Sicily

CHAIR: *Barbara Tsakirgis*, Vanderbilt University

Deep-Sea Shipwreck Investigation in Sicily: The Panarea III Shipwreck
Sebastiano Tusa, Soprintendenza del Mare, *Roberto la Rocca*, Soprintendenza del Mare, and *Alba Mazza*, University of Sydney

This paper explores the potential of a new methodology involving technical divers and submarines in the investigation of deep-sea shipwrecks in Sicily, Italy. Thanks to the recent development of new scuba-diving equipment and high-tech submarines, the exploration of the abyss investigation of deep-sea shipwreck is now less time-consuming, more accurate, and definitely safer than before for divers and archaeologists. Within this framework, the Sicilian Governmental Agency for Underwater Heritage Protection (Soprintendenza del Mare) in collaboration with foundations and not-for-profit organizations engaged with the exploration of the Aeolian Island seabed from ⁻50 to ⁻150 m depth, discovering and investigating dozen of shipwrecks. In this paper, we present one of the most significant: Panarea III.

The shipwreck lies at ⁻120 m off the coast of Panarea; it was identified in 2010 thanks to geoacoustic survey (SSS). ROV images and a test technical dive provided sufficient material to launch a proper research campaign that was conducted in 2014. The goal of the 2014 field season was to perform the first noninvasive archaeological investigation of the shipwreck. The research was accomplished by testing of a new methodology that involved technical divers performing survey, mapping, and recovery under the direct guidance of nondiving archaeologists in submarines.

Results of the 2014 field season were:

1) The real-time high-resolution photogrammetry and three-dimensional and four-dimensional reconstructions of the shipwreck.

2) The precision sampling of key archaeological materials allowing a rapid and exact date of the site.

3) The rapid evaluation of the conservation status and the immediate start of the protection procedures.

The shipwreck is composed of a mixed cargo of Punic and Greek amphoras, fine wares, and kalathoi. The preliminary study of these materials allows a possible date of the end of the third century B.C.E./beginning of the second century B.C.E. The discovery of a sacrificial altar richly decorated with sea waves drew the attention of the team. The precious object, inscribed in Greek on the base, gave a hint about the possible shipowner. It also provided substantial evidence in order to investigate navigation religious practices and on-board partition of ritual spaces.

In conclusion, the Panarea III shipwreck is a key site for investigating a crucial moment in the history of the Mediterranean Sea; it also provides the perfect scenario for undertaking pioneering research for further development of deep-sea archaeological investigation.

The Materiality of Science: Greek Bathing in Sicily in the Age of Archimedes
Sandra K. Lucore, Independent Scholar

The Hellenistic kingdom of Syracuse was home to Archimedes, whose ideas and discoveries revolutionized the science of the day and influenced a period of unprecedented invention and innovation. The prosperous reign of the Syracusan king Hieron II created fertile conditions for royal patronage of the great scientist and mathematician and for support of the application of new technologies more broadly. Hieron II was directly involved in the construction of civic and religious buildings that enhanced the towns and cities in his realm. Among the most striking innovations in civic architecture is a completely new and more elaborate type of luxury bathing and a revolutionary form of architecture to house this new custom. Greek public baths existed in more rudimentary form long before bathing appeared in Sicily, yet it was precisely in towns of the Syracusan kingdom that new and experimental technologies were applied to the unprecedented appearance of domes and vaults and innovative systems of heating and water management, striking innovations that can be connected to the ideas of Archimedes. Greek bathing establishments are known in Syracuse itself, and Megara Hyblaea, but at Morgantina the North Baths currently constitute the best-preserved and technologically most innovative public bath in the Greek world. This paper thus presents a detailed discussion of the Morgantina North Baths, highlighting specifically the domed and vaulted construction and its relation to Archimedes' analysis of spheres while placing the new technologies applied to thermal architecture within the larger context of the science and technology of the time.

Trade and Adaptation of Ritual Objects in Western Sicily: Contextual Readings of Stamped Louteria
Andrew Farinholt Ward, Institute of Fine Arts, New York University

A central component of Greek sacrifice was the act of purification through water. The louterion, or perirrhanterion, a basin standing on a cylindrical shaft and base, was the most typical container for these lustral waters. Produced also for

domestic settings, contextual readings, with a consideration of their associated assemblages, are critical for interpretation. While material and formal differences
make generalizations difficult, the style of louterion developed in Corinth proved
particularly popular in the colonies of Magna Graecia and Sicily, and in the sixth
and fifth centuries a diverse series of basins with relief decoration were produced
and traded between Himera, Akragas, and Selinous in western Sicily. And yet,
trade of these objects exceeded Greek sites and speaks to a far more adaptable and
polyvalent ritual object.

Created with rolling stamps, the reliefs portray centauromachies, hunters,
charioteers, and other scenes—and the quality of this thoroughly Greek iconography has led to a great deal of scholarly attention. Largely restricted in the past to
typological analysis, the entire corpus was assumed to be largely for use in Greek
sanctuaries. Beyond the fact that a review of original field journals reveals that
their findspots varied to a greater degree, these louteria are also found in both
indigenous and Phoenicio-Punic sites, such as Mozia and Enna. Especially in these
new cultural contexts, while the iconography and forms remain homogenous, contexts can vary quite a deal, found not only in sanctuaries but also in ritual and
profane domestic contexts and, surprisingly, in burial contexts.

As has been done with imported sympotic pottery in recent years, a contextual
reading of louteria in their new settings allows one to chart the chain of transformations by which a Greek ritual object can become an indigenous ritual object for an
indigenous audience—avoiding the hermeneutic dangers inherent to colonial and
post-colonial approaches. Indeed, louteria seemed to be just as adaptable when
traded among the Greek colonies—the polyvalent nature of the objects reflected
in the generalized iconographies of victory, order, and other concepts found in
the relief decoration. These concepts, when agreeable to local schema, explain the
importation of stamped louteria to sites such as Mozia, where one finds reliefs
depicting Nikai crowning charioteers—in this instance especially compelling considering other adaptations of agonic motifs into the Phoenician vocabulary.

A Sicilian Divine Couple: Demeter Malophoros and Zeus Meilichios
Allaire B. Stallsmith, Towson University

The extraordinary two-headed stelae found in the sacred area of Zeus Meilichios
next to the sanctuary of Demeter Malophoros in Selinus, Sicily, appear to be without parallel in the cults of the ancient Mediterranean world. Their identification as
a divine couple has been generally accepted, although there is no agreement as to
their identity. The twin stelae are usually seen as evidence of a Graeco-Punic cult
practiced before and after Carthage's conquest of Selinus in 409 B.C.E.

A new interpretation of the stratigraphy of the sacred area (C. Grotta, *Zeus Meilichios a Selinunte* [Rome 2010]) argues that the stelae, even though undatable, are
not to be seen as having any relation to the archaic-classical cult of Zeus Meilichios, attested by the Meilichios stones, and are not a punicized form of that cult.
Accordingly, any un-Meilichian elements found there must have slid down from
the higher level of the Demeter Malophoros sanctuary or intrusive Punic deposits.

But this argument from silence does not convince. It is not possible to ignore the
evidence of Greek figurines and *defixiones* from the sacred area of Zeus Meilichios,

nor the presence of a sixth-century B.C.E. Punic "altar with three baetyls" in the center of that area. That 28 of the 81 twin stelae were found in the fill beneath the naiskos north of the sacred area is not dispositive, as the date of that fill and of the building of the *naiskos* is disputed. Indeed, one of the Meilichios stones, dated to the late sixth century by its Greek lettering, was found in the same fill. Finally, the sanctuary area has yielded evidence of indigenous (Elymian?) and Punic elements throughout its history, which makes it impossible to rule out a Phoenician origin for the two-headed stelae, whose few parallels derive from the Neolithic and Bronze Age Levant.

The syncretic artistic style of the twin stelae and their use in the contested "middle ground" of Sicily makes their identification an attractive puzzle. I suggest that these Graeco-Punic underworld deities were addressed by the euphemistic Greek *epicleseis* Meilichios (sweet) and Pasikrateia (all-powerful) in Selinus, just as, at Eleusis, they were euphemized as Theos and Thea.

A Case of Archaeomusicology in a Greek Colony in the West: The Aulos from Selinus

Angela Bellia, Institute of Fine Arts, New York University

The aim of this paper is to combine the methods of archeology and musicology for the study of musical instruments by considering their specific findspots and overall contexts. The archaeomusicological approach can place instrumental and choral activities within a well-defined space and relate them to a specific occasion that could shed light on the political, religious, and social meaning of musical performance in antiquity.

This is the research methodology of the TELESTES project that has been funded by the Marie Curie Actions program of the European Commission. The project is dedicated to the musical culture of Selinus, one of the most important of the western Greek cities. My goal is to present a very important part of TELESTES: it is the study of an actual aulos that was found in two pieces in Temple R at Selinus in the summer of 2012 during the Institute of Fine Arts, New York University Selinus Mission. This was uncovered in a classical to archaic level that had been sealed by a deep fill of the Hellenistic period fortunately left untouched by earlier archaeological research at the site. Among the discoveries made in this fill were a series of votive depositions in situ located against the walls and dating to the sixth century B.C.E. It was within one of these deposits that two parts of the bone aulos were found. The primary character of the deposit enabled the aulos to be dated to ca. 570 B.C.E. because of its association with a Corinthian amphoriskos that was found next to it.

This discovery at Selinus is very significant, particularly with regard to the performance of music and ritual dancing associated with the cult activity of Temple R. The performance of choral dancing in this part of the main urban sanctuary of Selinus is also suggested by the discovery in the area of Temple R of a series of fragments of Corinthian vases featuring chains of dancing women that conform to the so-called *Frauenfest* iconography. These discoveries show the importance of music at Selinus, the city of the poet and musician Telestes, already in the Early Archaic period. As can be seen in other Greek cities, the architecture of the sanctuaries at

Selinus could reflect the kind of spatial organization that was necessary for both choral and instrumental practices, as well as for ritual performances.

SESSION 2G
Etruria and Latium in the Archaic Age

CHAIR: *Gregory Warden*, Franklin University Switzerland

New Evidence for the Early Phases of the Temple at Poggio Colla (Vicchio di Mugello)
Michael Thomas, University of Texas at Austin

Since 1995, the Mugello Valley Archaeological Project has conducted a broad systematic study of the site of Poggio Colla and its environs. Large-scale excavation ended with the 2015 season as the focus of the project moves toward study and publication. Over the duration of the project, survey and excavation have produced evidence of an expanded settlement centered on a hilltop sanctuary. Material culture points to constant occupation of the site from as early as the late eighth century B.C.E. until the early second century B.C.E. This paper presents evidence from the final five seasons of excavation that has broadened our view of the architecture in the sanctuary, specifically the construction history of a monumental temple at the site.

Though the site preserves remains of at least five phases of occupation over its long history, the first three phases provide the focus of this paper. An early premonumental phase may have been associated with hut foundations discovered at the site. Evidenced by a significant amount of late Orientalizing to mid Archaic-period bucchero, this phase can now be associated with an inscribed stone stele discovered in 2015. The Late Archaic period saw the construction of the first monumental temple. This building utilized massive sandstone blocks—which included molded column bases and podium blocks—in the construction of what new evidence suggests may have been a peripteral or semiperipteral temple oriented on a northeast–southwest axis. Associated with this phase of the temple is a ritual deposit that included an inscribed statue base and several bronze statuettes. The builders of the second monumental phase reused many of the blocks from the first phase and shifted the temple's orientation to align with the natural orientation of the plateau. Included with this phase are several ritual deposits and the remains of a rectangular altar, most of which seem datable to the fourth century B.C.E.

When combined, the architecture and material culture associated with these three early phases at Poggio Colla provide robust evidence of more than 300 years of religion and ritual. Despite its seemingly liminal location in Etruria, the scale of the construction and the nature of many of the finds suggest that the Poggio Colla sanctuary may have benefited, at least in part, from the patronage of wealthy and literate elites.

New Excavations in the Necropolis of Crocifisso del Tufo (Orvieto, TR, Italy)
Claudio Bizzarri, PAAO, and *David George*, Saint Anselm College

This year marks the recommencement of excavations at the Etruscan Necropolis of Crocifisso del Tufo after 15 years. The research design of the project is threefold: to understand a series of features to the north of the site that needed further investigation from earlier scientific excavations, to clear and remap the site to have a clearer understanding of the relationship of features that came to light in previous excavations as well as the 19th-century activity, and to map and understand the structural issues that have emerged from anastylosis projects of the 19th and 20th centuries to facilitate preservation and reconstruction projects in the tombs.

This paper reports on the results of this season's excavation as well as the results of its mapping (traditional total station surveying, in addition to LIDAR and photogrammetry). Of particular note is the excavation of an intact *tomba a cassetta* dating to the sixth century B.C.E. in close proximity to earlier scientific excavations. It contained a disarticulated set of skeletal remains, a redisposition from the sixth-century tombs with bronze vessels and black bucchero decorated vases in a striking condition of conservation. This paper gives an overview of these finds and discusses their significance. It also discusses the long-term conservation plan for the site.

The Struggle Is Real: Herakles and the Caeretan Hydriae
Joseph S. Woldman, Columbia University

The corpus of vases known in scholarship as the Caeretan hydriae has been considered a singular group of vessels based on certain criteria. It is for this reason that scholars have grappled with developing a convincing methodological framework and interpretive schema that applies to the entire body of vessels. Additionally, the use of these vessels has been largely overlooked in scholarship. Created between 530/20 and 500 B.C.E., all the hydriae that compose this classificatory group share vivid polychrome decoration and shape and were mostly discovered within the Etruscan city of Caere (modern Cerveteri). The hydriae also display various nonfigural motifs and figural scenes, prominent among which are mythological ones. Interpretations of these representations range from the historical to the social; however, several questions remain unresolved even in the most recent studies of these vases. Why were hydriae chosen and produced? Why was production terminated so suddenly?

This paper seeks to propose both a modified methodology and an interpretive lens based on iconographical and archaeological evidence in order to address these questions. By looking specifically at scenes of Herakles and drawing connections to the cultic landscape of the S. Antonio region of the Caeretan Plateau, a more holistic interpretation arises. Connecting the imagery on the vessels to the life and development of the Temple of Hercle/Herakles in Caere lends a contextual weight to the production of the hydriae. This paper suggests that a prevailing theme of confrontation and struggle is relevant to the vessels' use in cult activities. Furthermore, these vases may have been important in rites of passage based on the transformative aspect of a struggle, the use of hydriae in ritual, and the significance of the Temple of Hercle/Herakles in Caere.

Human-Mask Cups: Egyptian Models for Etruscan and Roman Craftsmanship
Daniele F. Maras, Pontificia Accademia Romana di Archeologia, and *Friederike Bubenheimer-Erhart*, Universität Wien

Human-mask cups are a peculiar group of vases known from about 40 exemplars in bucchero and Etrusco-Corinthian pottery, which spread over south Etruria and Latium in the early and mid sixth century B.C.E. Our analysis of the models that inspired the production of these cups shows that they derive from Egyptian plastic vases decorated with the face of the god Bes. This is a class of ritual vases of ancient tradition, originating from the New Kingdom (18th Dynasty, late second millennium B.C.E.) and produced until the Graeco-Roman period. In particular, the Etruscan human-mask cups derive from a stylized type of vessels manufactured in Upper Egypt in the 26th Dynasty (seventh to sixth centuries B.C.E.). Notably, this is the period of a major opening of Egypt to foreign travelers, especially Greek traders and visitors. Not by chance, in the early sixth century a number of pottery shapes and iconographies stemmed from Egyptian prototypes, especially in Ionian and Attic craftsmanship. It is worth mentioning the derivation of the Greek Silens from the iconography of the Egyptian Bes.

On the basis of a survey of the Etruscan human-mask cups, we identify the workshops where these vessels were manufactured, along with further types of plastic vases of Egyptian inspiration, such as flasks shaped as monkeys, rams, and antelopes, as well as of Cypriot inspiration, such as head-shaped hanging containers. The principal production center was the city of Veii, from where plastic vases were exported to the neighboring cities of southern Etruria, Rome, and Latium. The stylistic features and decoration patterns of the so-called Human-Mask Group stem from the earlier workshop of the Rosoni Painter, originally operating in Vulci and later migrating southward. Minor productions of the Veian workshop, such as painted cups, spread over the Mediterranean, with findspots as far as Carthage and Massalia thus being the objects of overseas trade. This international opening provided the grounds for the workshop to update its repertoire with exotic forms, drawing inspiration even from prototypes of faraway lands.

From the last decades of the sixth century B.C.E. onward, the overwhelming influence of Attic pottery prevented Etruscan craftsmen from drawing on other models. It is remarkable, therefore, that a new production of human-mask cups, with features extremely similar to the Etruscan archaic types, dates from the Early Imperial age in Italy and Roman Europe. As a matter of fact, the Roman face pots could have been inspired by the renewed Egyptian influence from the Augustean period onward.

SESSION 2H
Mimesis, Repetition, and the Aesthetics of Roman Art

CHAIR: *Ellen Perry*, College of the Holy Cross

Optical Games and Spiritual Frames: A Reassessment of Imitation Marble Mosaics in Roman Africa

Nathan S. Dennis, Johns Hopkins University

Toward the end of the second century C.E., a new type of mosaic pavement design emerged in Roman houses and bath complexes among the cities of Roman Africa, most notably in the provinces of Africa Proconsularis (Tunisia) and portions of Numidia and Mauretania Caesariensis (Algeria). Imitating larger, more monolithic slabs of variegated, book-matched, or otherwise brecciated marble, mosaic tesserae were arranged in designs that mimicked the striations and patterns of larger marble slabs or *opus sectile* inlay. Quite often, these same tesserae were fragments of the exact same marble they attempted to represent pictorially, making each tessera a *pars pro toto*: a full representation of the materiality it sought to imitate, thus creating a form of visual play. Early Christian basilicas and baptisteries in the region would later extend the design phenomenon well into the fourth and fifth centuries. Variegated marble slabs or column shafts were widely recognized in antiquity as symbols of luxury and imperium, and their abstract striations, varied palette of colors, and reflective properties gave rise to a rich tradition of *ekphraseis* on the relationship between inanimate stone and perceptible movement, optical illusion and the manipulation of the senses. Previous attempts to explain the rise of this mosaic development in North Africa on the basis of economic viability have failed to account for other, more ideological factors that suggest an aesthetic appreciation for the materiality of mosaic tesserae over larger revetment slabs and, in some instances, an intentional replication of the fluid, water-like striations of brecciated marble that accentuated the optics of aquatic spaces, such as domestic impluvia, public baths, and Christian baptisteries. The concept of imitating marble slabs in fresco existed in Italy well before the development in North African mosaics, with examples appearing in Roman houses in Pompeii and elsewhere along the Bay of Naples. Mosaic, however, offered a medium rich in paradox, where stone could imitate stone, and both materiality and iconography became inextricably connected. Using theoretical models of viewer engagement with mosaic pavements, this paper examines the rise and use of imitation marble in North African mosaic pavements. Moving beyond positivistic and economic explanations for the phenomenon, the paper argues that the mosaics were part of a traditional Graeco-Roman trope of visuality, and as such they were designed to facilitate visual play and contemplation, as well as blur the lines of agency between animate viewers and the seemingly inanimate spaces they occupied.

Mimesis and Material(ity): The Use of "Metallic" Stones in Roman Imperial Sculpture

Emily Margaret Cook, Columbia University

It has often been claimed that black, gray, and dark-greenish limestones and marbles were exploited by Roman sculptors both to imitate the material effects of bronze sculpture and, it is frequently added, to imitate a specific bronze prototype. However, this assertion rests solely on a perceived visual similarity; there are no ancient Roman literary sources or systematic modern scholarly studies that support it. In this paper, I critique and contextualize the potential relationships between dark-colored stones and bronze and, to this end, focus on the so-called Furietti Centaurs made in nero antico and found in the second-century C.E. villa of the emperor Hadrian in Tivoli. I provide a historiographic analysis of the proposal that their material was selected to imitate the qualities of their hypothetical bronze prototype; the well-documented ancient and modern lives of the centaurs reveal the tangled nature of the study of Roman materials and materiality. Expanding this study to consider both the context of their display in Hadrian's Villa and the other replicas of the Old and Young Centaur type, in various materials, I suggest that the primary resonance for an ancient viewer of such dark-colored stones was not an imitation of bronze but rather the character of the stone and, in some cases, its relationship to other stones. I draw attention specifically to the Roman preference for pairing black and red stones as pendants and in composite sculpture.

With these examples, I show that the identification of material mimesis must not be based solely on visual observation of similitude but rather must make use of investigations of ancient surface treatments, patterns of material selection and sculptural display, and histories of quarry exploitation and restoration practices. Through this analysis, I demonstrate the context-specific nature of materiality in two ways: first, by tracing relationships between materials in a certain time and culture and, second, by highlighting several instances when the modern reception of Roman sculptural materials has stood in the way of an understanding of ancient practices and impressions. Both of these aspects are crucial elements for a more thorough understanding of Roman materiality and a renewed sensitivity to the physical character of Roman sculpture.

Roman Wall Painting as Evidence for Egyptian Luxury Imports

Stephanie Pearson, Humboldt-Universität zu Berlin

The mid first century B.C.E. sees an explosion of Egyptian motifs in Roman wall painting. Drawing on pharaonic art (the art of Egypt under the pharaohs until the Hellenistic period), these motifs carefully reproduce the iconography and even artistic style such that the miniature pharaonic figures, crowns, and animals stand out prominently from their surrounding framework. Although once interpreted as a sign of the homeowner's adherence to Isiac cult, these motifs are now more commonly thought to reference Octavian's conquest of Egypt or to be simply a new development in fresco "fashion." Yet none of these readings is satisfactory: the paintings overlap in no way with religious and political imagery, and even a "fashion" needs to be explained within its historical context. How, then, can we make sense of them?

Comparing select wall paintings in Rome and the Bay of Naples with other archaeological material reveals that the paintings, including their pharaonic interpolations, in fact depict actual luxury objects—objects that were highly prized by Roman collectors and sometimes even stood within the same rooms that the painters were decorating. Indeed, that painters reproduced such precious items in fresco has already been recognized in the vessels and candelabra depicted in Second Style schemes (ca. 45–20 B.C.E.); this paper demonstrates that the same artistic practice informs the pharaonic motifs. Moreover, it shows that these motifs draw on a great range of prestige objects: not only vessels and candelabra but also jewelry, metalware, statuettes, and even textiles. Addressing each category in turn, this paper concludes that pharaonic motifs owe more to painterly process and the booming trade in luxury goods than to any religious or political agenda. In this respect, the motifs are actually analogous to many Greek elements in the paintings, which until now have been treated as a discrete and unrelated phenomenon and rarely interpreted in terms of politics. That Roman collections of precious objects inform both sets of material requires us to rethink the widespread political readings of pharaonic motifs and, indeed, Roman wall painting more generally.

Copying Across Time and Space: The Case of the Roman Isis

Lindsey A. Mazurek, Duke University

In this paper, I examine how sculptures of Isis from the northern Mediterranean advance scholarly discussions of ancient copying. As Robert Bianchi's lifelong study of Isiac sculpture has demonstrated, there is no "original" Isis image. With few exceptions, Roman sculptures of Isis from the northern Mediterranean did not imitate Egyptian art but created new naturalistic images appropriate to Graeco-Roman audiences. Scholars have regularly referred to this process as part of a "hellenization" of Isis. Rather than seeing Isis' new images as part of an intellectually problematic cultural process, I argue that we should analyze statues of the Egyptian gods as part of a broader tendency to reuse old images to represent new concepts. I argue that these images adapt existing Graeco-Roman sculptural types as a way to connect Isis with desired divine traits while integrating new symbols that required cult-specific knowledge to interpret.

Much of the past discussion surrounding copying focused on establishing types, arguing that sculptors of ancient gods and goddesses sought to emulate and adapt preexisting models. More recent scholarship by Elaine Gazda, Julia Habetzeder, Ellen Perry, and Miranda Marvin integrated the idea of cultural memory, suggesting that eclectic integration of previous types allowed statues to allude to specific meanings in many settings.

I am interested in exploring how viewers used similar practices of reading long-standing meanings into innovative images of Isis. Since statues of Isis draw from a particularly eclectic mix of established types and invented symbols, viewers needed to consider a range of cultural phenomena to "get" the Egyptian gods: well-known artistic types, secret religious rituals, and varied textual descriptions. I begin my paper with an overview of Isis' images in Italy, Greece, and Asia Minor, establishing Isis' formal characteristics during the Roman period. Next, I deconstruct these images to establish their relationships with Greek and Roman ideal sculpture. I conclude my paper with an examination of Isis sculptures found in situ, specifically the statue of Isis Pelagia from the theater at Messene and the cult statue of Isis from the temple at Pompeii, to consider what kinds of meanings statues of Isis conveyed to Graeco-Roman audiences.

Repetition as a Social and Aesthetic Strategy in the Group Reliefs of the Late Republic and Early Empire
Devon Stewart, Georgia State University

The group reliefs, popular tomb monuments produced primarily in the Late Republic and Early Imperial periods, have become emblematic of their prosperous freedman patrons in many ways. These monuments resonate particularly because the portraits they bear are potent examples of self-representation from a group of people whose voices otherwise are represented poorly in the historical and archaeological records. However, the monuments are largely formulaic in typology, iconography, and epigraphy. As a result, scholars often elide the formula and the patrons, interpreting the group reliefs as evidence for homogeneity within Rome's broader freedman population. This paper approaches the repetition seen within the monuments as a deliberate attempt to express membership within a particular stratum of the freedman population. Within a generation of the group relief's genesis, a basic visual formula emerged that formed a template for this type of monument, which remained relatively unchanged through the second century C.E. The repetition of a basic visual formula provided a stable visual anchor that united the subjects of these monuments under an umbrella of shared status, social values, and art historical knowledge. Each subsequent repetition of this kind of image further reinforced the legitimacy and authority of the type as a source. I argue that freedman patrons who commissioned group reliefs participated actively in the social and artistic dialogue attached to these images. Moreover, the absence of group reliefs from some contemporary nonelite tomb contexts, such as the Via Salaria necropolis and the Vigna Codini *columbaria*, reflects the diversity of social and commemorative interests within the population of Roman freedmen. Some freedmen remained within the circle of the patron's *familia* after death, choosing burial within household *columbaria* for social, personal, or financial reasons. The patrons of the group reliefs instead used their tombs and tomb monuments to reify the new identities they forged after manumission. In doing so, they aligned themselves with others of similar ambitions and distinguished themselves within the broader freedman population and the community at large.

SESSION 2I: Colloquium
AIA Presidential Plenary Session: Climate Change and Human Society, Past, Present, and Future

ORGANIZER: *Andrew M.T. Moore*, Rochester Institute of Technology

Colloquium Overview Statement

The increasing pace of climate change is having a marked effect on human society today and is expected to have an even greater impact in the future. Archaeologists have determined that climate change contributed importantly to the development of human societies in the past. Paleontologists consider that fluctuations in environment during the Quaternary influenced the evolution of hominins. Successive episodes of warming and cooling conditioned the peopling of Eurasia, Australasia, and the Americas from Africa. Climate change was a critical element in two major transformations in human society and economy: the development of farming and the formation and demise of civilizations in western Asia and elsewhere. Lower sea levels during the last Glacial Maximum connected East Asia and North America across the Bering Strait, facilitating the peopling of the New World. Rising sea levels today caused by atmospheric warming are destroying many coastal archaeological sites. Melting ice sheets at high altitudes are exposing others. Thus, climate change is having a direct impact on the archaeological record. The speakers in this colloquium present case studies that will highlight the interactions between humans and a changing environment in deep time and more recently. They discuss the implications of these insights for human societies in the present and in the future.

Archaeologists and Climate Change: There's More to This than the Birth of Frankenstein
Brian Fagan, University of California, Santa Barbara

The study of ancient climate change has come a long way from the environmental determinism of a century ago. In recent years, archaeologists have begun the task of factoring climate change into their studies of ancient societies. This requires highly sophisticated, fine-grained research, for we now know that the impacts of long- and short-term climate change are as much a local as a more global phenomenon. A new generation of field and laboratory inquiry is casting new light on such events as El Niños and major drought cycles. This exciting research has profound implications for our present concerns with global warming and potentially catastrophic climatic shifts in the future. Archaeology is unique among the social sciences in its ability to study both long- and short-term cultural change at global and local levels. This presentation presents examples of how ancient climatic events changed ancient societies and long-vanished civilizations. Using rising sea levels as an example, it argues that rising population densities in floodplain and coastal environments have made humanity far more vulnerable to the kinds of extreme climatic events that are forecast for the future. Archaeologists have an important role to play in making broader audiences aware of the hazards presented by rising seas and other changes. Do we yield to the ocean or build cities that are adapted to both wet and dry landscapes? What are the social consequences of sea surges, El Niños, and other such short-term events? Archaeology is no spectator in a world beset by accelerating climatic shifts. It provides a unique and vital perspective on the options that face humanity and the ways in which our forebears coped with droughts, sea-level changes, climate change caused by volcanic eruptions, and other such events. All of this gives much of our research a compelling urgency.

Climate and Life: A Human Retrospective from North Africa
Peter de Menocal, Columbia University

Climate shapes life across a range of time and space scales—seasons pace the cycle of death and renewal, and biodiversity is bounded by latitude. Did climate also shape us? The African Humid Period is one of the best and oldest examples of human cultural responses to climate change. Between 15,000 and 5,000 years ago, the Saharan Desert supported grassy, wooded plains, large lakes, and clusters of human settlements as a result of orbital increases in monsoonal rainfall. While there is an ongoing debate whether the end of this wet phase was fast (centuries) or slow (millennia), the rich archeological record shows that this region was depopulated and, within centuries, the first settlements appeared along the Nile River, near 5 ka B.P. Many "firsts" are associated with these predynastic cultures of the Naqada III period, including the first named kings, pyramids, and hieroglyphs, resulting in political unification and dynastic rule along the Nile.

Climate Change, Water Resource Availability, and Migration in Prehistoric North Africa
Jennifer Smith, Washington University in St. Louis

Populations in marginal environments are particularly vulnerable to environmental change, which reduces already limited resources. Where water is a key limiting factor, technological advances or shifts in subsistence base can only offset declining water supplies to a degree, at which point migration becomes the only viable adaptive mechanism. Successive populations of inhabitants of North Africa have faced such challenges repeatedly over the last several hundred thousand years, as the Sahara has oscillated between arid-hyperarid conditions (consistent with those of the present) and significantly more humid climates.

Understanding the availability of resources for Early, Middle, and Later Stone Age occupants of North Africa requires local environmental reconstruction, as spatial variation in access to water would have been high, even during wetter (generally, semiarid) periods. Lacustrine, fluvial, paludal, and spring-derived deposits provide a datable record of the distribution of water sources, which can be paired with archaeological survey data to understand the use of habitable environments through space and time. Geochemical and sedimentological analyses of these deposits generate qualitative records of the persistence (seasonal vs. annual) and quality (salinity) of the water bodies in which they were formed.

Compilation of such records from regions of North Africa, or across the entire Sahara, allows for a basic understanding of the extent to which mobility throughout the region was possible at different times. Marine Isotope Stage 5 (the last interglacial) was a particularly humid period across the extent of the Sahara and could have supported significant migrations along now-dry fluvial networks and between biologically productive lacustrine and wetland environments. During more arid times, occupation would have contracted to coastal, oasis, and major river (i.e., the Nile) floodplain habitats or moved out of the region altogether. The nature of environmental changes in the Sahara relative to its surroundings—the Sahel, the Arabian Peninsula, the Levant—could create a climatic pump, variably drawing inhabitants into or out of the region. This nature shifts from humid phase to humid phase, presenting different challenges and opportunities to Early, Middle, and Later Stone Age inhabitants.

Climate Change and Human Society: Beyond Crisis to Opportunity and History
Sturt Manning, Cornell University

This paper wishes to address some of the limitations (and missed opportunities) in much current literature on climate change and history and archaeology.

The first issue is to move beyond crisis. Much of the work to date on climate change and history/archaeology has focused on finding climate change causing apparently overwhelming crises—such as "mega-drought." While this work is undeniably relevant in some regions at some periods, I suggest that we would benefit from escaping from the crisis model. To begin, it is only occasionally that such a crisis can be successfully delineated. But more importantly, we should also look actively at the opportunities afforded by climate context. This might sometimes be a positive climate trajectory, but it might also be the lack of any significant climate change over a sustained period, contrary to the present emphasis on identifying extremes (usually bad and occasionally good).

The second issue I focus on is chronology. At present, despite much work, it remains the case that chronological resolution hampers attempts to identify robust linkages between human history and archaeology and climate change for many periods before the recent past. Many claims for climate relevance are based on poorly dated or resolved records and lack any secure association with human history and its material correlates. Speculation and hypothesis replace tightly constrained evidence associations. Some examples and approaches to improvement are considered.

The third issue I consider is regional focus. Climate change is regional: there are differing impacts of the same wider climate forcings at both the regional and intraregional levels. Available individual climate records also reflect different mechanisms; some are local, some regional or global. There is a need to move away from simplistic models and toward considerations of regions and of the mosaic of interlinked responses to climate and climate changes for any region(s) or period(s).

Nature's Naughty Child: El Niño in Peruvian Prehistory
Daniel H. Sandweiss, University of Maine

El Niño is a major cause of climatic variation throughout the Pacific Basin and beyond. Mega-Niños of the late 20th century caused billions of dollars of damage, cost thousands of lives, and reduced health. In the Internet age, El Niño became a household term and a popular whipping boy for all sorts of environmental and societal ills, as Dr. Elmo put it in his cult hit, "Blame it on El Niño." The future likely holds an increased incidence of this phenomenon, but El Niño also rampaged through Peruvian prehistory. Archaeologists working in the region have pursued two major lines of inquiry. First, they have used the archaeological record to study variation in El Niño frequency over time, which is important both for assessing impact on past peoples and for helping test the models that predict future events. Second and more commonly, archaeologists have sought to understand how El Niño affected the course of history in this region. When were events so severe or so frequent that societies were forced to respond and perhaps to change permanently? How did past peoples cope with these events, and are there lessons for a modern world facing growth in Niños? Were all events entirely negative in their consequences, or were there upsides to El Niño? This talk briefly reviews some highlights of recent research on these topics. El Niño is no deus ex machina to explain all aspects of Peruvian prehistory, but at the same time we musn't throw out the baby with the bathwater: El Niño is severe enough that people were often forced to react, and we can learn much from those reactions.

SESSION 2J: Colloquium
Landscapes of Death and Remembrance in Ancient Greece

ORGANIZERS: *Renee M. Gondek*, The George Washington University, and *Carrie L. Sulosky Weaver*, University of Pittsburgh

Colloquium Overview Statement
Upon burying the dead in ancient Greece, families erected funerary monuments that were sometimes quite lavish in nature. Not only did friends and loved ones gather to visit these burials, but strangers also would have been beckoned from the roads to marvel at their splendor. Thus, funerary monuments permanently altered the landscape to provide mourners with a focal point for their grief and ensure that the deceased would be preserved in the social memory of the community. To further our understanding of this topic, the proposed panel applies interdisciplinary approaches to the study of burial, commemoration, and remembrance in ancient Greece (seventh century B.C.E. to second century C.E.), and it explores the role of artifacts and landscape in documenting the relationship between the living and the dead.

While previous studies on ancient Greek burials have taken into account long-term changes in the landscape, the development of social groups within funerary complexes, and chronological shifts in funerary markers, papers included here incorporate current approaches to aspects of commemoration that involve interdisciplinary methodologies and use GIS for reconstruction purposes. "Mound Construction and Remembrance at the Seventh-Century Kerameikos" considers the spatio-temporal development of the Kerameikos. Upon careful reexamination of the stratigraphic evidence, the author argues that as the seventh century wanes burials become more individualized and these mortuary practices point to a shift in how the dead were memorialized. "Kroisos in Context: Sixth-Century B.C.E. Tumuli in Southern Attica" adopts the anthropological and literary methods of "locational" framing and "inscriptional" framing for a well-known archaic funerary monument. With the inclusion of previously overlooked archaeological and epigraphic evidence, this paper suggests that viewers of Kroisos associated his death with both political and Panhellenic concepts. "The Dead Among the Living: Mapping Classical Attic Tombstones" uses the findspots of and epigraphic information from classical grave tombstones to reconstruct the locations of burial plots of distinct populations (e.g., foreigners, demesmen, children). Applying GIS technology, this author demonstrates for the first time how Attic cemeteries expand, shift, and contract over time. Finally, "Commemorating the Dead: Dark Tourism in Ancient Greece" applies tourism theory to our understanding of ancient practices. Not only were burials deliberately aesthetically pleasing in order to draw in visitors, but also ancient literary sources tell us that macabre sites like the Athenian public cemetery and Marathon were described as "must see" attractions for the ancient traveler.

Mound Construction and Remembrance at the Seventh-Century Kerameikos
Cicek Beeby, University of North Carolina at Chapel Hill

The Kerameikos cemetery was home to an intriguing cluster of seventh-century graves. Each grave was usually covered by a large mound that was marked by a vessel at its peak. These mounds are built directly on top of one another in an agglutinative fashion and create a palimpsest that spans more than a hundred years.

The Kerameikos mounds provide us with an unparalleled chronological resolution in terms of understanding the spatio-temporal development of mortuary contexts. Based on the stratigraphy of the mounds, German excavators of the site were able to offer a sequence in approximately 10-year increments. Furthermore, the meticulous publication of plans and section drawings enables us to recreate the building sequence with precision. As a result of my analysis of the diachronic development of the mounds using GIS, I believe that the sequence can be divided into subphases that follow different patterns. In the first half of the seventh century, the mounds are more collective in their accumulation: new mounds replace the existing ones, creating a continuous vertical layering. Individual mounds or markers are not discernible; what a visitor observes is more akin to a single mound. This agglutinative palimpsest is created through constant reconstruction that highlights the assimilation of the individual into a larger collective. In contrast, the mounds in the second half of the seventh century show a growing tendency to preserve individual identities. New mounds saddle the existing mounds and fill in the gaps, thereby leaving the peaks of the mounds, and the markers that stood at the top, untouched. Instead of creating a more vertical palimpsest, the second group of mounds forms a cluster with multiple peaks, not to mention multiple markers.

The preservation of the markers perpetuates the memory of the individuals and fights against the tendency to turn them into anonymous members of a collective.

I argue that these differences are the result of deliberate choices that reflect a shift in how the personal memory of an individual is preserved. These mounds were probably constructed by a social group—perhaps an extended family—within a couple of generations of each other, and many of the deceased in this compound would still be within the limits of the personal memory of the living; but the way that memory is preserved changes. Throughout this sequence of mounds, we see a delicate balance between intrusive and reconstructive behaviors, as well as the simultaneous formation of individualizing and collective identities.

Kroisos in Context: Sixth-Century B.C.E. Tumuli in Southern Attica
Cameron Pearson, City University of New York

This paper uses both "locational framing" and "inscriptional framing" to explore how the viewer of Kroisos' grave tumulus from southern Attika would have been directed to look beyond the local burial and toward political and Panhellenic concepts.

Regarding locational framing, the monument was positioned facing a road that carried people north to Athens or south to Sounion. Part of a large tumulus 28 m in diameter, the grave would have stood out on the plain and would have signaled to the viewer that Kroisos was part of an important local family. Some have even argued that Kroisos was an Alkamaionid. If so, his grave could have framed the area as Alkmaionid territory. Nearby, two other large grave mounds have been excavated, and two more have been excavated about 3–4 km south in Anavyssos proper and Palaia Phokaia; scholarship tentatively dates all tumuli here to the sixth century B.C.E. Additionally, between Kroisos' tumulus and those at Palai Phokaia lie several earlier geometric cemeteries. I argue that Kroisos' tumulus and the four other tumuli were positioned so as to emphasize their importance over earlier burials and that they were part of a trend in the sixth century of using grave tumuli to frame political territory. To highlight the political context of the area, I include a stele (*IG* 1 3 972) found just north of Kroisos' tumulus in my spatial analysis of the region. Dated to the mid sixth century, the marker displays the names of "archontes" or "demarchs."

As has been noted previously in scholarship, Kroisos' epigram has resonance with martial elegy and *kalos thanatos*. Less commented upon is that this is the only funerary epigram of this period that mentions a deity: Ares. Using inscriptional framing, I argue that Ares gives Kroisos' death a larger Panhellenic significance. Kroisos was not someone killed by another human being; he was felled by a larger cosmic force, often encountered in *epos* and *elegos* as performed at symposia or public festivals. Thus, his death represents a larger loss to his whole community and is connected to events in Panhellenic poetry.

I conclude that an ancient viewer of Kroisos' grave monument would have been spurred not only to mourn but also to associate his death with political and Panhellenic concepts that transcended the place and time of burial.

The Dead Among the Living: Mapping Classical Attic Tombstones

Timothy Shea, Duke University

Classical tombstones are treated in the same way that most ancient sculpture is. Scholars gather the thousands of monuments that survive, assign each a date between 430 and 317 B.C.E., and arrange them in groups based on iconography. Where a tombstone was found has played a small role in their interpretation. Meanwhile, studies on ancient cemeteries focus mainly on the distribution of burials and the grave goods deposited in them. By constructing studies of cemeteries in this way, one tends to think of cemeteries as existing only belowground, as a place for the dead. If we consider the tombstones and their relationship to these burials, we can begin to reconstruct these cemeteries as they appeared to the living.

What I have done is systematically plot in a GIS database the findspots of archaic and classical tombstones in Attica. In many cases, tombstones have an archaeological context; they are simply recorded in varying degrees of specificity. Some are found under houses built in the late 19th century, others in rescue excavations undertaken by the Greek Ministry of Culture; others still are mentioned by Alexander Conze as being in houses in certain neighborhoods.

When the locations are viewed in conjunction with burials and settlement remains found in rescue excavations, such as those undertaken during the construction of the Metro system, it becomes clear that the findspots of tombstones are located in the immediate vicinity of burials from the same period. Tombstones form distinct groups along the periphery of the Themistoclean walls, and as a result, tombstones can be studied as coherent groups as parts of cemeteries in different areas of the city. Using information in the inscriptions on these monuments, I am able to show where foreigners, demesmen, and children are buried and how they are represented. This gives us a more complete picture of the cemeteries of Athens, and for the first time we are able to see how cemeteries expand, shift, and contract over time.

Commemorating the Dead: Dark Tourism in Ancient Greece

Carrie L. Sulosky Weaver, University of Pittsburgh

"Dark tourism" is defined as travel to sites associated with suffering and death. In the modern world, popular dark tourism destinations include bloody battlefields such as Gettysburg, sites of disaster like the Flight 93 Memorial, and scenes of genocide such as the Holocaust concentration camps. Although some scholars in the field of dark tourism maintain that travel of this sort is a phenomenon of the 20th and 21st centuries, humans have long been drawn to places of disaster, and dark tourism arguably has its roots in antiquity.

For the ancient Greeks, it was important to be remembered after death. Their cemeteries were extramural, flanking the roads leading to the gates of their cities. This placement was strategic, as it ensured that grave monuments were visible to travelers as they moved in and out of the city. Some cities, like Athens, took additional measures to ensure that their cemeteries were attractive to visitors. Thucydides (2.34, 43) states that the Athenians placed their cemetery in a picturesque district of the city and implies that citizens were actively encouraged to visit the graves of fallen heroes. Furthermore, excavations in the public cemetery of Athens have revealed sculpted grave markers that are among the finest examples of High Classical art, such as the "Stele of Hegeso" (ca. 400 B.C.E.). Thus, through the use of cultivated landscape and exceptional funerary art, the Athenians encouraged travelers to linger among the monuments, ensuring that the memory of the dead would be preserved. This practice of travel to sites of death and commemoration was not unique to the Greeks, and it persisted into the Roman period. In his *Description of Greece* (second century C.E.), Pausanias recorded personal observations from his visits to the Athenian public cemetery and the burial tumulus at Marathon (1.29.2–16, 1.32.3–5). Pausanias' travel account is selective, and he chose to discuss monuments and sites that he thought were "must see" attractions. The inclusion of two Athenian burial grounds on his itinerary is significant and revealing, suggesting that they were well-established sites of ancient tourism.

This paper explores the evidence for the practice of dark tourism in ancient Greece. It begins with an introduction to the anthropology of tourism, then focuses on a series of case studies. In particular, sojourns to ancient battlefields and visits to cemeteries and cenotaphs are considered, ultimately providing a foundation for future studies of dark tourism in the ancient Mediterranean world.

SESSION 2K
Poster Session

Tutankhamun's Shields: Historical Context and Digital Documentation
Islam Shaheen, Grand Egyptian Museum Conservation Center

Among the military equipment found in the tomb of Tutankhamun were eight shields, four of which are ceremonial and are of openwork wood, incised and gilded. These finds provide a lot of information related to the activity of usage of shields by the king as a symbol of the power and strength of the royal authority at that time. Shields were made of wood in several pieces pegged and glued together, the border and central panel covered with gesso and gilt, the remaining field covered with the hide of a cheetah (see spots), the hair well preserved.

The goal of this study is to identify the structure of shields. Indeed, this study gives us great semantics to confirm that the king use these pieces or not, as well as an image for development of weapons in the new kingdom.

This study also investigates the feasibility, effectiveness, and overall value of reflectance transformation imaging (RTI) in documenting the shields of Tutankhamen impressions. From where, the ability to manipulate the light source and enhance surface attributes with RTI facilitates identification of important shield features from documentation of shield impressions. Also, this paper compares RTI, digital photography, and multispectral imaging (ultraviolent [UV] and infrared [IR]) for documentation of the shields of King Tutankhamen.

Finally, the shields of Tutankhamen were documented by AutoCAD 2D to obtain a more detailed observation of the structure and plan of condition.

Peripheral Centers? Regional Urban Connectivity in the Xanthos Valley and Kibyratis Highlands

Rachel L. Starry, Bryn Mawr College

This study is part of a broader research project investigating the Roman impact on processes of urban development, practices of civic benefaction, and changes to regional urban networks in two microregions in southwestern Anatolia: the Xanthos River valley and the Kibyratis highland zone. This comparative case study focuses on the cities of Xanthos in the valley and Oinoanda in the highlands and considers how specific details of urban planning and architectural design can speak to the existence of dynamic regional urban networks that fluctuated across space and time.

On the basis of a detailed, diachronic comparison of architectural forms at each site, I propose that changes to regional urban networks during the first to third centuries C.E. are only partially related to Roman interference and that ultimately such networks are strongly shaped by the sociopolitical goals of the local elite families and individuals who sponsored major urban architectural projects. The Roman provincial reorganization that administratively joined the cities of the Kibyratis to Lycia (first century B.C.E.) likely encouraged a reorientation of the attention of the elites of Oinoanda away from their traditional northern and eastern connections and toward coastal Lycia as they began to compete with Lycian cities for regional and perhaps even supraregional prominence. The situation appears to have changed during the second century C.E., when Oinoandian elites began to return their attention to the north, especially toward the city of Aphrodisias. A more stable connection can be demonstrated between Xanthos and Pergamon, via the city of Perge in neighboring Pamphylia, which appears to show that Xanthian elites were primarily engaged in agonistic exchange with other Anatolian coastal cities.

These dynamic regional networks can be visualized through a series of interconnected maps, diagrams, and photographic overlays, and I conclude that the cities' respective topographical situations played a significant role in the development of both their urban plans and their regional connectivity throughout the Roman Imperial period. The Kibyratis is located at the intersection of four regions: Caria, Phrygia, Pisidia, and Lycia. Oinoanda likely participated in urban networks that were less stable in the long term because its inhabitants were constantly reacting to changes in the social, political, and economic environments of the many geopolitical zones surrounding them, as local elites sought to achieve (and maintain) sociopolitical status through competition with different cities at different times. In contrast, Xanthos was deeply rooted in coastal communication routes that persisted throughout the Roman period.

Lights, Camera, Archaeology: Documenting Archaeological Textile Impressions with Reflectance Transformation Imaging

Emily B. Frank, Institute of Fine Arts, New York University

This work investigates the feasibility, effectiveness, and overall value of reflectance transformation imaging (RTI) for documentation and analysis of archaeological textile and basketry impressions. The ability to manipulate the light source and enhance surface attributes with RTI facilitates identification of important textile features from documentation. This is especially important for ephemeral material, like archaeological soil impressions; the original material is often destroyed during ongoing excavation, and documentation becomes the sole record of the object. The interactive RTI files provide an alternative way to study textile impressions that minimizes object handling during examination. In this study, RTI images of impressions in ceramic, mudbrick, and soil were captured and then compared with digital photography based on standards for good documentation of archaeological textile impressions. The findings demonstrate that RTI can provide superior information to digital photography for documentation and analysis of textile impressions. Particularly exciting is the ability of RTI to provide a lasting digital artifact of short-lived archaeological information for in situ archaeological textile impressions.

Of Wine and Residues: Materials and Methods from the Tel Kabri Palatial Storerooms to the Chemistry Laboratory

Alison M. Crandall, University of California, Los Angeles, *Assaf Yasur-Landau*, University of Haifa, *Eric H. Cline*, The George Washington University, and *Andrew J. Koh*, Brandeis University

The 2015 season of the Kabri Archaeological Project at the Bronze Age Canaanite palace of Tel Kabri has continued to unearth storage jars from rooms adjacent to the wine cellar found in 2013. This season, the ARCHEM team and Koh Group at Brandeis isolated and analyzed 80 organic residue analysis (ORA) samples by gas chromatography-mass spectrometry (GC-MS) using ARCHEM's nondestructive extraction protocol to continue characterizing what was stored in the palace and how these rooms relate to ancient palatial economy. Because of the quantity of well-preserved and undisturbed storage jars with anticipated patterns of palatial organization, Kabri also presents an uncommon opportunity to test the limitations and potential restrictions of organic residue preservation and analysis.

Unlike modern experimental archaeology studies, which do not have comparable timeframes and depositional histories to fully mimic the absorption of organic residues into a ceramic matrix or the degradation that occurs through time and immediately after excavation, Kabri sherds sampled from disparate locations of a single vessel, as well as adjacent sherds subjected to different analytical techniques, allow us to compare the quality and variability of ancient ORA results. This particular study focuses on the potential difference in results between a base and rim of a single jar and that of adjacent base sherds extracted both destructively and nondestructively. Sherds from several vessels were also taken at initial vessel discovery for comparison with those taken after full articulation. Other experiments, such as storing sherds adjacent to those presently analyzed for future extraction, have been prepared.

ORA is a powerful technique to help interpret archaeological contexts and establish narratives of ancient social behavior and practices. As a science, it must be approached with care and attention to even the smallest of details, as established in modern scientific protocol. But a purely scientific approach can compromise the entire enterprise since the interpretation and contextualization of results are inseparable from the conditions of excavation. Moreover, the degradation processes over millennia must be taken into account, which simultaneously requires the scientific skills to read the data and the archaeological ability to deconstruct what is empirically there in order to reconstruct the past using informed and insightful reasoning. As archaeological science grows as a field and incorporates more intricate analyses, it must continue adapting to these latest scientific tools, providing a seamless bridge between archaeologist and scientist to obtain the most accurate and reliable results.

Curating and Preserving Digital Archaeological Data: A Guide to Good Practice
Jodi Reeves Flores, Center for Digital Antiquity, and *Adam Brin*, Center for Digital Antiquity

Archaeologists generate large numbers of digital materials during the course of field, laboratory, and records investigations. Maps, photographs, data analysis, and reports are often produced digitally. Good curation of digital data means it can be discovered and accessed, and preserving these materials means they are accessible for future use. In many ways, managing, curating, and preserving digital materials involves similar steps as those taken with physical artifacts, samples, and paper records. However, the digital materials are different, and the process can appear daunting at first.

In this poster, we outline some simple steps for managing and curating digital materials that can be integrated into existing or future project and that can be applied to digital materials from completed projects. We also use real-world examples from the Digital Archaeological Record (tDAR) to illustrate how people are preserving their digital materials for access and future use.

tDAR is a domain repository for archaeological resources, investigations, and related materials. Data and information are curated, are discoverable and accessible, and are preserved for future use. tDAR is developed and maintained by the Center for Digital Antiquity, a not-for-profit center at Arizona State University.

Three-Dimensional Field Documentation: Millimeter Accuracy at the Locus Level
Michael Ashley, Center for Digital Archaeology, and *Adam Prins*, Jezreel Valley Regional Project

The Jezreel Valley Regional Project (JVRP) has developed a workflow by which each individually excavated locus is documented in three-dimensional images with millimeter accuracy. The method demonstrates that it is now possible to reliably document all archaeological contexts, at any scale, in the field, in real time, without needing overly expensive equipment or a team of computer scientists. The workflow produces color-accurate, "born-archival" images, three-dimensional data sets in real-world coordinate space, orthographic photographs for annotation and drawing, and a full accounting of the archaeological process.

Structure from Motion is gaining traction as a viable tool for archaeological documentation, but its use has generally been limited to large features or fully exposed layers. This past summer at its excavations at Legio, a Roman legionary fort in northern Israel, the JVRP successfully experimented with producing a full three-dimensional model of each locus, every time a locus was changed, in under 10 minutes of total recording time. This allows for significantly greater methodological control, as every step of excavation is preserved in photo-realistic three dimensional images. These models reflect field decisions while providing a permanent data-rich record of every discovery—before, during, and after exposure.

While still in the field, two-dimensional orthophotographs generated from these models are used to produce final plans of the site with significantly better accuracy than manually measured hand drawings. Contexts are thus fully documented and ready for publication within hours, all in the field. Moreover, the multidimensional data captured will yield untold benefits for years to come as new processing methods are refined and invented.

Medieval Household Ceramics in 3D: An Inventory of Vessel Shapes from Nemea, Greece

Effie Athanassopoulos, University of Nebraska–Lincoln, and *Kim S. Shelton*, University of California, Berkeley

The University of California, Berkeley, excavations at the Sanctuary of Zeus at Nemea have revealed that the area was intensively used in the Medieval period, in the 12th and 13th centuries C.E.; farming plots, an irrigation ditch, agricultural implements, coins, and a large quantity of ceramics have been found throughout the area. This poster presents a selection of medieval ceramics from Nemea, specifically pottery from a series of closed deposits recovered in the 1970s and 1980s. Here, we employ quantitative methods and three-dimensional modeling to present an inventory of shapes, of coarse wares as well as tablewares. Pottery sherds are sorted according to shape and part of vessel (rim, neck, handle, base, etc.). Each group is then counted and weighted. The goal is to document the variability of vessel shapes and estimate the total number of vessels present in each deposit. Complete vessels provide the weight figures for calculating the equivalent number of vessels in each assemblage. The inventory of shapes facilitates the functional identification of vessels—for example, for storage, cooking, food consumption, and transporting water and other liquids. The quantitative procedures establish the frequency of these shapes in each closed deposit. For example, in a large pit located near the basilica, water jugs/amphoras, in a variety of sizes, are the most common type of vessel, with few other shapes represented. The ceramics are the key in understanding daily activities that took place here. Transporting water, probably for rituals associated with the basilica, indicates that this area played an important role in the life of the medieval rural community, a fact that is reinforced by the presence of burials inside and outside the structure.

Finally, the three-dimensional models of ceramics, created with a three-dimensional laser scanner, allow the visually effective documentation of ceramic variability in these deposits, reduce the need for a descriptive presentation of the pottery, and facilitate analysis, interpretation, and sharing of results. By employing a variety of methods, this project contributes to the study of medieval ceramics derived from a rural context and aims to document consumption patterns and reconstruct trade networks that connected the area of Nemea with the broader region of southern Greece.

Bronze Age Bottle Caps: A New Approach to Ceramic Stoppers in the Late Bronze Age Aegean

Trevor Van Damme, University of California, Los Angeles

Disk-shaped artifacts made from reworked ceramic sherds and tile, despite their widespread occurrence in Late Bronze Age Aegean contexts, have received little attention as a unified corpus. When published at all, they are typically relegated to catalogues of small finds and classed as stoppers, unfinished blanks intended for further reduction into other artifacts or dismissed as inscrutable with little further discussion. In this paper, I argue that the findspots of such artifacts in primary contexts confirm their intended use as stoppers and furthermore that the use of reworked ceramic sherds as stoppers makes them reliable proxies for the study of consumption practices.

Drawing on detailed studies of sealing practices in the economies of New Kingdom Egypt, as well as the large corpus of Hellenistic and Roman-period stoppers from sites such as Berenike and Mons Claudianus, I propose a more rigorous methodology for the study of stoppers in the Late Bronze Age Aegean. Because of their expedient manufacture from broken ceramics, they can safely be considered to have been low-value objects. As such, ceramic stoppers were frequently discarded at the site of their use. Concentrations of stoppers, on account of their ability to be easily recorded and quantified, can therefore be examined to assess the relative consumption of sealed vessels across a given site, as well as changing consumption patterns across time.

Focusing on a case study of ceramic stoppers excavated from 2011 to 2014 at the site of ancient Eleon in Boeotia, I argue that their distribution highlights the utility of this approach and suggests differential consumption of sealed vessels across the site. A comparison of the stoppers from ancient Eleon with other published examples from Mycenae, Thebes, the Menelaion, and Gla suggests that many are quite uniform, indicating that they were used for sealing a restricted number of vessel types. In this paper, I suggest that the majority of such stoppers in Late Helladic (LH) IIIA2–IIIC (early) contexts can be associated with transport stirrup jars (TSJs) and thus are an important archaeological indicator of the movement and consumption of bulk liquid commodities, such as oil and wine. This interpretation is supported by a significant reduction in stopper size after the LH IIIC (early) period, following the disappearance of TSJs from the archaeological record, as well as the observable correlation between stopper concentrations and TSJs at the aforementioned sites.

Southern Balkan Regional Variety and Connectivity: Results of a New International Collaboration

Tobias Krapf, Swiss School of Archaeology in Greece, *Esmeralda Agolli*, University of Tirana, *Ole Aslaksen*, University of Gothenburg, *Ekaterina Ilieva*, New Bulgarian University, *Stoyan Ivanov*, New Bulgarian University, *Christos Kleitsas*, Ephorate of Antiquities of Ioannina, *Giannis Papadias*, University of Thessaloniki, *Aleksandra Papazovska Sanev*, University of Skopje, *Evgenia Tsafou*, University of Thessaloniki, *Akis Tsonos*, University of Ioannina, and *Evangelia Vliora*, University of Thessaloniki

This poster aims at presenting the results of the international mobile workshop "Balkan Bronze Age Borderland: Along Ancient Routes from the Aegean to Albania, F.Y.R.O.M. and SW Bulgaria," which was held from 28 June to 11 July 2015. It brought together 11 young scholars, all specializing in pottery or other aspects of material culture of the Late Bronze Age/Early Iron Age in one of the above-mentioned regions. The workshop, covering Greece, Albania, F.Y.R.O.M., Kosovo, and southwest Bulgaria, was made possible with the support of the Max Geldner Foundation at the University of Basel. Through the collective visits and discussions of the archaeological sites and respective material evidence each of the participants focuses on in their research, the venture encouraged a reinvigorated insight into interregional comparison and contacts. Most significantly, it set the foundation for a network of young researchers and academics and their future collaboration in a region that is nowadays characterized by fragmentation, not only political but also in terms of language and research traditions. As a result, first steps toward the translation of terminologies, the comparison of classification systems, and chronological links have been established. A follow-up project has been envisaged for 2016, along with the publication of the results of 2015.

The visit of a selection of 19 relevant sites and 27 museums/storerooms (mainly involved were the teams of Toumba of Thessaloniki, Apsalos, Ioannina, Apollonia, Lofkend, Sovjan, Maligrad, Tren, Kamenica, Plaosnik, Skopje, Prizren, Kamenska Chuka, and Bresto) allowed a detailed examination of distribution patterns of different pottery styles as well as of settlement types and cultural developments. With the fundamental contribution of the workshop, many of the so far published distribution maps can be complemented by a series of new sites. Pottery decoration styles and motifs along with distinctive shapes proved to be valid criteria for the definition of different regional zones and the identification of interaction. Common traditions spread over a wider area as well as microregional differentiations have been discerned. Furthermore, our results can foster a renewed discussion regarding communication routes, prehistoric exchange networks, and ways of mutual influence.

This paper presents a selection of general conclusions on regionality and connectivity in this broad geographical area based on this joint effort of a group of scholars working on the major archaeological sites currently under study. It also aims at promoting this newly established network that intends to continue cohesive interaction.

The Shared Classical Heritage of East and West in the Monumental Art of the Early Islamic Middle East

Elizabeth Macaulay-Lewis, The Graduate Center, The City University of New York, and *Judith McKenzie*, University of Oxford

The recent focus of the Smithsonian's Freer and Sackler Galleries on Palmyra has highlighted the shared classical legacy resulting from the influence of Palmyra's classical ruins on Neoclassical architecture. Still less well known is how the Middle East and the West have a common classical heritage that continued from Graeco-Roman art into the Early Islamic monumental art of the Umayyad caliphate (661–750 C.E.), with its capital in Damascus. This poster aims to introduce some new observations on this classical heritage, reflecting its different strands (local and imported) and the roles of local architects as creators rather than imitators or synthesizers.

The "desert castles" are the most substantial surviving examples of secular Umayyad architecture. Unlike contemporary Islamic religious buildings, their floor mosaics, wall paintings, and relief carvings include figures and animals. Their sculptors used the "language" of classical architecture but broke away from its "grammar" to create new forms combined with Sasanian and other features. Our research has revealed how the sculpture of two of the "desert castles" of the southern Levant (Khirbet al-Mafjar and Qasr al-Mshatta) demonstrates connections to earlier Nabataean sculptural traditions at Khirbet et-Tannur and Khirbet edh-Dharih (70 km north of the Nabataean capital, Petra), suggesting a role of long-term regional influences and artists.

The redeployment of classical iconography and forms also occurred on the most iconic Umayyad religious monuments: the Dome of the Rock in Jerusalem and the Great Mosque in Damascus, with some motifs, such as acanthus leaves and scrolls, long recognized, alongside Sasanian elements. The architects of both buildings displayed a genius in how they designed structures closely integrated with their decorative programs to meet the requirements of the new religion. For example, the architect of the Great Mosque envisioned the decoration as relating to the structure when he designed its arcaded porticoes with the appearance of two stories, but without floors on their upper levels, so that their back walls provided a monumental canvas for mosaics, such as the famous landscape panorama. Further evidence has also been uncovered concerning the possible sources of its iconography, including an Alexandrian component.

Extensive images of the monuments and details presented in this poster are available on the open-access Manar al-Athar photographic archive (www.manar-al-athar.ox.ac.uk) for teaching and research, at a time when the use of such images in the classroom will increase understanding of the endangered heritage of the Middle East and appreciation of the importance of its preservation.

Revealing the Potters of Petsas House, Mycenae

Lynne A. Kvapil, Butler University, and *Kim S. Shelton*, University of California, Berkeley

It has been suggested that variation in vessel shape, size, and methods of fabrication occur within ceramic assemblages because the vessels were obtained from different workshops, where potters may have had their own perception of vessel shape, methods of measurement, and understanding of consumer needs. The picture changes, however, when variation is observed in a pottery assemblage excavated from within a ceramics workshop where vessel forms and fabrication are more likely to depend on workshop organization and the individual potters throwing therein.

This poster presents preliminary results from an ongoing study of production techniques and organization at Petsas House, a residence and ceramic workshop in the Late Bronze Age settlement at Mycenae that was in use throughout the 14th century B.C.E. After Petsas House was destroyed by an earthquake and fire at the end of that century, debris from the house, including material from the potters' workshop, was dumped in a well located in Room Pi in a futile effort to clear the ruined house. The Room Pi well deposit constitutes one of the largest known assemblages of LH IIIA2 pottery and is a rare example of a closed deposit from a ceramic workshop in the prehistoric Aegean.

Although a variety of wares is represented in the deposit, the majority of the pottery consists of undecorated fine ware vessels, especially open shapes used for drinking, eating, and serving. Because the vessels were unpolished and unpainted, they preserve traces of forming techniques and technical gestures used by potters during the fabrication of each pot—a sort of potter's signature that tends to be removed or obscured on painted fine ware vessels. Statistical analyses of vessel dimensions suggest that variation within vessel types was the result of modular production undertaken by multiple potters, and the analysis of patterns in the residual smoothing marks from the attachment of handles suggests that these potters were of differing skill levels. Differing degrees of variation between vessel types, however, indicate that some potters may have specialized in the production of vessel types that had different functions or that were intended for a particular set of consumers. Overall, results suggest that the organization of production depended on a variety of personal, technical, and cultural factors.

Occupation Over Time at the Gault Site

Bonnie Etter, Cornell University

It is my goal to use geographic information systems (GIS) applications to map and analyze the distribution of material created by the use life of the Gault site, in order to better understand the ways in which the site was reused.

By attempting to understand the scatter of material culture as a site is continually used over a period of centuries, I hope to better understand the reasons that the site was being occupied, including what sorts of activities were taking place and how previous activities affected those of later populations. Using the ability to map and analyze material scatter of a site, it will be possible to draw comparisons between different stratigraphic layers of excavation, which will serve as definitive levels of separate occupations. The comparisons of these artifact distributions will assist in the interpretation of many aspects of understanding at the site level, including an increased understanding of those materials that are left behind after the occupation of a site and what that reflects about its use during occupation.

The first series of maps produced will be focused on creating density distributions for each type of artifact across the site. At this stage, the data will be analyzed for high artifact concentrations or lack thereof, with the hope of defining specific locations for the discarding of objects. The two most likely outcomes for this stage of investigation are concentrated locations in which an object is being disposed of or an even distribution across an area. In either case, this series of maps will be compared in the second phase of this research project.

The second series of maps produced will be an overlay of the previous series, in which it will be possible to compare the concentrations of each type of artifact. Through this data it will be possible to understand whther specific locations within were being used over multiple stratigraphic layers or whether these high artifact density areas change. The information gathered will be compared with previously identified products of activity to better understand whether these materials are middens resulting from the accumulation of debris from the site or reflect specific activities that were taking place during different occupation phases.

Landscape Archaeology and New Technologies at Tel Akko and in the Plain of Akko

Jane C. Skinner, Yale University, *Ann E. Killebrew*, Pennsylvania State University, *Jamie Quartermaine*, Oxford Archaeology, Inc., and *Michal Artzy*, University of Haifa

The renewed excavations at the ancient port site of Tel Akko commenced in 2010, under the direction of Ann E. Killebrew (Pennsylvania State University) and Michal Artzy (University of Haifa). Located on the only natural bay in the southern Levant, Akko is frequently mentioned in historical sources ranging from the Bronze Age through the present time. Among the Tel Akko Total Archaeology Project's primary goals is the development and implementation of new technologies devoted to three-dimensional documentation and to a high-resolution investigation of the environs of Tel Akko and the site within the context of the Plain of Akko. These include sophisticated and effective three-dimensional recording of the ongoing excavation on the tel, an intensive test-pitting survey of the mound, and a regional survey of the Plain of Akko using LiDAR, three-dimensional photogrammetry, and pedestrian survey. This poster presents the results of our three-dimensional documentation from the excavation, the test-pit survey on the mound, and the application of LiDAR and photogrammetry to interpreting the Plain of Akko's ancient landscapes.

Studying Households and Tracing Cultural Practices in Northeast Spain (Second and Early First Centuries B.C.E.)

Alejandro G. Sinner, York University, *Kimberly McCullough*, York University, *Ashwyn Grewal*, York University, and *Daniel Jankulovski*, York University

The aim of this poster is to present the archaeological project together with the results of the first excavation campaign that York University (History Department, Faculty of Liberal Arts & Professional Studies) is conducting at the Ibero-Roman city of Ilduro (Cabrera de Mar, northeast Spain).

Scholars have typically taken two different positions regarding the function of this settlement and the ethnicity of its inhabitants. The first associates the foreign material culture with a stable foreign occupation of the settlement. The second, usually called romanization, takes a diametrically opposite approach and understands the presence of foreign material culture as proof of a high degree of hybridization of the indigenous population. The two theories derive from two very different approaches that share a common need to build a grand narrative that explains the multiple rapid, ongoing changes that occurred in the settlement in the wake of the Roman conquest. However, it makes little sense to draw such conclusions without knowing how the inhabitants of these households were and consuming and living.

Our research aims to solve the aforementioned problem by focusing on the detailed analysis of three complex domestic spaces and their material culture: two of them excavated during the 1990s and one that will be fully uncovered by the York University archaeological team. The houses, inhabited approximately between 135/125 B.C.E. and 90/80 B.C.E., when they were abandoned, are located near the public baths and seem to occupy one of the most privileged spaces within the urban layout. Therefore, a household archaeology study of these domestic spaces should reveal some of the cultural practices, consumption patterns, and other relevant aspects of their inhabitants' lives.

Our poster shows how analysis of the most relevant new data obtained from our first archaeological campaign in June 2015 combined with significant revision of some key findings from the previous excavations can usefully address questions of the cultural horizons of the inhabitants of these urban domestic spaces.

Gold from the Sea: A Cargo of Coins from a Fatimid Egyptian Shipwreck at Caesarea Maritima, Israel

John R. Hale, University of Louisville, *Jacob Sharvit*, Israel Antiquities Authority, *Robert Kool*, Israel Museum, Jerusalem, *Dror Planer*, Israel Antiquities Authority, and *Bridget Buxton*, University of Rhode Island

This poster reports on the discovery of Fatimid Egyptian gold coins in the harbor at Caesarea Maritima, Israel, in 2015. The authors describe the identification and dating of the coins and their chronological and historical context. We also document the subsequent underwater search for remains of the Fatimid shipwreck that may have been the source of the coins. The dates of the newly discovered coins span approximately a century and a half, from the late ninth to the mid 11th century C.E. At that time, Caesarea was an important port under the control of the Fatimid caliphs, a Shiite dynasty that built an empire in North Africa and the eastern Mediterranean.

In February 2015, after a storm stirred up sediments on the floor of Caesarea's ancient Roman harbor, recreational divers discovered a few gold coins. They notified underwater archaeologists of the Israel Antiquities Authority, who found 2,000 additional coins that same day. The Caesarea discovery is the largest find of coins ever made by archaeologists in Israel.

More than 3,000 gold coins have now been recovered from the site. The earliest is a quarter-dinar minted ca. 850 C.E. in Palermo, Sicily, which was an early Fatimid maritime base. The latest coin was probably produced at the Cairo mint in Fatimid Egypt no later than 1036, so the loss of the coins at sea presumably happened shortly after that date. Similar coins remained in circulation even after the Crusader conquests.

Two denominations are represented in the Caesarea find: dinars and quarter-dinars. The condition of the coins ranges from seemingly uncirculated to extremely poor, with some coins worn completely smooth. The presence of human bitemarks as well as bent coins shows evidence for testing the gold's purity, which is 23–24 carat. Fatimid merchants were considered wealthy if they carried even 100 gold dinars at a time.

Archaeological survey of the area where the coins were discovered has revealed the presence of three iron anchors that appear to be contemporary with the coins and that may have derived from a Fatimid shipwreck. Formal underwater excavations began at the site in June 2015, using the Research Vessel KADMONIT as a base for the diving operations. This poster summarizes the results of these ongoing investigations.

Assessment of Iron Age Lydian Tumulus Distributions Through GIS-Based Spatial Analysis

Daniel Plekhov, Boston University, *Christina M. Luke*, Koç University, and *Christopher H. Roosevelt*, Koç University

The Iron Age Lydian burial mounds of Bin Tepe, in western Anatolia, are the defining characteristic of the local landscape, within which around 140 mounds have been documented, about one-quarter of all the known mounds within Lydia. This area has long been identified as the burial ground for the rulers and elites of the nearby Lydian capital, Sardis, with several of the largest mounds constructed in places clearly visible from the city across the valley. Most of the mounds are, however, difficult to see unless in close proximity, often disappearing entirely from view as one moves across the rolling and hillocky landscape. As such, visibility to and from Sardis was likely not the only criterion when deciding on building locations for new burial mounds.

This poster uses a wide variety of data sets, integrated in a GIS, to study the distribution of the Bin Tepe burial mounds in relation to a variety of other considerations that may have influenced the location of their construction. Inter-visibility, topography, proximity to natural resources and features, and proximity to contemporary archaeological surface finds are all considered for each of the mounds. Clusters of mounds and outliers are identified through spatial and attribute queries that detect similar sets of considerations for their placement. In this way, this study addresses the environmental and cultural factors that influenced where burial mounds were constructed, identifies mound groupings on the basis of similar attributes and spatial relationships, and demonstrates the value of combining varied and independent data sets within a GIS.

Portable X-Ray Fluorescence Spectrometer Analysis of the Pylos Linear B Tablets
Billy B. Wilemon, Jr., Mississippi State University

More than 1,100 clay tablets were found at the Mycenaean palace at Pylos in Messenia, western Greece. These are generally economic in nature, and most were stored in the archives room. There are none to be found in any quantity outside the palace. About 40 different scribes have been noted. Stamped clay sealings were used to track containers of oil, wine, etc., as well as to label baskets of tablets.

Over the summer of 2015, 500 Linear B tablets and sealings from Pylos were analyzed at the National Archaeological Museum in Athens using a portable X-ray fluorescence spectrometer (pXRF). This poster presents results of this analysis, which point to significant chemical-compositional variation.

There are a number of questions that careful interpretation of pXRF data may help us address:

- Did the sealings travel with material goods, or were they manufactured at the palace as materials arrived?
- When inscribed sealings are related to tablets, do they use the same or different clays?
- Does one scribe use more than one clay for sealings and tablets, or are the clays the same?
- Do the tablet manufacturers use different clays, and can it be determined whether these manufacturers were at the palace or located elsewhere?

Answers to these questions inform models of political-economic exchange in Mycenaean states related to regional control and distribution of wealth. They also may help clarify how the tablet writers interacted with one another and managed goods entering the palace, and how information made its way into and through the official record.

This project, supervised by Kevin Pluta of the University of Texas–Austin and Michael Galaty of Mississippi State University, is taking place under the auspices of Sharon Stocker and the University of Cincinnati Department of Classical Studies.

Visibility Networks in the Castro Culture of Northwestern Portugal
Jordan Bowers, University of Texas at Austin

This project examines the extent of visibility networks in the areas of northwestern Portugal occupied by the Castro Culture, a culture group that existed from the Late Bronze Age until the Roman conquest in the first century B.C.E. The most notable physical feature of the Castro Culture is the existence of fortified hilltop settlements, known as *castros*.

The geography of northwestern Portugal is dominated by numerous rivers that generally flow from east to west and are separated by chains of prominent hills rising above the river valleys. The *castros* were generally built at the tops of the hills or on prominent spurs, which benefited them with a large viewshed that included other settlements. Visibility between settlements would have allowed for forms of visual communication, circumventing the need for travel to relay simple messages. What was the extent of the visibility network between *castros* and how, in terms of number of sites visible, do major sites compare with smaller sites?

To discover the lines of visibility between *castros*, I use the "Viewshed" tool in ArcGIS to find the viewshed of each individual site and then identify which sites fall within that viewshed. Lines are then drawn from the observer site to the observed sites. As this is done for each site, the network through which visual communication was possible becomes evident. The results of this analysis demonstrate that the majority of *castros* share visibility with at least one other site, with known major sites exhibiting the highest number of sites visible and a network that theoretically could allow sites more than 50 km apart to convey information quickly.

Alpine Lichenometry as a Relative Dating Mechanism in Archaeology
Patrick Hunt, Stanford University

This presentation explores preliminary successes of testing field lichenometry in the Alps for relative dating. Since 2003, Stanford teams have noted and recorded many contexts in the Alps where identifiable lichens are present on human-modified stone monuments from Bronze Age through Roman and medieval contexts, especially where the variables of stone type, climate, elevation, and solar azimuth are in common; multiple statistical analyses show the applicability of lichen growth over time. Prior methodology has been applied from glaciology on geological surfaces. One basic assumption in lichenometry is that lichens grow at known rates over long time periods. Another assumption is that optimal measurements of lichen thalli on human-modified stone surfaces aim for the largest single lichen, preferably one growing radially. Lichen speciation is implemented by noninvasive chemical (K-C-P) and UV light testing. *Rhizocarpon* and *Xanthoria* genus lichens are the most reliable for alpine lichenometry to date and can be cross-correlated when on the same stone surface. Thus, many site contexts in the Alps have corroborated lichenometric rate of growth as parallels of dates known by other means. Material from several of this researcher's forthcoming peer-edited archaeometry papers are referenced in this paper, and sponsorship for several years of research came from the National Geographic Expeditions Council.

Reuse of Roman Material at the Iglesia de la Asunción, San Vicente del Valle (Burgos, Spain)
Scott de Brestian, Central Michigan University, and *Victor Martinez*, Arkansas State University

The Iglesia de la Asunción is an Early Medieval church located in the small village of San Vicente del Valle in the province of Burgos, Spain. The church was overlooked by scholarship until 1990, when a fire damaged the fabric of the building and revealed that it was far older than had previously been thought. In addition, the damage brought to light a large number of reused Roman inscriptions and architectural blocks that were preserved under later plasterwork in the interior and exterior walls of the church.

Recent scholarship has focused on the contested question of the date of the structure, and dates in both the sixth century and ninth century have been vigorously defended. Relatively little attention has been paid to the Roman material incorporated into the church and its potential to shed light on the early occupation of a region previously thought to have been largely devoid of substantial Roman presence.

This poster summarizes the preliminary findings of a field project begun under the auspices of Central Michigan University in 2015. The first season consisted of a detailed inventory and documentation of the Roman blocks and inscriptions from the church, including both material found in the walls of the church as well as a series of 10 Roman inscriptions reused to form the base of a baptismal font in the south portico of the church. By correlating the positions of each block with the reconstructed building phases of the structure, we are able to identify different "procurement groups" representing different phases of spoliation. This allows us to tentatively identify a number of buildings and inscription groups that were appropriated to construct or expand the church, as well as to document the changing availability of Roman architectural material in the valley over the course of the Middle Ages.

Digital Etruria: Three New Projects to Update the Study of Etruscan Archaeology
Orlando Cerasuolo, University at Buffalo, SUNY

Today much of Etruscan archaeology has kept an "old-fashioned" spirit. This is primarily due to the predominant use of traditional methods concerning documentation and study. Generally, Etruscan archaeologists have been reluctant to take advantage of new approaches and technologies or even to discuss theoretical issues that enliven other fields of archaeological, historical, and heritage studies.

Up to this point, few projects have challenged this norm and advanced the field of Etruscology. Some of them are presented and discussed in this paper—that is, the "International Etruscan Sigla Project" (G. Bagnasco and N. De Grummond) or the "EAGLE Project" within Europeana.

Recent years have been characterized by innovation in the field of Etruscan archaeology. Three novel projects are presented. They share some general points: (1) an inclination to digital documentation; (2) an emphasis on the spreading of recent studies and archival data; and (3) the development and testing of new technologies.

The first project, Etruscans@EXPO, is devoted to digital dissemination. It was carried out by the University of Milano, under the patronage of the Istituto Nazionale di Studi Etruschi ed Italici, during the EXPO 2015 Universal Exhibition. Over a six-month period, the international event led many international Etruscologists to get involved and publish short presentations about their field research and studies. Numerous contributions to the project have been collected and exhibited in a virtual stand with three-dimensional screens, touchscreens, and holograms, as well as published on a dedicated website.

The second project—the Landscape of Vulci WebGIS Project—is run by University at Buffalo and Roman Archaeological Association (GAR). The project is an integrated approach to the different data already available in the territory of Vulci, in a multidisciplinary and international environment, which allow us to address new methodological issues and guide future research in the area. The project aims to disseminate the results and data by developing an open webGIS interface, which will foster the discussion of more general issues in Mediterranean archaeology.

Finally, the "Tablet Archaeology Project" is designed to define new methodologies and increase the use of tablets and smartphones in archaeology. It was created by Rofalco Excavation and Outreach Project together with PRISMA (Florence). The development of software and procedures especially designed for archaeology allows a more efficient, complete, and cost-saving process of documentation and study; furthermore, the tablets can be used as promoting devices as well as useful tools for documenting excavation and field activities.

Three-Dimensional Virtual Archaeology Exhibits for Public Outreach
Veronica M. Morriss, University of Chicago

Photogrammetry is a powerful tool for public outreach, as well as traditional archaeological analysis. Since 2012, the Rockley Bay Research Project, under the direction of Kroum Batchvarov (UCONN), has been investigating shipwrecks in Scarborough Harbour, Tobago (Caribbean). During the 2014 season, the archaeological team excavated a 17th-century ship, discovering numerous rare and unique objects important to the history of Tobago—including ornate smoking pipes, delicate pottery vessels, and weapons of war.

To give everyone throughout the islands of Trinidad and Tobago a chance to take part in the ongoing discoveries, our team dedicated the 2015 season to public outreach and three-dimensional recording. We used photogrammetry and structured light scanning to create three-dimensional models of the TRB-5 shipwreck site and artifacts. The three-dimensional artifact models allow students and researchers to physically manipulate, rotate, and handle 340-year-old objects from Tobago's history in ways they never could in a museum. A three-dimensional model of the shipwreck site gives the public a chance to virtually dive beneath the waves, explore excavation areas, and even see where archaeologists discovered important artifacts.

Instead of simply posting models online, our team developed a virtual archaeology exhibit for the project. This exhibit consists of both a web portal and a custom iPad app that integrate the three-dimensional models with video, imagery, local interviews, and history to create a story-based approach to presentation. The goal of our project was to engage the public and get people excited about protecting Tobago's cultural heritage. In addition to developing the virtual archaeology exhibit, we provided small groups of students with hands-on demonstrations of cyberarchaeology's tools and methods to help energize the next generation of scientists and historians.

This poster addresses the importance of placing archaeology and artifacts in context and the social significance of making archaeology accessible to the public.

Morphological and Archaeometric Analyses of Daub at Poggio Civitate

Daniel W. Moore, Indiana State University

Evidence for earthen architecture is often found during archaeological excavations in the form of fired daub, but no defined methodological approach exists for its investigation. Daub can be treated as a subgroup of ceramics and subjected to the archaeometric testing typical of ceramic studies (e.g., V. Tine, ed. *Favella: Un villaggio neolitico nella Sibaritide* [Rome 2006]), or it can be analyzed solely as an architectural material whose morphology is its defining characteristic (e.g., B. McConnell, "The Early Bronze Age Village of La Muculufa and Prehistoric Hut Architecture in Sicily," *AJA* 96 [1992] 23–44). More than 400 fragments of fired daub were recovered from the destruction level of the seventh-century B.C.E. Etruscan building complex at Poggio Civitate, Italy. This poster describes the system developed to classify the daub morphologically and the archaeometric and petrographic tests performed on samples retained for further study. Study of the morphology of the fired daub reveals that wattle and daub was the primary method used to construct the walls of the complex. Petrographic and archaeometric analyses (thermogravimetric analysis [TGA] and laser ablation inductively coupled plasma-mass spectrometry [LA-ICP-MS]) of the daub fragments indicate that lime was used both in the formation of the daub itself and in the white plaster facing used to protect the wattle-and-daub walls from erosion. This study demonstrates that only an integrated approach to the study of fired daub that includes both morphological and laboratory analyses can provide a comprehensive understanding of the processes involved in the formation of this common architectural material.

Organic Pottery Residues at Ayia Triada Cave: A Preliminary Analysis

Rachel Vykukal, University of Tennessee

Details about the Early Bronze Age inhabitants of southern Euboea, the island that flanks mainland Greece to the east, have remained elusive to researchers. Only scant settlement remains dating to the Early Bronze Age have been excavated in the region. However, the well-preserved site of Ayia Triada Cave presents an exceptional opportunity to expand what we know about these inhabitants. Evidence for multiple burials were found in the cave dating to the Early Bronze (EB) II period. Curiously, they were buried atop burned macrobotanical and faunal remains, smashed pottery, and bronze items. It has been suggested that feasting occurred in the cave prior to the burials, but this remains speculative.

This study explores food and drink consumption at Ayia Triada through chemical residue analysis of its pottery. Samples of jars, storage pots, and bowls were analyzed to determine their original organic contents using gas chromatography and mass spectrometry (GC/MS), a technique that separates complex organic mixtures into smaller compounds for identification. Organic residue results were incorporated into previous analyses of the plant, animal, and human remains for a comprehensive analysis of EB II rituals in the cave. This aims to shed light on Early Bronze Age diet, burial traditions, and exploitation of plant and animal resources in the region. Preliminary findings from this ongoing analysis will be presented.

SESSION 3A: Colloquium
Integrating Community and Education into Archaeological Research
Sponsored by the AIA Outreach and Education Committee

ORGANIZERS: *Rebecca Sgouros*, Jackson Hole Historical Society and Museum, and *Matthew Stirn*, Jackson Hole Historical Society and Museum

Colloquium Overview Statement

The integration of local communities and K–12 students into archaeological field research offers a powerful tool for fostering heritage preservation, developing a connection to place, combating looting, and preparing young students for a career in the field. While most academic field projects include some aspects of community engagement and educational outreach, the extent to which these objectives are integrated into the main research model varies. By directly involving non-academic populations and precollegiate students in the discovery of archaeological materials and the research process, it is possible to move beyond a preliminary introduction to archaeology and nurture a reciprocal relationship that jointly impacts students, the local community, and archaeologists. The projects presented in this colloquium place education and community collaboration at the core of their research objectives and are strong models for future community and education-focused field research.

"It Was Just Like Finding Treasure": Archaeology, Heritage, and Community Partnership at Little Bay Plantation, Montserrat, West Indies
Jessica Striebel Maclean, Boston University

In 2012, the Little Bay Archaeology and Heritage Project launched a "preservation through education" initiative at Little Bay Plantation, a small-scale 18th-century sugar plantation and heritage site on the island of Montserrat in the eastern Caribbean, funded by an AIA Site Preservation Grant and developed in association with the Montserrat National Trust. The project set out to establish the foundation of a community-based archaeological, interpretive, and education program at the heritage site. The initiative included the integration of secondary-school students into active excavations and the development of a student-led walking-tour program intended to provide educational programming for the local museum and employment for students. A core value of the project is sustainability. This paper shares the successes and challenges associated with the program's development and implementation, and the importance of time, patience, creativity, long-distance trust, and the radio in creating a lasting community partnership and sustainable program footprint.

Public Involvement at the "Epicenter of Rocky Mountain Archaeology"
Richard Adams, Colorado State University

In 2010, American Museum of Natural History archaeologist David Hurst Thomas called the small town of Dubois, Wyoming, the "epicenter of Rocky Mountain archaeology." Dubois—with a summertime population of about 2,000—is a model of community involvement in participatory archaeology. Local avocational archaeologists found alpine villages in the Wind River Mountains, discovered ancient butchered bison bones in alpine ice patches, found wooden wickiups and sheep traps, engaged in experimental archaeology, created museum displays, and wrote books and magazine articles about their experiences. It is not uncommon for 10% of the town's residents to attend a public lecture by a visiting archaeologist. I believe that students—future archaeologists—need more exposure to community archaeology to avoid winding up cloistered in Ivory Towers on college campuses. It takes a village to train an archaeologist.

The Aguacate Community Archaeology Project: Convening Archaeology and Heritage in a Q'eqchi' Maya Village
Claire Novotny, University of North Carolina, Chapel Hill

Emphasizing how historical knowledge is produced, and for whom, is a cornerstone of community-based archaeology. In this paper, I present a model for community-based archaeology that was developed in collaboration with the village of Aguacate in the Maya Mountains region of southern Belize. Villagers' daily lives and practices are performed on the landscape that also contains the archaeological record; as contemporary locals, they have a stake in how projects are carried out on their land. The model presented here outlines my strategy for collaborating with the village of Aguacate, which is rooted in the concept of communities of practice. Communities of practice are constituted by people with a common goal who engage in joint activities and discussions to share information. In the case of Aguacate, the shared domain was archaeology and heritage, and the community included archaeologists and local Maya people. In this paper, I present the activities engaged in by the Aguacate Community Archaeology Project, such as excavations, meetings, site visits, capacity building, and educational initiatives. The result of the collaboration is a site-conservation project and a community-heritage center opening in 2015. The goal of this model is to illustrate how community-based research can be integrated into archaeological method, theory, and research design.

Providing Multiple Pathways to Community and Archaeology Education
Kathy Stemmler, Crow Canyon Archaeological Center

Integrating community archaeology and education into archaeological research involves developing cooperative, respectful relationships with a diverse range of community members. Crow Canyon Archaeological Center located in Cortez, Colorado, is proactive in establishing multiple pathways for community members ages 9–99 to participate in archaeological interpretation, preservation, and cultural continuation.

For more than 30 years, the mission of the center has been to advance and share knowledge of the human experience through archaeological research, education programs, and partnerships with American Indians. Crow Canyon seeks to broaden and enrich the perspectives gained through archaeological research, incorporate indigenous voices in its education curriculum, and initiate research and education projects that are relevant to the concerns of local community members and American Indian communities today.

Through our research, we hope to learn more about the settlement of the Mesa Verde Region. What impacts did early farmers have on the landscape? How and when did the earliest communities form, and what were they like? On a broader scale, researchers seek to understand not only early Pueblo society but also the development of other early agricultural societies around the world. Crow Canyon's programs provide an experiential, integrated curriculum to cultivate 21st-century skills. Community-based archaeology is essential to our research.

We provide a pathway for participants beginning with fourth-grade students to stay on our residential campus and work alongside our archaeological staff. Our high school and college field schools as well as adult research programs allow community members a wide variety of opportunities to conduct participatory research in addition to preparing students for a professional archaeological career if they choose.

Recently our educational programming has changed its focus to sharing the past and human heritage through empowering communities to create their own approaches to local archaeology and heritage management using methods that are most appropriate to their local cultures. Our K–12 Education Community Program, which began last year, works with selected local teachers to create an archaeological curriculum that best meets their needs. It is in contrast to the traditional approach that relies on expert knowledge that is prepared for teachers to deliver to their students.

Crossing Boundaries: Archaeology Across Cultures and School Levels
Eleanor M. King, Howard University

In 2004, Howard University began a program of archaeological research in the southwest United States on the interaction of the Buffalo Soldiers and the Apache during the last of the Apache Wars in the late 1870s. This program was part of a larger National Park Service initiative, the Warriors Project, which seeks to encourage discussion between African Americans and American Indians about their mutual past on the frontier. Warriors Project Archaeology comprised two sequential projects, one in Guadalupe Mountains National Park in Texas (2004–2006), the other in the Gila National Forest in New Mexico (2008–2011). From the outset, these projects involved members of the Mescalero Apache Tribe, who were later joined by representatives of other Apache nations, including the Warm Springs, White Mountain, and San Carlos Apache. Typically, Mescalero high school students worked alongside African American undergraduates from Howard University. Rounding out the crews were high school, college, and graduate students from a mix of backgrounds, including Hispanic and European Americans and even some international students. Every year, representatives of different Apache nations visited for several days, and, in the last year of the program, San Carlos college students participated alongside the Mescalero. For both Apache and African American students, archaeology was a way to explore a past to which they felt deeply, if distantly, connected. Visiting Mescalero adults would point out to their children the resources in the Guadalupe Mountains that their ancestors had once exploited and that were different from those familiar to them from their home farther north. African American students wrote about understanding that archaeology was not just about "old white men in khakis" and lost worlds. The mix of age levels and backgrounds seemed to work especially well in encouraging participants to explore beyond their comfort zones. Community support was also essential to the project's success. In fact, many of the students went on to work or study further in archaeology. The major lesson from this program is that, if we are to encourage diversity in the archaeological profession, we need to engage both different communities and different age groups in exploring a past that matters to them.

Ancient Lod: A Community Archaeology Project
Yuval Gadot, Tel Aviv University

In this paper, we present a unique community archaeology project to rehabilitate the old city of Lod with the cooperation of the city's diverse, multicultural Jewish and Arab population. This project was initiated by the Israeli Institute of Archaeology (IIA).

Lod was settled continuously from the Neolithic period to modern times and is most likely the only ancient city to maintain such settlement stability. During the Roman period, Lod-Diospolis was a major crossroads in the Levant. Saint George was born and buried in this city, which was consequently named Georgioupolis. During the Muslim occupation, Lod was the civil capital of Palestine. A cathedral was built by the Crusaders followed by the Mamluks, who built the al-Umari mosque and Jindas Bridge. During the Ottoman period, Lod became an important center for the production of olive oil.

Since 1948, the city of Lod has suffered from an economic and social crisis, and most of the heritage sites are neglected. The IIA is currently designing an archaeological tourist site in the Old City of Lod and promotes conservation and restoration of important monuments in the city. These monuments include Khan al-Hilu, the Arches Building, Masbanet al-Far and the Roman-period mosaic floor excavated by the Israeli Antiquities Authority. We are also conducting archaeological excavations to reveal other monuments and remains of the city's glorious past. The project is based on the principles of community archaeology, which have proven to be beneficial for the mixed Jewish-Arab population. Residents of the city are full partners in all stages of the project, including design, archaeological excavations, conservation work, site development, ongoing maintenance, and presentation of the Old City to the public.

10,000 Years of History: Community Heritage and Place-Based Learning at the Linn Site, Idaho

Rebecca Sgouros, Jackson Hole Historical Society and Museum, and *Matthew Stirn*, Jackson Hole Historical Society and Museum

David Sobel defines place-based education as "the process of using the local community and environment as a starting point to teach concepts in language arts, mathematics, social studies, science and other subjects across the curriculum, emphasizing hands-on, real-world learning experiences. This approach to education increases academic achievement? [and] helps students develop stronger ties to their community." We believe that archaeology, taught both in the classroom and in the field, offers a powerful platform for place-based learning and can provide a curriculum that connects students to their environment and local heritage. Furthermore, by instructing K–12 students in archaeological methods, ethics, and problem solving, it is possible to prepare students for a career in the field before they enter higher education and to foster an early understanding of cultural heritage and preservation. During the summers of 2014 and 2015, the Jackson Hole Historical Society and Museum (JHHSM) conducted excavations at the Linn Site in eastern Idaho. These preliminary investigations identified multiple prehistoric occupations ranging from the Early Holocene through the Late Prehistoric period (ca. 1300 BP). The fieldwork conducted at the Linn Site was run through the JHHSM's Mercill Archaeology Center and incorporated gifted and talented students from the local middle school and elementary-age Latino students from a local educational nonprofit. The students first participated in a variety of introductory cultural history and archaeological classes and then joined professional archaeologists in excavation, lab analyses, artifact curation, and report writing. This paper investigates the Linn Site excavations as a case study for place-based archaeological education and explores how this model can be applicable to other community-oriented field projects.

SESSION 3B: Colloquium
Social Spaces and Industrial Places: Multiscalar Approaches to Production in the Ancient Mediterranean

ORGANIZERS: *Katherine B. Harrington*, Brown University, and *Linda Gosner*, Brown University

Colloquium Overview Statement

From massive industrial installations, such as the large terra sigillata kilns at La Graufesenque or the mountains collapsed by imperial gold mining at Las Médulas, to neighborhood-level production of bread at Pompeii to the metal workshops associated with many Greek sanctuaries or the household-level production of textiles across the Mediterranean, people made things at many different scales and in many different places in the ancient Mediterranean, with varying social and economic consequences and benefits. As interest in the archaeology of production increased in the 1980s and 1990s, innovative scholars like van der Leeuw,

Peacock, and Costin sought to develop models to aid comparative archaeological study of the organization of production, producing typologies that included scalar categories such as "household industry," "nucleated workshops," and "community specialization." These models directed attention to often-overlooked aspects of productive activity and inspired many new approaches in subsequent years.

One unintended consequence of this work, however, has been the reification of scalar categories as a hierarchy of development. Thus, in many studies, production activities at either end of the scale are not subject to the same types of analysis as workshop production; domestic production is assumed to make very little impact on the larger economy while, conversely, major industrial works are often subsumed within the study of empire and political economy, obscuring the complicated reality of how very large-scale industrial ventures worked on a human level. Following a recent call for more rigorous integration of data at different scales of analysis by Dietler, among others, in this session we juxtapose ancient production at different scales to examine the role(s) of production in larger social and economic processes in the ancient Mediterranean world. We present a series of papers that draw on geographically and chronologically diverse material from Greek, Roman, and other Mediterranean traditions. The first four papers present a series of case studies of production sites—including glass production, metallurgical production, fish salting, and mining—and examine the dynamics of production at different scales as they relate to topics such as labor organization, patterns of consumption, and empire. The final three papers examine the role of production in wider communities and cities, illuminating commonalities and differences in production at the household, neighborhood, workshop, and industrial levels. Together, these papers not only present new archaeological research but also promote comparative and multiscalar analyses of production and situate the role of production in wider debates in Mediterranean archaeology.

DISCUSSANT: *Eleni Haskai*, University of Arizona

"But There is No Hellenistic Glass": A Multiscalar Analysis of the Late First Millennium B.C.E. Glass Industry
Katherine A. Larson, University of Michigan

Depending on the geographic area and chronological period in which they work, Mediterranean archaeologists have very different attitudes toward and experiences with ancient glass. Roman and Late Antique specialists tend to view glass as rather commonplace, less meaningful but more irritating than pottery, while Greek archaeologists hardly ever find glass at all, except when excavating later deposits. This divergence in modern experience illustrates an ancient reality: glass was extremely rare, especially for everyday domestic use, prior to the Roman period. The question, therefore, is when, how, and why glass transformed from a luxury material with limited distribution and use, as it was in the classical Greek world, to a widespread commodity with a diverse array of functions and contexts of use.

This paper argues that the answer is a matter of scale. At a Mediterranean-wide level, glass is quite rare until well into the first century C.E., but in the eastern Mediterranean, glass drinking bowls become increasingly common over the course of the second and first centuries B.C.E. The concentration of these bowls in Syro-Palestine and evidence from later literary sources point to the emergence of a new glass industry, likely along the Phoenician coast, which used sagging and casting methods that had been in practice since at least the fourth century B.C.E. The novel availability of glass tablewares in the marketplace further spurred consumer demand and fostered workshop experimentation, which in turn led to the invention of glassblowing in the first century B.C.E.—not the other way around, as has long been argued. My research documents the increasing magnitude of the Hellenistic glass industry by collating, mapping, and analyzing published and unpublished glass from the final three centuries B.C.E. throughout the Mediterranean, before glassblowing was widely adopted. A scalar approach to the late first-millennium B.C.E. glass industry undermines deterministic narratives of industrial development as resulting exclusively from new technologies, and it demonstrates how shifting local productive practices can affect larger cultural patterns of consumption.

Industrial Intensification and Abandonment at Neo-Punic Zita
Brett Kaufman, Brown University

Empires use colonial appropriations to expand their base of surplus production, and the industrial pollution that follows can be measured by multiple proxies. This is demonstrated at the global scale through the Greenland ice cores that show a spike in heavy-metal contamination during the Roman empire, peaking ca. 300 C.E. Long-term unsustainable resource-exploitation practices can also be witnessed at the local, urban scale. At the Neo-Punic mound of Zita in Tripolitania, Roman imperial authorities oversaw two centuries of industrial intensification before the city was abandoned also ca. 300 C.E.

There were likely multiple factors responsible for the desertion of Zita, but the hypothesis tested here argues that environmentally and colonially exploitative industrial activities exceeded the ecological metabolism of the urban area, which in part contributed to the abandonment of the ancient city. Nine kilns and two metallurgical precincts are still visible on the surface of the site today, 1,700 years later. Slag (or metallurgical production debris) covers at least 10% of the abandoned urban area. Excavations of one industrial precinct contained upwards of 24–28 kg of slag and crucible debris per cubic meter. Preliminary in situ analysis of excavated industrial soils revealed heavy-metal contamination at elevated levels, with lead, cadmium, arsenic, tin, copper, zinc, silver, and iron remnant from industrial intensification.

The Scale of Production of Salted Fish and Fish Sauces at the Roman Site of Tróia (Portugal)

Inês Vaz Pinto, Tróia Project, *Ana Patrícia Magalhães*, Tróia Project, *Patrícia Brum*, Tróia Project, and *David Gerald Pickel*, Stanford University

The archaeological site of Tróia, on the southwestern coast of the Roman province of Lusitania (modern Portugal), is a remarkable example of a Roman settlement that specialized in the production of fish products. The site was active between the first half of the first century until mid fifth century C.E. Although the 25 workshops found at Tróia vary in architectural type, dimension, and production capacity over the course of the site's long history, together they form the largest production center known in Lusitania. The results of excavations at Tróia have demonstrated that productive activity can be divided into two main periods, the first through second centuries C.E. and the third through fifth centuries C.E., with a significant interruption in production at the end of the second century. During the second phase, many of the larger workshop areas and fish-salting vats were divided into smaller units, yet Tróia seems to have maintained a significant volume of production in both periods. The aim of this paper, then, is to draw on evidence from recent excavations conducted under the auspices of the University of Arizona and TroiaResort to discuss the possible models for the organization of production in each of the two main phases observed. It also discusses how the organization during each period relates to the overall scale of production at Tróia, especially in comparison with other known fish-salting workshops in Lusitania and in the wider Mediterranean, and the likely economic impact such production had on both the local Sado river valley and those areas that consumed its products.

Life and Labor on the Edge of Empire: Roman Mining Communities in Southwest Iberia

Linda Gosner, Brown University

The southwestern corner of the Iberian Peninsula was famous in antiquity for its natural richness in metals and has even been jokingly referred to by modern scholars as the "El Dorado" of the ancient world. Strabo (3.2) wrote of Iberia, "Up to the present moment, in fact, neither gold, nor silver, nor yet copper, nor iron, has been found anywhere in the world, in a natural state, either in such quantity or of such good quality." Many of these ores were mined as early as 4000 B.C.E.; later, as a result of demand brought about in part by Phoenician and Roman colonization, the scale of mining increased dramatically. This has been demonstrated by environmental studies of Greenland ice cores and European peat bogs, which show a spike in pollution attributable to Roman-period mining, particularly mining of ores from the Iberian pyrite belt. Additionally, archaeometric studies of Roman imperial coinage, ingots, and pigments have demonstrated both the empire-wide distribution of products originating from these mines and the role of Iberian mining in the wider Roman economy.

Despite these recent scholarly advances, the local social impacts of this increased scale of production, including necessary shifts in the organization of production and the composition of the labor force, are understudied. While the Iberian pyrite belt is a unified geological zone, it spans an area divided from the time of Augustus between the Roman provinces of Baetica and Lusitania, and today between Spain and Portugal—divisions that have resulted in somewhat fragmented scholarly traditions. In this paper, I bridge these divides to discuss the impacts that increased mining activity had on local communities and the landscapes. Using archaeological and epigraphic data from both Spain and Portugal, I discuss the distribution of mines and mining settlements from the late first century B.C.E. through the second century C.E. and their role in wider social and economic networks. I then look closely at three case studies including Vipasca (Aljustrel, Portugal), Cerro del Moro (Nerva, Spain), and Cortalago (Riotinto, Spain) to investigate the local efforts as well as imperial directives that shaped mining communities during these centuries. Burial, household, and epigraphic evidence demonstrates the mixed labor force in such communities, including women, children, slaves, contract laborers, and army personnel. Examining the logistics of life and labor in these productive communities, so often marginalized in scholarship, provides a better understanding of Roman imperialism and its localized effects.

The Purpose-Built Workspaces of the Classical Agora and Scales of Urban Production
Alison Fields, University of Cincinnati

The Agora Excavations of the American School of Classical Studies at Athens have explored the Athenian Agora since the 1930s. The excavations have exposed the market square, with its associated civic buildings, as well as parts of the neighborhoods surrounding the square. Evidence for craft production within this area northwest of the Acropolis dates as early as the Sub-Mycenaean period. A large quantity of industrial debris—especially potters' and metal-casting waste—has been found in a number of wells and refuse pits. In many cases, permanent architecture cannot be associated with these early traces of industrial activity.

However, in the second half of the fifth century B.C.E., a new type of industrial building emerged in the Agora: the purpose-built, multiroom workspace. These buildings were constructed of well-cut poros blocks and featured a similar spatial syntax: a row of single or double-room units, accessed either directly from the street or via a shared corridor. This paper explores the historical context for the emergence of these purpose-built workspaces and how their unique architectural footprint may indicate shifts in urban scales of production and consumer experiences in the mid fifth century B.C.E.

Industry and Interaction: Crafting Neighborhoods as Communities in Classical and Early Hellenistic Greece
Katherine B. Harrington, Brown University

The concept of the neighborhood has recently received more attention from archaeologists interested in ancient urban settings. As a spatial unit smaller than the city but larger than a single house, the neighborhood has particular relevance for the study of ancient Greek craft production, because Greek cities are often assumed to have dedicated industrial quarters. According to conventional wisdom, these quarters are typically located outside the city walls for reasons of safety and pollution. In some cases, like the Kerameikos of Athens, this may have been true, but in many Greek cities, traces of craft production can be found clustered in urban neighborhoods within the city walls, well-integrated with the other activities of everyday life. Some craft production occurred in dedicated workshops in urban settings, but many craftspeople worked from their homes. Yet the contribution of these domestic workshops has been underestimated, and the relative scale and economic contribution of residential and nonresidential workshops is rarely considered. Considering a wider range of craft activities and examining different scales and settings of production exposes the dynamic nature of life in Greek crafting neighborhoods.

I explore these settings at the sites of Corinth, Isthmia, and Olynthos. Each site provides different insights into the ways that craft production affected the rhythms of daily life and bound craftspeople and their neighbors together in communities. At Corinth, potters maintained a connection to their past through specific religious rituals. In Isthmia, a group of rural farmers collectively developed a nucleated settlement and to continue producing agricultural products. At Olynthos, light industry is found in many houses in the neighborhood north of the agora; it was clearly planned for as a part of the city expansion.

Living and working in densely packed neighborhoods provided craftspeople with opportunities for face-to-face interactions with their neighbors and competitors as they went about their daily business of acquiring supplies, making objects, and selling them. In this paper, I explore the dynamic types of communities that formed when craftspeople lived in close quarters in urban neighborhoods in mainland Greece. I examine the neighborhood as a potential site for the formation of communities, with a particular concern for how crafting activities of various scales both engendered and complicated social relations. Crafting communities were essential to the transmission of technical knowledge, fostering both tradition and innovation, and played an important economic role in many Greek cities.

The Social Space of Production in the Northern Part of the Iberian World (Sixth to Third Centuries B.C.E.)

Alexis Gorgues, University Bordeaux Montaigne

Archaeologists of the western Mediterranean Iron Age often oppose, a bit schematically, workshop production and domestic production. The first is associated with dynamism, with a growing social complexity enhanced from the sixth century B.C.E. onward by overseas trade and then reaching the shores of this Mediterranean "cul-de-sac." The latter is considered a remnant of the previous, primitive, social organization, whose overall economic significance is negligible. In this paper, we propose another point of view. The analysis of specific contexts allows us to discuss the relation between productive activity and space and how production inserted itself within the Iberian social space and time. We first show that "workshop" is not a convenient concept to describe the Iron Age reality, as it is rather difficult to identify a "shop" (or even a room) predominately used for specific "work" requiring a high degree of technical skill. Instead, we can determine the existence of temporary "workplaces" that were inserted mainly into domestic buildings. Some of these workplaces were linked with specifically domestic activities, such as food processing. But in others, complex technical processes took place. Some of these processes, such as weaving, are considered as mainly domestic and related to household consumption, but others, such as blacksmithing, are usually regarded as typical workshop production aimed at commercial distribution. The apparent paradox resulting from this observation can be resolved if we accept that the segregation between maintenance activities and works of high technicality was not as clear in the actual working of Iron Age societies as it is in the archaeologist's mind. We would like to show that Iberian Iron Age domestic units developed unitary strategies of production encompassing all activities, from maintenance activities to highly skilled ones. These strategies were clearly multiscalar: they aimed at obviously guaranteeing the reproduction of the domestic cell from one generation to another but also at gaining the upper hand in the social competition for power. This last goal could have been achieved in two ways. The first was a horizontal "don/contre-don" exchange involving the more complex objects, the goal of which was the consolidation of political alliances. The second was a redistribution process, from the most "productive" domestic cells toward the others, to build a clientele.

SESSION 3C
Archaeology of Crete

CHAIR: *Kevin T. Glowacki*, Texas A&M University

Hosting and Toasting as an Arena for Cooperation and Competition
Luke F. Kaiser, University of Arizona

As Malcolm Wiener has recently pointed out (in the 2014 Ellen Davis Memorial Symposium), the use of paired vessels is an archaeologically significant activity that needs further investigation. It not only appears in the Aegean Bronze Age but is a cross-cultural, diachronic phenomenon. The use of such vessels often occurred during feasting ceremonies, ranging from regional celebrations to small gatherings, that provided a stage on which socioeconomic and political roles were defined. Ritualized meetings between paramount individuals involving eating and drinking with paired vessels acted as a simultaneously communal and competitive event that provided an opportunity to develop social, economic, and political complexity in the Aegean and elsewhere and assisted in the emergence and maintenance of stratified society during this period.

Well-known examples of paired vessels in the Aegean include gold sauceboats from the mainland of Greece, the gold Vapheio cups, and cups shown on the Campstool Fresco from Pylos. More recently, two large tankards were uncovered in an Early Minoan (EM) IIB deposit at Mochlos alongside a set of eating and drinking vessels and two ceramic boat models. The context of the Mochlos vases associates them with feasting, and the boat models suggest that the participants in the paired feast traveled to take part in these reciprocal activities. Ethnographic parallels suggest that the two participants of the feasting event used this paired set of vessels to generate cooperative bonds that created an even social playing field. One of these participants was obviously from Mochlos, and it is quite likely that the other was from Gournia, which was the primary rival of Mochlos at this time.

Paired vessels of this sort illuminate the manner in which Aegean and other societies increased ties with other cultures in the area, particularly with neighboring families in Mochlos and regional rivals within the Mirabello. The interaction of paramount individuals through paired feasting created reciprocity and promoted cooperation and trust that set the groundwork for competitive standards in the Mirabello region regarding economic activity and social ranking.

A New Protopalatial Ceramic Deposit: Exploring Local Pottery Production and Consumption in Mochlos in the Middle Minoan IB–IIB Period
Georgios Doudalis, Ruprecht-Karls-Universität Heidelberg

This paper explores a recently excavated Protopalatial deposit from Mochlos to better understand local aspects of production and consumption at the site from Middle Minoan (MM) IB to MM IIB (ca. 1900–1650 B.C.E.). Earlier studies have discussed the control of larger "palaces" over sites in the Gulf of Mirabello during the Protopalatial period, with Gournia operating as a provincial center of closed vessel production, but newly studied material from Mochlos reveals a more complicated picture of production and consumption at this time. This stratified deposit from House C12 demonstrates a tradition of pottery production with uniquely local flavor and provides evidence that Protopalatial Mochlos was not completely dependent on these other, larger sites.

This local production is proven using three methods of analysis: macroscopic analysis of coarse ware pottery, potters' marks, and tracing the formal evolution of carinated cups. The high frequency of local fabrics and inclusions such as phyllite, micaceous phyllite, and calcite, in addition to potters' marks placed on handles of closed vessels and rims of open vessels such as flaring bowls, indicate the presence of at least one local workshop. Carinated cups, one of the most distinctive vessels of the MM IB to MM II periods, were formed from local coarse fabric as well as local fine clay at Mochlos. During MM IB and in MM IIA, fine carinated cups feature deep banded ridges, red or black slip, and low carination. In the MM IIB period, the carination shifts to sit relatively higher on the body of the cups, and the ridges become thinner and finer. These later cups are still produced locally, though they are formally evolved to imitate the aesthetic of carinated cups in larger centers.

Throughout the duration of the Protopalatial period, Mochlos seems to have developed a distinctly local tradition of coarse and fine ware production and consumption. This reading of the deposit complicates our understanding of the role of Gournia in the Mirabello area and suggests that Mochlos did not rely on Gournia but had its own workshop and its own pottery production that served the Mochlos community with products of a uniquely local character.

The Western Magazines and the West Facade of the Palace at Malia (Crete) During the Protopalatial Period
Maud Devolder, TOPOI-FU Berlin

This paper presents unpublished results of a new architectural study of the palace of Malia. It focuses on specific building techniques and materials that indicate the existence in the West Wing of a series of parallel rooms devoted to storage from the Protopalatial period onward. These early magazines are formed by walls erected in layered rubble masonry, some of which survived the destruction of the building ca. 1700 B.C.E. and were later incorporated in the Second Palace. This study moreover suggests that the Protopalatial facade of the West Court is made of large blocks of *sideropetra*, the local gray-bluish limestone, built on a leveling course of imported crystalline limestone. Such blocks were thoroughly reused in the Neopalatial complex in different forms (column bases, thresholds, lintels, and a kernos) and are now spread all over the building. The proposed restitution of the West Wing, including the facade of the West Court, indicates the quality in both layout and execution of the First Palace at Malia. In addition to its importance for the reconstruction of the architectural sequence of the palatial complex of Malia, this restitution has important consequences for the understanding of the sociopolitical background of the Protopalatial settlement. Indeed, it questions the primacy of agents outside the palace in architectural innovation, an aspect that is explored by considering architectural developments at the scale of the whole site.

Excavations at Palaikastro 2014–2015
Carl Knappett, University of Toronto, *Nicoletta Momigliano*, University of Bristol, *Alexandra Livarda*, University of Nottingham, *Tim Cunningham*, Université Catholique de Louvain, *Quentin Letesson*, Université Catholique de Louvain, and *Hector Orengo*, University of Sheffield

We report on two seasons of excavation at Palaikastro in east Crete, site of a large coastal town occupied through most of the Bronze Age. While much of the town has already been uncovered in previous campaigns, many questions remain about the organization of the urban environment and its relationship to the wider landscape. Our work in 2014 and 2015 has focused on a previously unexcavated part of the town site, which appears to be a discrete neighborhood separated from the urban core by a gully. Three houses and two streets have come to light in this neighborhood, which is on the edge of town closest to the Petsophas peak sanctuary. House MP1 sees occupation in the Middle Minoan (MM) III to Late Minoan (LM) IA periods and may have been abandoned around the time of the Theran eruption, as we find deposits of volcanic ash just outside the building and no subsequent activity. Building AM1 is a large structure with a series of rooms preserving in situ floor deposits from the LM IB period, including pithoi in storage rooms, a grinding installation for food preparation, and stone vases and a frit necklace on the floor of a central paved room. AM1 also sees further occupation in LM III; an extensive deposit of *Hexaplex trunculus* for producing purple dye is particularly noteworthy. Our third building in this quarter is AP1, which presents a complex history of reuse during LM III, including a complete larnax lid, a fragment of a gold bucranium earring, and a griffin sealstone inside the building, as well as extensive dumps of pottery, shell, and animal bone outside. Trials outside the facade of AP1 revealed fine pottery of the MM IIB period, suggesting the building may have been constructed in MM III. Thus, we have evidence for a previously unknown neighborhood, occupied from at least MM II until LM IIIA2. When combined with our on-site micromorphology work, off-site paleoenvironmental reconstructions, and landscape analysis, a clearer picture begins to emerge of how the site's urban fabric developed over time and how it was sustained.

The Magic and the Mundane: The Function of Talismanic Class Stones in Minoan Crete

Angela Murock Hussein, Eberhard Karls University, Tübingen

The so-called Minoan Talismanic Class stones are a distinctive group of incised beads, often classified as seals, dating from Middle Minoan III through Late Minoan I. They are made primarily of colored quartzes and decorated with rapid rotary tool cuts. The compositions that appear on them consist of a limited number of recurring symbolic motifs. Because of their distinctive appearance and the evidently symbolic nature of their decorative compositions, Arthur Evans considered Talismanic Class stones to have served an amuletic rather than a sphragistic function, a hypothesis followed by Kenna and others. More recent scholarship has stressed that the group is distinguished by its manufacturing technique rather than its function.

The disparity between their evident popularity and their rare representation in sealing archives has been raised as evidence for their being merely decorative, or imitations of seals. However, by tying together evidence from the tools used, the contexts in which they were produced, and their actual use as seals, we can extrapolate a picture of the function of Talismanic Class stones in the Neopalatial Minoan economy. This paper examines not only the excavation contexts of Talismanic Class stones but also the techniques of seal manufacturing in Late Bronze Age Crete and the societal and economic needs for seals in the Neopalatial period to finally discover the owners of these important objects.

Edifis at Work? A New Court-Centered Building at Sissi: Results from the 2015 Excavation Campaign

Simon Jusseret, University of Texas at Austin, *Sylviane Déderix*, University of Arizona, *Maud Devolder*, TOPOI-FU Berlin, and *Jan Driessen*, Université catholique de Louvain

Located on a low coastal hill (locally known as the Buffos or Kefali) only 4 km east of Malia, the Minoan settlement and cemetery of Sissi have been under exploration by the Belgian School at Athens since 2007. The strategic location of the hill along overland communication routes, as well as its proximity to Malia, make the settlement an important barometer to understand the relationship between a palatial center and its assumed hinterland.

During the last weeks of the 2011 campaign, the possible presence of a Neopalatial court-centered building on the southeast summit of the hill was noted of which Building F would have formed the east wing. The new five-year program allowed further investigation. Preceded by GPR, geomagnetic, and geoelectric surveys undertaken by IMS-FORTH, excavations west of Building F revealed a large trapezoidal court of approximately 250 m², made of white *tarazza*. Facing it on the northwest, a short stretch of an ashlar facade was seen to have a fine square room (ca. 3.0 x 2.5 m) behind it. This room shows a degree of architectural elaboration that is reminiscent of palatial architecture (low bench coated in red-painted plaster, "mosaico" floor in ironstone, rectangular plaster floor partition). Immediately south of this room and accessible from it was found a collapsed stepped structure built of finely cut sandstone blocks. The square room and stepped platform form an isolated unit built against an imposing Prepalatial terrace wall above which Early Minoan II rooms are quite well preserved, largely untouched by later construction activities. South of the stepped structure, an ashlar facade with a different orientation from the ashlar wall flanking the square paved room was found. There was at least one plastered room behind it. Moreover, large rooms with special architectural features (plaster, pavings) were also found to the north of the court. A sunken building to the south comprises a massive ashlar tumble. Although the complex was found largely empty, preliminary examination of the pottery suggests that it was abandoned early in the Neopalatial period (Late Minoan IA) and that it collapsed soon afterward.

The Dessenne Building in the Protopalatial Settlement at Malia (Crete)
Maud Devolder, TOPOI-FU Berlin, and *Ilaria Caloi*, Université catholique de Louvain–AEGIS

The 2012–2015 project of the Dessenne Building aimed at publishing the remains of a Protopalatial complex situated near the palace of Malia. Discovered in 1960 by André Dessenne, the complex was interpreted as a storage unit depending on the palace (Dessenne Storage Area), soon to be abandoned and left unpublished. A new architectural study has allowed us to reconsider the phasing of the building and to question the primacy of storage. Complementary work included the study of ceramic material excavated in 1960, which provided large numbers of Middle Minoan IIB vases destroyed at the end of the Protopalatial period on the site. This paper provides the synthesis of the work accomplished between 2012 and 2015 to publish the edifice, focusing especially on soundings led under its floors. These indicate the Dessenne Building was erected later than usually suggested during the Protopalatial period, on early architectural remains sometimes incorporated in the building. A sounding along the eastern side of the complex has also provided the earliest element of the road network at Malia, as well as a fill linked to the preparation of the paving of the West Court of the palace, thus offering stratified material for its dating. Such discoveries add to the initial publication project by contextualizing the Dessenne Building within late Prepalatial and early Protopalatial Malia.

SESSION 3D: Colloquium
Gold Medal Colloquium in Honor of Malcolm Bell III

ORGANIZERS: *Barbara Tsakirgis*, Vanderbilt University, and *Carla Antonaccio*, Duke University

Colloquium Overview Statement

With this panel, we celebrate Malcolm Bell III, who has been scholar, teacher, excavation director, and vice-president of the Archaeological Institute of America. In his 38 years as professor of art history at the University of Virginia and four years as Mellon Professor-in-Charge at the American Academy in Rome, Bell taught and mentored many students on Jefferson's stately campus, at the archaeological sites of the eternal city, and in the golden-brown fields of central Sicily. For more than 30 years, Bell has directed excavations and scholarly inquiry at Morgantina in central Sicily, where many of his students learned to excavate, many of them going on to research archaeological material at Morgantina and other sites across the Mediterranean.

Bell's scholarly interests have focused on architecture, whether that of the Greeks and Romans or that designed by our third president, Thomas Jefferson. Architecture of any scale and use has caught Bell's eye and inquiring mind, from a water mill on the Janiculum Hill to the monumental stoas in the agora at Morgantina. His scholarship on sculpture similarly has an all-encompassing scope, from the terracotta figurines of Morgantina to the monumental marbles of classical and Hellenistic Sicily, an animated satyr and a cocksure charioteer. Many of his architectural and sculptural studies have focused on the kingdom of Syracuse in the third century B.C.E.

Importantly for this organization, Bell served as Vice-President for Professional Responsibilities from 2003 until 2007. Before, during, and after his tenure, he has fought tirelessly for cultural patrimony, working closely with Italian colleagues and successfully orchestrating the return to Italy of numerous looted antiquities. His efforts alone on behalf of our shared history merit recognition from the AIA.

For all the speakers on the panel, Bell has been a colleague and friend, an interlocutor on the art of ancient Greece writ large and on the history and monuments of Morgantina, and a fierce protector of Italy's cultural heritage. With each of us, Bell has discussed and debated, always graciously, and thereby expanded our understanding of the topics at hand. Bell also delights in the present-day produce from Sicily's fields, an appreciation that has influenced the choice of topic in our last paper. Speakers represent all walks of Bell's scholarly life, including a former student and colleagues from Morgantina, the American Academy, and the AIA.

New Developments in the Handling of Cultural Property in the Wake of Malcolm Bell's Vice-Presidency of the AIA
Patty Gerstenblith, DePaul University College of Law

The past 20 years have seen considerable developments in the law applicable to the market in archaeological objects and to voluntary practices, especially in museum policies for the acquisition of archaeological objects. This paper examines these developments, beginning with the forfeiture of the Sicilian gold phiale purchased by the collector Michael Steinhardt and also considering the recognition of national ownership laws in the Schultz prosecution as well as other legal developments in both international and U.S. domestic contexts. During this same period, the two major U.S.-based museum organizations (the American Alliance of Museums and the Association of Art Museum Directors) formulated new policies and guidelines for the acquisition of ancient art and archaeological material. Malcolm Bell's contributions in the cultural heritage arena, including his work with the Morgantina silver that had been acquired by the Metropolitan Museum of Art in New York and the cult statue acquired by the Getty Museum in California, are situated within these broader developments.

While this paper presents an overview of past progress toward greater protection of archaeological heritage, it also turns to the issues that confront us today. At this time, armed conflict poses the greatest threats to archaeological heritage, including both intentional destruction of archaeological sites and monuments and industrial-level looting of sites. Bell's work as AIA Vice-President for Professional Responsibilities during the lead-up to the 2003 Iraq War also touched on issues of cultural heritage during armed conflict. This paper concludes with suggestions as to what changes in international law and in market practice might help better preserve the archaeological heritage in the Middle East and elsewhere.

Not Sloppy but Hasty: Late Athenian Black-Figure
Kathleen M. Lynch, University of Cincinnati

The figural decoration of some Athenian black-figure lekythoi and cup skyphoi became increasingly impressionistic in the years after 500 B.C.E. until the demise of the shapes in the decades after the Persian Wars. Scholars describe these late lekythoi as "mass produced" because of the hastiness of the figural decoration, and their uninspired imagery has received little art historical attention. This paper considers what the hastily executed scenes can reveal about visual literacy and mass production of pottery in Athens.

The Marathon Tumulus and deposits associated with the cleanup following the Persian destruction of Athens provide a snapshot of black-figure lekythoi and skyphoi in use in Athens ca. 500–480 B.C.E. Lekythoi from domestic and public contexts indicate that this shape was not solely funerary. The hastiest of scenes are attributed to the Haimon Painter and the CHC Group workshops, which produced the majority of the late lekythoi and skyphoi. The images on these vessels feature chariots, Dionysos and his retinue, and a few stock scenes of warriors and Herakles. The degenerated scenes received limited or sometimes no incision, and chariot teams frequently have extra legs.

The impressionistic images work because of the conventionalization of vase painting. Thus, the painters could assume that viewers in Athens, at least, were familiar enough with these recurring compositions that they could identify them from their barest elements. The decoration is not designed to be didactic; the subjects have become decorative and emblematic of generic cultural values more than narrative stories. Herakles and the lion reduced to wrestling figures and a tree prompts "hero" just as the unspecified warrior and charioteer do. Dionysos conveys the convivial world of the symposium. Moreover, the late black-figure scenes share compositional features that make them well suited to the space of the vessels. Herakles wrestling the lion fits better than combat with the Hydra or Geryon. The rhythmic marching of superabundant horses' legs suits the straight walls of the lekythoi and cup skyphoi. Finally, the potting is unexpectedly good, signaling that vessel function is more important than decoration, which contrasts with the usual emphasis we place on vase decoration over function.

These late black-figure scenes are often dismissed as "sloppy," but the hastiness of their execution reveals the painters' confidence in the visual literacy of their viewers.

Sauroctonos Corinthius
Jenifer Neils, Case Western Reserve University

Based on an epigram of Martial (14.172) that describes an anonymous bronze statue of a youth killing a lizard, it is here proposed that the sculpture known as the Apollo Sauroctonos is in fact not Apollo and not attributable to the fourth-century sculptor Praxiteles. Ever since Winckelmann (1760), the marble statue in the Borghese Collection of a youth leaning on a tree on which a lizard is poised has been inextricably associated with Pliny's (*NH* 34.69–70) description of a bronze original by Praxiteles of Apollo about to stab a lizard. However, the eroticized pose, the eccentric hairdo, and the genre subject matter are fitting neither for the god nor for the fourth-century date. Arguably this statue type that was so popular in Roman times began as an Early Hellenistic personification (not unlike the youthful Hypnos, Pothos, or Agon), was adapted to a genre theme (not unlike the Boy Strangling the Goose), and owed its considerable popularity to the Roman taste for "sexy boys" and villa decoration. Like many ancient authors, Pliny may have mistaken the attribution (as he did the Tyrannicides) or made it up, and Praxiteles' reputation for divine statuary made the designation as Apollo acceptable. If we had only the epigram of Martial, we would have no problem assigning this statue type to the realm of Hellenistic genre figures.

Playing in the Dirt: Earthen Walls in Hellenistic Architecture
Elizabeth Fentress, International Association for Classical Archaeology

Walls made in earth have been little noticed in the archaeology of Italy for a number of reasons, of which the most obvious is that they have often dissolved into a uniform stratum of earth over the stone foundations on which they stood. This is as true of mudbrick as it is of walls in cob (*bauge*), or rammed earth (*pisé de terre*), whose dissolution hides a series of different traditions. Yet, because building techniques are perhaps the most conservative of practices, they have the most to tell us about the origins of the people who use them. Building on the work of the French excavations at Lattes, where earth walls were shown to be consistently built with the cob technique, this paper presents an outline of the problem for the central Mediterranean—Italy, North Africa, and Spain. Using evidence from central Italy (Murlo, Torre di Satriano, Fidenae, Cosa, Pompeii), I suggest that cob, or *bauge* walls were current in central Italy from the seventh century B.C.E., when they were used together with posts. In the fourth century they were replaced by walls in *pisé* in central Italy. Although the third-century B.C.E. rammed-earth walls at Punic Kerkouane remain an outlier, the cases of Ampurias, Utica and Heraclea Minoa in the second and first centuries B.C.E. and the military sites of Lambaesis and Verulamium tie this phenomenon to Roman colonization. A way forward for recognizing the techiques is a sampling program and micromorphological examination of the material, designed to distinguish between rammed-earth, cob and mud-brick walling.

Salute a Mac: Dining and Drinking at Hellenistic Morgantina
Barbara Tsakirgis, Vanderbilt University

Our symposium in honor of Malcolm Bell is an appropriate setting to examine the symposium at Hellenistic Morgantina. Evidence for the consumption and enjoyment of food and wine at Hellenistic Morgantina comes from the physical remains of both the dining rooms and their interior decoration as well as the vessels used for storage, preparation, and service. While the square *androues* of classical houses, with their raised platforms for couches and off-center doorways, were out of fashion in Sicily in the third century and later, the practice of convivial dining in a decorated setting continued into the Hellenistic period. Rooms for entertainment in the houses of Morgantina are handsome in their dimensions, pavements, and wall paintings. That elaborated setting was enhanced by the serving vessels, including the moldmade bowls often used in the wine service.

Literary evidence enhances our understanding of the Morgantina banquets and symposia. For example, the Sicilian tables used to hold the vessels and foodstuffs for the meals no longer exist, but they are mentioned by Athenaeus. Literature also provides information about the possible sources of inspiration for the Morgantina feasts and their entertainments. The Syrakosia was the luxury barge of Hieron II, king of Syracuse, and was decorated with mosaics, a garden, indoor baths, and Atlas supports (Moschion ap. Athenaeus). In its lavish display, it anticipated by more than 200 years the Liburnian pleasure galleys of Caligula (Suetonius). We can only guess whether statues such as the Priapos from Syracuse are evidence of similar decorative additions to the dining rooms of Morgantina.

Archaeological comparanda from throughout Sicily similarly enrich our understanding of the Morgantina symposium. Dining rooms in the Hellenistic houses at Iaitas (Monte Iato) provide evidence of the windows used to illuminate and ventilate the symposia held there. Pavements recovered from Capo Soprano (Gela) and the Hellenistic houses at Megara Hyblaia show that the habit of adorning convivial space was alive and well in Hellenistic Sicily. The drinking vessels recovered at all these sites similarly prove the widespread popularity and longevity of the convivial banquet in Sicily in the Hellenistic period.

SESSION 3E: Colloquium
From Castellina to Cetamura: Recent Developments in the Archaeology of Chianti

ORGANIZERS: *Lora L. Holland*, University of North Carolina at Asheville, and *Nancy T. de Grummond*, Florida State University

Colloquium Overview Statement

A few Etruscan sites in Chianti (region of Tuscany) were known in the early 20th century, such as the famous Montecalvario tomb at Castellina. But it was not until Alvaro Tracchi, an amateur archaeologist from San Giovanni Valdarno, investigated the area in the 1960s that its importance per se and as a link between major cities in northern and central Etruria could be demonstrated beyond the Archaic period. The archaeology of this region even today remains largely unknown outside of Italy. This colloquium highlights the most significant discoveries in the archaeology of Chianti, from the Etruscan Orientalizing period to the period of the Roman empire, giving particular emphasis to recent work at Castellina and Cetamura.

The session begins with a paper on Tracchi's contribution and an overview of past and current work at some of the sites he documented. Next, a survey of early tombs in Chianti, particularly at Castellina, reveals a vibrant emerging aristocracy near the places that would become the principal towns of Chianti in the Medieval era. The remaining papers focus on what Tracchi regarded as his most important discovery: Cetamura, a nonelite site of the Late Etruscan and Roman periods and the only site in Chianti excavated by Americans. Cetamura has yielded a sanctuary and an artisans' quarter dating to the fourth to first centuries B.C.E., Roman baths of the first century C.E., and a medieval castellum. The excavator of a deep well recently completed at the site discusses the innovative engineering techniques required to recover its wealth of archaeological artifacts and organic material. Two scientific teams report on their ongoing floral and faunal analyses of this organic material from Cetamura, which is of wider significance for the environment and agriculture in Chianti in general. The first paper is part of a larger study of Tuscan environmental history through scientific analysis of carpological materials, to which Chianti now contributes. The second discusses the results of zooarchaeological evidence at Cetamura, particularly for domesticated animals and the significance of the avifaunal remains. Of particular interest is the abundance of chickens during the Roman period, which demonstrates a break in cultural continuity at the site during the last phase of active use of the well in the first half of the first century C.E. The panel concludes with a study of some uses of deer remains at Cetamura, particularly during the Etruscan phases of the site, in sacrifice and feasting, in tool-making, and in divination, in the larger context of this understudied phenomenon in Etruria.

The colloquium thus situates significant new discoveries in Chianti within relevant current issues concerning society, religion, economy, faunal and floral remains, and environment.

Exploring Chianti with Alvaro Tracchi

Nancy T. de Grummond, Florida State University

In 1978, the book *Dal Chianti al Valdarno* (*From Chianti to the Arno River Valley*) by Alvaro Tracchi was published, only a few months after his death. He had spent many years conducting surface surveys of diagnostic materials in this area and had identified some 200 Etruscan and Roman sites. This classic work remains an important guide to the archaeology of the area.

This paper presents a review of the issues concerning the identity of the areas that use the term "Chianti," beginning with the heartland made up of the territories of the three towns that formed the original "League of Chianti," also known as "Chianti Geografic" in the Middle Ages—Castellina, Radda, and Gaiole. The name of Chianti, closely associated with the great wines of that name, has been extended, sometimes by government decree, to surrounding or adjacent areas where the requisite grapes are grown and the characteristic wines are made. For the purposes of archaeology, there are several ways to parse the geographical term Chianti, which is discussed in the paper. This paper privileges sites in Chianti Geografico that have actually undergone excavation, such as Montecalvario, Fonterutoli and Salivolpi (Castellina), Poggio la Croce and Malpensata (Radda), and Cetamura and Monti (Gaiole), but it also makes references to sites in nearby areas, especially those around Castelnuovo Berardenga.

The publication of the first volume of a *Carta archeologica della provincia di Siena* by Marco Valenti in 1995 features the abovementioned area of Chianti but includes sites farther south, resulting in a title for the whole volume as *Il Chianti senese*. This volume expands enormously the surface surveys of Tracchi, noting some 524 sites (many of which, however, are largely or wholly medieval). The recent creation of a Museo Archeologico del Chianti Senese and the publication of a guidebook by Marco Firmati (2014) helps create a closer focus on the major sites and provides yet another tool for studying Chianti.

We are now in a position to ask more pointed methodological questions and work toward a new synthesis, building from the base established by Tracchi. Besides determining geography and chronology, we can make distinctions about class status, trading connections, religious and funerary activities, and workers' practices. We can also deal with the ever-vexing questions of when and how Etruscan sites became Romanized.

Etruscan Princes from Chianti

Massimo Pianigiani, Museo Archeologico del Chianti Senese, Castellina in Chianti

During the Orientalizing and Archaic periods (seventh century B.C.E. to the end of the sixth century B.C.E.), a rich Etruscan aristocracy developed in the Chianti area, basing its power and wealth on land ownership and the trade of valuable commodities. As it is nowadays, ancient Chianti was a favored place for wine making. This paper focuses on the Etruscan princes of Chianti and their relationships with the elites from northern Etruria, in particular the ones from the territories of Siena, Volterra, and Fiesole.

The wealth of the Etruscan princes of Chianti is displayed by the notable funerary objects found in tombs at Radda in Chianti near La Malpensata, at Castelnuovo Berardenga near Il Poggione, and at Maciallina. The extensive necropolis of Poggino Fonterutoli and the magnificent tumulus of Montecalvario are located in the area of Castellina in Chianti. These sites are a significant testament to continuity in the geographical centers of power in this region.

Jewelry and sumptuous jars are among an array of funerary objects conserved in the Museo Archeologico del Chianti Senese of Castellina in Chianti, together with a reproduction of a princely chariot of the seventh century B.C.E. found during the excavation in the tumulus of Montecalvario and recently restored, more than 100 years after its discovery. These aristocratic commodities attending the dead in their travel to the afterworld have much to tell us about both public and private life, especially the emerging symbols of aristocratic power and the relationship to the sacred in early Etruscan culture.

Engineering the Well Excavation at Cetamura del Chianti: Innovative Solutions in a Confined Hypogeum Environment

Francesco Cini, Cooperativa ICHNOS: Archeologia, Ambiente e Sperimentazione, Montelupo Fiorentina (Italy)

A well located on the summit of the ancient hilltop settlement now known as Cetamura was dug from the sandstone bedrock during the Late Etruscan period and reached a depth of about 32 m below ground level. Modern excavation, begun by Alvaro Tracchi in the 1970s and continued by Florida State University (FSU) stopped in 2004 when the water level had reached a depth of about 27 m. The excavation resumed in 2011 as a collaborative effort between FSU and ICHNOS and was at last completed in May 2014.

This well showed from the beginning great potential for the recovery of archaeological data but posed numerous logistical and safety problems. As a result, ICHNOS had to approach the excavation using a combination of technical engineering solutions typical for extreme environments and the ordinary techniques of archaeological excavation. The most significant deviation from standard archaeological practice was our development of an artificial stratigraphy for distinguishing the division of layers within the well.

The conditions inside the well necessitated further innovations. To ensure the safety of the excavators as well as provide safe transport for the archaeological artifacts, we used mountaineering ropes, harnesses, and carabiners set up in a type of belay and winch-and-pulley system. The damp environment and depth of the well required the installation of low-voltage lighting that was also water resistant.

The water that constantly accumulated in the well was removed daily with a special hydrodynamic pump. The air was circulated with a large industrial fan. The discovery of unusual objects, both in shape and material, forced us to adjust the recovery techniques many times. Sediments, once pulled out, were fully floated with a system of nozzles and water/air mixers specially designed and built entirely by ICHNOS. The water was further recycled via a recirculating system that permitted the archaeological teams to do a preliminary rinsing of objects onsite.

Thanks to these innovative excavation techniques, we were able to recover thoroughly the materials of archaeological interest from the well. As the following papers demonstrate, the results that are emerging from the excavation of the well of Cetamura demonstrate the importance of the excavation of these challenging structures. Not only do we gain a better understanding of the settlement at Cetamura as a whole but we are also poised to learn important information about the ancient environment and its climate.

Tracing the History of Human-Plant Relationships: A Case Study at Cetamura del Chianti

Gianna Giachi, Soprintendenza Archeologia della Toscana, Firenze (Italy), and *Marta Mariotti Lippi*, Dipartimento di Biologia, Università di Firenze (Italy)

The primary aim of archaeobotany is the reconstruction of the ancient landscape, focusing on human-plant relationships and plant exploitation. Indeed, most landscapes are the result of the interaction between the human cultures and the natural environment. Therefore, the history of peoples is also the history of their relationship with the environment where they lived. Moreover, archaeobotanical studies offer contributions to other topics, such as diet, medical preparations, and commerce, and they can contribute to the development of new methodologies to study various materials. Research carried out in different archaeological contexts of Tuscany offer examples of the information that can be gathered. They also underline the advantages of comparing data coming from different archaeobotanical analyses inside the same archaeological context. Starch and pollen analyses in the Paleolithic site of Bilancino (Florence, Italy) allowed us to gain insights into food processing, revealing the use of local plants to produce flour (Revedin et al., "Thirty Thousand-Year-Old Evidence of Plant Food Processing," *Proceedings of the National Academy of Sciences of the United States of America* 107 [2010] 18815–19). Pollen and charcoal analyses at Follonica (Grosseto, Italy) provided evidence for how the Etruscan industry modified the forest vegetation, probably enhancing its xeric features (Mariotti Lippi et al., "Studi sulla vegetazione attuale e passata della Toscana meridionale (Follonica-Italia) e considerazioni sull'impatto ambientale dell'attività metallurgica etrusca nel VI–V secolo a.C.," Webbia 55 [2000] 279–95). A multidisciplinary approach, including starch, pollen, and microcharcoal analyses (Giachi et al., "Ingredients of a 2,000-Y-Old Medicine Revealed by Chemical, Mineralogical, and Botanical Investigations." *Proceedings of the National Academy of Sciences of the United States of America* 110 [2013] 1193–96), furnished precious information about the ingredients of an ancient medicine recovered in the Baratti Gulf (Grosseto, Italy).

To this large study of sites in Tuscany, we now add Cetamura del Chianti. The archaeobotanical materials recovered between 2011 and 2014 from a well on the site include pollen, charcoal, seeds, and other plant materials, as well as a large quantity of worked and unworked wood. The results of our ongoing analyses, carried out over the summer and fall of 2015, are presented here and add to our knowledge of the history of the Chianti region and the settlement of Cetamura itself in its ancient context.

Animals in Rituals? Etruscan and Roman Evidence from Cetamura del Chianti

Chiara A. Corbino, University of Sheffield, *Ornella Fonzo*, Laboratorio Civico Museo Archeologico of Villanovaforru (Italy), and *Umberto Albarella*, University of Sheffield

A substantial quantity of animal bones was recovered from Cetamura del Chianti (Tuscany, Italy) during excavations undertaken between 2011 and 2014. The material derived from a rock-cut well located in the highest part of the settlement. The archaeological evidence indicates that it was used for dining and ritual activities during the Late Etruscan period (third century B.C.E.) as well as the Roman period (first century C.E.). The faunal remains belong primarily to mammals and birds, and there is some evidence for fish and amphibians. Domestic species are dominant, but there is also a great diversity of wild animals, especially birds.

Taxonomic diversity, anatomical frequencies, ages at death, and butchery patterns underline significant differences between the Etruscan and the Roman contexts. In the Etruscan layers, there are many types of wild birds, including owls. Evidence for chicken is absent, whereas it becomes the most important species in the following period. Mammal remains of both adults and young individuals from the Etruscan period show a wide range of mortality patterns, and the high frequency of butchery marks is similar to that identified in the ordinary domestic refuse. Sheep/goat remains predominate, but there are also cattle, pig, and deer. By contrast, in Roman times very young individuals predominate, especially piglets, and large articulated portions of animals appear to have been disposed of, with minimal butchery evidence on display.

Those differences suggest a break point in cultural beliefs and practices rather than continuity between the Late Etruscan and Roman contexts. This study throws light on the use of animals in ancient dining and religious rituals and indicates that initial apparent similarities in Etruscan and Roman practices in fact speak to significant differences.

Antlers and Astragali: Sacred Deer at Cetamura del Chianti

Lora L. Holland, University of North Carolina at Asheville

Worked and unworked deer bone and antler deposited in sacred contexts are part of a widespread, but understudied, phenomenon in Etruria and beyond. Among some notable examples: worked deer antler as a votive offering is known as early as the 10th century B.C.E. in the Area Sacra at Tarquinia (Bonghi Jovino, "The Tarquinia Project: A Summary of 25 Years of Excavation," *AJA* 114 [2010] 161–80); at Poggio Civitate, bone and antler remains suggest that deer were part of elite consumption and ritual in the seventh century B.C.E. (Kansa et al., "Etruscan Economics: Forty-Five Years of Faunal Remains from Poggio Civitate," *Etruscan Studies* 17 [2014] 63–87); and worked deer bone and antler were inscribed and used in divination ritual at Treviso and other sites in the Veneto during the Hellenistic period (Gambacurta, "Manufatti iscritti in osso o corno, " in *I tempi della scrittura: Veneti antichi, alfabeti e documenti* [Montebelluna 2002] 121–26). This study is focused on the evidence for the use of deer remains in sacrifice and feasting, for making artisan tools, and for divination at Cetamura del Chianti, a nonelite site of the Late Etruscan through early Roman Imperial period located on a hill only a few kilometers distant from other, earlier sites in the Chianti region.

Excavations at Cetamura del Chianti in 1980 uncovered worked deer bone and antler in a votive pit near a deep well whose final excavation in 2014 is a major topic of discussion in this panel. Numerous deer bones and antler fragments were also present in the well, including a number of astragali (knucklebones). The analysis of the remains by Ornella Fonzo in Florence revealed several individuals, suggesting that these deer were slaughtered for feasting or perhaps as part of a religious ritual. The worked antler falls into two distinct categories. Some of the pieces from Cetamura had been used for artisanal purposes, including one piece as a handle for a tool. Deer antler worked as tools are known from many sites, including republican levels at Pompeii, but have not been studied as a group. Other antler fragments from Cetamura that were cut into slices offer the tantalizing possibility of divination ritual along with the deer astragali mentioned earlier.

The new evidence from Cetamura suggests that unlike in Greek and Roman religion, where they are primarily associated with the cults of Artemis/Diana, deer played a more fundamental role in Etruscan culture and religion.

SESSION 3F
The Economics and Logistics of Roman Art and Architecture

CHAIR: *Brenda Longfellow*, The University of Iowa

Pigment Prices: Costs, Fraud, and the Concerns of Roman *Pigmentarii*
Hilary Becker, University of Mississippi

Little is known about the supply industry that allowed painters to create Roman frescoes. *Pigmentarii* were traders that sold pigments and other tools needed by fresco artists. These very supplies offer an unusual opportunity to explore how the use of color in the Roman world furnished opportunities to display conspicuous consumption or to save money. Two valuable sources, which bookend the Imperial period, Pliny the Elder and the Price Edict of Diocletian, allow us to look carefully at the prices for ancient pigments, as well as supply and demand in the Roman world.

In addition, certain commercial conventions developed that stated who could buy the more expensive pigments (such as cinnabar and lapis lazuli). These conventions were most likely developed to protect all of the stakeholders in the Roman painting industry: *pigmentarii*, artists, and those who commissioned frescoes. Both artists and unscrupulous *pigmentarii* had incentives to adulterate more expensive pigments. For instance, the value of one pound of cinnabar was equivalent to 56 pounds of red ochre. There was indeed ancient concern that profit-minded people might adulterate or even fake painting and other artists' supplies. For this reason, the ancient Roman buyer had recourse to a number of preventative measures, rough chemical tests, and other sensory checks that might help determine whether certain pigments and other supplies had been correctly labeled. Thus, the pigment industry, long neglected, offers an opportunity to understand the commercial concerns of Roman artists as they sought to get the correct products.

Lapis Gabinus: Quantifying the Economy of a Roman *Tufo* Quarry
Jason Farr, University of Michigan

Augustus may have boasted that he left Rome a city of marble, but for many archaeologists working in the city today, Rome is a city of *tufo*. *Tufo*, or tuff, is a type of volcanic stone quarried in and around Rome itself and can be found in nearly all its ancient monuments. The majority of studies on Roman stone quarrying, however, have focused on marbles and other decorative stones, ignoring the more mundane, unpolished blocks that were absolutely crucial to the local construction industry. Some *tufo* quarries, moreover, are relatively well preserved and accessible, as are the ancient structures built with *tufo* blocks, making it possible to reconstruct the transportation routes between the two. As such, there is untapped potential for quantitative analyses to illuminate this important sector of the ancient economy.

In this paper, I present my research into the quarrying of *lapis Gabinus*, a hard, coarse-grained gray *tufo* that served as an excellent building stone and was extracted near the city of Gabii, 18 km east of Rome. Blocks of *lapis Gabinus* appear in structures at Gabii itself, but in the first century B.C.E. they were being transported to Rome in large quantities for the construction of important monuments such as the Tabularium, Forum of Caesar, and Forum of Augustus. Recent excavations at Gabii have revealed new evidence of quarry activities, prompting a survey of *lapis Gabinus* blocks in extant Roman monuments. Using the results of these investigations and relying on supplementary data from a wide array of sources (19th-century construction manuals, experimental archaeology, and Egyptian papyri), I present an analysis of estimated labor requirements for the quarrying and transportation of these blocks to building sites in Rome. Results demonstrate that the resources and manpower dedicated to these operations were considerable and that quarrying may have served as the principal economic activity at Gabii during this period. I argue that the "decline" and "abandonment" of Gabii bemoaned in textual sources obscures ongoing economic activity like quarrying and that these developments are better seen in the broader context of the changing economy of suburban Rome. The quantitative approach of this study thus illuminates the economic ties between the city and its hinterland and provides a more complete understanding of the economy of urban construction at Rome.

Extracting Economics from Roman Marble Quarries
Leah Long, Virginia Commonwealth University in Qatar

Recent research on manufacturing industries of the Roman world has begun to fill in new information on the expansion of an urbanized agricultural society. Urbanization in Rome and across the empire created a demand for building materials on an unprecedented scale, which was in large part conducted by municipalities, institutions, or landed aristocrats, who owned or inherited the land from which the stone was extracted. In the last decade, quarry surveys in Turkey have revealed the prevalence of these small-scale operations managed by urban polities. To flesh out various scenarios for the economics of local markets, I apply theories of economic rationality and natural resource economics to historical and archaeological sources, which includes Roman jurists writing about the extraction of marble on private land in the *Codex Iustinianus* and eight new quarries discovered in the region of Aphrodisias during an archaeological survey. By using principles of economics as a guide, and with greater coordination among theory, written sources, and archaeological data, I examine the processes involved in the decision to open a quarry. In light of current studies, the paper offers an alternative model for resource acquisition in which the exchange of local building stone took place in a competitive market. According to the legal rulings, private citizens could oversee quarrying operations on their land and profit from trade. While landowners actively tried to improve their financial situation, they also did so at considerable risk. Roman jurists, primarily interested in protecting property value, made landowners calculate whether the potential for profit outweighed the degradation of agriculturally productive land. At Aphrodisias, examples of failed attempts at quarrying exist alongside long-running and successful enterprises. Entrepreneurs involved in civic building at the city did not extract a homogenous set of marble resources but chose to exploit stone with inconsistent physical properties. According to resource economics, substitution is initiated because as the higher-grade materials vanish, the time comes to move on to inferior deposits. Yet Aphrodisias' higher-quality sources were never depleted, suggesting that both demand and price had risen to such an extent as to make the exploitation of alternative sources viable.

The Cost of Building Rome: Architectural Energetics and Labor-Time Estimates at the Basilica of Maxentius

Brian Sahotsky, University of California, Los Angeles

Cost computation for architectural building is severely complicated by the ancient world. Material costs, wages paid, and transportation prices are often difficult to ascertain, and layered restorations and extant remains obscure original building plans. However, the discipline of architectural energetics provides a means to translate monumental construction into "labor-time" estimates. Energetics is not only useful for assigning a specific cost to building, but it also allows for the articulating of hierarchical power structures and behavioral patterning within construction labor. The concept of translating architectural building into units of power, energy, and structure proves useful in an ancient Roman context and can be used to understand the construction of the fourth-century Basilica of Maxentius. The fortuitous amount of archaeological evidence and the contemporaneous "Edict of Maximum Prices" informs the relative cost of labor and resources in the Late Roman empire, and the basilica can be roughly translated into a cost estimate based on total volume of material used during construction, replication, and diversification of on-site tasks and overall energy expenditure. Identifying the variability and limitations of resources allows an energetics analysis to forecast overall project organization and possible exigencies of scale. Based on archaeological remains, economical studies, and discipline-specific estimates, we find that Roman construction was environmentally unfriendly and incredibly costly. For example, the sheer volume of constituent masonry elements required to construct the basilica yielded an additional need of 1,040 tons of wood to fire the lime and bricks.

The large marble columns of the central halls came from more than 2,400 km away. Given this level of cost hemorrhaging, the only way construction could proceed was if the state controlled the urban prefect, quarries, forests, kilns, and monetary coffers. This paper uses architectural energetics to interrogate the constituent elements and comparative benefits and detriments of large-scale Roman building.

Beasts of Burden: Animal Power for Public Construction in Rome
Christina Triantafillou, University of Southampton

In the burgeoning field of Roman construction, much focus is being devoted, and rightly so, to the size and scale of manpower for construction. However, what has yet to be more fully addressed is animal power, which was necessary not only for materials transport from production site to building site but also as the power for lifting mechanisms for large loads on the building sites themselves. This paper seeks to better understand the size and scale of the animal workforce in public building projects undertaken in Rome and the practicalities and logistics involved with the presence of these creatures in a bustling urban environment. During the heyday of imperial public construction in the early second century C.E., the streets of Rome were inundated with hundreds to thousands of additional animals for power and transport purposes. This paper calculates the minimum animal power needed for several major public building projects in Rome undertaken by Trajan during the course of his principate. It examines the organization and potential routes these transport animals and vehicles would have taken to and from the building sites. With these minimum animal power figures, it is possible to address the scale of the issues associated with the presence of these animals in an urban environment and how these factors may have affected the planning and logistics of urban construction sites. The presence of animals raises two concerns in particular: corralling and pollution. Where would the animals have been housed after completing their outbound journey from the production site or after a day of powering lifting cranes on the building site? The presence of animals also implies large quantities of fresh manure supplied on a daily basis. Was this by-product seen solely as a waste material to be removed or as a valuable resource to be reused for agricultural, fuel, or other purposes? To answer these questions, this paper examines the available archaeological and literary evidence, supplementing it with comparable historical examples to explore further the potential ways in which the Romans would have dealt with and benefited from the use of animals in public building construction.

Monolithic Columns: Spolia and the New Architecture of Late Republican Rome
Peter D. De Staebler, Pratt Institute

Monolithic columns are a hallmark of the so-called "marble-style" architecture of the Imperial Roman period. Each shaft represents a tremendous expenditure of effort and money to quarry, transport, and install. Over time, columns were manufactured in an increasingly standardized range of sizes to facilitate their incorporation into grand civic and religious projects. Many columns were sponsored by the emperors and flowed toward Rome or were destined for favored projects in the provinces; many were locally produced as well. After the third century C.E., these columns were created in ever smaller numbers, and new Late Roman and Early Christian buildings recycled precious monolithic columns from among the stock carved in prior centuries.

In this paper, I focus on how monolithic columns played a central role in the formation of a distinctively Roman architecture in the period before they were widely produced. Significant is the forgotten detail that the earliest monolithic columns used in Rome during the Republican period arrived as spoils of war—as literal "spolia"—taken along with art, cash, weapons, and slaves from cities in the Hellenistic east. The columns were premade, with set dimensions, and removed from other structures, not ordered in specific sizes and numbers for defined projects. From the beginning, builders in Rome found ways to integrate these impressive blocks into their architectural schemes and even, I suggest, to invent new building types (such as the columnar scaenae frons) to accommodate the vast number of columns.

The Marzamemi "Church Wreck": New Excavations and Heritage Management off Southeast Sicily

Justin Leidwanger, Stanford University, and *Sebastiano Tusa*, Soprintendenza del Mare

The Marzamemi Maritime Heritage Project is a collaborative excavation, survey, and heritage management initiative focusing on the maritime landscape and seaborne communication off the southeast coast of Sicily. Since 2013, fieldwork here has centered on the famous "church wreck," which sank while carrying prefabricated architectural elements for the construction of a late antique church— possibly alongside other cargo—from the northern Aegean region during the sixth century. In addition to three field seasons of survey and excavation, efforts have centered on documentation and conservation of previously raised materials, including those excavated in the 1960s by pioneering underwater archaeologist Gerhard Kapitän, as well as complete three-dimensional recording of the dispersed site and individual finds, both in situ and raised. Together, the vessel and its cargo offer insight into the character and patterns of maritime connectivity between the divergent eastern and western Mediterranean worlds and the possible complementary roles of imperial agency and local patronage in the ambitious programs of (re-)construction in sixth-century Italy. Equally important to this research, however, is the development of collaborative heritage management and outreach strategies, particularly centered on the development of the new local Museum of the Sea, designed to engage the public and promote responsible cultural tourism in the area.

SESSION 3G: Colloquium
Current Developments in North African Archaeology: AIA/DAI New Projects and Joint Efforts

ORGANIZERS: *Susan E. Alcock*, University of Michigan, *Michelle L. Berenfeld*, Pitzer College, *Ralf Bockmann*, Deutsches Archäologisches Institut, Rome, and *Ortwin Dally*, Deutsches Archäologisches Institut, Rome

Colloquium Overview Statement

North Africa has lived through an academic "renaissance" in recent years. The region has a remarkable heritage of archaeological sites in an exceptional state of preservation, albeit often hampered by a lack of stratigraphic data, owing to the specific historic contexts and academic traditions in the region. Recently, North Africa has seen considerable, if variable, political change in the course of the "Arab Spring"; while Libya is suffering from the breakdown of political institutions in a long civil war, with its own effects on archaeology and the role of researchers, Tunisia has become a young democracy, possibly opening up, despite painful setbacks, to international academia and new cooperations in a way never seen before.

There is a great potential in North Africa, with its very particular archaeological situation, for large-scale surveys and urban topographic studies using noninvasive reconnaissance techniques. This potential has been developed in a number of recent research projects. The pre-Roman period and Late Roman, Byzantine, and Early Medieval periods have also begun to receive increasing attention, in addition to the more usual emphasis on the Roman Imperial period. However, archaeological research today, especially in troubled regions such as this, is inseparably linked to current realities. With the opening up of North African archaeology to collaboration, a stronger (and understandable) demand for conservation, site and museum management, and education is directed toward international cooperative partners, who are asked to engage in a more intensive way with local communities. The preservation and management of cultural heritage in North African countries today demands from researchers clear strategies about how to deal with sites and finds beyond simply their investigation and publication.

Recent work by members of the AIA and the Deutsches Archäologisches Institut (DAI) reflects growing interest in the region. The ties between the two institutions reach back several years and are supported by an exchange program between the AIA and DAI. In our joint session, we present current trends in archaeological research in and on North Africa as represented by archaeologists from our institutions and researchers connected with them in active projects. Through this second joint AIA/DAI session, we would like to promote European-American and North African cooperations and inspire new joint projects.

DISCUSSANT: *Steven Ellis*, University of Cincinnati

"Where are Those Great and Splendid Cities?" Urbanization and Landscape Change in North Africa Across the Longue Durée (500 B.C.E.–800 C.E.)
Corisande Fenwick, University College London, and *Andrew Dufton*, Brown University

North Africa was one of the most densely urbanized regions of the Roman empire, and its history has long been told through the rise and fall of the classical city. The traditional orthodoxy held that North Africa experienced a period of unparalleled urban prosperity under Roman rule, with many new cities founded in this period. For Quodvultdeus writing in the 430s, as for modern commentators, this Roman world of hundreds of cities and towns began to unravel in late antiquity and had disappeared almost entirely by the Muslim conquest of Carthage in 697/8. Recent work in northern Tunisia suggests that this model—rooted in colonialist discourse and based on exceptional archaeological cases such as Carthage, Leptis Magna, or Timgad—needs a complete reevaluation. Sites such as Althiburos in northern Tunisia reveal far earlier indigenous precedents for urbanism, while a far more complicated picture of urban collapse has emerged at the other end of the chronological spectrum.

These new findings raise fundamental questions about the dynamics of urbanization and landscape change in North Africa between 500 B.C.E. and 800 C.E.—and the exceptional nature of the Roman "urban boom"—that can only be answered from a diachronic landscape perspective. This paper draws on new survey and excavation evidence to chart changing settlement patterns in northern Tunisia from the first Numidian and Phoenician towns, through Roman rule, to the emergence of new urban networks in late antiquity and beyond. Examining urban boom and bust across the longue durée provides new insight into some of the big questions currently being asked by Roman archaeologists in North Africa: when and why did such a concentration of urban sites emerge? Why did these towns flourish under the Romans? How did the surrounding countryside support the growth and specialization of such a densely urbanized landscape in the Roman period? And what are the implications of a much-reduced urban network in late antiquity and the Early Middle Ages?

Research, People, and Politics: The Tuniso-German Archaeological Project at Chimtou (Ancient Simitthus, Tunisia)
Philipp von Rummel, Deutsches Archäologisches Institut, Berlin, and *Stefan Ardeleanu*, Universität Heidelberg

Recent activities at Chimtou, undertaken by a combined team from the Tunisian Institut National du Patrimoine and the Deutsches Archäologisches Institut focus on periods of the urban history that hitherto have not received the attention they deserve. To date, archaeological research on the site chiefly centered on the imperial quarries of the *marmor Numidicum* (giallo antico) and on selected monuments in the town. The current project studies Chimtou's urbanistic evolution from its Iron Age origins well into the Medieval period—without, however, neglecting its urban development in Roman times.

A core goal is to study and publish the results of excavations conducted between 1968 and 1984. This work is accompanied by new stratigraphical, ceramological, geophysical, archaeobotanical, archaeozoological, and geomorphological studies, which have yielded astonishing new insights into Chimtou's pre-Roman, Roman, and medieval history. Other important aspects of the project include the enhanced integration of the archaeological site into the local community, the intensified training of archaeologists, architects, and conservators as well as of local craftsmen, and the valorization of the site. This paper presents an overview of our most recent activities and their results.

Urban Neighborhoods in North Africa
Michelle L. Berenfeld, Pitzer College

Roman imperial and Late Antique houses in North African cities have long been the object of intense and fruitful scholarly attention, yielding a rich body of work on domestic architecture and interior decoration, particularly mosaics. While many studies have noted similarities between elite houses in multiple North African cities, few have explored how interior decoration, architecture, and spatial organization intersect in specific urban contexts. This paper examines the impact and function of houses on the urban scale in selected North African cities, with an emphasis on Tunisia, and proposes a model for approaching urban domestic buildings in new ways.

Building on existing data—published reports and excavated remains—I explore the formation and development of neighborhoods as social complexes within the city and how these aggregations of (for the most part, elite) property interacted with streets and other public spaces. At Dougga and Thuburbo Maius, for instance, elite houses of varied shapes and sizes, occupying irregular plots of land, were clustered together, often with little space between them. The limits of individual properties would have been difficult to discern from the outside and would have occupied a large and perhaps seemingly collective elite footprint on the city that was far more prominent than any one individual house. At Carthage and Bulla Regia, on the other hand, where elite neighborhoods developed within more regularized grid plans, the spatial relationships were somewhat different but had a similar effect of presenting the neighborhood as an elite precinct.

This paper argues for an approach to the study of urban housing that considers relationships between houses within urban neighborhoods by examining physical connections and movement between buildings and the integration of mosaics and other interior decorations into the discussion. This should include analysis of patterns in the use of iconographic elements, stylistic choices, materials, and positioning of images among multiple houses. Using selected Tunisian cities as case studies, this paper demonstrates how the examination of decisions made in individual buildings (decorations, room arrangements, etc.), in combination with patterns among contemporary neighbors, may shed new light on elite self-presentation and conceptions of status as well as their place within urban social life more generally.

On Current Archaeology in Libya: A Remote-Sensing Project in Research and Heritage Management
Ralf Bockmann, Deutsches Archäologisches Institut, Rome

Some years ago, a cooperative effort between German, Italian, Libyan, and Tunisian archaeologists was inaugurated to study changes in settlement topography and resource management between late antiquity and the Early Middle Ages in North Africa, specifically a region in the hinterland of Leptis Magna in Libyan Tripolitania. Owing to political developments and a constantly deteriorating security situation, the survey that was originally planned could not be carried out by partners from the Deutsches Archäologisches Institut in Rome and Durham University, United Kingdom.

Instead, a remote sensing study was undertaken to gain basic data that could be combined with photographic and ceramic material collected on the ground by archaeologists working for the Libyan Antiquities Department. Training courses in GIS methodologies are held in Tunisia for the Libyan project partners, so that data collected on the ground can be linked to digital images and maps. By following this strategy, it has been possible to carry out some of the research originally planned in the project, while at the same time contributing to capacity building for local archaeologists.

The data gathered by remote sensing has turned out to be extremely helpful for heritage management, providing the opportunity not only to identify possible sites but also to monitor third-party interventions in archaeological zones. In this paper, I present results of the project first and then, taking our project as an example, discuss the possibilities for using remote-sensing data as part of heritage-management strategies in regions suffering from issues of accessibility.

An Archaeology of Rights: Cultural Heritage in the Medjerda Valley, Tunisia
Kathryn Lafrenz Samuels, University of Maryland, College Park

Cultural heritage is today a social force producing meaningful claims in the full spectrum of contemporary life, but especially in struggles against injustice involving social difference and inequality. Because of the power of heritage as a social tool for effecting change, increasingly cultural heritage is articulated within national and international legal frameworks as a type of human right. However, the universalizing ethos of human rights faces difficulty when confronted with the specific historical trajectories and contextual sensibilities implicated in a category like "heritage rights." Human rights also bear their own conceptual history, deriving from a western liberal tradition keyed to property rights.

In this paper, I offer an "archaeology of rights" to draw out in sharp relief the historical constitution of rights. Archaeological, textual, epigraphic, and ethnographic evidence ground this account of rights in the valley of the Medjerda (ancient Bagradas) River, which flows through northwestern Tunisia. The bulk of international attention in the region is directed to the UNESCO World Heritage Site of Dougga (Thugga), an important Libyco-Punic capital and Roman administrative center. Leading up to and during Tunisia's 2011 revolution, Roman and Punic archaeological material was variously mobilized within broader political conversations about Tunisian sovereignty vis-à-vis western intervention and integration. International interest in the classical heritage of Tunisia follows from earlier reclamations of the Roman empire under French and Italian colonialism. The degraded state of classical remains—as evidence of decay and neglect of a once flourishing ancestral civilization—provided legal legitimation of French colonial rule over a *terra nullius* in need of rebuilding and preservation. Traditional Islamic property regimes in the region, such as *habous* (perpetual inalienable endowments), were stripped away as a central strategy of broader land grabs. *Habous* arrangements overlay the earlier grand estates of agricultural production staked out by Roman centuriation, which in turn had constrained preexisting indigenous rights, marking them as "customary" and "traditional" and relegating their domain to marginal and uncultivated lands.

Each system of rights had to be legitimized vis-à-vis already existing claims, through distinctive strategies that variously embraced or neutralized these historic claims. Examining rights over the longue durée renders visible the multiple, overlapping regimes of rights and obligations as they articulate and contend with one another. If "heritage rights" are incorporated into the international human rights system, I argue that this diversity must be at the core of their formulation, showcasing the legal pluralism and historic constitution of rights.

The German-Algerian Research Project in the New National Museum of Cherchel
Ortwin Dally, Deutsches Archäologisches Institut, Rome, and *Ulla Kreilinger*, Universität Erlangen

The fourth-century B.C.E. Phoenician foundation of Iol/Jol (modern Cherchel, Algeria), after forming part of the Numidian kingdom, became the seat of the client kings of Mauretania, Juba II, his wife Cleopatra Selene II, and his son, Ptolemy (25 B.C.E.–40 C.E.). With this change, the city was renamed Caesarea or Caesarea Mauretaniae. In 44 C.E., the city in turn became Colonia Claudia Caesarea, the provincial capital of the Roman province of Mauretania Caesariensis. The city flourished until late antiquity, with notable buildings including a theater, the Port Island, and a now-vanished palace. Civic prosperity is also reflected in the discovery of some 400 statues and colorful mosaics. These were discovered both in several bath facilities and in private homes and villas, especially of the first to third centuries C.E.

We present here results of a German-Algerian research project that aims not only to publish the statues themselves (four volumes have so far appeared) but also to contextualize them within the specific topography, history, and cultural development of the city; we focus particularly on those dating to the reign of the client kings of Mauretania and the Roman Imperial age as partially documented by the first French excavators (19th century).

In addition, we address the presentation of the city's material record (esp. the statues) in the Archaeological Museum of Cherchel. Because of their number and high artistic quality, the Algerian Ministry of Culture decided in 2009 to name this the second National Museum, after that in Algiers. Since then, the collection has been undergoing reorganization and reinstallation by the Deutsches

Archäologisches Institut, in cooperation with Algerian and German partners. The project is supported not only by the German and American Embassies in Algiers and the Algerian Ministry of Culture but also by the German Ministry of Foreign Affairs. The project includes the presentation of a didactic, globally unique assemblage of sculpture as part of an overall effective exposition of the cultural and historical development of Cherchel, as well as of the conservation and care the objects require. Given the quantity and quality of the exhibits, the recruitment and training of local experts in support of the project is of considerable and especial significance in cultural policy.

SESSION 3H: Colloquium
Sailing with the Gods: The Archaeology of Ancient Mediterranean Maritime Religion

ORGANIZERS: *Sandra Blakely*, Emory University, and *Amelia R. Brown*, University of Queensland

Colloquium Overview Statement

Archaeological evidence for ancient maritime rituals casts light on the range of social behaviors designed to mitigate the risks and celebrate the success of voyages fundamental to life in a networked Mediterranean world. Seaside sanctuaries, votive dedications, and shipwrecks all bear witness to a wide range of rituals related to safe seafaring and the gods and heroes carried from port to port around the Mediterranean Sea. These explorations are relevant to debates on the origin, diffusion, and development of Greek, Roman, and Eastern cults; the everyday lives of fishermen, sailors, merchants, and pirates of varying classes and origins; and the mechanics of Mediterranean connectivity. They also cast light on perennial questions in maritime archaeology: Do the risks of seafaring shape social practices that are qualitatively distinct from those of land-based cultures? What data, beyond shipwrecks, may contribute to understanding the experience of seaborne travel?

The papers in this session situate the exploration of maritime ritual in the context of economics, trade, and connectivity from the Late Bronze Age through the Hellenistic period: they reflect methodologies ranging from iconographic studies to network modeling. "Phoenician Maritime Religion" explores the relationship between maritime and nonmaritime rituals, arguing for an essential distinction in the rites that addressed the risks and liminality of seafaring. "Praying and Singing" analyzes the scene inscribed on the Dor scapula and argues for a Cypriot rather than a Phoenician setting for its festival invoking the Great Goddess' protection over an outbound ship. "Aphrodite Euploia" focuses on the network of sanctuaries devoted to the maritime aspect of the goddess of love; "Testing the Gods" proposes that the human social network created by the Samothracian cult was a practical way to fulfill the rites' promise of safe sea travel for its initiates. "Love and Money" foregrounds the insights gained through analysis of financial markers in Hellenistic cults of Isis, Cypria, and Aphrodite on Kos, Thera, Delos, Rhodes, and Cyprus, while "Perati" explores the diverse ritual practices in the

Late Bronze Age East Greece and their evidence for the intersection of ritual and economic exchange. "Naukratis" explores ritual in the contexts of archaic emporia, as the sea brought diverse communities together and enabled the transmission of new forms of religion—Egyptian, Greek, Phoenician, and Carian.

DISCUSSANT: *Denise Demetriou*, University of California, San Diego

Phoenician Maritime Religion
Aaron Brody, Pacific School of Religion

Phoenician seafarers faced dangers and fears posed by the sea, weather, reefs, and other hazards of sailing on the Mediterranean Sea and Atlantic Ocean. Accordingly, specialized sacred beliefs and ritual practices developed among mariners that were a subset of their home culture's religion. Sailors honored deities whose maritime, celestial, or meteorological attributes could either benefit or devastate a voyage. While on land, these divine patrons were worshiped in harbor temples and at promontory shrines. While at sea, divine protection came from the ships themselves, which were considered to be imbued with the spirit of a god or goddess; these vessels also contained sacred spaces that allowed for continued contact with tutelary deities. Mariners performed religious ceremonies on land and at sea to enlist and ensure divine protection and success for their voyages. Specialized maritime features are also found in the funerary practices and mortuary rituals of seafarers. These maritime sacred beliefs and practices were a subset of more general Phoenician religion, which were generated by the liminality of the waters of the deep and the unique uncertainties and perils experienced while at sea.

Praying and Singing When Departing: A Cypriot Maritime Ceremony to the Great Goddess
Caroline Sauvage, Loyola Marymount University

The unique scapula found at Dor and published by E. Stern is often cited as illustrative of maritime celebrations characterizing the Phoenician coast in the mid first millennium B.C.E. However, the exact nature of these celebrations as well as the associated deity have been somehow glossed over. This paper reexamines the iconography of the maritime scene and provides a new reading and interpretation of the scene. It argues for the Cypriot origin of the object and for the identification of the scene as the representation of a ritual to the Great Goddess celebrated before the departure of a Cypriot ship. The paper demonstrates that two scenes of a ritual aimed at securing her protection over navigation are depicted.

The Maritime Network of Aphrodite Euploia
Amelia R. Brown, University of Queensland

The goddess Aphrodite, long the subject of literary and iconographic studies, has only recently gained attention for her ancient network of temples, cults, and sanctuaries. However, many aspects of these remain highly controversial, from her connection with courtesans to the architectural form of even her most famous shrines at Paphos and Cnidus. In this paper, I suggest that a neglected aspect of her patronage, her protection of mariners, may help explain some common aspects of her sanctuaries and cults around the coasts of the Mediterranean Sea. Material evidence for votive dedications, seaside shrines, and acropolis temples from southern Italy to the Levant can, with some caution, be combined with the evidence of Herodotus, Strabo, and Pausanias. Offerings made by hopeful or grateful seafarers, colonists, and travelers of multiple ethnicities occur at many of Aphrodite's shrines. Maritime Aphrodite's cult was practiced both at the port and atop sites with a view of the sea, with a focus on enclosures, statues, and dedications rather than monumental buildings. A better understanding of Aphrodite's network of maritime sanctuaries can therefore cast light on otherwise immaterial rituals of travel by sea and the interlocking networks of colonization, trade, and belief in the power of the gods that linked Magna Graecia with Greece, Cyprus, and the eastern Mediterranean.

Testing the Gods, Saving Your Ship: A Digital Approach to the Samothracian Ritual Network

Sandra Blakely, Emory University

Initiates into the cult of the Great Gods of Samothrace were given a promise unique in the world of ancient mystery religions: assurance of safety in travel at sea. The promise was famous long before the site attained its architectural and economic floruit in the Hellenistic period and is attested in monumental and epigraphic as well as literary form. The Nike of Samothrace stands on the prow of a Rhodian trihemiolia; Diagoras reported that the sanctuary was full of *pinakes* thanking the gods for safe travel (Cic., *Nat. D.* 3.37.89); a spectacular Neorion greeted visitors as they walked into the sanctuary from the shore. Inscriptions thanking the Samothracian gods for salvation at sea are found in Anatolia and Egypt—some so far inland that they must remind the reader of the tale of Odysseus and his oar. All of these symbolically rich data reflect the agency of individuals who chose to advertise the gods' interventions on their behalf. Grants of *theoria* and *proxenia*, recorded on the island's inscriptions, open the door to the structures through which the cult's promises were realized. These grants provide the basis for tracing the human social network among poleis who shared Samothracian affiliation. Shared festival attendance was a mechanism for increasing communication and cooperation, solemnized by the gods widely famed for their protection of travelers at sea. Arguments from Weber onward have argued for the effectiveness of *proxenia* as a legal counter to piracy and aid to maritime commerce. Inscriptions from the town of Samothrace underscore this aspect of the island's proxeny, listing its benefits as safe entrance (*eisploun*), safe exit (*ekploun*), representation in city councils, *asylia*, and freedom from taxes.

All of these raise the hypothesis that the Samothracian promise worked: the human social network generated by the cult ensured communication, cooperation, and counters to piracy along the Asia Minor coast, the islands, and the shores of the Black Sea. The Samothracian Networks project (https://scholarblogs.emory.

edu/samothraciannetworks/) has undertaken a test of the hypothesis, using GIS technology to track human cultural operations in real geographic space, and Social Network Analysis to map the frequency, intensity, and direction of human interactions in virtual space. The combination of these approaches opens up a new methodology in the investigation of ancient ritual systems that linked harbors and sailors from one side of the Mediterranean to another, enabling visualization, integration of qualitative and quantitative data types, and models of the information flows enabled by the cult's emergence as a supraregional center. This paper demonstrates the results of our work to date, contrasting two different visualizations of the information flows: the first based on a purely quantitative analysis of the epigraphic data, the second on a qualitative analysis that integrates historical practices associated with the *theoria*, *proxenia*, creation of monuments, and institution of priesthoods.

Love and Money: Financial Documentation for the Cults of Aphrodite, Cypria, and Isis in the Eastern Mediterranean

Isabella Pafford, Willamette University

Recent scholarship has improved our understanding of the Hellenistic Sanctuary of Aphrodite Pandemos and Pontia, located close to the harbor on the island of Kos. Inscriptions documenting building expenses, sales of priesthoods, and cult fees, as well as references to offering boxes or *thesauroi*, provide insight into the financial administration of the cult, as well as much-needed documentary evidence regarding the social practices of the citizens. More interesting, however, are the parallels between administrative mechanisms on Kos and related cults located on the nearby islands of Thera, Delos, Rhodes, and Cyprus. In all of these places, local cults incorporate ritualized coin use into mechanisms for regulating sanctuary access by citizens as well as noncitizens and in validating marriage contracts. This paper considers how the incorporation of additional financial markers from the neighboring islands can improve our understanding not only of the administrative mechanisms used by the Sanctuary of Aphrodite Pandemos and Pontia but also of the changes in social organization in the islands during this time of transition in the Hellenistic period.

Maritime Trade, Cult, and the Community of Perati in Late Helladic IIIC East Attica

Sarah Murray, University of Nebraska–Lincoln

Maritime trade in Late Bronze Age Greece has most frequently been cast as an economic and political institution, through which exotic finished objects and locally unavailable commodities were transferred among elites and empires. In this paper, I consider instead the evidence for religious diversity that both facilitated and grew out of maritime contacts in early Greece. In particular, I examine the context, nature, and significance of imported objects from the Late Helladic (LH) IIIC necropolis of Perati in east Attica and argue that these objects overwhelmingly suggest that this key port of the Postpalatial Aegean was a locus of economic transactions and harbored a wide-ranging array of cult activities and diverse religious beliefs.

First, I present the evidence for diverse ritual practice among the community members interred at Perati. The assemblage of finds from this extraordinary necropolis contains 42 imported objects (60% of the total number of imports known from the LH IIIC mainland), suggesting not only that Perati was wealthy during the Postpalatial period but that its inhabitants retained an unusual intensity of maritime contact with the outside world at a time during which Greece is usually thought to have become increasingly isolated. Surprisingly, the majority of imported objects from the tombs do not suggest that this community represented a native political elite. Rather, Syro-Palestinian amulets, Egyptian amulets, and figurines of Egyptian gods, as well as Cypriot and Syro-Palestinian weights, are prominent and correlate poorly with overall tomb wealth. Moreover, the assemblages are remarkably homogenous within discrete tombs. Egyptian amulets and figurines, for example, are contained primarily within a distinct group of contemporary tombs. A careful examination of the distribution and context of these imports within the cemetery suggests that Perati is likely to have hosted a group of resident traders or merchants, each practicing a bespoke set of funerary rituals and beliefs, rather than a homogenous Greek community profiting from preferential access to trade routes, as is usually assumed.

In closing, I consider the implications of this analysis. In the context of finds demonstrating imported ritual practice from other prominent ports in LH IIIC Greece, including Tiryns in the Argolid and Kanakia on Salamis, the evidence from Perati should cause scholars to take seriously the religious context within which economic exchange was situated in the Late Bronze Age and the active role that the diversity of religious practice in the Aegean may have played in shaping maritime contacts in this period.

Religious Cults and Archaic Emporia: Cross-Cultural Interaction and Religious Change Through Naukratis
Megan Daniels, Stanford University

In the Archaic period, coastal trading settlements, or emporia, formed vital nodes of commercial and cultural exchange within larger networks of connectivity. I argue that the religious cults within these settlements provided common loci of identity and cohesion amid various cultural groups engaged in overseas migration and seaborne trade and, on a broader level, played significant roles in transmitting new forms of religion throughout the wider Mediterranean world. I take the *emporion* of Naukratis as my case study, building off recent reassessments by the British Museum on the material remains and cultural patterning of the settlement, and specifically the epigraphic and votive material from the Sanctuary of Aphrodite. I situate my analysis of religion in Naukratis within recent models from cultural evolutionary psychology, which see religion, along with its attendant rituals and symbolisms, as an adaptive mechanism for human groups that both reflects and enables growing social complexity in human societies.

I first present recent arguments on the definition and function of the *emporion* in the ancient world, focusing on their multiethnic character, as argued, most recently, by Denise Demetriou (*Negotiating Identity in the Ancient Mediterranean* [Cambridge 2013]). I then outline the development of the Sanctuary of Aphrodite at

Naukratis, examining its architectural elements, spatial location, and the iconography of its votive offerings. I relate these material components and practices to the cultural groups present at Naukratis from the seventh century onward—namely, Egyptians and Greeks but also Phoenicians, Cypriots, and Carians. Finally, I step back and consider the broader sociopolitical meanings behind the Near Eastern origins of Aphrodite, particularly her relation to Cypriot and Levantine goddesses worshiped as the Queen of Heaven across the Bronze and Iron Ages. With this broader outlook, I demonstrate that the unique mixture of populations engaged in trade and settlement at Naukratis formulated new conceptions of the Queen of Heaven, reflected most of all through Aphrodite's main epithet at Naukratis, that of Pandemos ("All the People"), and her connections to seaborne activity.

SESSION 3I: Colloquium
Recent Excavations on Roman Provincial Sites: New Data for Understanding Regional Differences in the Provinces
Sponsored by the Roman Provincial Archaeology Interest Group

ORGANIZERS: *Elizabeth M. Greene*, University of Western Ontario, and *Alexander Meyer*, University of Western Ontario

Colloquium Overview Statement
The Roman Provincial Archaeology Interest Group (RPAIG) hopes to build on the success of the AIA Program Committee's new "recent work" sessions by offering a colloquium focused on current excavations in the Roman provinces. The session includes three papers concentrating on the western provinces and two on the eastern Mediterranean. If this session is successful, the RPAIG intends to plan similar sessions on different geographic regions that are just now seeing a great deal of modern excavation work, such as the Balkans, for future meetings. While the mandate of the current session is Roman provincial archaeology, individual papers do not concentrate exclusively on "Roman" material. Provincial archaeology spawns discussions about cultural hybridity, especially as pre-Roman settlements are affected by conquest and cultural change either directly or by proximity to the Roman empire, and it also includes the effect of provincial cultures on the Roman conqueror. These issues are becoming clearer as new data emerge from the recent and ongoing excavations discussed here.

The papers highlight recent work at six important sites. Each paper discusses the current excavations before considering the site's new contributions to regional trends with regards to social, religious, and economic trends. The first paper presents the results of the excavations at Idol Hill (*Der Götzenbühl*) in Germania Superior, a prehistoric tumulus with long-term use and implications for our understanding of religious change by way of the reuse of these sites in the Roman period. The second paper offers an overview of the very exciting Deutsches Archäologisches Institut excavations at Waldgirmes toward a discussion of Roman urbanism east of the Rhine in the late first century B.C.E. The third paper reports the discovery of an industrial complex outside the military fort at Vindolanda on the British frontier and its broad implications regarding the military role in production and consumption in the region of Hadrian's Wall.

The papers on eastern provincial sites also highlight recent work and the implications this work has for our understanding of regional trends. Andrew Goldman uses the recently excavated material from three Roman cemeteries at Gordion to understand mortuary practices in Roman Galatia. Robyn Le Blanc places the Roman remains of Ascalon into a broader understanding of the Mediterranean koine and discusses the communal sacred city of the elites in the Roman period. All the papers in this session have a goal to understand the evidence emerging in recent excavations in the context of their regional environment.

Idol Hill and Prehistoric Monuments in the Roman West
Philip Kiernan, University at Buffalo

Tumuli are long-term monuments that simultaneously define landscapes while changing in meaning over time. From 2011 to 2013, the University at Buffalo explored the tumulus known as Idol Hill (*Der Götzenbühl*) in southern Germany. This funerary monument was first built in the Middle Bronze Age and was re-constructed on a much larger scale in the Hallstatt period. It was probably in this second phase that a statue or standing stone was added to the site, for which the site was later named. A small number of finds suggest continued activity in the Roman period, as do Roman sites in the vicinity. The monument is attested in several early modern documents as a land marker. The Idol Hill site invites a reconsideration of the role of prehistoric tumuli and standing stones in Rome's western provinces. Prehistoric tumuli and standing stones were still present in the landscape throughout the Roman period, and some seem to have retained a cult function. At sites such as Avenches En-Chaplix and Folly Lane, Romano-Celtic temples have been connected to pre-Roman burials and cremation sites. At Antigny and Triguères, prehistoric standing stones were actually incorporated into Roman temple structures. The Menhir of Kernuz and the Gollenstein, both prehistoric standing stones, were augmented with relief carvings of Roman divinities. These examples of the reuse of prehistoric monuments show that they could retain a sacred character many centuries after their initial construction.

Germany East of the Rhine, 12 B.C.E.–16 C.E.: The First Step to Becoming a Roman Province
Gabriele Rasbach, Deutsches Archäologisches Institut Römisch-Germanische Kommission, Frankfurt

In the territories east of the Rhine, the Roman forces encountered completely different conditions than they had in Gaul. Political, administrative, and economic centers that could support Roman rule no longer existed, and a peasant subsistence economy prevailed. This economy was barely able to support the sometimes sudden needs of the Roman army campaigning and occupying territory in the provinces. If the Romans actually wanted to rule the conquered territories, they had to develop their own infrastructure rather than rely on existing frameworks of supply and settlement. This was done by the rebuilding and expansion of existing military camps, where additional buildings for administrative and economic purposes were built, such as at Haltern. Furthermore, Dio Cassius reports the foundation of cities. The forum in the settlement of Waldgirmes was excavated by the Deutsches Archäologisches Institut between 1996 and 2009. It was built over the top of stone foundation walls and represents the first proof of such a city foundation east of the Rhine. In its very earliest phases, the forum was equipped with a group of bronze statues.

The dendrochronological dating of timbers of two wells within the site showed the onset of Roman activity as early as 4 B.C.E. The Roman settlement in Waldgirmes existed for only about 20 years (from no later than 4 B.C.E. to 16 C.E. at the latest). This exceptional situation makes the place an excellent research object for the urbanization of a rural landscape. It is above all the central administrative building in Waldgirmes that allows a purely civilian interpretation of the site rather than an understanding of it as a military complex. This Roman forum is unique among buildings on the right bank of the Rhine River, and it is the oldest timber building with stone foundations in Germany. This paper presents these recent discoveries at Waldgirmes and places them in the broader context of the Roman occupation and urbanization east of the Rhine.

A Military Kiln Complex at Vindolanda: Production for the Local and Regional Military Economy

Alexander Meyer, University of Western Ontario, and *Elizabeth M. Greene*, University of Western Ontario

In the summer of 2014, a large kiln complex was discovered at Vindolanda in an industrial area of the site to the north of the fort and settlement. The complex appeared initially to have produced brick and tile, presumably for local use in the stone structures of the nearby fort and extramural settlement in the second century C.E. (petrographic analysis is currently under way). After further excavation, however, the kiln and the associated work areas produced wasters of much finer ceramics, which appear to be potential knockoffs, for the local economy. Also discovered was a mold for a small figurine, a bust of a figure in a classical style with a fillet in its hair, which was probably an appliqué for the body of a fine ceramic vessel. The complex was quite large with evidence for extensive use over a long period of time, and there were at least two different areas of work. Another notable find was the preservation of two-thirds of a wooden potter's wheel.

The discovery of this industrial complex brings into question the role played by the military forts on a frontier such as Hadrian's Wall in the local economy of production. The Roman army is more often considered the consumer in these military zones, and one often hears that the garrisons created an immediate market for local production. We should consider, however, that the military was as much a producer of some products, especially for the regional market present in the military zone along Hadrian's Wall. Initial dating results (radiocarbon) suggest that the complex was in use for an extended period of time in the second and third centuries, and the advantageous location of Vindolanda at the center of Hadrian's

Wall on the Stanegate Road made it an ideal location for supplying the region to the coasts to the east and west. This paper sums up the discoveries of 2014 and considers the new evidence within its local and regional context toward a discussion of the military role in supplying the regional economy.

Thinking Globally, Acting Locally: The Communal Sacred Identity of Roman Ascalon

Robyn Le Blanc, University of North Carolina, Greensboro

This paper investigates the formation of collective public sacred identity at the former Phoenician port city of Ascalon on the southern coastal plain of Roman Palestine. Using architectural, sculptural, numismatic, and epigraphic evidence, some of it recently excavated on the site, I argue that elites at Ascalon attempted to form and maintain relationships with the larger Mediterranean world through the adoption of elements of the Hellenistic visual koine. This is especially evident in the area of public cult and the presentation of the city's relationship with universal and particular deities. Previous studies have emphasized the ways in which cult, myth, and images of gods in Ascalon demonstrate a particular persistence of a Phoenician culture and religious identity beneath a thin "veneer" of hellenization. I problematize this conclusion and instead frame the adoption of elements of the Hellenistic koine as a conscious strategy undertaken by the elites of Ascalon. By tapping into the cultural and mythological networks and practices of the Roman empire, the Ascalonians fostered a communal identity based on their close relationships to the Greek and Roman world.

This exploration of the city's communal sacred identity is set against the urban plan of the city as revealed during the nearly 30 seasons of excavation at the site by the Leon Levy Expedition to Ascalon. Two bath buildings, a multiperiod bouleuterion, a theater, Roman domestic structures, a sewer system, and portions of the city wall have been uncovered from the Roman period. Although no temples or sanctuaries were found in the modern excavations, there is ample evidence for the civic spaces of the city participating in the creation of Ascalon's communal sacred identity through their sculptural and architectural decoration. This imagery was reinforced by the appearance of Ascalonian and universalized deities on coins and weights.

I argue that we should move beyond categorizing elements of the visual imagery of deities and the sacred at Ascalon as "Greek" or "Phoenician" and instead contemplate the ways that these images were used to form relationships within the city and between the city and other groups in the region and in the Mediterranean. Ultimately, I argue that many of the strategies and negotiations evident in the archaeological record at Ascalon are similar to those undertaken by elites in other cities from the Roman world, pointing to larger structural and systemic factors at work.

Roman Gordion and Its Cemeteries: Constructing a Model for Rural Burial Practices in Central Anatolia
Andrew L. Goldman, Gonzaga University

The population of Roman Galatia was largely a rural one, composed of nonelite subject peoples who lived outside the region's few urban centers. Relatively little is known about the rural inhabitants of Galatia during the Imperial period, owing both to a dearth of excavation within the province and to its relative paucity of literary and epigraphic records. Even less is understood about rural burial practice in this central Anatolian region, where the funerary landscape is an elusive one, relatively unpopulated with the types of monuments (i.e., elaborate rock-cut tombs, decorative sarcophagi, mausolea) found so plentifully in western and southern Turkey. What is evident from the surviving sources is Galatia's high level of ethnic diversity, with a mixed population that included people of Phrygian, Pisidian, Lycaonian, Persian, Greek, and Celtic descent.

Excavations at Gordion between 1950 and 1995 have provided a promising means of inquiry into the character of Galatia's rural, mixed ethnic population and its associated material culture, in the form of nearly 150 Roman-period burials belonging to three necropoleis and dating between the mid first and early fifth centuries C.E. These new data have permitted an initial identification of possible local patterns of nonurban funerary activity, several potential signature markers of "Galatian" character, such as the concurrent use of multiple construction types in a single necropolis. On the basis of this evidence, this paper offers up an initial diachronic model of rural burial practice for Roman Galatia.

Until recently, this model has remained necessarily tentative: Gordion functioned at least in part as a Roman auxiliary base, and the temporary or permanent stationing of non-Anatolian garrison troops at the site might well be responsible for the introduction of nonlocal funerary rites and burial patterns into its necropoleis. However, a means of testing independently potential "Galatian" patterns of funerary activity has recently become available with the publication of new fieldwork at Çatal Höyük as well as a spate of recent rescue projects in other Galatian necropoleis (e.g., at Haymana, Golbaşı/Boyalık). Examination of these new data appears to strengthen the case for certain common, widespread patterns of funerary activity in Galatia as well as to suggest that local variations did exist among the province's ethnically diverse population.

SESSION 3J: Colloquium
Cycladic Archaeology: New Approaches and Discoveries

ORGANIZERS: *John A. Tully*, Independent Scholar, and *Erica Morais Angliker*, University of Zurich

Colloquium Overview Statement
Scholarly approaches to the Cyclades have traditionally diverged by period. The Bronze Age Cyclades were early recognized as distinctive through cities such as Akrotiri, and they formed an early core for peer-polity interaction (Tsountas,

Renfrew). For later periods, however, Cycladic studies have a far lower profile. With rare exceptions (Delos), they are considered "stepping stones" of little intrinsic merit as much to modern scholars as to ancient outsiders.

This panel aims to change this situation in two ways: first, it shares recent developments in Cycladic scholarship with a broader audience. It draws on recent recognition of the greater economic potential of the Aegean Islands and new concepts of insular space as able to generate multiple connections. In addition, recent excavations have brought to light important sanctuaries, some absent from written sources (e.g., Despotiko, Kythnos). We illustrate how these sanctuaries and new epigraphic finds are enabling the revision of previous theories.

Second, this panel is also deliberately diachronic. Starting in the Bronze Age and ending in late antiquity, it aims to draw out common themes applicable across period boundaries. Each paper thus addresses a core historical or archaeological question but also contributes to core questions addressed by multiple papers. How did island identity change through the years? How did the Cyclades relate to other neighbors and to each other? Which social and religious forces underpinned these connections at different times?

Cumulatively, this session argues that the greater connectedness and dynamism that each paper reflects do not each reflect an unusual period or untraditional aspect of Cycladic life but instead were intrinsic to its form. By presenting new case studies of archaeological materials from each historical period, including unpublished materials just recently excavated, we hope to drive continued attention to this area of Greece.

DISCUSSANT: *François de Polignac*, EPHE

Storage and Sociopolitical Complexity in Middle and Late Bronze Age Ayia Irini, Kea

Evi Gorogianni, University of Akron

Storage, especially storage of surplus commodities, has been closely connected with emerging socioeconomic complexity in sedentary agricultural communities. Therefore, a detailed examination of storage facilities and their role in a community's economy is germane to furthering our understanding of local socio-economic organization, as well as a community's potential in engaging in trade and exchange. Hence, this paper assesses the issues in question using raw and interpretive data from the northern sector of Ayia Irini, specifically from the Northeast Bastion, which includes a storage gallery of pithoi attached to a kitchen and a dining room. Since this complex does not have the only storage room at Ayia Irini, the character, size, and capacity of this facility is analyzed and compared with others at the site (e.g., House A).

The goal of this research is to make inferences about the socioeconomic organization of the Ayia Irini community during the Middle and Late Bronze Age and to gain some resolution into the economic basis of social groups that had enough surplus to allow them to be active in maritime trade and exchange. These activities were conducted within the context of a complex and far-reaching trade and exchange network that connected the site to other key island and coastal communities of the Aegean. It also facilitated the exchange of metals and other commodities sought after by the established palatial polities on the island of Crete and by the emerging palatial elites on the Greek mainland. So far, these key communities (often collectively referred to as the Western and Eastern String) have been treated as monolithic entities managed by a group of elites who benefited from a special relationship with palatial societies. Thus, a study of the economic makeup of Ayia Irini not only elucidates the intrasite sociopolitical dynamics but also provides a clearer picture of the actors operating within this network.

Miltiades at Paros? New Evidence from Despotiko

Yannos Kourayos, Paros Archaeological Museum, *Robert F. Sutton*, Indiana University–Purdue University Indiananapolis, and *Kornilia Daifa*, University of Thessaly

A Late Archaic destruction at the Parian sanctuary of Apollo on Despotiko sheds light on Miltiades' puzzling attack on Paros in 489 B.C.E. and provides a new fixed point in Late Archaic chronology. The historical scene is set mainly by Herodotus (*Histories* 6.132–136), who tells us that Miltiades after leading the Athenians to victory at Marathon in 490 B.C.E. invaded Paros with his fleet, besieging the city and ravaging the countryside. Critical here is Miltiades' foray into the Thesmophorion, indicating his willingness to violate sacred sites, together with Ephoros' claim that Miltiades attacked other islands before Paros. This paper interprets the material evidence from Despotiko that clearly shows that the island suffered a violent attack in the light of Ephoros' statement.

First, we demonstrate the commercial importance of Despotiko and argue that the island was a suitable goal for an Athenian attack. Despotiko, which in antiquity was linked to Antiparos and was part of greater Paros, had a large bay protected from wind that was suitable for many ships. We point to ceramics at the sanctuary that document long-term commercial ties to Thasos and the north Aegean, and we argue that the attack on Paros was motivated by a long-standing rivalry in the region with Miltiades' Philiad and other Athenian interests.

Second, we analyze the material evidence from Despotiko that points to an attack specifically ca. 489 B.C.E. and, by extension, by Miltiades. Two data points are critical: first, mutilated fragments of several archaic kouroi were built into classical walls, indicating that the site sustained a major destruction. The stratigraphic evidence points to a Late Archaic date. Second, the north part of Building A, whether temple or *hestiatorion*, received a marble Doric facade dated by Manfred Schuller and Aenne Ohnesorg "circa 500 B.C.E. or a little later." With no obvious damage after construction, it must have been erected after the widespread Late Archaic destruction. This evidence suggests that the sanctuary sustained extensive damage during the Athenian invasion of 489 B.C.E. and immediately after received the new Doric facade.

In conclusion, we review the evidence for reconstruction across Paros at this time. For example, in the same decade, 490–480 B.C.E., the extramural Delion on Paros overlooking the city was refurbished with a new temple, altar, and colossal marble statue of Artemis. We interpret this also as a repair of Athenian damage and as an indication of the size of the Athenian threat.

The Cult of Demeter in the Cyclades: A Case Study of Kythnos and Naxos

Erica Angliker, University of Zurich, and *John A. Tully*, Independent Scholar

The cult of Demeter in the Cyclades, one of the most ancient in the archipelagos, is well attested by epigraphic, literary, and archaeological materials, which include a vast array of items from sanctuaries recently discovered (e.g., Kythnos). Despite this availability of sources and materials, there has been little attempt to synthesize the varied cultic practices of Demeter in the Cyclades, and the evolution of the cult is still not fully understood. This paper addresses this gap and argues for contact with Eleusis as a key driver of cult practice in the cult of Demeter on two Cycladic Islands for which there is abundant archaeological material: Naxos and Kythnos.

First we evaluate the evidence from Naxos. In the Archaic period, the cult of Demeter on Naxos had simply a sacred spot in the open air and was focused on ground pits to receive chthonic sacrifices. At first glance, these pits recall the cult of the Sanctuary of Demeter on Tenos. We argue from a closer consideration of the arrangement of the pits in Naxos that they recall the ritual of the *plemochoai* performed during the Eleusinian mysteries. This link continued when the Temple of Demeter was inaugurated ca. 530 B.C.E. Although the pits are erased, we argue that the general layout of the temple remained suitable for the celebration of the mysteries of Demeter as the one celebrated at Eleusis.

Second, we address the evidence from the recently excavated Sanctuary of Demeter on Kythnos. Preliminary excavations indicate the presence during the Classical period of a type of kernos used exclusively at Eleusinian sanctuaries. In addition, two inscriptions mention lands owned by Eleusis on the Sanctuary of Demeter in Kythnos. In the Hellenistic period, the kernoi and other artifacts disappear from the Sanctuary of Demeter. We argue this points to a change in cult practices between the high days of the sanctuary during the Classical period and the Hellenistic era. Nevertheless, the combined evidence from Naxos and Kythnos shows that both islands were in contact with Eleusis (Naxos during the Archaic and Classical periods, Kythnos during the Classical period) and that the interactions were central to the cult practice at that time.

The Port-City of Delos and Its Commercial Cityscape

Mantha Zarmakoupi, University of Birmingham

This paper focuses on the harbor facilities and commercial infrastructures of Delos to address the ties between economic change and urban growth. By analyzing the development of the harbor areas in relation to public and private commercial infrastructures on the island, I examine these areas as microcosms of the broader developments that the island underwent in this period. In doing so, my aim is to address the factors that shaped the dynamic commercial cityscape of the port-city of Delos.

Delos became an important commercial base connecting the eastern and western Mediterranean after 167 B.C.E., when the Romans made it a "duty free" port under Athenian dominion. Between 167 B.C.E. and the sacks of 88 and 69 B.C.E. by the troops of Mithridates and the pirate Athenadoros, the island became an intermediary step in Rome's commercial relations with the Hellenistic east. Although the literary sources stress the importance of the Delian *emporion*, the archaeological record has not provided sufficient evidence for the ways in which the commercial center operated. In addition, although numerous archaeological excavations over the last century have probed into the city of Delos, its port infrastructures remain a surprisingly understudied topic, which has hindered the understanding of its development in the Late Hellenistic period.

To date, research has focused on the harbor facilities and commercial infrastructures of the central harbor area of the island, on the west side of the island. The submerged structures of the central harbor of the Delos area have, however, suffered irreversible changes, as the 19th- and 20th-century excavations deposited the archaeological rubble on the sea floor and the new harbor installations were constructed over it. A new underwater fieldwork project (2014–) focuses on the northeast side of the island, examining the submerged area of the Stadion District—one of the new neighborhoods that were created in this period. It has provided evidence for commercial activities as well as harbor facilities at the eastern end of the district. The results of this project change the predominant assumption that this neighborhood did not have an instrumental role in the operation of the Delian *emporion*. Taking into account the preliminary results of this new project, I analyze the ways in which the harbor facilities of the island of Delos were related to the private and public commercial infrastructures on the island.

Interaction vs. Isolation: Rethinking Island Identity in the Roman Cyclades
Enora Le Quéré, University of Rouen (France)

Both ancient writers and modern scholars frame the Cyclades as a place of desolation and poverty in Roman times. Indeed, ancient writers used the decline of Delos during the first century B.C.E. as a model for describing the situation for all the surrounding islands. Thus, until recently the Cyclades were deemed unworthy of historical study.

Recent work suggests reality was quite far from this traditional perception of the Cyclades. First, I argue that Romans were highly integrated in the culture and the daily life of the poleis. I draw on a series of recent surveys and excavations on Melos and Paros, together with systematic analyses of Latin inscriptions on Parian marble blocks and Melian amphoras, to demonstrate that the exploitation of the islands' mineral resources was entirely controlled by Romans and to show from epigraphic evidence how the same Roman citizens and freedmen had often become magistrates, priests, or evergetes.

Second, I argue that, despite their apparent geographical insignificance, the Cyclades engaged in constant interaction with other cultural entities within the Roman empire. This is reflected in the rich material culture discovered, which includes the building of several remarkable baths on Delos and Tenos, as well as the reconstruction of monuments on Thera and Melos in the second century C.E. (i.e., Basilika Stoa, theater, agora, Hall of Mystae). The characteristics of these constructions suggest that, even though traditional architectural techniques were preserved, the models of the buildings came from Cyprus and Asia Minor, and their function was modified according to the needs of a new "Romanized" way of life. In the same way, I argue that the Roman sculptures from these islands (e.g., the *imago clipeata* from Amorgos, the honorific and funeral statues from Andros and Thera, the female busts from Melos) were up to date with the contemporary artistic trends in Rome and the rest of the empire while still also preserving strong traditional characteristics of the local culture.

My combined analysis of archaeological and epigraphic material allows a deep understanding of an emerging new insular identity. I argue that this identity should be understood as a dynamic process that results from a complex dialogue and interaction between Greek and Roman culture in the specific context of a micro-insular environment.

Networks and Christianization in the Late Antique Cyclades

Rebecca J. Sweetman, University of St. Andrews

While new research on the Cyclades in the Roman period is challenging traditional ideas of the islands as pirate-infested backwaters, little is known about them in the Late Antique period (ca. 400–700 C.E.); in fact, they have been sidelined by ancient and contemporary historians because of their reputation of being isolated and provincial. Moreover, the 41 Late Antique churches known from 12 islands indicate a contrary view, but the synthesis and contextualization of this data have been lacking. Consequently, detailed analysis of the Christianization of the eastern Mediterranean is restricted by a significant gap in the evidence. Scattered data from the Cyclades suggest that they were Christianized earlier than many of the surrounding areas. Other than the Christian catacombs on Melos (first to fourth centuries), there is literary evidence of an early and energetic Christian community on the islands. For example, some of the islands, such as Amorgos and Santorini, had early bishoprics. A number of Cycladic bishops also attended the early ecumenical councils (bishops from Paros and Naxos attended the third and fourth councils). Excavations at the church of Panagia Ekatontapyliani, Paroikia, Paros, indicate a fourth century foundation, and literary sources tie its establishment to Ayia Eleni of the imperial family. These positive data are bolstered by recent research on surrounding areas, such as the Peloponnese and Crete, which provides clear indications that the Cyclades were conduits for Christianization in the Aegean. However, the processes of how and why this was the case were unknown in part because of the skewed perceptions (often from an imperial top-down view) and the difficulties of synthesizing the data from the islands. To address this issue, we undertook an architectural and topographic survey of the churches to understand how Christianity was adopted on the islands. It became clear that locations were chosen to draw on tradition and memory to help peacefully situate the new religion in the community. This analysis, combined with a study of associated material culture (including mortuary and epigraphic) sheds light on the diverse local communities as well as agents of conversion. Rather than insularity, the innovative aspects of church building and early conversion indicate the receptiveness to new ideas on the part of island communities. Altogether, this paper provides an original synthesis of the Late Antique Cyclades from the perspective of the islands themselves, which highlights their vibrancy, their innovativeness, and the important roles they played on network routes in the Aegean.

SESSION 4A: Joint AIA/SCS Colloquium
Digital Resources for Teaching and Outreach
Sponsored by the Digital Classics Association

ORGANIZER: *Neil Coffee*, University at Buffalo, SUNY

Colloquium Overview Statement

Digital resources are increasingly opening up new opportunities for classics education and outreach. Some, like MOOCs, have been intensively discussed. The goal of this session is to highlight new and less familiar approaches and encourage reflection on how we can best achieve our educational mission in this changing environment. We now have access to free online language textbooks with exercises. Students can play online games in which they guide animated characters through Roman history. They can also contribute to research by publishing translations and annotations in major online repositories. Papers are invited that introduce these and other sorts of tools and techniques and/or reflect on the present and future use of digital methods for pedagogy and outreach.

Dumbarton Oaks Byzantine Seals Online Catalogue
Lain Wilson, Dumbarton Oaks, and *Jonathan Shea*, Dumbarton Oaks

Lead seals are among the most numerous artifacts to survive from the 1,100 year history of the Byzantine empire: between 70,000 and 80,000 individual specimens are estimated to have survived. Until recently, however, their publication was limited to specific categories—for example, seals with place names, family names, and particular iconographies, offices, and titles. These publications are expensive and are not widely available outside of university libraries with extensive Byzantine studies sections.

The Byzantine Seals Online Catalogue (www.doaks.org/resources/seals) is an effort to catalogue all the seals in the Dumbarton Oaks and Fogg Museum of Art collections' almost 17,000 specimens. The online publication of these seals is important for undergraduate and graduate students as well as subject-area specialists, and in three respects their online presentation is especially useful for the purposes of teaching and outreach.

First, for undergraduate and early graduate students, the limited Greek inscriptions provide a useful starting point for the subject of Byzantine Greek epigraphy. High-resolution photography together with diplomatic and expanded transcriptions of the inscription, translations, and commentary allow students with no experience to see the steps by which sigillographers read a seal and interpret the often-abbreviated inscription.

Second, the catalogue gives students with limited Greek the opportunity to make use of a large corpus of primary materials. For many students, Byzantine history is necessarily limited to translations of chronicles and histories along with, perhaps, art historical or archaeological materials. The online catalogue introduces students to an important and ubiquitous element of material culture that intersects, and thus can serve as a primary source for, numerous topics in Byzantine studies: prosopography and family networks, personal piety, art history, and military and administrative history, to name a few. A faceted search of various metadata fields allows users to find quickly all seals matching the criteria relevant to their research interests.

Finally, an integral part of the catalogue's development has been the creation of ancillary materials, such as online exhibits related to Byzantine emperors and New Testament narrative iconography, as well as an extensive bibliography. The exhibits, along with the catalogue, have been added to multiple undergraduate and graduate course syllabi. They together serve as one entry point available to students and specialists everywhere for the study of a rich and complex civilization.

Using Online Tools to Teach Classics in a Small or Nonexistent Classics Program
Kristina Chew, Rutgers University Online

The Internet offers many tools, from online texts to scholarly resources to technologies, making it possible to communicate with—and teach—students who are thousands of miles away, to enhance the teaching of classics. Classicists at colleges and universities with very small programs, or without a classics program at all, can especially benefit from these. Classicists such as Barbara McManus and Carl Rubenstein have shown just a few of the ways Internet resources can be used to promote the study of the ancient world. They and more than a few other scholars have also expressed reservations about overreliance on e-learning, citing concerns about academic integrity, practical issues such as how to evaluate students, and reduced opportunities for interaction (Guerlac, O'Donnell). As the sole classicist at two smaller universities, and as an online instructor for a variety of classics courses, I have very much relied on the creative use of Internet resources to provide students with a well-rounded foundation in classics. Online tools such as those designed by Google can be adapted to provide students with as personalized and attentive a learning experience as possible in online courses on topics ranging from Latin to medical terminology. The ready availability of resources about the ancient world, Latin, and ancient Greek on the Internet can be of use in developing lessons about ancient history, culture, and literature for community college courses, to bring classics to a wider audience of students.

I discuss specific strategies to (1) use Google tools to facilitate online instruction and (2) infuse classics into community college writing and reading courses, as examples of how, even in the absence of an official classics program, the teaching of the ancient world can be accomplished.

Collaborative Annotation and Latin Pedagogy
J. Bert Lott, Vassar College

Over the past two years I have used a collaborative annotation tool, Annotation Studio, developed at the MIT Hyperstudio with support from the National Endowment for the Humanities (AnnotationStudio.org), to have students in intermediate and advanced Latin classes annotate digital versions of Latin readings before and after class sessions. My approach is inspired by recent interest among humanists in digitally supported "social reading" but remains grounded in the traditional form of the textual commentary, which, I believe, naturally lends itself to collaborative work. In this paper, I present my use of the tool through examples from my own classes. I also discuss both why and how I use Annotation Studio for Latin instruction.

Technology is providing classicists with powerful new tools for study and scholarship, most notably easily accessible online versions of ancient texts linked to powerful research and linguistic tools. While this is opening up new possibilities, it is also altering Latin pedagogy and language acquisition. We have relied on a particular model of student work—involving memorization and difficult-to-navigate reference tools—to direct students into slow, engaged reading. Now, students click straight to answers, without doing the work we saw as a primary mode of pedagogy. I use Annotation Studio to replace that work with other kinds of focused attention to the text while also taking advantage of the interactivity made possible by digital collaborative annotation. Annotation Studio, accessed through a web interface, allows students to write comments linked to individual words and phrases of a text and respond to comments others have made. Students write extended posts investigating the use and meaning of individual words. They ask and answer questions about syntax or grammar. They make interpretive comments tied to very short selections of text. Importantly, the interactive nature of the work requires students to stretch out their contact with the text, asking questions, getting answers, and discussing ideas as part of their preparation, activities that are normally confined to a single session of "doing homework."

My use of Annotation Studio adapts some aspects of the "flipped classroom" approach. It requires that students use collaborative annotation to read more actively and to engage more deeply outside of class time; thus, more class time is devoted to discussion and less to problem solving. The goal, however, is not to free up class time by moving noninteractive activities out of class using technology. Collaborative annotation is active and interactive. It teaches close and engaged reading by requiring students to anchor their ideas in specific words and passages rather than just thinking about broad themes and plot; it enhances memory of the texts and helps students make connections across different parts of the text; and it teaches them to take effective notes and then use those notes to develop bigger ideas.

From Stone to Screen to Classroom
Gwynaeth McIntyre, University of Otago, *Melissa Funke*, University of British Columbia, and *Chelsea A.M. Gardner*, University of British Columbia

Inscriptions are one of our most useful and abundant sources of information about the ancient world. Considering that inscriptions are most commonly located on immovable stones, however, it is difficult to engage with the physical reality of epigraphic evidence in the classroom. Epigraphic squeezes, made using a pre-digital technology that remains instrumental to classicists, offer an affordable and practical solution to this problem by allowing scholars to virtually transport the stone to institutions worldwide. Yet there are still challenges to overcome when attempting to incorporate the physical squeezes into the classroom, the least of which is the fragility of the filter paper of the squeeze itself. One option is to transform the physical artifacts by means of digitization. In the case of the graduate student-launched initiative presented here, digitization is accomplished through an innovative photographic technique, which results in crisp, detailed images that retain the three-dimensional nature of the original inscribed words.

This paper describes how these digitized squeezes have been incorporated into the undergraduate classroom, in both language and nonlanguage courses, and it showcases the type of experiential learning that typically has been limited to archaeological sites and museums. It argues that the use of these digital artifacts helps overcome the challenges of bringing ancient subjects to life in the classroom through two case studies. First, we address the use of digital images of a fourth-century Athenian inscription (*IG* 1 3 969) in an intermediate Greek course and how this exercise provided a means of contextualizing the language in a way that was not possible through literary texts alone. Second, we discuss the implementation of the images of an inscription from the Temple of Athena Nike in Athens (*IG* 1 3 35) in an introductory archaeology course and an intermediate Greek religion course. Both classes studied the letterforms on this inscription from detailed images projected in the classroom and from this learned how individual letters affected our understanding of historical timelines and the contexts of particular sites.

These two case studies show how the transformation of a predigital technology into a digital technology allows for easy incorporation of artifacts into a variety of courses at the undergraduate level. We conclude our paper by discussing our creation of open access teaching modules, such as those discussed above based on our collection of digitized squeezes, and their potential use throughout the classics teaching community.

Dependency Syntax Trees in the Latin 1 Classroom
Robert Gorman, University of Nebraska–Lincoln

Those attending past panels sponsored by the Digital Classics Association have been introduced to the Ancient Greek and Latin Treebanks and the digital tools that support them. These databases have been discussed primarily for their value for research. But their implications for language pedagogy have also been touched on, and with good reason. The technology of treebanking can be a valuable classroom resource throughout all stages of the Greek and Latin curriculum. I propose to discuss treebanking as a teaching method and illustrate how it can be integrated into language instruction.

I have been incorporating treebanking into our Latin sequence for more than 5 years at all levels of instruction from the first week of Latin 1 to our most advanced classes. In my paper, I discuss aspects of treebanking at all these stages, but I concentrate on how the technology works in the first-year classroom.

I will begin with a few words about the nature of dependency syntax and the characteristics of a dependency graph. Then I will introduce the Perseids Collaborative Platform and the Arethusa Annotation Framework. I focus in particular on the features of most value to teachers. The system offers tremendous flexibility rather than forcing a single approach to language on its users. This quality is apparent, for example, in its handling of syntax labels. The labels used by research scholars are not well suited to the classroom, where the paramount concern is that textbook and technology should agree. The Perseids/Arethusa system makes such agreement easy, since it supports user-defined tag sets. I will demonstrate how these labels are set up. Likewise, it allows great latitude in handling morphology. For beginning-level students, one may turn off Arethusa's morphological analysis, so that the students must supply the lemma, part of speech, and form for each word. At the intermediate level, one may set the parser to offer choices of possible forms for the students to select. My advanced students have used the system several times in lieu of a textbook and lexicon.

I will also demonstrate how the student interface allows one to grade student homework automatically against a gold-standard template. For each word, data from a wide range of student choices (both correct and erroneous) are recorded and displayed. I will close by touching on the efforts currently underway to determine a rating of sentence difficulty and make these data comparable among different college language programs.

SESSION 4B: Joint AIA/SCS Colloquium
Standardization and the State

ORGANIZERS: *Robert Schon*, University of Arizona, and *D. Alex Walthall*, University of Texas at Austin

Colloquium Overview Statement

One nearly universal concern of states is the standardization of measures. On one hand, the state's involvement with standardized measures is a form of exercising power. By establishing official standards, and curating the physical prototypes that define those standards, state authorities attempt to impose themselves into the economic transactions that take place within a state's territory. On the other hand, by regulating standards and ensuring widespread compliance to them, these same authorities help reduce transaction costs, thus providing a public good. Because there are concomitant competitive and cooperative motivations behind standardization, then, there are myriad ways in which it can be implemented. The ways in which states approach standardization, moreover, shed further light on the nature of statecraft practiced in them.

In this set of papers, we seek to better understand how states go about establishing, implementing, and regulating standards. Our primary concern is the political economy of ancient states in Greece and Italy from the Bronze Age through the Roman empire. Previous research on the economies of ancient states has tangentially touched on standardized measures, but none has explored them as the primary focus of study. Similarly, scholars who focus on weights, measures, coins, and other things that get standardized have rarely positioned their research in broader discourses concerning statecraft. In contrast, this has been a fruitful field of investigation in later periods, especially in Europe during the Renaissance and early modern periods. This set of papers seeks to fill this lacuna and contribute to our increasing understanding of the long-standing relationship between statecraft and standardization.

The papers assembled here explore varying facets of how states approach standardized measures from a range of perspectives and theoretical orientations, including performance, political power, finance, and law. Our case studies, set throughout the ancient Mediterranean world, are selected to illustrate the range of contexts in which standardization affected economic activity from the individual transaction to the economy as a whole.

The session begins with an introductory paper by the session organizers that provides a review of scholarship until the present day, offers future directions, and contextualizes the papers that follow. The second paper, focusing on materiality and performance of measurement in the Aegean Bronze Age and the Athenian Agora, traces how standards are adopted and what their adoption reveals about the emergence of ancient markets. The third paper examines the manner in which standards were set in the first place using Greek numismatic evidence, and it argues that the process of adopting standards was a hotly contested one. The author of the fourth paper focuses on Hellenistic and Roman weights and measures from Sicily and further explores the contested nature of standardization, highlighting the politics behind the implementation of a common standard throughout a region. The fifth paper explores a range of contexts in which Roman law mediated the use of standards among parties who did not necessarily wish, or need, to adopt them. The sixth paper conceptualizes measurement as a performance and argues that it was the repetition of measurement tasks, rather than the imposition of specific units, that promoted the adoption of standards in Roman Egypt.

Collectively, the papers reveal how the process of standardization in the ancient Mediterranean was selective, contested, inconsistent, and met with mixed results. Despite these limitations, standardized measures endured as essential institutions of the political economies of states well beyond the ancient world.

DISCUSSANT: *Ian Morris*, Stanford University.

Materiality and Performance in the Use of Standardized Measures
Robert Schon, University of Arizona

One way to trace the emergence and development of markets in the ancient world is through the adoption of standardized measures. The archaeological record of the ancient Mediterranean is replete with evidence of standardized measures ranging from the measuring devices themselves to artifacts that reveal the use of standards in their design and documents that list commodities being measured. Identifying such measures is straightforward, but determining how they were incorporated into a given economy is a more challenging task. Although researchers have made great strides in identifying the standards that were in use in ancient states, little work has been done to establish the relationship of those standardized measures to their political economies.

The goal of this paper is to show how certain physical characteristics of measuring devices, such as their form, regional distribution, and degree of state-level regulation, can provide insights into how they were used and how measurement, more broadly, functioned in the ancient economy. To illustrate this point, I examine two cases: one from the Bronze Age Aegean, where centralized intervention is indiscernible, and the other from classical Greece, where it is unambiguous. The paper treats measurement as a performance, focusing on three of its aspects: the context in which measurement takes place, the materiality of the measuring instrument, and the act of measurement itself. Context determines what kind of measuring instrument is appropriate. Characteristics of the instrument, along with the manner in which measuring is performed, can reveal information about the relationship of the participants. Take, for instance, the weighing of commodities for the purpose of exchange. In reciprocal exchange, transactions are generally carried out by parties who know each other well and have a history of mutual trust. In such circumstances, commodities may be exchanged without any formal measurement at all. On the other hand, in market-based exchange, where transactional partners may not be acquainted, commodities are more often measured using instruments that are standardized, accurate, and possibly guaranteed by the state. Thus, the materiality of measuring devices and the performance of measurement are connected to the economic contexts in which they occur. Moreover, applying Butler's concept of performativity (as Callon has done for markets writ-large), I argue that materiality and performance in turn define the transactions in which they are employed. The mass of a commodity, for example, is economically meaningless unless it can be measured.

The case studies presented here illustrate how archaeologists can assess the performance capabilities and appropriate uses of measuring instruments and thereby infer their economic roles. The first consists of a series of lead discoid weight sets used throughout the Aegean during the Bronze Age. I argue that their standardized form, similar degrees of accuracy, and depositional range reveal a koine of the practice of measurement that emerged without any state intervention. The second case study focuses on the Athenian Agora and examines how the institutionalization of measurement as a public and transparent act became an essential pillar of the Athenian polis. Here, standardized measures were labeled as belonging to the demos. This public display of an official prototype was a strategic move by state officials that served multiple functions. On one hand, it materialized the state's claim of possessing the authority to set the standard in the first place. On the other, it reduced transaction costs, thereby providing a public good that furthered the viability of private enterprise in the marketplace. These are but two examples of how the materiality and performance of standardized measurement can provide further insights into the functioning of ancient economies.

Who Benefits? Incentive and Coercion in the Selection of Greek Monetary Standards

Peter van Alfen, American Numismatic Society

Coinage in the ancient Greek world was produced in accordance with a weight standard selected by the political authority within a state ultimately responsible for the production of that coinage. This standard served as both a money of account (e.g., Attic drachm) and as the basis for the denominational structure of the coinage (e.g., tetradrachm, drachm, obol). This much is clear. How authorities came to select a particular standard is much less obvious, however. Metrological studies of Greek coinage, along with the occasional insights provided by epigraphic or textual evidence, suggest that authorities could follow one of a number of different paths in selecting a standard. They could, for example, adopt or modify an existing epichoric standard; they could voluntarily borrow a standard from elsewhere; they could acquiesce to hegemonic demands to use an imposed standard; they could modify a borrowed standard either independently or as part of a collective of other authorities. Scholars generally reduce the motivations authorities had for selecting one path, or standard, over another to a somewhat limited range of political and economic incentives: their desire to generate fiscal revenues in currency exchanges; their desire to reduce transaction costs in international trade, taxation, or joint military endeavors; their relative political strength within the international arena. For those hedging, the more vague explanations of "maintaining tradition" or "being influenced by" offer crowded refuge.

While cold economic rationalities and cross-border power plays no doubt had a role in some choices about standards, this cannot be all there is to the story, a supposition that the recourses to "tradition" and "influence" would seem to affirm. In this paper, I suggest that as with all decisions concerning archaic and classical coinage—whether to mint or not, which metal, which denominations, etc.—those concerning weight standards likewise had larger social and political ramifications. Some within the community stood to benefit by the decision, others did not. Some could put pressure on decision makers, other could not. Thus, our interpretation of how coin weight standards were selected must be expanded to include a process that was potentially a great deal more problematic, contentious, and internally divisive than is usually suggested. By doing so, we can begin to see that standards were not necessarily selected for the greater public good but rather for the good of those able coerce their selection.

Measures and Standards in Hellenistic and Roman Sicily
D. Alex Walthall, University of Texas at Austin

"Cicilia ae piu salme," complained the 15th-century merchant Giovanni da Uzzano, reflecting on the multiplicity of capacity measures one routinely encountered in Sicily, measures that all shared the name "salma." Such variation in "standard" units of measure was not uncommon in medieval and early modern Sicily, where an island-wide standard for measuring grain, for instance, remained an elusive goal until the early 19th century. Adherence to local and feudal standards was, in fact, the norm until 1809, when the Bourbon king Ferdinand III, compelled by a need to raise taxes, dispatched technicians to Sicily with the task of enforcing metric units across the island. For both merchants and monarchs, the diversity of metrological units stifled vital aspects of their respective livelihoods' trade and taxation.

Of course, the desire to mobilize the island's agricultural resources through taxes and trade has a long history on Sicily and with it efforts to enforce common units of measurement. This paper addresses some such earlier efforts to achieve metrological unification across parts or the whole of Sicily, focusing on two major political transformations of the Hellenistic period—namely, the consolidation of eastern Sicily under the authority of the Syracusan monarch Hieron II and the incorporation of the island within Rome's growing administrative empire. For both Hieron and the Romans, Sicily's renowned agricultural fertility offered a source of great wealth. One need only look to Cicero's account of the *Lex Hieronica* to grasp the centrality of the agricultural tithe within the political administration of the island. It follows that, for both Hieron and the Romans, a unified metrological system was desirable for the efficient assessment and collection of agrarian taxes. Yet, while sovereign authorities endorsed the official standards of the state, we have little by way of surviving documentary or literary evidence to account for how this process was carried out under Hieronian or Roman authority. Judging from later medieval and early modern sources, metrological standardization was not a particularly simple or organic operation, especially in the highly segmented political and geographic landscape of Sicily.

Here, archaeological evidence can help further our understanding of the role ancient states played in the endorsement and adoption of metrological standards. The appearance of uniform weights and measures at different sites across a broad geographic area, for instance, may be used to track the spread of metrological standards endorsed (and enforced) by state authorities. In this light, the many hundreds of weight and volume measures recovered in the course of the American excavations at the central Sicilian city of Morgantina offer rich testimony to the adoption, dissemination, and use of standard measures in the Hellenistic and Roman Republican periods. In this paper, I present a selection of unpublished weights and measures from ancient Morgantina, which appear to document both the swift adoption of state-sponsored standards in eastern Sicily during the reign of Hieron II and their gradual replacement by Roman standards of measure throughout the first two centuries of Roman rule. At the same time, the Morgantina material reveals the coexistence of weights and measures belonging to different standards at a single location, a fact that may shed light on the limits of state-sponsored standardization in antiquity.

State Standards and Metrological Culture in Imperial Rome
Andrew M. Riggsby, University of Texas at Austin

As the organizers point out, standardization of weights and measures is a near-universal operation of states, but it would be surprising if all states carried this out with equal zeal and efficiency. This paper explores the limits of standardization in the Roman empire, particularly (though not exclusively) in terms of the incentive structure created by the legal system. Appeal to universal standards was rarely required by the state, whether in its own interactions with private persons or between two such parties. Nor were persons who voluntarily relied on such standards rewarded indirectly by the commercial law. These limits are then located in a broader metrological culture, which was not only nonstandardized but anti-standardization, and this context shaped and limited the state's interventions.

(1) Prior to the question of use, even the broad spatio-temporal availability of standards is subject to doubt because the very diversity of available options undercut the value of any individual one. (The evidence on this point is weak and better studied in previous scholarship than most of what follows. I simply note briefly that a minimalist reading is at least plausible.)

(2) Mechanisms for direct enforcement of standards in transactions between two private parties by state officials were weak, localized, and quite literally something of a joke. Market standards were (apparently) only enforced by local authority (and perhaps to local standards) and without penalty, and even then enforcement actions seem to be regarded ipso facto as overzealousness on the part of the magistrates concerned (Juv. 10.100–2; Pers. 1.129–30; Ulp., D. 19.2.13.8).

(3) Interactions between state and individual, such as payment of taxes and distribution of water, were often arranged so as not to require measurement to a universal standard. Instead, they operated by proportion, and indeed often by proportions valid only within a fairly local context (e.g., *OGIS* 2 674; *IGRP* 3 1056 [tax]; *CIL* 6 1261, 8 4440, 14 3676 [water]). While there are numerous exceptions, when the state could (and in fact did) dictate the terms of interaction, it did not systematically impose standardized weights and measures.

(4) The indirect effects of how measure was treated in commercial law similarly did little to privilege standardization. The law allowed parties to choose their own measures and particularly recognized regional diversity (*Pap. D.* 18.1.71). More indirectly, but perhaps more importantly, Roman law appears not to have recognized generic sale by quantity (*Gaius D.* 18.1.35.5; Zimmermann, *Law of Obligations* [Oxford 1996] 236–39).That is, no merchandise was understood to have been sufficiently well identified to be an object of sale until it had actually been measured. (Such controversy as exists on this point in the legal literature seems to stem not from real evidence but from raising the present question of standardization.) Individual transactors were not rewarded for conforming to state standards.

The last two points relate to a broader feature of Roman metrological culture. That culture operates to a significant extent by approximation and proportionality, because even simple measurement had not become what Latour and Woolgar's *Laboratory Life* (Princeton 1986) has called an "inscription device." That is, there was no community of agreement that the written output of some mechanical/procedural operation should be allowed to stand in for a real property of a physical object (as in a modern laboratory, a spectrogram stands in for real properties of some chemical). Treating various weights and measures as inscription devices is a technological development that cannot simply be assumed just because it would suit various purposes of the state.

Performing Measurement in the Roman East

Melissa Bailey, University of Maryland, Baltimore County

In this paper, I argue that measurement was only selectively standardized in many parts of the Roman empire and that we can best approach this selectivity by conceptualizing the act of measurement as a performance, which the government controlled or coopted at key moments, rather than as (only) the production of uniform units, which often dominates ideas of standardization in the modern world. Using this model, we can then see how, for example, taxation in kind relied not only on specific kinds of containers but also on repetitive labor tasks, quality checks, and transition points leading in a chain to Rome or Constantinople and largely ignoring lateral economic encounters (encounters that did not involve the state) between citizens or subjects. I argue this point using documentary texts (taxation documents, leases, and loans in kind) from Roman Egypt, particularly the site of Oxyrhynchus, and further argue that here, measuring transactions do seem to have become more widely standard over time; less, however, through the direct interest of the imperial government than because of the increasing symbiosis between the government and large estates in matters of taxation.

With reference to modern states, standardization is often conceptualized through the production of uniform units. By imposing exact units of money, weight, capacity, and time, states created a standardized system encompassing every transaction for all their citizens. Scholars have also emphasized how the modern transactional world involved entirely new modes of transporting, storing, counting, and loading/unloading commodities like grain. This latter perspective is the most useful for evaluating the different approaches of the Roman government to measurement. The Roman empire produced some kinds of standardized units (e.g., coinage) on an extremely massive scale. Nevertheless, specifically Roman units of measure were not imposed in many areas, and a wide variety of local named grain measures persisted—for example, in Roman Egypt. Grain intended for the state followed a path of standardized measuring encounters bringing not only particular capacity (and possibly weight) units but also labor (such as the grain one person, donkey, or ship could carry), repetitive movement (loading, unloading, and counting), and quality of grain into play. But transactions between individuals still cited a wide variety of local measures, with a high disconnect between how each measuring encounter was arranged.

I compare and contrast these sets of encounters (those along the taxation path of the state and those between individuals), asking what modes of verification were used, how quality was evaluated, and whether different overall priorities were at work (e.g., one such priority for the state might be massive transport, thus prioritizing weight, wagonload, or repetitive tasks over or in addition to uniform units). I furthermore suggest that the scope of the chain of measuring encounters could change over time. In particular, the increasing symbiosis between the government and large estates in the Late Roman period (at least in certain areas, such as Oxyrhynchus) meant that more people in transactions beyond taxation encounters measured grain in the same way. However, this was again less due to the Roman government's interest in widespread standardization than to increasing chains of dependency at the local level. Where the government did attempt to produce exact standard units, meanwhile—in coinage—the careful standardization of one unit (gold) coupled with the instability of other units (billon and bronze) caused estates to exploit unstable transactions rather than increasingly standardize them.

SESSION 4C
Prehistoric Aegean

CHAIR: *Susan Allen*, University of Cincinnati

Early Humans in the Aegean Basin: First Excavation Results from the Paleolithic Site of Stélida, Naxos

Tristan Carter, McMaster University, *Demetrios Athanssoulis*, Cycladic Ephorate of Antiquities, *Kathryn Campeau*, McMaster University, *Daniel Contreras*, University of Aix-Marseille, *Justin Holcomb*, Boston University, and Danica Mihailović, Belgrade University

The chert source and knapping floors of Stélida (northwest Naxos) were first discovered in 1981; this project and later rescue excavations suggested that the site was of early prehistoric date. In 2013, we initiated the Stélida Naxos Archaeological Project to geoarchaeologically characterize the site. After two years of intensive survey, our interpretative limit had been reached; our detailed claims for Lower to Upper Palaeolithic and Mesolithic activity needed to be grounded by absolute dates, not least because of the potential implications such purported early finds might have with regard to early hominin dispersal routes and their potential maritime migration. We thus began excavating in 2015, our first aim to locate undisturbed, stratified deposits we could scientifically date.

Sondages were established in areas with the best potential soil retention in what is an erosion-prone landscape. Upslope, adjacent to the chert outcrops, four unfinished 2 m^2 trenches have up to 1.5 m of cultural deposits. Two major artifact-rich lithostratigraphic units were revealed, both representing major colluvial events. The upper stratum can be tentatively dated to the early Upper Palaeolithic, with blades, cores, and retouched elements that correspond to the Eurasian Aurignacian cultural tradition that dates elsewhere to 42,500–34,000 BP. Significantly, many associate this culture with the first appearance of *Homo sapiens* in Europe. The second stratum generated a very different large, flake-based assemblage, whose diagnostics include a Quina scraper and proto-biface. The material has many Lower Paleolithic characteristics and may share elements with the Levantine Yabrudian tradition. In both instances, these data might thus provide us with an alternative—potentially seaborne—route for hominin migration from Africa via Anatolia, alongside that of the long-accepted Thracian land bridge.

Closer to the modern coast, some 1 m^2 trenches immediately revealed more Upper Paleolithic activity; in this flatter off-quarry area, we hope to find the base camps of those exploiting the source, the upslope sondages "only" producing masses of knapping debris and few modified tools. We also documented beachside stratified fossilized sand dune (aeolianite) deposits within which were embedded a few stone tools. Cultural material was photographed and mapped prior to extraction and a series of samples taken for optically stimulated luminescence (OSL) dating. OSL samples were also taken from the deepest upslope trench.

Stélida thus provides the first stratified and datable Pleistocene deposits in the Cyclades and suggests the Aegean Basin played a major role in early human migration.

Preliminary Report on the 2014 and 2015 Excavation Seasons in the Pelekita Cave, Zakros, Crete

Susan C. Ferrence, INSTAP Academic Press, *Athanasia Kanta*, Mediterranean Archaeological Society, *Lily Bonga*, INSTAP Study Center for East Crete, *Dimitra Mylona*, INSTAP Study Center for East Crete, *Tristan Carter*, McMaster University, and *Costis Davaras*, University of Athens

Pelekita Cave is located north of the Minoan palace at Kato Zakros on the eastern coast of Crete. It is one of the largest caves on the island at ca. 310 m long and an area of approximately 4,500 m². Deeper portions of the cave contain many impressive stalactites, stalagmites, columns, and a freshwater source at the local water table.

It was previously excavated during three seasons by Kostis Davaras and Athanasia Kanta (1979, 1982, 1985). Two recent excavation seasons (2014 and 2015) by Athanasia Kanta and Susan Ferrence tested the stratigraphy of the cave and collected sediments and other samples to investigate the economy, flora, fauna, and paleoclimate history of the area. In addition, a new visitors' access route was completed to isolate the excavated area from access.

Occupation of the cave began as early as the Middle Neolithic and culminated in the early Late Neolithic. A gap in occupation occurs during the Final Neolithic, but use of the cave continues from the Early to Late Minoan (LM) periods. It was a temporary shelter for humans and animals. A layer of volcanic tephra likely associated with the LM IA eruption is also present.

In the Neolithic, both informal and built hearths were superimposed on one another and found in situ with ground and chipped stone tools, seashells, bones, and pottery. A double hearth built of local stones was unearthed along with tools and several seashells of spiny oyster (*Spondylus gaederopus*). Obsidian artifacts and tephra samples are being chemically analyzed using pXRF techniques to determine provenance.

The meticulous mapping, collection, and processing of sediment samples yielded rich archaeobotanical remains, which will shed light on the human interaction with the landscape. Additionally, the excavation has produced one of the largest and best-preserved fish-bone and seashell assemblages in the Aegean, including many large fish such as grouper. The rest of the excellently preserved animal bones include the typical Neolithic domestic mammals—that is, sheep, goat, pig, and cattle, as well as birds and microfauna, such as rodents. They were contemporary with the human occupation of the cave. Many of the remains from the larger mammals come from young specimens, indicating that the cave probably sheltered animals and humans.

The results of the excavation will illuminate the poorly understood Neolithic period on Crete in terms of its formation, identity, and economy. Early study of the Neolithic pottery demonstrates the mobility of these agriculturalist-seafarers as the pottery exhibits both Knossian and Dodecanesian affinities. The wealth of organic and inorganic finds will shed light on the Neolithic economy of eastern Crete.

Mavropigi-Filotsairi: An Early Neolithic Settlement in Western Macedonia
Lily Bonga, INSTAP Study Center for East Crete

Mavropigi-Filotsairi is an Early Neolithic site in Western Macedonia, Greece. Rescue excavations were carried out in 2005 and 2006 by Georgia Karamitrou-Mentessidi (then Ephor) and the 30th Ephorate of Prehistoric, Classical and Byzantine Antiquities over a period of 10 months in 1995 and 1996. An area of 4,000 m² of the flat-extended settlement was excavated. Although later remains from the Late Neolithic, Roman, and Hellenistic periods were found on the site, the majority of the occupation and subsequently the focus of the excavation was on the Early Neolithic settlement, which dates to ca. 6590–6450 to 6200–6010 (2σ) B.C.E.

The remains of three earlier pit dwellings and seven later free-standing, post-framed, and waddle-and-daub houses sunk in foundation trenches were discerned. The houses range from 50 to 90 m². Seventeen burials of adults, teenagers, and infants were found throughout the site, in pits inside and around houses after the house had been abandoned. The large areas of horizontal exposure of the site, burials, architectural types, and small finds provide fresh information into settlement organization, technological knowledge, and cultural choices of the inhabitants.

Given the early radiocarbon dates and the geographic location of the settlement on a natural crossroads between the Balkans and southern Greece, Mavropigi-Filotsairi is positioned as a key site for understanding the process of "Neolithization" of Greece and into the Balkan Peninsula by early farming groups. This paper introduces the site of Mavropigi-Filotsairi and highlights the current, ongoing study of ceramic assemblage, conducted at the Archaeological Museum of Aiani (Aiani, Greece), which reveals some challenges to the established chronologies for both painted pottery and "Impresso" pottery in both Greece and the neighboring regions, which have ramifications regarding the direction and rate of Neolithic expansion in southeastern Europe.

New Perspectives on Neolithic Agricultural Villages in Eastern Thessaly (Greece) Through Remote-Sensing Applications
Apostolos Sarris, FORTH, *Tuna Kalayci*, FORTH, *François-Xavier Simon*, FORTH, *Jamieson Donati*, FORTH, *Ian Moffat*, FORTH, *Carmen Cuenca García*, FORTH, *Meropi Manataki*, FORTH, *Gianluca Cantoro*, FORTH, *Nikos Nikas*, FORTH, *Nassos Argyriou*, FORTH, *Sylviane Dederix*, FORTH, *Georgia Karampatsou*, FORTH, *Evita Kalogiropoulou*, FORTH, *Cristina Manzetti*, FORTH, *Konstantinos Vouzaxakis*, Archaeological Ephorate of Karditsa, Greek Ministry of Culture, *Vasso Rondiri*, Archaeological Ephorate of Magnesia, Greek Ministry of Culture, *Polyxeni Arachoviti*, Archaeological Ephorate of Magnesia, Greek Ministry of Culture, *Kaliopi Almatzi*, Archaeological Ephorate of Magnesia, Greek Ministry of Culture, *Despina Efstathiou*, Archaeological Ephorate of Magnesia, Greek Ministry of Culture, and *Evangelia Stamelou*, Archaeological Ephorate of Magnesia, Greek Ministry of Culture

The Neolithic period in Europe (7000–2000 B.C.E.) is widely considered a key epoch in the evolving relationship of human beings and their livable environment. Migrant hunters and gatherers gave way to permanent agrarian societies preoccupied with animal husbandry and the cultivation of food crops for sustenance. Carbon isotope dating and artifact analysis indicate that the earliest European farming communities appeared in the southern Balkan Peninsula and the Aegean Islands from populations originating in southwestern Asia. Recently, interdisciplinary studies have combined traditional forms of archaeological exploration with evolutionary biology, archaeozoology, phylogeography, and predictive models to provide novel insights into the patterns of Neolithic culture and the behavior of Neolithic peoples. The field now attracts the attention of a wide range of theoretical archaeologists, social scientists, statisticians, and scientists in the applied fields.

Within this new scientific framework of investigating Neolithic cultures, this paper presents the preliminary findings of a multiyear geophysical and remote-sensing campaign to study the physical landscape and living dynamics of Neolithic settlements within the coastal hinterlands of eastern Thessaly (Greece), where a rich sequence of Neolithic culture is known most famously at sites such as Sesklo and Dimini. Although hundreds of Neolithic settlements have been identified in Thessaly through nonintensive field survey and archaeological excavations, the broader characteristics of these early farming communities still remain vague, such as the extent and makeup of the built environment; the internal social hierarchy, production capabilities, the exploitation of the natural environment; and the intercommunal contact of Neolithic peoples on a localized and regional scale. Remote-sensing methodologies have been successfully used to document the diverse spatial composition of dozens of Neolithic sites in Thessaly. Some sites are core habitation mounds of modest proportions, while others are sprawling communities several hectares in size with more than 50 individual buildings. The variability in the size and internal organization of buildings at certain settlements raises important questions on the social hierarchy of these communities. Despite the great range in settlement size and internal composition, the habitation zones of the majority of sites are surrounded with concentric ditches and/or walls. Taken as a whole, this new evidence for early farming communities is an important contribution to the study of the Neolithic period in Europe.

SESSION 4D
The Northeast Peloponessos

CHAIR: *Joseph L. Rife*, Vanderbilt University

Sikyon Excavations: 2013 and 2014 Seasons
Yannis Lolos, University of Thessaly, *Scott Gallimore*, Wilfrid Laurier University, *Sarah James*, University of Colorado, Boulder, *Nicola Nenci*, University of Edinburgh, *Matthew Maher*, University of Winnipeg, *Susan-Marie Price*, University of British Columbia, and *Martin Wells*, Austin College

Since 2013, the Archaeological Society of Athens has resumed excavations at a large scale in ancient Sikyon after a hiatus of six decades. The current excavations followed upon an intensive urban survey carried out between 2004 and 2009.

Two areas were now targeted, to the southeast and the northwest of the agora of the city, with the trenches covering an overall surface area of almost 1,200 m². In this talk, we present the results of the first two seasons (2013 and 2014): further excavation of the Hellenistic stoa to the southeast of the agora, first explored by A. Orlandos in the early 1940s, has produced important evidence for the dating and construction technique of that stoa. A section of a second stoa, hitherto unknown, and a probable street were brought to light to the southeast of the Hellenistic stoa. In the area to the south of the Hellenistic stoa, we exposed abundant remains of residential and industrial nature, spanning a period of six centuries, from the first to the seventh century C.E. To the northwest of the agora, we have excavated a small temple built in the Late Classical or Early Hellenistic period and later surrounded by a Π-shaped complex of which we exposed its northeastern corner. The new excavations have tremendously increased our knowledge of the built landscape around the ancient agora and of the Sikyonian material culture, particularly of the Roman and Late Roman eras.

Trading and Transporting Timber in the Peloponnese: The Special Roles of Sikyon and Corinth
Morgan T. Condell, University of Pennsylvania

This paper discusses the existence of a robust timber trade based in the Peloponnese during the Classical period, in which Corinth emerged as a specialist in transport and Sikyon demonstrated the capacity to extract timbers of extraordinary size and quality from its hinterland.

Scholarship on the trade in timber during the Classical period has largely focused on imports of timber to Athens from Macedon and the suggestion of imports from southern Italy. Very little attention has been given to the capacity of Greece to supply timber from within, perhaps driven by the misperception that Greece was largely deforested in antiquity. However, a substantial body of epigraphic evidence points to the fact that a sophisticated timber industry existed in the Peloponnese during the late fifth and fourth centuries B.C.E., with timbers being sourced from within and then traded around the Saronic and Corinthian Gulfs.

The accounts of the *naopoioi* from the rebuilding of the Temple of Apollo at Delphi in the late fourth century B.C.E. record a large purchase of cypress wood, much of it thought to be for the construction of the temple roof beams. The likeliest source of cypress in Sikyonian territory is Mount Cyllene, which Ovid (*Fasti* 5.87) would later call "cypress-bearing." Crete is a better-attested source of cypress during this period, prominently featured in the building records at Epidauros; however, the choice of Sikyon enabled the *naopoioi* from Delphi to participate directly in the purchase, as they apparently traveled to Sikyon together with the architect to select the timbers in question.

Corinthians also feature prominently in temple building records from Epidauros, Eleusis, and Delphi as participants in the timber industry. The area immediately around Corinth was never forestland; however, Corinthians are frequently found fulfilling timber contracts and providing transport to the sanctuaries. The Corinthians therefore must be acquiring the timber from other territories, either by securing permission to extract it themselves or serving as resellers. I argue that the

Corinthians capitalize on their control over the ports of Kenchreai and Lechaion, turning the port sites into a marketplace for timber and positioning themselves as experts in heavy transport.

By understanding the role of these two cities in extracting and supplying timber to Greek sanctuaries, we can begin to reconstruct the broader geographical, political, and economic dynamics of the timber trade in the classical Greek world.

Athena at Corinth: Revisiting the Attribution of the Temple of Apollo
Angela Ziskowski, Coe College

The attribution of the temple at Corinth to Apollo has been disputed many times. Compelling cases have been presented for making the argument that Apollo was the god to whom the archaic temple in the center of Corinth was dedicated. However, archaeological evidence, patterns in Corinthian iconography, and trends in cultic significance build a case for attributing the temple to Athena, and not Apollo.

Pausanias' reference to passing the Temple of Apollo in the second century C.E. remains the strongest piece of evidence for connecting Corinth's central temple with the god. However, this association relies on locating the city's agora underneath the Roman Forum, an assertion that is debated. Once this cornerstone of evidence is challenged, few logical reasons remain to connect the archaic temple with the god Apollo.

This paper makes the case that Athena was worshiped at the central temple in Corinth. First, a lead fragment of a sacred calendar from Temple Hill specifically names Athena in its text. Another calendar fragment makes reference to "Φοινι[---]," which can be the month of Phoinikaios or the epithet of Athena Phoinike, which is attested at Corinth. Athena also appears very frequently in Corinthian iconography. The same cannot be said for Apollo in the Archaic period. Religiously, Corinth is dominated by female protectors in the Archaic period. Hera, Demeter, Kore, and Aphrodite all have major sites of worship in or near the city. Athena is surprisingly absent from this group, especially since she is likely the figure depicted on the city's coinage in reference to the bridling of Pegasos, which myth says occurred not far from the temple.

Athena can be tied to the area around the temple in other ways as well. Worship of Athena Hellotis was attested in the early work of Pindar. Hellotis and her sister supposedly were burned to death in a temple of Athena during the Dorian sack of Corinth. The festival of Hellotia, established in honor of the girls' deaths, may have had a connection to the Sacred Spring, which is just meters away from the temple. Such references tie the history of Athena very closely to the physical area around Temple Hill.

Investigation of a variety of types of archaeological and literary evidence warrants reconsideration of the designation of the temple of Corinth to Apollo. With respect to cultic trends at Corinth, Athena offers a logical alternative.

Outreach in Ancient Corinth: Educational Enrichment in the United States and Greece

Katherine Petrole, Corinth Excavations, American School of Classical Studies at Athens, and *Ioulia Tzonou-Herbst*, Corinth Excavations, American School of Classical Studies at Athens

Over the last 119 years, research at Corinth Excavations, conducted by the American School of Classical Studies at Athens (ASCSA), has produced a wealth of academic publications. Part of the mission of the ASCSA, however, in addition to producing research, is to disseminate the results to wider audiences. Since 2007, Corinth Excavations has facilitated educational programs in the museum and on the site of ancient Corinth for Greek schoolchildren and teachers on a variety of subjects; for example, a program held at the Asklepieion included a dramatic interpretation of Epidaurian healing inscriptions. The purpose of the outreach is twofold: to create communication between archaeologists and historians who produce new and exciting results with the general public, and to increase awareness of the questions and interests that inspire outside audiences to continue to learn about the legacy of ancient Greek, Roman, and medieval culture.

Since the fall of 2014, thanks to the generous support of the Steinmetz Family Foundation Fellowship, Corinth Excavations has had a dedicated staff member for educational outreach; our Museum Fellow is designing enriching lesson plans for Greek and American curricula. Largely following Grade 6 Common Core Learning Standards, when American students learn about the entire Eastern Hemisphere, the lesson plans are adaptable for use in other grades as well as non–Common Core curricula. We present selected examples of our lesson plans based on materials from the Corinth Excavations, representing periods from antiquity to the present. Themes covered include water management, healing practices, mysterious rituals, literary vs. archaeological evidence from the Classical period, cultural achievements of the Roman empire, pottery designs and styles of the Byzantine empire, the development of Christianity, and interpreting Frankish skeletal material.

Feedback and collaboration with teachers in the United States is ongoing in order to shape the lessons to best fit the needs of diverse audiences. The lesson plans and supporting digital materials will be freely available online with an invitation to extend learning via a Skype interview with Corinth Excavations staff, allowing for valuable post-lesson discussions and opportunities to ask classroom-generated questions.

To highlight more than a century of research, the uniting theme of our outreach efforts is that Corinth was and continues to be a crossroads of cultural, religious, and economic activities for thousands of years. Outreach in ancient Corinth aims to communicate these interactions among peoples through time and share the legacy of ancient Greek, Roman, and medieval culture with future generations.

The Antonine Julian Basilica in Corinth

Paul D. Scotton, California State University, Long Beach

Over the course of several meetings of this forum, I have presented various aspects of the Julian Basilica, including its form and function. All of those, however, have focused on the original or Augustan phase of the building. In the mid second century C.E. the building underwent significant remodeling, at least on the interior. Those modifications were primarily decorative, and what once was a structure largely of stuccoed and painted poros became one of marbles and fine stone.

The major structural modification was in the south aisle of the cryptoporticus where a vault was added. This was not a cistern but rather a replacement of the joist and beam system that had supported the main floor. That system had been jacked in several places following the earthquake of 78 C.E., but by the time of Antoninus Pius that solution was abandoned and the vault installed. This was done to better accommodate the increased load caused by multiple statues, altars, and aediculae associated with the imperial cult. The tetrastyle Doric tribunal of poros and stucco was replaced by a marble hexastyle Corinthian one. The statue of Divus Iulius remained on the tribunal, and the statue of Augustus was kept nearby.

The stuccoed and painted walls were revetted in various marbles and stones from the floor up to the archivolts of the clerestory. The original superimposed Doric and Ionic half columns along the interior of the exterior walls were cut back and faced with superimposed Corinthian and Pergamene pilasters of marble. Before them stood freestanding, superimposed columns of the same orders, tied to the walls by projecting epistyles. The result was a series of *ressauts* along all four walls, which provided a more elaborate framing for whatever other statues, altars, and shrines were displayed in the building.

At least some of the Julio-Claudian statues were removed but not discarded. This was certainly the case with the statue of Gaius, adopted son of Augustus. His statue was found lying on its back on the floor of the cryptoporticus, buried under approximately 1.5 m of earthen fill below the debris from the collapse of the basilica. The statue of his brother Lucius was found nearby but at a higher elevation built into a medieval wall. It is likely that statue had had similar treatment to that of Gaius but that it had been discovered by later robbers and reused as building material.

SESSION 4E
Archaeometric Approaches to the Mediterranean Bronze Age

CHAIR: To be announced

Chemical Characterization of Early Bronze Age/Middle Bronze Age Pottery from Ognina (Sicily): A Comparison of XRF and pXRF for Analysis of Ancient Pottery

Davide Tanasi, Arcadia University, *S. Hassam*, University of Wisconsin–Milwaukee, *F. Pirone*, University of South Florida, *A. Raudino*, LaTrobe University, *P. Trapani*, Independent Researcher, *Robert H. Tykot*, University of South Florida, and *A. Vianello*, Independent Researcher

The archaeological exploration of the Ognina islet, near Syracuse, Sicily, carried out in 1964 provided the evidence of a long-term prehistoric occupation between the Neolithic and the Middle Bronze Age. Maltese-style ceramics were found in the Early and Middle Bronze Age layers. The small group of imports, belonging to the Thermi Ware, was found in connection with the local Castelluccian Ware (Early Bronze Age), while the Borġ in-Nadur Ware, also Maltese in style, was related with local Thapsos ceramics (Middle Bronze Age). The interpretation of the Maltese-type artifacts as imports resulted in the Ognina islet being considered a Maltese "colony" in Sicily, a controversial hypothesis never dismissed.

In 2012, Arcadia University carried out a new exploration of the area. During the fieldwork, a large number of ceramics were recovered, among which were some new examples of Thermi and Borġ in-Nadur wares, as well as large amounts of Castelluccian and Thapsos pottery. To ascertain whether the Maltese-type pottery was imported from that small island, a program of archaeometric analyses was established. Out of a group of 114 sherds collected, 43 diagnostic samples were selected for scientific analyses. Due to the small size of many sherds and the concerns related to the application of destructive analyses, just 11 samples, among them two supposedly Thermi Ware and four Borġ in-Nadur samples, were subjected to destructive thin sectioning and X-ray fluorescence spectrometry (XRF). The same samples were analyzed then with nondestructive portable XRF, in order to compare the results between laboratory-based and portable instruments.

The study continued with 32 additional samples of local pottery, which were analyzed with the pXRF together with a sample of Sicilian clay taken from the source most likely used in prehistoric times by the inhabitants of the islet. The analyses demonstrated that the two Thermi Ware samples were locally produced, while three out of four Borġ in-Nadur pieces were produced in Malta and one was produced in Sicily. These results strongly suggest some mobility of artisans from Malta to Sicily, an interpretation that could reinforce the hypothesis of Ognina having been an emporium with different cultural groups present, if not a "colony."

This study assessed an old interpretation adding targeted new data, which revealed the presence of both Maltese pottery imports and local imitations. Its methodology demonstrates also that pXRF analyses, despite some technical limitations, are effective in investigating certain research questions.

Rub-a-dub-dub: Organic Temper and Shared Practice in the Production of Bathtubs in the Late Helladic IIIB–IIIC Saronic Gulf

William D. Gilstrap, Missouri University Research Reactor, and *Peter M. Day*, University of Sheffield

A multitechnique study of pottery around the Saronic Gulf at the end of the Mycenaean period has identified a number of major production centers with wide product distribution and has reconstructed their technological practices. Although these centers feature different choices made in raw material procurement and manipulation, as well as in surface treatment and firing, there are intriguing examples of shared technological practice across otherwise seemingly different production traditions.

We focus here on the shared use of organic temper in the characteristic bathtubs, as well as in some large storage jars. This distinctive choice is observed at a number of production centers, the location of those in Attica, Corinth, and Aegina being known. Organic temper is not used in the production of other vessels of the period, and its use spans quite different potting traditions, showing the horizontal transmission of technological practice in the manufacture of specific type.

The use of organic temper affects several aspects of production: forming, green strength, and effective drying, in addition to creating a very different ceramic body in terms of its weight and porosity. The social and technological implications of the adoption of this practice across a number of centers are discussed.

Provenance Determination of Mycenaean Pottery from Alalakh

Sıla Votruba, Koç University

This paper elucidates the maritime connections of Alalakh, particularly with the Aegean region and Cyprus, through the archaeometric analysis of Mycenaean pottery found at the site. Excavations yielded Mycenaean pottery from the Late Helladic (LH) IIIA2 and LH IIIC periods. In addition, the recent discovery of an enigmatic sherd of the LH IIIB period has the potential to provide crucial information regarding the site's networks within the 13th century B.C.E. A selected group of Mycenaean pottery from all mentioned periods was analyzed through petrography and ICP-MS to determine their provenance. The results are discussed in the context of the wider Mediterranean and the site's networks, tracking their continuity or diachronic change throughout the Late Bronze Age. Intercity dynamics of Alalakh are also illuminated, such as the relation of the Mycenaean pottery with other pottery groups—namely, Cypriot, Nuzi, and the local groups found at the site.

Metals and Metallurgy at Bronze Age Ayia Irini, Kea

Myrto Georgakopoulou, University College London Qatar, and *Natalie Abell*, University of Michigan

Metallurgy is frequently attributed a central role in explaining the prominence of the settlement of Ayia Irini during the Aegean Bronze Age. This idea emerged because of the wealth of metal and metallurgical remains recovered during extensive excavations in the late 1960s and 1970s, as well as the proximity of this coastal Keian site to the rich polymetallic ore deposit of Lavrion. The earliest known copper production evidence in the southern Aegean has been identified in the neighboring Final Neolithic site of Kephala; deposits of the same phase are known also at Ayia Irini. In the Early Bronze Age, metal production and circulation flourish in the southern Aegean, with Attica and the western Cyclades in particular considered primary sources for copper, lead, and silver. The role of Kea, and Ayia Irini in particular, located in the center of this metal-bearing zone, remains to be clarified. Following a hiatus of occupation, Ayia Irini emerges in the Middle Bronze Age as one of a few prominent settlements outside Crete, with intense and characteristic "Minoanizing" features. Its position, as a gateway to Lavrion, is considered a primary driving force for this development. Despite the likely economic and social importance of metallurgy for the community at Ayia Irini, publication of metal and metallurgical finds to date has been limited. Sporadic finds have been mentioned in publications of particular periods or parts of the site, while a few artifacts have been featured in reports of scientific analyses, primarily focused on Aegean metal circulation.

A new project by the authors constitutes the first systematic analysis of the entire collection of metals and metallurgical remains at the site. The methodology used so far involves archival research, macroscopic examination of all finds including fabric categorization of metallurgical ceramics, and noninvasive portable XRF analysis of metallic artifacts. Our research has so far identified more than 1,000 objects, spanning all Bronze Age periods of occupation, as well as subsequent historical periods.

Using this data set and previously collected analytical data, our paper summarizes the emerging picture with regard to spatial and chronological distribution of Bronze Age metal and metallurgical finds at Ayia Irini. In doing so, it discusses changing patterns of metal procurement, working, and consumption across the site and considers typological and technological changes over time.

Alloying with a Purpose: Comparing Object Typologies and Chemical Compositions at Neopalatial Mochlos

Jesse Obert, University of California, Berkeley

This paper presents new conclusions about Minoan bronzeworking in the Neopalatial period. Using a Bruker TRACeR-IV portable energy dispersive x-ray fluorescence unit, the author scanned more than 150 bronze objects from Neopalatial Mochlos. The goal of this project was to discover whether an object's typology and purpose correlated to its chemical composition, thereby implying that Minoan metalsmiths understood the intrinsic differences between arsenic bronze and tin bronze and chose one alloy over the other when forging a specific object.

Arsenic and tin behave similarly in low quantities, but tin produces a harder alloy. Tin bronzes are more brittle and cannot be hot worked, and tin may have been an expensive commodity in the Neopalatial period. Although arsenic bronzes were more reliable and cheaper, arsenic produces a toxic gas when smelted. Aesthetically, the alloys look very different, as tin-bronze objects have a golden hue while arsenic-bronze objects are silvery gray.

Each object was cleaned and scanned multiple times. While this sort of surface analysis cannot produce accurate chemical compositions, it can confirm the presence or absence of specific chemicals. Based on a series of parameters, each object was categorized as an arsenic bronze, tin bronze, or unalloyed copper object. These data were then studied alongside the official object descriptions and typologies that will be published in forthcoming Mochlos volumes.

Ultimately, there is no direct correlation between an object's function and its chemical composition. However, the data revealed two important trends. First, it is clear that Neopalatial Minoan metalsmiths understood inherent alloy attributes, as Soles and Giumlia-Mair suggested in their publication on the Mochlos sistrum. Within the Mochlos bronzes, tin bronzes were more likely to be cast in a mold than worked and annealed. This statistical trend suggests the Minoans understood the versatility of arsenic bronze and the limitations to tin bronze. Second, jewelry had the highest percentage of arsenic bronzes in the Mochlos collection. This conflicts with our first conclusion: because jewelry was predominately cast from a mold, we would expect tin-bronze alloys to dominate. However, bronze was often used to imitate precious metal in antiquity. While tin bronze was probably a substitute for gold, the scarcity of tin on Neopalatial Crete may have made it an uneconomical imitation. However, arsenic bronze, with its silvery exterior, would have been an economical substitute for silver jewelry. Therefore, these data suggest that Minoan metalsmiths understood the inherent production benefits of arsenic bronze over tin bronze, but only actively employed arsenic bronze for its cosmetic attributes.

Slags and Ores: Archaeometallurgy and the Geometric Settlement of Zagora, Andros, Greece

Ivana G. Vetta, University of Sydney

On a windy promontory on the southwest coast of the Cycladic island of Andros lies the Geometric-period settlement of Zagora. The lack of later development on the site has preserved the early remains, with settlement occupation at Zagora now known to span the sub-Protogeometric period (ca. 900–850 B.C.E.) through to the Early Archaic period (ca. 700 B.C.E). The most extensive and intensive occupation period of the site was the eighth century B.C.E., with the site being almost completely abandoned in the following decades.

Seven seasons of excavation conducted by the University of Sydney, in the 1960s and 1970s and more recently from 2012 to 2014, have found tantalizing evidence for a robust metalworking industry, yielding an abundance of metallurgical slags, a waste product of metal production, with to date no centralized location for metalworking activity being identified. The wealth of metallurgical material may indicate a rich and diverse metalworking industry within the settlement, but can we really reconstruct an industry from only its waste?

The original excavations at the site found various stratigraphic deposits containing metallurgical slag such as floor deposits within structures as well as packing fills within the fortification wall. The distribution of this material was further clarified during intensive survey of the site carried out in 2012, which found some 223 slags, consistently spread across the settlement, and included smithing hearth bottoms and evidence of hearth lining.

Slags are present as a waste product from various stages of metal production, and relics of this process are trapped within the physical matrix of these artifacts. Through both macroscopic and microscopic analysis of this metallurgical waste, we can begin to outline the techniques that were available to the ancient smiths of Zagora, the ore sources that they used, and what other materials were employed in the process of metal production. This analysis will be viewed in light of the *chaîne opératoire* and how Zagora in turn fits into the wider landscape of Iron Age metallurgy.

SESSION 4F
Western Mediterranean and Adriatic Prehistory

CHAIR: *Michael L. Galaty*, Mississippi State University

The Projekti Arkeologjikë i Shkodrës (PASH), Northern Albania: Results of the 2014 Excavation Campaign

Michael L. Galaty, Mississippi State University, *Lorenc Bejko*, University of Tirana, *Sylvia Deskaj*, Michigan State University, *Richard Yerkes*, Ohio State University, *Susan Allen*, University of Cincinnati, and *Rachelanne Bolus*, University of Cincinnati

The Projekti Arkeologjikë i Shkodrës (PASH), the Shkodër Archaeological Project, is an international, collaborative, regional research project focused on the Shkodër province of northern Albania, a strategically important region located in the western Balkans along the Adriatic coast. To understand better the transition to social complexity in Albania, and in Europe generally, we conducted five years (2010–2014) of interdisciplinary archaeological field research, followed by a study season (2015). Our study region encompasses the Shkodra Plain and surrounding hills and is situated along the eastern shore of Shkodra Lake, the largest freshwater lake in the Balkans. This paper reports preliminary project results, with a focus on excavations conducted in 2014 at three prehistoric settlements—Kodër Boks, Zagorës, and the large hill fort at Gajtan—and two burial mounds, in Shtoj and Shkrel. We describe the results of archaeobotanical and archaeofaunal analyses as well as programs of radiocarbon dating and human bone strontium analysis. Radiocarbon dates from Gajtan indicate an initial occupation in the Eneolithic ca. 3765–3645 B.C.E. calibrated. This is the first absolute date for the Copper Age from north Albania, and it points to an unexpectedly early founding of what would become in the Bronze Age—one of Albania's largest hill forts. Kodër Boks and Zagorës also experienced growth during the Bronze Age and both are associated with large fields of tumuli, at Shtoj and Shkrel, respectively. Excavation of a large tumulus at Shkrel produced remains of at least three individuals, one of whom was a juvenile. Radiocarbon dating of two adult molars produced dates of 1740–1610 B.C.E. and 1885–1690 B.C.E. calibrated. Strontium analysis of the latter molar indicated a nonlocal origin. Finally, the mound excavated at Shtoj generated a remarkably rich array of artifacts dating from the Eneolithic through the Late Roman period, including pottery, coins, and beads. It may have served as some kind of long-term ritual installation. Archaeozoological analysis of faunal remains from the mounds, one used for burial and the other used for ritual, produced different profiles, with the Shtoj mound much more focused on equid and cattle remains. Archaeobotanical remains indicate a prehistoric diet rich in domesticated and wild plant foods, including wheat, millet, lentils, and vetch. In summary, PASH's preliminary results point to a dynamic prehistoric landscape in Shkodra, one with Eneolithic roots, a Bronze Age expansion, and complex patterns of economy, exchange (including migration), and ritual.

An Iberian House at Cástulo: Results of the First Season of American-Spanish Collaborative Excavations
Justin St. P. Walsh, Chapman University, *Diego López Martínez,* Cástulo Siglo XXI, *Ildefonso Martínez Sierra,* Cástulo Siglo XXI, *Enrique Peregrin Pitto,* University of Granada, *Francisco Arias de Haro,* Conjunto Arqueológico de Cástulo, and *Alfonso Luis Montejo Ráez,* Cástulo Siglo XXI

As reported at last year's AIA meetings, a Spanish group (FORVM MMX/Cástulo Siglo XXI, operating under the supervision of the Conjunto Arqueológico de Cástulo) has been excavating the Ibero-Roman town of Cástulo since 2011, with the goal of recovering archaeological information about various aspects of urban life in a city suggested by ancient authors to have been the most important indigenous settlement on the Iberian Peninsula prior to the coming of the Romans. The city controlled a major riverine trade route from interior Andaluca to the Atlantic, as well as silver and lead mines. Cástulo Siglo XXI's work itself follows on several decades of earlier investigation by the Complutense University of Madrid in the area immediately outside the city walls.

The 2015 season marked the first season of collaboration between Chapman University and the Conjunto Arqueológico de Cástulo. The specific target of our new partnership has been the excavation of one or more Iberian houses. Up until now, this period (ca. 700–200 B.C.E.) has been known at Cástulo only from numerous extramural tombs, whose assemblages often included Greek ceramics, including the Athenian stemless cup shape named for this site. Our interest lies in understanding the characteristics of assemblages from domestic contexts at Cástulo, and especially the relationship between imports and locally produced goods—if any— within Iberian homes. Cástulo's reputed commercial significance in the ancient sources, combined with what is already known about its actual consumption of imports from the tombs, makes it a good location for this kind of study.

This paper presents the results of eight weeks of joint excavation by the American and Spanish groups. Our work yielded a significant portion—more than 45 m²—of an Iberian house dating to the Late Iberian period (fourth or third century B.C.E.), remains of a neighboring house dating to the same period, and strong evidence for housing in the same areas during preceding phases, including the Middle Iberian period (ca. fifth century B.C.E.) and the Final Bronze Age (ca. eighth to seventh centuries B.C.E.). Comparison is made to houses of similar date from other Iberian sites, such as Puentetablas. The paper concludes with some discussion of data-recording techniques employed at Cástulo.

Potters' Choices and Vessels Performance on the Island Gran Canaria (Canary Islands, Spain) During Aboriginal Times: First Results

Miguel del Pino Curbelo, University of Sheffield, *Noémi S. Müller*, British School at Athens, *Jaume Buxeda i Garrigós*, University of Barcelona, *Amelia Rodríguez Rodríguez*, University of Las Palmas de Gran Canaria, *Peter M. Day*, University of Sheffield, *José Mangas Viñuela*, University of Las Palmas de Gran Canaria, and *Vassilis Kilikoglou*, National Center for Scientific Research "Demokritos"

The indigenous culture of Gran Canaria flourished from the third century C.E. until the conquest of the island by the Castilians (15 to 16th centuries C.E.). During this period, the aboriginal population of the island remained isolated from the rest of the world, an isolation that is reflected in the uniqueness of its material culture and especially its pottery, which is clearly different from contemporary ceramics produced on the other islands of the archipelago.

Morphological and technological differences that are attested within the aboriginal pottery of Gran Canaria (reflected in variation in surface treatment and decoration patterns) seem to be influenced by vessel function. The continuity in morphology and surface-treatment differences between cooking ware, decorated pots, and big storage jars over centuries points to the existence of knowledge transmission mechanisms among aboriginal potters that conditioned their production strategies for generations. This paper explores the relation of those main functional groups with potters' technological choices during the manufacture of the vessels, examining paste recipes and resultant mechanical properties. Based on a detailed macroscopic study, 60 samples from two aboriginal archaeological sites (La Cerera, sixth-seventh century C.E.—13th century C.E. and Cueva Pintada, 13th century C.E.—16th century C.E.) were analyzed through optical petrography. Moreover, a subset of samples from Cueva Pintada were further tested for mechanical strength.

Probably because of its use as a domestic area, the assemblage from La Cerera was composed mainly of cooking ware and decorated pots. Four clearly different petrographic groups were identified at this site. Coarser fabrics were used only for cooking ware, while finer-grained pastes were employed preferentially for decorated pots. Petrographic analysis confirmed macroscopic observations that technological choices and in particular patterns in paste selection remained largely unchanged during the six centuries the site was inhabited.

A different picture arises at the later site of Cueva Pintada: here, most of the individuals recovered were decorated pots along with some big storage jars. Unlike in La Cerera, petrographic results showed a high heterogeneity, with fabrics represented mostly by only one or two individuals. No clear pattern of paste selection could be attested for the different vessel types; however, mechanical tests revealed that production strategies employed by potters at Cueva Pintada led to clear differences in affordances for the two different vessel types.

We discuss the implications of these findings on our understanding of the sites studied and on pottery production in precontact Gran Canaria more generally.

The Passersby of the Western Mediterranean: Considering the Informal Migration of Traders, Merchants, and Laborers

Sam J. Lash, Joukowsky Institute of Archaeology and the Ancient World, Brown University

There have been several attempts to situate trade, craftsmanship, labor, and industry within discussions of migration, often under the controversial label "diaspora." Within this framework, "diaspora" is extended beyond the often violent and forced dispersal from a homeland to include expansion associated with pursuits of labor, trade, and colonial ambitions. This fails to account for individuals who are not "permanently dispersed." While permanent or continuous movements of substantial groups of people fall within this framework, consistent movement of multiple individuals embedded within their home communities does not. By subsuming these types of movements under the umbrella of migration, we are obscuring the relationship between them. Thus, this paper focuses on the question of how to examine, archaeologically, "small-scale" or informal migration.

This paper introduces the concept of "aggregate fluctuations" in order to account for the collective impact of individuals' movement within consistent trade, labor, and production networks. The intention is not to quantify but to consider the nature of this movement in its own right and subsequently its relationship with migration through the examination of the development of trading posts, extraction and production site, and "weigh-station" communities in the western Mediterranean, with a particular focus on Sardinia, Iberia, and southern France in the Iron Ages. Therein we see the pervasiveness of consistent movement associated with trade, industry, and labor by a subset of individuals. Whether these individuals stayed a single night or an off season or became resident traders, their collective presence would have been substantial. These individuals correspond to permanent structures, institutions, and communities (such as family, land ownership, civic responsibilities, and citizenship); their mobility is inherently tied to the success and productivity of these more permanent components. These mobile individuals are temporally participating as members of their own communities in the practices of a number of given "nodes." It is their presence and interactions in aggregate that contributes to a constant negotiation of local and "global" knowledge and the connectivity that is subsequently enhanced by larger migratory movements.

These interactions, repeated with an incredibly high frequency by individuals within the framework of resource exploitation, industry, and trade, in aggregate form material connections and networks in much the same way as migration or colonization and may foreground these community-wide scale movements. This concept of "aggregate fluctuations" picks up on numerous threads and overarching questions prompted in recent debates on material connections, mobility, materiality, and identity.

Resisting Change: Distributive Networks and Social Inequality in the Central Mediterranean, Fourth to Second Millennia B.C.E.

Clive Vella, Joukowsky Institute for Archaeology and the Ancient World, Brown University

By the fourth millennium B.C.E., well after the establishment of Neolithic life-styles, central Mediterranean communities began to undertake localized cultural developments while maintaining a varying level of interconnectivity. In this setting of broad social transformations, cultural developments were meant to resist and counter the potential for change, which can overturn the benefits reaped by those leading their communities. This paper addresses social inequality in prehierarchical societies by outlining strategies of exploitation and unequal access to broadly distributed objects.

Academic approaches to distribution networks in the prehistoric Mediterranean oscillate between claims of high interconnectivity to the physical isolation of some places, like islands. By concentrating on shifting object quantities, such approaches run the risk of limiting insights into social inequality across physical regions and in different communities. In this paper, social inequality is seen as a social stratagem meant to curb the effects of potential change. Through often subtle processes, distribution networks reveal inequality in the ability/inability of groups to participate in such interactions as well as the uneven distribution within groups themselves. These inequalities reflect a fluctuating collective spirit, which experienced a particular diminishment in the second millennium B.C.E.

After the Neolithic period, central Mediterranean communities scattered across the continental Italian mainland, three large islands, and small archipelagos remained interested in broad connectivity. However, that connectivity offered an avenue for the increase in social inequality. Certain communities across this region had an influential effect on the flow of objects, often only a temporary position. On the edges of distribution networks, other communities relied on other desired objects while facing an unpredictable availability. In this setting of disparate connections to broad distribution networks, prehistoric groups attempted to create stable lives in a world prone to continuous change.

2013–2015 Survey of Neolithic Agricultural Sites in the Tavoliere (Italy): A Report on Ceramic and Lithic Finds as well as Aerial- and Ground-Based Remote Sensing

Robert H. Tykot, University of South Florida, *Craig Alexander*, University of Cambridge, *Keri A. Brown*, University of Manchester, *Kyle P. Freund*, Indian River State College, and *Italo M. Muntoni*, Soprintendenza per i Beni Culturali della Puglia

Over the past three years, our team has surveyed 25+ sites in the Tavoliere (northern Puglia) to investigate perhaps the earliest agriculturalists in Italy. The Tavoliere was an area of dense settlement in the early Italian Neolithic (ca. 6200–5000 B.C.E.). A sample of sites was selected from the more than 700 ditched enclosures identified from World War II (and later) aerial photography, representing different sizes and areas. The pottery includes nondiagnostic coarse wares, Impressed Wares, painted coarse and medium wares (e.g., La Quercia), and Passo di Corvo fine wares, while the lithics include flint as well as obsidian. All finds were georeferenced and incorporated into GIS. Clay samples were also taken from many rivers in the region and analyzed both raw and after firing. In 2015, a remote-controlled aerial vehicle as well as ground-level magnetometry/electrical resistance tomography were used at two sites to further assess the preservation of ditches and other structures for future excavation.

About 1,270 ceramic artifacts were collected from the sites surveyed and, along with more than 70 clay samples and additional ceramics in the collections of the Soprintendenza per i Beni Culturali della Puglia, were analyzed using a Bruker portable X-ray fluorescence spectrometer, specifically for trace elements. On five example sherds, 25 readings were taken on the same spot to determine the precision of the instrument. Two or three spots were tested on all sherds to address any potential heterogeneity, and the results were calibrated against international standards. This nondestructive method allowed us to put the ceramics and clay samples into different groups using multivariate statistics. More than 100 obsidian artifacts were also tested, with most matching Lipari and some Palmarola.

All data consisting of pXRF readings, pottery descriptions, GPS locations, and photographs were entered into an Excel spreadsheet, constituting the largest body of data for Neolithic ceramics in southeast Italy. The data obtained provide profiles of ceramics and clay sources that can be used to identify linkages between raw material sources and production areas and to investigate the distribution of finished ceramics across villages in order to address social archaeological issues such as craft specialization and mobility. One hypothesis tested is that a polycentric mode of production was used in the Neolithic, in which each site produced its own ceramics from local clay sources. Along with lithic and other data, this project expands our understanding of socioeconomic development in the Tavoliere during the early agricultural Neolithic.

SESSION 4G: Colloquium
Out and Around Houses in Eastern Mediterranean Cities

ORGANIZER: *Fotini Kondyli*, University of Virginia

Colloquium Overview Statement

Household archaeology has come to be recognized as a fruitful avenue for exploring different dimensions of the past, such as identity formation, gender and social diversity, economic and social networks, and community building. Household archaeology focuses mainly on domestic architecture, spatial organization, and social and economic activities within houses. Less attention, however, is paid to the archaeology of spaces immediately outside and around houses. Are these spaces part of the household? If households are understood as "shifting sets of relationships," how can we describe the spaces that surround them? Who is responsible for the use, maintenance, and design of such spaces?

These are spaces in between, bridging and dividing the private and public spheres, the house and the settlement, the family and the community. They are spaces of social construction and experience of daily life where shared experiences, daily deeds, and rituals take place. These may also be places of contestation among different agents who claim these spaces for their own economic and ideological purposes. A wide range of archaeological evidence, such as alleys, drains, wells, benches, burials, and damping deposits speak to the variety of activities that occurred outside of houses. Ethnographic evidence further highlights these spaces as pivotal for the formation and negotiation of social and economic networks. Yet because they are spaces between house and settlement with limited or no architecture, they are often excluded from the study of houses and do not find their way to publications on household and settlement archaeology.

This session aims to explore the nature, role, and archaeological signature of spaces around and outside houses. Papers in the session present culturally and chronologically diverse case studies and explore different methodologies and theoretical frameworks for understanding the economic and sociopolitical functions of such spaces. A prime goal of the session is to identify the range of activities taking place in such spaces and discuss the relationship between architectural form and human behavior. Emphasis is also placed on the relationship between these spaces and houses—specifically, how are these spaces affected by household cycles, family history, and the architectural biography of the houses around them? Ultimately, this session will contribute to a better understanding of ancient societies and their settlements on a macroscale through the study of microhousehold histories.

Probing the Development of Exterior Domestic Spaces: Patterns and Strategies
Lisa Nevett, University of Michigan

From at least the eighth century B.C.E., the exterior space between the residential buildings in Greek settlements represented an important activity area that supplemented the roofed space provided by the structures themselves. These "courtyards" were either open to passersby and the occupants of neighboring buildings (as at Emborio, on Chios), or demarcated by boundary walls or periboloi that defined a specific area as connected with a particular dwelling (as at Skala Oropos or Eretria). By the sixth and fifth centuries B.C.E., the conceptualization of exterior space was undergoing a radical shift: in the larger properties, a substantial open area became enclosed between the walls of the house itself—an internal courtyard. At the same time, a move toward the coordinated construction of rectilinear buildings sharing party walls decreased the amount of space around individual dwellings, which became limited to the area immediately in front of, and on occasion, to one side of, the building.

These changes in architectural design can be identified in settlements across the Greek world (albeit they happen at different times in different places), but a major question that has not been addressed is to what degree the change in location of exterior space may have been accompanied by alterations in the roles it played. One of the most interesting and important aspects of exterior space is its flexibility—its capacity to host a wide range of different activities. But while this flexibility is attractive to users (at least in clement weather conditions), it poses particular problems for any archaeological analysis aimed at understanding the roles of such spaces. Historically, classical archaeologists have been much better at evaluating architecture than analyzing other forms of data to understand patterns of activity. Yet the relative paucity of fixed features in courtyard and street spaces means that architecture alone cannot give much insight into their use. In this paper, I argue that when viewed in chronological perspective, changes in the exterior space around individual houses need to be understood in tandem with the appearance of the internal courtyard. I review what current evidence suggests about the roles of each type of exterior space. I then explore the potential of additional methods aimed at providing a more in-depth understanding of the use of the exterior spaces of Greek houses, including piece-plotting of artifactual remains, soil micromorphology, geochemistry, and analysis of environmental remains.

Pigs in Space: Zooarchaeology and Spatial Patterns in Ancient Households
Michael MacKinnon, University of Winnipeg

Analyses of zooarchaeological remains at ancient Greek and Roman sites have a relatively long tradition of providing data about changing dietary and economic patterns throughout antiquity, but it is important to note that they also yield information about cultural behaviors surrounding where and how such deposits are formed. Indeed, the spatial distribution of faunal remains acts as an integral component of our reconstructions of activities among households across Graeco-Roman times. This paper surveys the range of such spatial data from various households to determine how faunal waste was disposed of or otherwise used within such settings, with particular attention placed on deposits collected from areas immediately outside and around houses. Rural and urban settings are compared, with focus principally on Roman contexts. Among urban households, with examples here drawn primarily from excavation work at larger centers including Pompeii, Athens, Carthage and Ostia, variations often register across households, underscoring individuality at each. Stalling or raising animals (including equids, dogs, and domestic fowl, among other taxa) occurs at some houses, but not all. Depositional patterns indicate some households were relatively clean (removing most waste), while others disposed of rubbish by other means (internally in garden pits, in latrines, and along edges of walls, and externally in streets, gutters, and outside wells). Rural households provide a second level of investigation, with a distinction here noted between larger-scale, rural villa settlements and smaller, arguably less-elite, rural complexes. Investigation of zooarchaeological data from "peripheral" spaces at larger villa sites sometimes reveals specialization and compartmentalization in activity, as witnessed in relatively large volumes of faunal waste and often a greater degree of bias in the representation of skeletal parts and species frequencies than compared with similar deposits from smaller-scale rural settlements. Such patterns presumably reflect differential organization of household activities in rural areas that are arguably linked with greater population densities and wealth, and an enhanced range of complexity in processing and using animals among larger settlements.

Antioch, Daphne, and the Transformation of Domestic Space
Andrea De Giorgi, Florida State University

With their harvest of mosaics, the 1930s Princeton excavations catalyzed attention on the houses discovered in Antioch, Daphne, and Seleucia Pieria. Although hastily explored and crippled by centuries-long spoliation, these buildings are the silent testimonies of the relentless modifications of the city's built environment. More to the point, they effectively reflect the local social fabric and its transformative character during the Middle to Late Roman empire. A cluster of buildings in Daphne, in particular, needs to be brought into sharper focus, as it attests to the radical overhaul of an entire sector of this community. This process demarcated first a clear-cut departure from previous architectural traditions and second the redesigning of curb, street, drainage systems, and ultimately the space between units in order to accommodate the expansion of households. How these transformations appear in the archaeological record and how they may inform the evolution of Antioch's social landscape—with the concomitant rise of a new rampant aristocracy—is the subject of this paper.

Connective Spaces at Roman Kourion
Thomas W. Davis, Southwestern Baptist Theological Seminary

The Kourion Urban Space Project (KUSP) is focused on understanding the domestic urban fabric of a major Roman-period site on Cyprus. Ongoing excavations have revealed intriguing uses for the interconnections in the urban neighborhood we are sampling. The placement of cisterns into exterior alleyways, refuse deposits outside the doorways, and deliberate filling to create access ways indicates a dynamic and understanding of connective spaces in the city. This paper documents the variety of uses and suggests some reasons for the patterning observed at Kourion.

Life in the Streets: Placemaking and Collectiveness in Byzantine Athens
Fotini Kondyli, University of Virginia

Between the monumentality and visibility of public buildings and the complex and rich biographies of houses, small-scale alterations and additions outside houses and in open spaces often remain unnoticed and certainly underrepresented in scholarship. This paper argues for a microscale approach to the study of ancient cities that encompasses spaces outside and around houses as key focal loci of social interaction, identity negotiation, and political action. It focuses on Byzantine residential quarters in the Athenian Agora, overlying the ancient Greek and Roman layers, and discusses preliminary results from the study of the Byzantine settlement based on unpublished material from the Athenian Agora excavations. This paper seeks to understand the nature of activities taking place in spaces in-between and around houses and their impact on the living conditions and built environment of Byzantine Athens. It also considers the expansion of the household outside house walls to reassess notions of public and private in intensely populated areas of Byzantine Athens. This paper thus focuses on a series of architectural features and interventions in open spaces and streets, such as encroachment on public spaces, access and control of movement in streets and alleys, burials around houses, and construction and maintenance of public amenities. This paper argues that the architectural alterations and related activities around and inbetween houses speak to placemaking events that enhance collectiveness and a sense of belonging in Byzantine Athens. Furthermore, it points to the significance of daily practices and the role of ordinary people in transforming urban architecture and reconfiguring the rules of urban living, thus offering a bottom-up approach to the study of Byzantine Athens.

SESSION 4H
Roman Emperors: Their Images and Their Spaces

CHAIR: To be announced

The Roman Emperor as Jupiter: Jovian Concepts and the Polyvalent Image
Zehavi V. Husser, Biola University

How does one represent a Roman emperor when there previously was none? One early solution involved creating images that connected him with various aspects of Jupiter's character and identity. As a result, there exist a significant number of statues, cameos, gems, and coins that depict the emperor in the guise of the Roman god. To directly link a mortal with the Romans' highest deity, however, was risky. Both innocuous and more threatening interpretations were possible when assessing images, and viewers could potentially react negatively to blatant associations with the god. How were Romans, then, meant to interpret images of the emperor as Jupiter when they encountered them? We can glimpse some existing options for interpretation by uncovering prevalent concepts relating the emperor to the god as evidenced in literature. In this paper, I assess the predominant concepts likening the emperor to Jupiter in Early Imperial literature. I then show how this conceptualization worked in the art and coinage of the first Roman imperial dynasties.

Jovian concepts formed a useful framework for understanding imperial rule by providing a means of describing the differing ways an emperor could exercise his power. The living emperor was presented as the earthly counterpart of Jove, as one paternally benevolent to his people yet wrathfully authoritarian when crossed. He was a Jovian protégé and conquering victor. Quasidivine in life, his exceptional deeds generally could earn godhood after death. Circulating ideas like these formed some of the conceptual options for understanding assertions of an emperor-Jupiter connection in other media, such as art and coinage.

Images of the emperor as Jupiter were polyvalent. As in the literary evidence, multiple concepts of Jupiter tend to be depicted together in an image. Using specific examples, I demonstrate various ways of interpreting such images and show how visual cues presented in a given object were intended to direct viewers to particular Jovian associations.

Harvard's Emperor in Fragments: An Old Trajan Reconsidered

Anthony R. Shannon, Harvard University

This paper represents a reevaluation of Harvard's cuirassed statue of the emperor Trajan (1954.71), relying on three separate facets of preservation ancillary to the statue itself for new data: conservation, archival documentation, and reproduction. Conservation work undertaken in the 1980s revealed the use of iron rods, hidden since the 18th century, holding together ancient fragments and modern restorations. The restoration of the statue has been acknowledged in recent museum publications, but its revelation raised further questions that required further investigation. For example, a noteworthy restoration was used to connect the statue's head to the statue's torso. Both fragments joined by the restoration are assuredly ancient, but their connection as original parts of the same statue is spurious, as the head has no secure connection to the rest of the statue.

In addressing the restorations revealed by conservation, this paper approaches the statue from two angles: history and iconography. The former approach, dealing more narrowly with the statue itself and its owners/patrons, addresses the issue of the statue's restoration in light of a larger question concerning the statue's modern provenance, using a recently discovered letter from the Shugburough Hall archives that serves to extend the succession of the statue's owners further than previously known and perhaps also provide the essential clue as to who restored the statue in the 18th century.

The latter approach investigates the statue's ancient credentials through a detailed analysis of the iconography used in its decorative program, particularly with regard to the overall milieu of imperial iconography. Analysis of the portrait shows that it was carved using an identifiable Trajanic type dated to the period between his two Dacian Wars, but the ambiguity of the iconography used in the decoration of the cuirass makes dating the rest of the ancient fragments more difficult, resulting in a broader date range to be considered. Aiding in the investigation of the iconography is a recently identified plaster cast in the Sir John Soane Museum in London, a reproduction of the main torso motif of a central figure engaging two griffins in combat, which has been preserved in an extremely weathered state on the statue but in a more pristine state in the casting.

A New Building Complex at the Center of Hadrian's Villa and Other Findings from Columbia's Fieldwork Season (Advanced Program of Ancient History and Art Tibur 2015)

Daira Nocera, University of Pennsylvania, *Francesco de Angelis*, Columbia University, and *Marco Maiuro*, Columbia University

The second excavation season carried out at Hadrian's Villa by Columbia University's Advanced Program of Ancient History and Art (APAHA) yielded significant new data through the expansion of the 2014 trenches, geomagnetic prospection of previously unexplored areas, paleobotanic analyses, and the study of the architectural fragments recovered from post-antique layers.

The team continued exploration in the area known as the "Lararium" adjacent to the Great Vestibule of the villa and was able to ascertain the original pavement level of the niched courtyard in front of its temple. Among other things, the excavation revealed the existence of a mosaic floor as well as traces of the staircase leading to the temple itself. Moreover, it retrieved hydraulic fixtures in different sectors of the site. The investigation was also able to identify a medieval phase, during which the floor of the courtyard was largely spoliated and pierced by long grooves, most likely for agricultural purposes. Finally, the systematic study of the numerous architectural fragments dumped in the Lararium in the course of the Middle Ages and the early modern period has shed light on post-antique accumulation dynamics in the area and has provided new data concerning the use of the Doric order in the villa.

Interesting data were also gathered in the second excavation site, the "Macchiozzo," located in a central area of the villa just south of the Piazza d'Oro. The expansion of the trench, intended to further investigate the walls uncovered in 2014, brought to light a large and articulated Hadrianic building complex. The exceptionally well-preserved decoration of the rooms includes mosaic floors with both vegetal and abstract patterns, marble revetments, wall paintings, and an entire ceiling fresco. A garden area and water channel, evidenced by in situ lead pipes and dating to a later period, were discovered immediately outside the building. Stratigraphic analysis further allowed the team to identify a fourth-century phase, which demonstrated partial building collapse, followed by the removal of sections of the mosaic floors.

Geomagnetic prospections carried out in the immediate surroundings of both excavation areas revealed the existence of further networks of walls and buildings that allow us to better determine the spatial and functional relationship of both the Lararium and the Macchiozzo complexes to previously known sectors of the villa.

A New Interpretation of Hadrian's "Province Series" Coinage
Martin Beckmann, McMaster University

Hadrian is known for his journeys and one of the most prominent artistic manifestations of these is—or at least appears to be—the extensive series of coins depicting provinces, cities, and geographic areas of the empire produced late in his reign. In addition to personifications are images of Hadrian's arrival in various locales, his restoration of some of them, and the military units stationed there. This "province series" has generally been interpreted as a memorial to Hadrian's travels earlier in his reign and as reflecting the emperor's concern for the well-being of the empire's various parts. Toynbee's summary is representative: the province series was produced when Hadrian "had settled down after his final return to Rome after the Jewish war and had leisure to turn his attention to art and to formulating a retrospective of his life's work." The interpretation of the province series turns on its dating, and this is uncertain. This paper presents results of a die analysis of this coinage that yields new and concrete evidence for its chronology. It shows that the province series was relatively long-lived, began in 133 (thus before Hadrian's final return to Rome), ended before the adoption of Aelius in 136, and dominated the coinage within this period. This new dating demonstrates that the production of this coinage coincided closely with the high point of the four-year-long Bar Kokhba rebellion in Judaea, which raged probably between 132 and 136.

Werner Eck has argued that the revolt was much more serious than commonly as-sumed, constituting a "state of emergency" in the empire. There was conscription in Italy, enrollment of noncitizens in the legions, the award of triumphal regalia to three generals, and the eventual erasure of the name of the province itself. Seen in this context, the province series of Hadrian—including its associated military types—takes on a dramatically new meaning. These coins were not a contented celebration of the past achievements of an elderly emperor but instead a massive exercise of imperial communication in a time of grave crisis. The message was multilayered and included components (e.g., images of Judaea being restored by Hadrian) that did not correspond to the reality of the crisis. The overall theme was one of reassurance, demonstrating the breadth, power, and stability of the empire in the face of rebellion.

New Discoveries at the "Villa of the Antonines": The 2015 Season

Deborah Chatr Aryamontri, Montclair State University, *Timothy Renner*, Montclair State University, *Carla Mattei*, Independent Scholar, *Carlo Albo*, Independent Scholar, and *Alessandro Blanco*, Independent Scholar

The 2015 excavations at the "Villa of the Antonines," located along the ancient Via Appia in Genzano di Roma, shed important new light on the nature and histo-ry of this archaeological site. Since the early 18th century, this site, once part of the ancient Ager Lanuvinus, has been commonly identified, on the basis of a group of Antonine portrait busts currently in the Capitoline Museums, as the imperial villa *apud Lanuvium* of this second-century dynasty. The two areas investigated so far contribute to an emerging picture of the architectural design and spatial develop-ment of this villa complex, which is probably the one mentioned by the *Historia Augusta* as the birthplace of Antoninus Pius and Commodus.

Our 2015 work at the amphitheater, located immediately west of the thermae, confirmed the presence of underground passageways inside the arena and includ-ed the partial excavation of an apsidal, barrel-vaulted room, oriented west–east and intersecting a central north–south subterranean corridor at the crossing of the two axes of the amphitheater. Explorations in previous years drew attention to the presence of a spiral staircase and a cross-vaulted room on the east side of the building. Although the full extent of these subterranean rooms must await further excavation, the 2015 explorations, including the use of microgravimetry, have confirmed an articulated underground passageway system that is of note-worthy complexity for our amphitheater, one of the smallest in the Roman world. They strengthen the hypothesis that this is one of the venues where Commodus devoted himself to pleasure and gave himself up to fighting wild beasts and men, as described by Dio Cassius.

Further investigations in an area about 150 m upslope from the amphitheater, begun in 2014, have brought to light a series of rooms decorated with black-and-white mosaics. In addition to the one discovered the previous year, with a decora-tion of interlocking circles defining hexagons, of which a fine example is in the Hospitalia at Villa Adriana, we have uncovered two additional black-and-white mosaics, one with an elaborate hexagonal motif and the other with a head of a Gorgon. These decorations suggest that these rooms formed part of the residential quarters of the villa, given also their location with an impressive view of plain and sea.

Finally, the continuing finds of fragmentary *opus sectile*, colored glass tesserae, and particularly frescoes, although dispersed, contribute to validating the hypothesis of a lavishly appointed imperial residence.

Caracalla as Birdman? Proposing a New Imperial Identity for the British Museum's "Horus in Roman Military Costume"
Anne E. Haeckl, Kalamazoo College

In a striking hybrid of Egyptian religious and Roman military iconography, a painted limestone statuette in the British Museum (EA 51100) depicts an enthroned, falcon-headed human figure arrayed in the armor of a Roman imperator. A multicultural image of imperialistic command featured in recent exhibitions in Marseilles (1997), Frankfurt (2005), and on tour throughout Great Britain (2013–2015), the sculpture has been variously described as "Horus en empereur," "Horus wearing Roman military dress" and "Big Bird." As an alternative to such generalized appellations, this paper proposes a specific identity for the British Museum Horus, that of the emperor Caracalla, and a specific context for its creation as a work commemorating Caracalla's imperial visit to Egypt in 215 C.E. Despite the difficulties of identifying human facial features across species lines, the beetled brow and glowering gaze of Horus' avian visage seem intentionally to inscribe onto the head of a predatory raptor the furrowed physiognomy and expressive intensity of Caracalla's last official portrait type, the "Sole Ruler" or "Scowling Caracalla" type (215–217 C.E.).

A portrait of Caracalla in the guise of the Egyptian falcon-god Horus, son and successor of Osiris and divine incarnation of the living pharaoh, would be an appropriate addition to the corpus of Severan dynastic portraiture, a filial homage to the Serapis portrait type of Septimius Severus. Moreover, Horus' armor effectively reconciles Caracalla's paradoxical public image as both an ordinary Roman soldier and a latter-day Alexander the Great. Two elements of his painted uniform can be meaningfully associated with Caracalla. A short, light-green mantle fastened with a round brooch on the right shoulder suggests the Germanic military cloak (*caracalla*/*caracallis*) that gave the emperor his nickname, while the Egyptian blue *lorica plumata*, a mail shirt with overlapping, feather-shaped scales, is also worn by Caracalla on a sardonyx cameo in the Hermitage. Horus' *lorica plumata* further evokes the Alexander Aigiochus type, as replicated in numerous statuettes from Graeco-Roman Egypt. Here Alexander's aegis takes the shape of a Macedonian chlamys whose overlapping, feathery scales are formally identical to those of Horus' mail shirt. Magnificently armored, imposing, and intimidating, the British Museum Horus fiercely embodies Caracalla's two main activities during his visit to Alexandria in 215: a respectful pilgrimage to Alexander's tomb, where Caracalla dedicated colorful clothing akin to Horus' military uniform, and a brutal massacre of local ephebes, cruelly assembled under the pretext of mustering a new phalanx in honor of Alexander.

SESSION 4I
Change and Continuity in Italy and Sicily from the Republic to the Middle Ages

CHAIR: *Joanne M. Spurza*, Hunter College of the City University of New York

Update from the Field: Report on the 2015 Excavations of the Contrada Agnese Project (Morgantina, Sicily)

Randall Souza, Binghamton University, *Jared Benton*, University of Victoria, and *D. Alex Walthall*, University of Texas at Austin

This paper presents the results of the third season of the Contrada Agnese Project (CAP), a long-term research and excavation project conducted under the auspices of the American Excavations at Morgantina, Sicily. Since 2013, CAP excavations have focused on an insula (13W/14S) located at the western end of the classical and Hellenistic city and have documented construction beginning in the Early Hellenistic period. Two principal concerns drive CAP's investigations. First, our understanding of the city's fate in the second and first centuries B.C.E. remains generalized and can improve with more excavation data. Second, although the nearby discovery of two public bath complexes has illuminated our view of bathing culture in Sicily, little is otherwise known about the nature of occupation at the western limits of Morgantina in the area of the Contrada Agnese.

The 2015 excavations revealed larger portions of a building that occupied the northwestern lot of the insula and that was first excavated in 2014. Our most recent excavations have improved our understanding of the building's chronology, which can be broadly divided into two phases. In the earlier phase, dating to the third quarter of the third century B.C.E., the building exhibited notable architectural features including a monumental entrance along a major avenue. An abundance of terracotta column drums found in later layers (several belonging to a toppled column) suggests that the building possessed a courtyard and peristyle. Several extant doorways now permit a tentative reconstruction of access and circulation, and analysis of pithos fragments recovered in 2014 and 2015 indicates the presence of nearly a dozen large storage vessels. In the second phase, which postdates the Roman sack of the city in 211 B.C.E., the building was renovated and reused. A bread oven found in 2015 may be further indication of industrial activity belonging to this phase.

In its third year, CAP has already answered some of its original research questions and developed new ones. Monumental elements in the building's architecture are well-suited to an insula flanked by two public bath complexes. Moreover, the pithoi and bread oven offer new evidence for storage and food preparation in this area, and ongoing environmental analysis has revealed the presence of at least three types of wheat. Finally, modifications to the building indicate a shift in its function from the third to the second centuries B.C.E. and might imply a fundamental change in the urban fabric of Morgantina.

Masked Identities: Investigating Votive Rituals and Political Transformations at Narce in the Third Century B.C.E.

Jacopo Tabolli, Trinity College Dublin

This paper aims to investigate the transformations in the identity of an ancient community who celebrated a peculiar votive ritual in the first half of the third century B.C.E. at Narce, a Faliscan site, 25 km north of Rome. In October 2014, during the excavation of the Sanctuary of Monte Li Santi-Le Rote at Narce, a votive deposit consisting of more than 300 terracotta masks was found. The current excavation revealed that the deposit constitutes a collective ritual, filling the foundation trench of the "temple" which was rebuilt as an open-area temenos. The chronology of the deposit was assigned to the first half of the third century B.C.E. and is secured by the discovery of Roman coins in the deposit, dating to ca. 268 B.C.E. By presenting the archaeological record of this ritual, this paper investigates themes such as the definition of the links between war and religious places, preservation and transformation of memories, and reactualization of past identities. At the same time, the paper presents an innovative digital display of the archaeological record and communicates ancient identity and religious actions to a nonspecialist audience.

Notes of Roman Economy in Populonia

Carolina Megale, Universitá di Firenze, and *Stefano Genovesi*, Archeodig Project

The maritime settlement of Poggio del Molino is located in the heart of the former territory of one of the most important Etruscan cities, Populonia, overlooking the Tyrrhenian Sea. The Roman building was built on the northern side of a headland that acts as a watershed between the beach of Rimigliano in the north and the Gulf of Baratti in the south; it is situated in a strategic part of the bay, next to a navigable inland lake and the great Campiglia mines.

Populonia was for centuries (from 900 B.C.E. to 100 C.E.) one of the most important centers of iron smelting and trade in the Mediterranean. Anyway the transfer of the city to Roman rule (250/200 B.C.E.) and the related changes (politico-economical, architectural, religious) are still largely unknown in this part of the Etruscan coast.

In the second half of the second century B.C.E., the northern part of the promontory was occupied by a fortress placed to control and defend the territory of Populonia against pirates attack. The fortress, with a rectangular plan of about 55 x 56 m, has two gateways with control towers and a lookout tower facing inland. At the end of the first century B.C.E., the building was turned into a farm with adjoining *cetaria*, a handicraft factory for the production of garum (fish sauce), equipped with pools for soaking the fish. In the second half of the second century C.E., after a thorough renovation, the building takes on the characteristics of a maritime villa: a large open area set out as a garden with columns around surrounded by the bath complex and the living quarters with mosaic floors and painted walls, and a servants' area with the kitchen and housing. In the fourth and fifth centuries C.E., after the destruction, the site experienced a significant phase of inhabitation connected with the presence of a gathering place, probably linked to early Christian worship, and of a tomb set up on the ruins of the villa.

Recent Research on the Republican Phases of the Roman Sanctuary at Sant'Omobono

Daniel P. Diffendale, University of Michigan

The ancient cult place under the church of Sant'Omobono in Rome's Forum Boarium has been the focus of archaeological investigation since its chance rediscovery during demolitions in the 1930s. The bulk of scholarly attention since then has focused on the remains of the deeply buried archaic temple and its associated material culture. Most of the remains visible today, however, are dated broadly between the early fifth century B.C.E. and the second century C.E., and yet many basic questions about these "later" periods of the sanctuary lack satisfying answers. For instance, which elements on-site can be assigned to discrete architectural phases? What materials were used in these phases, and how can these phases be dated? The ongoing work of the Sant'Omobono Project, which aims at a definitive publication of the site, has included a total station survey of all visible remains in conjunction with chemical analysis of the types of *tufo* used and archival research on the past 80 years of archaeological exploration; I present preliminary results of this work and identify prospects for future research.

Recent Discoveries from a Mechanized Coring Survey of Rome's Forum Boarium

Andrea L. Brock, University of Michigan

This paper presents preliminary results from a mechanized coring survey of the Forum Boarium valley in the heart of Rome. This survey complements and builds on recent work at the Sant'Omobono sanctuary, which includes investigation of archaic and pre-archaic layers at the site. This project has provided much-needed context for the cult site at Sant'Omobono by producing new data on the topography and environment of the floodplain as well as early human activity in the area.

In the summer of 2015, our team produced 12 boreholes along the east bank of the Tiber River, in the regions known as the Forum Boarium and Forum Holitorium. Typically employed for geological and engineering projects, special machinery was used to drill each borehole to a depth of 15 m or more, providing access to the entire sequence of urban stratigraphy and the natural substratum below. Although this project is multifaceted with a variety of ongoing studies (pollen, paleomagnetometry, etc.), the stratigraphic and sedimentary record preserved in the boreholes has already provided a wealth of new insights. First, there is new evidence for the topographic and environmental conditions of the river valley as it existed at the beginning of human occupation at the site of Rome. This project has also documented the changing position of the Tiber River in prehistoric and historical periods as well as the overwhelming effects of floods and alluvial aggradation in the valley. These natural hazards challenged urban development and forced the early inhabitants of Rome to pursue landscape modification projects. Finally, with a greater understanding of the natural landscape, this project has begun to reveal the setting and structure of Rome's archaic river harbor and harbor temple.

In addition to addressing these preliminary results, this paper discusses plans for future research. It is expected that coring data will be incorporated into three-dimensional models, which will translate this complicated data set into a series of interactive graphics that depict the changing landscape of Rome's river valley during the first millennium B.C.E. Such results will not only demonstrate the potential of coring survey in urban archaeology but also offer invaluable new evidence for the development of early Rome.

Recent Finds from Excavations at Coriglia, Castel Viscardo (Umbria, Italy)
David George, Saint Anselm College, and *Claudio Bizzarri*, PAAO

This year marks the end of 10 years of excavations of an Etrusco-Roman site at Coriglia near Castel Viscardo, Italy. The site rests on four terraces descending northward toward the Paglia River to the north. Uncovered over the course of excavation in the last decade are various features associated with water: a large hypocaust, a series of very large *vascae*, as well as a number of monumental walls with channels and pipes for the routing of water and various hydraulic features in addition to walls and rooms dating from the Etruscan phase to the late Roman. There have been a range of artifacts recovered, including impasto ware, Attic black-figure and red-figure, archaic Etruscan black-figure as well as black and gray bucchero, *aes rude*, Roman coinage, Roman fresco, and various objects in bronze or other materials. Until last year, we could document the site's continuous use from the eighth century B.C.E. to fifth century C.E. The site's floruit seemed to be concentrated in the Hellenistic Etruscan phase and the early empire, especially the Neronian and Flavian period. However, in the last two years, excavations have brought to light a number of important features that aid in our understanding of the history and use of the site. We have recovered a number of barrel vaults—one, collapsed, associated with one of the *vascae*, another still partially intact running about 3 m and at present not associated with any other feature though having a set of stone stairs descending to it from the south. Both contain material, numismatic or stamped amphoras, all of which dates to the late first century C.E. We have also recovered a number of walls that indicate repair and expansion of the site during the third century C.E. based on numismatic evidence and evidence from foundation trenches. Of particular interest is an area built into the walls of two of the *vascae* to the south of the site that has well-built wells of tuff and a floor built of dressed stone and reused ceramic with Maiolica Ware datable to the late 14th and early 15th century C.E. recovered from it near the wells and corners.

The *Longue Durée* Development of the Porta Esquilina and the Church of S. Vito in Rome
Margaret M. Andrews, Brown University, *Seth G. Bernard*, University of Toronto, and *Simonetta Serra*, Sovrintendenza Capitolina ai Beni Culturali, Rome

We present the results of recent fieldwork focused on the extant Roman and Early Medieval structures below the church of S. Vito in Rome. Built in 1477 against the central bay of the Porta Esquilina/Arch of Gallienus on the Esquiline Hill, the church stands in a location that has been the subject of considerable topographical debate for centuries, as a number of important, but archaeologically elusive, monuments are attested in its immediate vicinity: the archaic and Republican circuit walls; the Anio Vetus aqueduct; the so-called Macellum Liviae; and the Early Medieval diaconia, monastery, and church of S. Vito. The entire church was excavated in 1971, revealing numerous ancient and medieval building phases. Despite their potential to clarify several topographical issues, however, the results were only summarily published, and there has been no attempt to interpret them since.

Starting from unpublished, archival plans made in 1988 by the Soprintendenza Archeologica di Roma, we undertook a new documentation campaign of the ancient and medieval structures below the church in 2015. The results allow us to determine the chronological relationship of the various structures beneath the church and to offer new interpretations of multiple phases spanning from the sixth century B.C.E. to the 15th century C.E. For the earlier periods, the structures show the relationship of the archaic fortification walls to the Middle Republican *agger* and *fossa* at one of the city's most important gates. In the Flavian period, significant hydraulic installations dated by newly discovered brickstamps and numismatic evidence were constructed, perhaps associated with the Anio Vetus and the construction of a nearby macellum. These structures remained in use until late antiquity, when two burials were inserted within them. Although an ecclesia of S. Vito is attested in documents beginning in the eighth century, the original structure is generally thought to have been located elsewhere. Our reexamination, however, reveals significant Early Medieval construction and may demonstrate the presence of a church here already in this period. We are able to identify a 13th century predecessor to the current church through new evidence for a narthex within the side bay of the Arch of Gallienus. Our work thus demonstrates not only the significant implications for several long-standing topographical and archaeological problems that the remains below S. Vito have but also the shifting urban importance of the Porta Esquilina across a wide chronological arc of Rome's history.

SESSION 4J: Colloquium
Deserted Villages, I: Before Abandonment
Sponsored by the Medieval and Post-Medieval Archaeology Interest Group

ORGANIZERS: *Deborah E. Brown Stewart*, Dumbarton Oaks Research Library, and *Kostis Kourelis*, Franklin & Marshall College

Colloquium Overview Statement

Overshadowed by more prestigious ancient sites nearby, deserted villages from the Medieval and early modern periods in the Mediterranean have been neglected by the archaeological community. This two-part colloquium presents data from recent fieldwork projects and new approaches to the investigation of both old and new data. It covers a wide geographical range (Egypt, Syria, Greece, and the United States) and chronological span (sixth to 21st centuries) and formulates new theoretical and methodological approaches to an endangered category of material culture.

The first part of the colloquium features new research into processes of formation and occupation at now abandoned villages. A paper on Late Antique villages from Syria challenges old interpretations and calls for an appreciation of abandoned houses as lived spaces and as key nodes in village dynamics. Combining papyrology, archaeology, and Arabic records, the second paper nuances the process of abandonment of the Fayum in Egypt. Turning from Egypt to Greece, the third paper illuminates the famous deserted villages of the Mani that have alluded historical analysis. With the aid of Ottoman archival records, aerial survey, and field reconnaissance, the paper sorts through the complex continuities of occupation across the centuries. Anavatos on Chios is one of Greece's most famous deserted villages. The fourth paper reconstructs the settlement's development from its foundation in the 16th century to its abandonment after the earthquake of 1881. Finally, a case study from the Western Argolid Regional Project uses tools from a pedestrian regional survey to investigate villages along two major land routes that connected the Corinthia, the Argolid, and Arcadia in the Medieval and early modern periods.

The "Dead Villages" of Northern Syria: Surveillance and Security at Déhès
Anna M. Sitz, University of Pennsylvania

The "Dead Villages" of the Limestone Massif (northern Syria) are exceptionally well-preserved because of their basalt masonry; these villages represent one of the largest repositories of Late Antique domestic architecture. Indeed, the permanence of the architecture and the richness of its carved decoration call into question our usual notion of a village. Tragically, the current conflict in Syria has inhibited fieldwork in the region, and the amount of damage incurred at these sites is unknown. Previously published material is therefore our only opportunity for further study. In this paper, I reexamine the architectural remains of a site called Déhès, excavated by J.P. Sodini et al. (*Syria* 57 [1980] 1–304), to better understand the nature of a village in the region and the social dynamics at work in this community.

Most studies of the Dead Villages have focused on the economy: agricultural production and the question of big landowners or autonomous villagers (e.g., G. Tchalenko, *Villages Antiques de la Syrie du Nord* [Paris 1953]). The few publications on the domestic architecture have suffered from a lack of contextualization: buildings have been categorized typologically, inscriptions have been published separately from the architecture, and the village setting has been ignored. The excavation undertaken at Déhès by Sodini et al. aimed to clarify a "typical" Late Antique settlement in the Massif, and the results undermined previous interpretations of the village: instead of civic features such as an agora and "andron," the excavation identified three courtyard houses dating from the fourth to sixth century C.E. (recently redated by J. Magness to the sixth century). Yet the excavators again focused primarily on the economy in their analysis of the remains.

I approach these houses as lived spaces and active agents in the social dynamics of the village. Techniques that have born fruit in the study of Roman and Late Antique towns elsewhere, such as spatial analysis and attention to sight lines, shed light on the concerns of the occupants. I have plotted inscriptions and carved cross medallions, usually written off as simple "apotropaic" devices against demonic forces, in their architectural settings—and their locations suggest that it was not only malevolent spirits that were meant to take notice. Inaccessible though the Dead Villages may be, this reassessment of the architecture and finds from Déhès uncovers the concerns and social strategies of a village in the region that saw P. Brown's "rise of the holy man."

The Center Holds: Village Desertion and Settlement Patterns in the Early Medieval Fayum, Egypt

Brendan Haug, University of Michigan, Ann Arbor

Located some 70 km southwest of Cairo, Egypt's Fayum is a vast geological depression in the Libyan Sahara whose settled area covers 1,850 km². Irrigated by the waters of the Bahr Yusuf, a natural side channel of the Nile, and formerly filled with a shallow lake, the region has been extensively inhabited since its reclamation by the early Ptolemies in the third century B.C.E. Following the expansion of settlement into this newly reclaimed territory, the Fayum enjoyed nearly 600 years of relative stability. Beginning in the fourth century C.E., however, the villages of its margins were gradually abandoned to the desert, a process that preserved thousands of papyri.

Excavation and survey has revealed that village abandonment, previously regarded as a regional crisis, was a protracted process whose pace and scale varied. And yet a synthetic study of this transitional phase of Fayum history remains unwritten despite the recent upsurge in interest in Egypt's Late Antique and Early Medieval periods. This situation cannot be blamed entirely on a lack of evidence, since hundreds of papyri from the seventh and eighth centuries have been published and thousands more remain unstudied. Still, the majority of these documents are small scraps derived not from villages but from the region's central capital, modern Medinat al-Fayum. Overwhelmingly concerned with minute matters of fiscal administration and published in archaic editions, these papyri have been neglected in favor of the far richer village documentation of the Ptolemaic and Roman periods.

A habit of early Arab administration nevertheless renders the later material uniquely suited to topographical analysis—that is, the division of the countryside into sometimes microscopic units of fiscal assessment (choria). As Jean Gascou has remarked, this administrative innovation results in the sudden appearance in Early Medieval papyri of hundreds of toponyms otherwise unattested in the Byzantine period.

This ongoing project, part of a longue durée environmental history of the Fayum, seeks to create a "relational" topography by linking these numerous and largely obscure toponyms to locales that have either survived to the present day or are securely located in other medieval sources. Through several microregional case studies, I demonstrate that the Fayum's central alluvial plain remained densely inhabited even after the desertion of the margins.

By highlighting the relative continuity in settlement patterns between late antiquity and the early Middle Ages, this research enriches our understanding of an era that otherwise marks a significant inflection point in Egyptian history.

New Insights into the Abandoned "Palaiomaniatika" from Ottoman Defters, Aerial Survey, and Field Reconnaissance

Rebecca M. Seifried, University of Illinois at Chicago

Four decades ago, the first studies were published about the enigmatic "palaio-maniatika" settlements in the Mani Peninsula, Greece. These Byzantine-period villages are characterized by a unique dry stone architecture that has been described as "megalithic" and "cyclopean." Until now, archaeological research has focused on identifying the locations of the villages (with more than 100 identified to date) and discussing their unique architectural style. Generally, scholars agree that the *palaiomaniatika* were inhabited during the broader Byzantine period until about the 15th century C.E.

This paper reviews the previous interpretations of the *palaiomaniatika* and discusses new information that I gathered as part of a larger project on the Medieval and post-Medieval settlements in the region. One important source of data is a series of newly translated defters, or Ottoman tax registers, from the years 1514, 1583, and 1715 C.E. As some of the earliest written records about the Mani, these administrative documents provide information about the past population, social organization, and potential agricultural output of the region. The toponyms listed in the defters can be used to trace the history of the modern settlements, as well as to assist in identifying unnamed *palaiomaniatika* villages. To supplement this archival research, I conducted aerial survey with historical aerial photographs and satellite imagery between 2014 and 2015 and field reconnaissance in 2014. One of the goals of the project was to identify abandoned settlements that may correspond to toponyms listed in the defters. In addition, selected settlements were chosen for detailed investigation and recording, resulting in full-plan maps of the residential structures and cisterns. The maps allow for a more thorough discussion of community layout, complementing the studies of domestic architecture published previously.

The results of this new investigation of the *palaiomaniatika* allow us to trace the development of Maniate villages from the Medieval to post-Medieval times, especially in terms of how communities were organized. Moreover, the toponymic research suggests that many of the now-ruined villages continued to be inhabited into the Early Ottoman period, perhaps as late as the 17th century. The *palaiomaniatika* are unique not just for their architecture but also because of their high number and overall state of preservation. It is hoped that the new insights presented here will help broaden our understanding of rural communities elsewhere in medieval Greece.

The Deserted Village of Anavatos on the Island of Chios, Greece

Olga Vassi, Ministry of Culture, Greece

The island of Chios is located on the opposite coast of Asia Minor, on the sea route leading from the eastern Mediterranean to Constantinople and the Black Sea. In the early 16th century, when Chios belonged to the Genoese, a settlement was founded in the mountains, invisible from the sea, in the forests. Either loggers or stock breeders were supposed to live there. The village was founded on the top of a steep hill, which made it partly inaccessible. Even its name expresses the difficulty that it caused to access principally for defensive purposes. "Anavatos" means "not passable."

The settlement, the streets, the public spaces, the churches, and the small terraces necessarily follow the relief. A high defensive wall, not very strong, follows the brow of the cliff, and in the single passable point the gate of the entrance to the small village can be found. The domestic architecture is almost primitive; the houses are small, with a narrow facade, two storied and with flat roofs. On the top of the hill, a large church dedicated to the archangel Michael was built in the 18th century. Another church, dedicated to the Dormition of the Virgin, was later erected in the lower neighborhood of the village. Beneath this church is placed the only water cistern of the village known thus far.

After the 18th century and the elimination of the fear of piracy in the Aegean Sea, the village began to spread outside the wall. It covered the entire slope, and new houses were built, significantly larger than those found in the old fortified village on the hilltop. The progress was violently cut off in the year 1822, when the Ottomans massacred the population of Chios and led to the devastation of the village for several years. The return of the residents took place ca. 1840; however, instead of inhabiting the fortified village on the top, they dwelled in the new one on the slope. In the late 19th century, in 1881, an earthquake caused irreparable damage and forced the few remaining inhabitants to settle at the foot of the hill, where they followed new architectural types for their houses. Little by little the new village in its turn was also abandoned, and today all the neighborhoods either in the old medieval village or on the slope are deserted and partly in ruins.

Roads, Routes and Abandoned Villages in the Western Argolid

Dimitri Nakassis, University of Toronto, *William Caraher*, University of North Dakota, *Sarah James*, University of Colorado, Boulder, and *Scott Gallimore*, Wilfrid Laurier University

This paper interrogates the archaeological relationship between roads, routes, and settlement in the post-Antique Argolid based on new fieldwork by the Western Argolid Regional Project in 2014–2015. Archaeologists often represent abandoned villages as disconnected dots in the Greek landscape that are left isolated by changing patterns of travel through the countryside. Mechanized agriculture, the construction of railways, and the spread of automobiles in the Greek world affected both the structure of rural settlement and the routes between sites in the countryside: routes suitable for animals or walking were increasingly abandoned, and sites located in relation to these routes were transformed by their new landscape context.

The Western Argolid Regional Project documents sites and artifacts in the upper reaches of the Inachos River, a region associated with a major east–west route connecting Arkadia and the Argolid and a north–south route connecting Argos to Nemea and the western Corinthia. The former route was part of a network of cart roads as early as the Classical period and was known as the Klimax. This road's Ottoman and early modern successor is a stone path used for a variety of purposes, from Ibrahim Pasha's raids in 1826 to modern transhumant pastoralists

moving their flocks from summer pastures in Arkadia to winter them at Kara-
thonas, near Nafplion. The most recent instantiation of this route is the Moreas
motorway constructed in the 1980s.

Intensive survey has complemented the study of these major routes with an
investigation of abandoned local routes. Over two field seasons we have gathered
evidence ranging from ceramic scatters to stone bridges, fortified rock shelters,
isolated churches, and paths between field walls. Whereas we can discern broad
continuity in settlement and road networks from classical antiquity onward at
the regional scale, at a more localized scale the archaeological evidence suggests
that very different networks of routes were used, connecting mountainous microregions to one another and to the Inachos River valley, where good agricultural
land and the major terrestrial route to Argos were located.

SESSION 4K
Macedonia and the Hellenistic World

CHAIR: *Josephine Shaya*, The College of Wooster

Pieria Capta: Methone, Pella, and the Urbanization of Macedonia
Sarah P. Morris, University of California, Los Angeles

In 354 B.C.E., Philip II defeated the northern Greek harbor city of Methone, an
Eretrian colony sited on an earlier settlement, and forced its inhabitants to leave
with only a himation on their backs. The Macedonian ruler lost an eye in the siege
but gained an invaluable advantage over southern Greece by terminating the life
of a major port, ally of Athens, and essential source of timber for the Athenian
fleet. A smaller garrison was established approximately 1 km north of the site and
may have lasted through Roman times, even after the Battle of Pydna ended Macedonian hegemony.

While hardly the only northern city to fall to Philip II (Olynthos, Torone, and
other independent poleis were forced to capitulate, evacuate, or relocate), Methone
bequeathed Macedon a particular legacy visible only in archaeology. Excavations
in Nea Agathoupolis by the IST' and KZ' Ephorates since 2003 have uncovered
extensive archaic and classical industrial activities in both the "Agora" (East Hill)
and the "Acropolis" (West Hill), dedicated to manufacturing pottery, figurines,
metal artifacts, bone, ivory, and glass. The Agora, with monumental buildings of
mudbrick on ashlar courses under tile roofs (one with a porch added to form a
stoa) framing open plazas, represents one of Greece's earliest public urban settings for the manufacture and sale of artifacts, near an ancient harbor engaged in
exchange.

With the defeat of Methone and the relocation of its inhabitants, both this model
of urbanization and its agents may have been attracted or absorbed into the expanding city of Pella, the largest city in Macedonia by the time of Amyntas III
(Xen., *Hell.* 5.2), linked to a major river port leading to the Thermaic Gulf. This
paper considers the possibility that Macedonian rulers deliberately replicated the
public spaces and workshops of defeated Methone in their new center at Pella,

recruited its craft specialists to new workshops adjoining an active harbor, and fused this model with the southern Greek orthogonal grid plan already in use at Pella, to create a new Hellenic-Macedonian city with a large open agora surrounded by workshops that manufactured and sold crafted goods near a maritime network. This also ultimately made Pella (and the ghost of Methone) the prototype for new or expanded urban centers in the north (e.g., at Dion, Thessaloniki, and Demetrias) that followed Greek models under Hellenistic rulers, as well as those exported back to southern Greece, as suggested for Sikyon.

The Gymnasium at Amphipolis, Peristyle Architecture, and Elite Civic Space in Early Hellenistic Macedonia
Martin Gallagher, Wolfson College, Oxford

The gymnasium at Amphipolis is incredibly important for the development of buildings with interior peristyles in Hellenistic Macedonian architecture, the role of this architecture in defining civic space, and the role of new buildings in the negotiation of Greek localism and the expansion of the Macedonian state. Unfortunately, this building has never been published, and its limited and sometimes opaque presentation in field reports (esp. *Prakt* and *Ergon*, 1982–1989) has hindered full consideration of the building. Skaltsa (*Hellenistic gymnasia* [2008]) noted that Amphipolis' gymnasium was unique for its inclusion of rooms on all four sides of the peristyle but did not discuss its comparability in this respect to the palaces and monumental houses of Macedonia.

The excavators dated the building to the reign of Philip II (359–336 B.C.E.), but I argue for a date in the last quarter of the fourth century, which is supported by a range of numismatic and ceramic evidence from foundation deposits. By comparison with the near contemporary gymnasium at Delphi, Amphipolis' gymnasium is much more integrated, with a *xystos* (covered running track) articulated to the main peristyle building. The *xystos* had to be shorter (87 m, compared with 175 m at Delphi), but greater emphasis is placed on the peristyle itself, which covers almost 1.5 times the ground area of Delphi's. The gymnasium of Amphipolis was designed to serve a function similar to other peristyle buildings in Macedonia, providing an interior context for activities that otherwise would have taken place outside. That it does this while fitting into more compact urban space is especially interesting because the area in which it was built was newly developed in the Hellenistic period, as if it was designed with major urban expansion in mind.

The two entrances to the gymnasium, the Doric pentastyle stoa, and the deployment of honorific and votive sculpture throughout the building support Robert's idea of a Greek gymnasium as a "second agora." Although caution is required because of the Early Roman date of the gymnasiarchic decree from Amphipolis, its similarity to the decree from Beroia suggests common Macedonian customs and their importance in elite life. Alternatively, the legend of the racing torch on Alexander the Great's coinage produced at Amphipolis, a prominent symbol on the city's earlier emissions, shows a continuity of athletic traditions stretching from the period of independence through that of Macedonian hegemony.

Macedonian Elite Tombs: A Shift In Perspective
Olga Koutseridi, University of Texas at Austin

This paper analyzes a particular type of elite burial structure known in modern literature as the Macedonian tomb. This tomb type first appears in the fourth century and continues into the second century B.C.E. The most succinct definition of a Macedonian tomb is a barrel-vaulted burial chamber found within the territory of ancient Macedonia.

The current pattern of scholarship on Macedonian tombs is centered on issues of chronology, topology, iconography, and identification of the tombs' occupants. In addition, the study of Macedonian tombs is often focused on "royal" tombs and is conducted without close consideration for their sociopolitical context. In light of these scholarly trends, this paper implements a new approach to the study of Macedonian tombs and presents alternative directions for future research.

This paper begins by contextualizing the construction of Macedonian tombs within the sociopolitical realities of the Macedonian kingdom in the late fourth and early third centuries B.C.E. This period is characterized by intense political instability due to a lack of a clear successor following the death of Alexander the Great and the ruthless ambitions of Alexander's commanders.

The latter part is dedicated to a holistic survey of the sepulchral structures made possible through the comprehensive catalogue of H. von Mangoldt (*Makedonische Grabarchitektur: Die Makedonischen Kammergräber und ihre Vorläufer* [Wasmuth 2012]). From this analysis, I was able to identify a lack of distinction between royal and elite Macedonian tombs. I believe that this uniformity played an important role in reaffirming an egalitarian image (among the Macedonian elite) by which they wished to project as a means of creating, perpetuating, and securing their elite status and identity in this politically unstable world. Thus, it becomes clear that through the use of this uniform tomb type the Macedonian elite created and displayed an image of cohesiveness, power, and most importantly solidarity as a response to the unstable political conditions at the turn of the third century.

Most importantly, this paper brings to the foreground the necessity of using Macedonian tombs as a source of evidence for understanding the often overlooked local Macedonian elites and their self-perception and self-representation. Through these monuments, we are able to reinstill local elites with a sense of agency by acknowledging their conscious participation in an architectural discourse with their fellow elites. Consequently, Macedonian tombs offer to some extent a reflection of local Macedonian elite solidarity.

Religion, Culture, and History: A New Assessment of Alexander the Great in Egypt
Marsha B. McCoy, Southern Methodist University

The recent publication of Ian S. Moyer's award-winning book, *Egypt and the Limits of Hellenism* (Cambridge 2011), new research on Alexander's architectural and sculptural program at Thebes, Elephantine Island, and elsewhere, as well recent archaeological work at Saqqara, Alexandria, and Siwa have shed new light on Alexander's activities, intentions, and accomplishments in Egypt. This paper analyzes the new evidence for Alexander's achievements in Egypt and situates them within Moyer's framework of the Greek view of Egyptians as an alien but sub-sumable culture on the one hand, as exemplified by the fifth-century B.C.E. Greek historian, Herodotus, and the Egyptian management of the Greek incursion with a policy of accommodation and incorporation on the other hand, as exemplified by the late fourth- to early third-century B.C.E. Egyptian writer, Manetho, who also rose to become the chief priest of the sun god Ra at Heliopolis and may have experienced Alexander firsthand as a young man. Alexander deployed a combina-tion of diplomacy, display, and a carefully coordinated building program to create connections to specific Egyptian gods, pharaohs, and key points in Egyptian his-tory. But he also used Egypt's place in Greek mythology (Iphigenia, Theseus, etc. all stopped in Egypt; Herakles and Perseus visited Siwa) and history (Herodotus and Plato spent time in Egypt) to subsume Egypt into Greek culture. His goal was to create a religious, cultural, and historical logic, acceptable to Greeks and also Egyptians, for his assumption of pharaonic powers and crowns and his incorpora-tion of Egypt into his growing realm.

Representing Royal Power: A Dark Stone Queen from Hellenistic Egypt
Rachel Kousser, City University of New York

Recent underwater excavations near Alexandria have brought to light an un-orthodox yet compelling statue of a Ptolemaic queen. Carved in diorite and with a traditional Egyptian visual format, the portrait has up-to-date touches of sensuous Hellenistic naturalism. It has been associated by its excavators with the prominent queen Arsinoe II, whose cult was energetically promoted in the early Ptolemaic era. But the sculpture does not resemble other, better-documented images of Ar-sinoe II, and its fusion of Greek and Egyptian elements has few parallels in the early third century B.C.E. This paper draws on archaeological and epigraphic evi-dence to propose an alternate context for the sculpture: that of the less celebrated yet artistically ambitious and hybrid court of Ptolemy VIII Physkon.

While the dark stone queen is unusually well preserved and well executed, it is one of a number of late Ptolemaic royal portraits in diorite. These include images of Physkon himself and his wife Cleopatra III, both represented with Greek-style individualized features combined with Egyptian iconography. Such portraits were popular commissions under Ptolemy VIII; the king's reign saw an extensive sculp-tural production of works notable for their high quality, their large, frequently colossal scale, and their hybrid nature, which fused Greek and Egyptian styles into a new synthesis. The dark stone queen fits well among such works; it should be redated and identified as one of the prominent royal women of the era—for instance, Cleopatra III or her aunt and stepmother, Cleopatra II.

This reevaluation of the statue has significant implications for our understand-ing of late Ptolemaic art. Scholars have frequently focused on the third century B.C.E. and have highlighted its extensive Greek cultural production in works ranging from the Sarapeion and Pharos lighthouse to the writings of Kallimachos, Theokritos, and Poseidippos. The dark stone queen serves as a useful reminder of the continued creative vitality of Egypt in the later Ptolemaic era, despite eco-nomic woes and dynastic strife. It also attests to the contribution made by native artists, since diorite was a material associated with traditional Egyptian craftsmen.

This study of the dark stone queen is thus important not only for our understanding of Ptolemaic self-representation but also for the investigation of materiality in Hellenistic art.

Mapping Female Space and Social Networks in Hellenistic Lindos and Priene
Machal Gradoz, AIA Member at Large

Over the course of the Hellenistic period, honoring individual benefactors with statues became prevalent, and the practice evolved into the common form of figure and inscription seen in imperial Rome. Though women increasingly took on the role of benefactors in the Hellenistic period, the extent and nature of their dedications—those made for them and those made by them—remains largely understudied. This is especially true for the physical impact of female-associated benefactions in public space. In other words, what does it mean for women to be dedicators and/or honorands in public space?

This paper analyzes the impact of female civic patronage in Hellenistic Ionia (where the evidence is best) via case studies of female benefactors and honorands in honorific monuments in two cities, Priene and Lindos. I argue that there are commonalities in how women shape public space via their patronage and how others honor them. Moreover, in these commonalities we can map female social space and discern female social networks to learn how they functioned within their respective city.

I show that the primary way by which women participated in Hellenistic public space was through their familial social network, by being both active patrons and passive honorands. While a statue of a woman is an obvious mark of female presence in public space, women also mark space as female via the dedications they make. John Ma (*Statues and Cities: Honorific Portraits and Civic Identity in the Hellenistic World* [Oxford 2013] 15–63) discusses the nominative-accusative formula often found on Hellenistic statue bases, wherein the honorand is the passive recipient of the action while the dedicator is the active party. As a result, a female dedicator actively marks female presence in city space, even if her image is not there.

In Lindos, all of the female-associated statues were placed in the Sanctuary of Athena Lindia. I demonstrate that the statues of women and statues by women serve to imbue female presence in one of the most important places in the city via family connections. In Priene, female-associated statues were found in both religious and political spaces, but, as in Lindos, family networks are at the forefront of these dedications. Consequently, it is through familial networks that women shape public space in Hellenistic Lindos and Priene, and this may in fact be part of a larger trend in the Hellenistic period by which women participated in public life.

SESSION 5A
Mycenaean Funerary Practices

CHAIR: *R. Angus K. Smith*, Brock University

TAPHOS, Tombs of Aidonia Preservation, Heritage, and Exploration Synergasia: The 2014 Pilot Survey and 2015 Excavation Seasons

Kim S. Shelton, University of California, Berkeley, *Konstantinos Kissas*, Korinthian Ephorate of Antiquities, Ministry of Culture, Greece, and *Lynne A. Kvapil*, Butler University

We present the preliminary results of the 2014 and 2015 seasons at the Late Bronze Age cemetery of Aidonia in the southern Corinthia. The TAPHOS project is a cooperative effort between the Corinthian Ephorate of Antiquities (Hellenic Ministry of Culture) and the Nemea Center for Classical Archaeology (University of California, Berkeley) and is a recipient of the 2015 AIA Site Preservation Award. These initial seasons represent a rescue program that will expand into a systematic multiyear cooperative project beginning in 2016. The Mycenaean cemetery of Aidonia, discovered through looting followed by excavation in the 1970s and 1980s, consists of 20 multiburial chamber tombs containing material dating to the 15th to early 13th centuries B.C.E. The tombs are remarkable for the high quality of construction and for the precious and numerous contents of the burials, including the so-called Aidonia Treasure, a group of objects that appeared illegally on the antiquities market during the 1990s.

The TAPHOS project was initiated in 2014 due to the resumption and intensification of looting over the last few years. A pilot survey and mapping of the Aidonia hillside revealed not just one but three distinct cemeteries and more than 30 examples of illicit activity. Moving forward, the project goals include the systematic excavation of tombs in areas where archaeological remains are in danger; the use of artifact and ecofact data, as well as newly recovered and legacy material, to better understand the people who used the cemetery; and the provision of future site security through outreach about the destruction of cultural heritage and the engagement of the local population in an interactive visitor center.

The 2015 excavation season focused primarily on the middle cemetery and consisted of the investigation of several areas with signs of illicit digging and two burial features, an unusual bedrock cutting probably associated with the Early Mycenaean period and a collapsed chamber tomb (T100). Although this tomb had been disturbed and partially robbed, three burial deposits containing the remains of several individuals were found undisturbed in layers of soft bedrock collapsed from the tomb ceiling. Pottery from these burials suggests that the tomb was in use from the Late Helladic II period, and one of the secondary burial groups contained a cache of bronze weapons. Altogether, these investigations add new chronological and cultural depth to the cemetery and emphasize the need for continued excavation at a site where the full extent of the looter's disturbance remains unknown.

Eleon 2015: Discovery of a New Early Mycenaean Funerary Structure in Eastern Boeotia

Brendan Burke, University of Victoria, *Bryan E. Burns*, Wellesley College, and *Alexandra Charami*, Ephorate of Antiquities of Boeotia

The Eastern Boeotia Archaeological Project (EBAP) continued its investigation of ancient Eleon near Arma in central Greece with six weeks of excavation and study beginning 1 June 2015. The chief goal of the Greek-Canadian synergasia this year was the full exploration of an Early Mycenaean funerary structure discovered within the multiperiod site. Limited excavation in 2014 identified the inward-leaning wall of an unusual construction that we dubbed the Blue Stone Structure, since its walls are capped with blue-gray limestone blocks. Ceramics of the Middle Helladic and Late Helladic I periods and fragments of human bone recovered in a test pit suggested that this enclosure contained Early Mycenaean burials.

The identity of the Blue Stone Structure as an Early Mycenaean funerary structure is now confirmed by the excavation of four cist graves. The four graves vary in their form and use. One was formed of clay slabs (like another Eleon burial discovered in 2013) containing the intact skeleton of a child, aged 2–4. The three other cist graves were of substantial size, with stone built walls and massive cover stones. Skeletal material from these burials was degraded, but preliminary analysis indicates multiple interments in at least two graves. The only grave goods recovered were one ceramic cup and one spindlewhorl. The Early Mycenaean date of all the graves is confirmed by ceramics from associated deposits and constructions. Most notable are a series of cobblestone platforms built at various levels above the shafts of individual graves. Clay packed above these paved levels formed a mound over the mass of the Blue Stone Structure, suggesting a tumulus of at least 10 m in diameter.

Through subsequent years of activity at Eleon, nothing was ever built over the Blue Stone Structure. In fact, remains of both the Late Bronze Age and the Archaic to Classical periods are found strikingly close to the artificial mound. The large polygonal wall of Eleon, which is the site's most prominent feature, may also be associated with the early burial, acting as a memorialization of classical Eleon's Mycenaean forebears.

Burial Landscape, Spatial Organization, and Societal Changes at the Mycenaean Cemeteries of Eleona and Langada on Kos

Calla McNamee, Malcolm H. Wiener Laboratory for Archaeological Science, American School of Classical Studies at Athens, and *Salvatore Vitale*, Università degli studi di Pisa

The study of burials has long been used to increase our understanding of multiple facets of prehistoric cultures, ranging from interpretations of sociopolitical and economic condition to reconstructions of identity and kinship. In this paper, we present the results of a reexamination of the landscape and stratigraphic data for the cemeteries of Eleona and Langada on Kos to better understand both macro- and micro-scale societal and cultural developments on the island during the Late Bronze Age.

Excavated by Morricone between 1935 and 1941, Eleona and Langada contain a total of 83 tombs, the vast majority of which are categorized as chamber tombs that span in construction and use from Late Helladic (LH) IIB through LH IIIC. In recent years, the material culture from these tombs has been extensively investigated in the context of the Serraglio, Eleona, and Langada Archaeological Project (SELAP). As part of SELAP's ongoing work, this study incorporates our current understanding of change at the cemeteries with modern methods of spatial and geoarchaeological analysis to reconstruct the funerary landscape, investigate the spatial distribution of tombs through time, and reassess the architectural features of the cemetery.

The material culture excavated from the tombs indicates that Kos maintained a rich and flourishing cultural tradition throughout all periods. Our work, however, identifies transitions in the use of the burial landscape. We note a gradual shift in the spatial patterning of tombs, from a general trend of more organized placement in LH IIIA2 and LH IIIB to more dispersed and chaotic placement in LH IIIC. Through time, the possible introduction of other tomb types in addition to chamber tombs and an increase in the variability of tomb shape are also observed, with the greatest diversity occurring during LH IIIC. We relate these patterns to three primary factors: (1) the broad sociopolitical transition from a well-structured society during the Palatial Period to a less organized society during the Postpalatial Period; (2) an increase in economic and sociocultural fluidity during LH IIIC; and (3) the practice of micro-traditions as a reflection of family and identity. In so doing, we emphasize the influence of both structured cultural practice and individual agency in the formation of the funerary landscapes on Kos.

SESSION 5B
Greek Votive Dedications

CHAIR: *Catherine M. Keesling*, Georgetown University

Little Gifts: Dedications at the Sacred Spring in Corinth
Theodora Kopestonsky, University of Tennessee, Knoxville

Corinth, a polis known for being "well-watered" (*IG* I3 1143), encompasses several springs associated with ritual activity dating from the Archaic to Hellenistic periods. While the Peirene Fountain may be the most well-known water source, the Sacred Spring is the most significant example of a water-related cult site in Corinth. Located in the lower Lechaion Valley, the Sacred Spring began as a natural spring but became a sanctuary as early as the eighth century B.C.E. and continued in use into the Hellenistic period. Its position across the road from the Peirene Fountain, just north of the racecourse and south of the Doric Temple, placed it in the heart of the polis and suggests that it may have had an important civic and religious role. During the majority of its existence, the Sacred Spring consisted of a two-level complex including an apsidal temple, a triglyph-metope retaining wall with a secret passage, a spring house, and an open area. It was one of the first major monuments excavated at Corinth and has a long history in the scholarship, but surprisingly the small finds have never been systematically studied. This paper presents an examination of the unpublished small finds from the Sacred Spring, provides fresh information about this intriguing sanctuary, and offers a new perspective on possible ritual activity.

While much of the material from the early excavations is difficult to recover, the small finds from the latter excavations conducted in the late 1960s and early 1970s offer a representative example of the types of dedications from the Sacred Spring. More than 30 types of terracotta figurines, including predominately articulated, seated, and standing females, animals, and horses with riders, along with loomweights, jewelry, styli, and even bronze arrowheads, were excavated from the area of the sanctuary. The majority date to the Classical period. An analysis of these finds in conjunction with the ceramics indicates that the dedicatory tendencies at this sanctuary have a predilection toward feminine objects, which seems to suggest female ritual activity. When compared with other similar assemblages and water-related cult sites, particularly the Caruso Cave, the association of the Sacred Spring to some sort of transitional rituals, possibly female maturation rites, becomes stronger. By understanding the character of the finds from the Sacred Spring, we can speculate more precisely on the use of the sanctuary and the use of water in the sacred sphere.

His and Hers: Gender and Appropriateness in Ancient Greek Dedicatory Practices
Nicole M. Colosimo, Bryn Mawr College

It has long been seen that votive offerings constitute an important group of artifacts, but it is less clear which factors influenced worshipers when they selected a gift for a deity. What was considered an appropriate dedication in ancient Greece? In this paper, I explore this question as it relates to sex and gender roles of both the dedicator and the deity. In modern scholarship, the idea that certain items were "appropriate" is pervasive and often applied to the types of dedications given by men and women. Such ideas find their roots in textual sources, such as *The Palatine Anthology*, which emphasized the perceived realms of men and women in relation to social roles and dedicatory practices. Thus, women are associated with dedications of garments, because of their connection to the production of clothing, and items like jewelry. Men, in contrast, are often presented as dedicators of arms and armor, since they carried them into battle. Such associations are then projected into the divine sphere: the clothing inventories from the Sanctuary of Artemis at Brauron and the offerings of arms and armor in sanctuaries, such as Isthmia and Olympia, have been used to justify a gendered separation of dedications.

In this paper, archaeological, textual, and epigraphical sources dating to the Classical and Hellenistic periods are reconsidered to determine whether sex and gender indeed played a significant role when selecting offerings. As dedications rarely carry inscriptions identifying the dedicator, the analysis relies mostly on the contents of various sanctuary assemblages. The textual evidence referring to dedicatory practices spans numerous genres, from the historical works of Herodotus to the comedies of Aristophanes and the epigrams of *The Palatine Anthology*, while relevant epigraphical material includes temple inventories, decrees, and dedicatory inscriptions.

The evidence provided by these sources indicates that a polarity of dedications along gender lines, mortal or immortal, is too simplistic. While there may have been more men dedicating armor and women dedicating clothing or jewelry, the fact that these gifts were also offered by the opposite gender cannot be overemphasized and calls for a more nuanced approach. It is suggested that these excep tions provide an opportunity to reconceptualize appropriateness in ancient Greek dedicatory practices.

The Parthenon Frieze as a Representation of Beneficiaries
Toshihiro Osada, University of Tsukuba

The scenes of the Parthenon frieze can be summarized as depicting a festival procession moving toward seated gods. Compositionally as well as thematically the frieze belongs to the category of votive relief. This paper explores the interpretive possibility that, like votive reliefs, the design of the Parthenon frieze was intended to depict the beneficiaries of divine protection as a reciprocal reward for the building of the Parthenon temple.

The practice of dedicating votive reliefs began at the end of the sixth century, and the composition of these reliefs typically included the following features: (1) god(s) and worshipers (usually family, relatives, or officials) represented facing each other; (2) framing of the scene by a male servant, *kanephoros*, with a victim at the head of the procession and a female servant, *kistephoros*, at the rear, giving clear definition of the worshipers in number, sex and age; (3) the representation of the worshipers as smaller than the god(s), and the servants still smaller.

Inscriptions were generally brief, and the typical formula, "X dedicates Y (to a god)" often referred only to a (few) name(s) as dedicator. The relief itself thus functioned as a visual display of the beneficiaries of divine grace who were not mentioned in the inscription. The primary intention of the design of the monument must therefore have been the specification of worshipers, especially when these worshipers were numerous and unidentified.

The same religious mentality should be inferred in the reading of the Parthenon frieze. It would seem that the design of the frieze was intended not as a picturesque or "generic" representation of the festival procession, as has often been supposed in previous studies, but as a display of the rightful beneficiaries of divine protection in return for, in this case, the building of the Parthenon. The actual Panathenaic procession included numerous and diverse people: citizens, both from the elite and nonelite classes, noncitizens, such as females and metics, Athenian overseas colonists, and delegations of the allied cities. Some iconographical incongruities between the frieze and the actual procession, such as the male *hydriaphoroi* in the frieze, suggest that citizens and their families were specified as the only beneficiaries of divine protection in the frieze, and metics were excluded. That 12 Olympian gods, not the goddess Athena alone, were represented on the frieze can also be explained by votive culture, in which deities were often represented with their family members.

Those Meddling Kids: Child Statuary and the *Oikos* Mentality in the Late Classical and Hellenistic Age

Alyssa A.S. Friedman, University of Colorado, Boulder

During the fourth century B.C.E. there was a noticeable shift in sanctuary dedications to include sculptures of children, from infancy to adolescence. Though children had been represented in art of earlier periods, this was the first known instance of a trend in commissioning life-sized sculptures of children and dedicating them in religious sanctuaries. This trend is significant in that it indicates that children became a subject worthy of representation in their own right, and in an expensive medium, further underlining their importance. The children are neither uniform nor generic but are sculpted in a range of stages of physical development and with a range of postures and attributes. Olympia Bobou, Lesley Beaumont, and others have demonstrated that the sculptures can be separated into distinct developmental categories, which can then be related to a social system of maturity between childhood, adolescence, and adulthood and to new votive habits comprising offering sculptures of children in gratitude after successful childbirth and protection for the child thereafter.

I argue that this new trend of dedicating child statuary at sanctuaries can be linked to the growing tension between *oikos* and polis and age-transition rituals during the fourth century B.C.E. The experience of the individual and the image of the family as a harmonious social unit became an important focus, which clearly permeated contemporary cultural expression. Funerary customs, epigraphy, art, philosophy, and literature of the fourth century B.C.E. all point toward the inward focus of Greek individuals. Specifically, grave stelae from Athenian funerary contexts and epigraphic evidence of honorific decrees point toward the solidarity of the *oikos* in the face of the polis and the rise of the individual through the fourth century B.C.E. The tension between *oikos* and polis is underlined further by the greater significance of the family unit in sanctuaries during the Hellenistic period, represented by child statuary, and thus the greater importance of the *oikos* in comparison with the polis. In effect, the commissioning and subsequent dedication of child statuary was tied to earlier Late Classical traditions to celebrate important family events, such as age transitions and maturation, which reflected the growing importance of the *oikos* and diminishing focus on the polis.

SESSION 5C: Workshop
Navigating the Publication Process

MODERATORS: *Maryl B. Gensheimer*, University of Maryland, and *Simeon D. Ehrlich*, Stanford University

Workshop Overview Statement

Graduate students and early career scholars are acutely aware of the importance of having their work published, yet little if any attention is given in formal settings to the process of publication. While the goal remains clear, the path to achieving it is obscured, elucidated only in part by anecdotal accounts from one's colleagues.

Horror stories of obstacles encountered on the way to publication leave one intimidated rather than confident. Unawareness of the resources available to an author and of different avenues of publication can lead to hesitancy or missteps. There is a need for a forum in which to provide students and early career scholars with an overview of the process of submission, revision, and publication and with insights from those involved in the process.

This workshop seeks to address that need by bringing together editors, reviewers, and authors to explain various aspects of the path to publication. Publications of various sorts, whether monographs or journal articles, will be discussed. Shorter pieces such as conference proceedings, handbook chapters, and encyclopedia entries will receive attention. Panelists will advise on best practices for adapting a dissertation into a monograph, drafting a book proposal, and choosing a suitable journal for submission. They will explain what goes on during the review process, where to look for publication subvention grants, and how to secure permissions and copyrights for images.

The panelists—published scholars, editors of journals, and representatives of presses and funding agencies—will contribute to a holistic understanding of the publication process. Recent and future Ph.D.s will benefit from hearing the experiences of those who have been in their position, as well as the perspectives of those whom they would not encounter in a traditional academic setting. A fuller understanding of the steps involved, the pitfalls to avoid, and the challenges to be encountered will build confidence and allow authors to share their work with the scholarly community more readily. Students and junior faculty, whether on the market, approaching it, or settling into a new job, all know the importance of publication to their careers. All stand to benefit from the insights offered regarding the path to publication.

PANELISTS: *Susan E. Alcock*, University of Michigan, *Jack L. Davis*, University of Cincinnati, *Sheila Dillon*, Duke University, *Susan Lupack*, American School of Classical Studies at Athens, *Sarah Pirovitz*, Oxford University Press, and *Jennifer Trimble*, Stanford University

SESSION 5D
Aegean Survey

CHAIR: *Alex R. Knodell*, Carleton College

Prehistoric Finds from the Survey of the Katsaronio Plain, Southern Euboea, Greece: A Preliminary Assessment
Zarko Tankosic, Indiana University, and *Katerina Psoma*, University of Illinois at Chicago

We present here the preliminary assessment of the results of four years of fieldwork (2012–2015) conducted in southern Euboea (the Karystia) by members of the Norwegian Archaeological Survey in the Karystia (NASK) project. In the course of the project, NASK discovered more than a 100 previously unknown archaeological sites. Of those, there are at least 24 that are either purely prehistoric or have a prehistoric component. The sites present considerable diversity, ranging from scatters consisting of a handful of pottery and/or lithics to sites with hundreds and, in some cases, even thousands of artifacts scattered over substantial areas. The prehistoric assemblages from the Katsaronio are characterized by large numbers of lithics, overwhelmingly obsidian, with some truly exceptional concentrations in terms of both quantity and quality. The ceramics, which provide the bases for most of our chronological assessments, can be dated to the Final Neolithic and Early Bronze phases. Evidence for prehistoric metallurgy was also found. The location of these findspots indicates the presence of a thriving community of people in this part of the Karystia during a part of Aegean prehistory, offering also clues on how the members of that community culturally structured and used the landscape they inhabited. Finally, we present a preliminary interpretation of the patterning of the material culture in the Katsaronio Plain and its wider socioeconomic implications.

The Thorikos Intrasite Survey: A Glimpse from the Top

Roald Docter, Ghent University, *Floris van den Eijnde*, Utrecht University, *Margarita Nazou*, Ghent University, *Andrea Perugini*, Ghent University, *Amber Brüsewitz*, Ghent University, *Lieven Verdonck*, Ghent University, *Sophie Mortier*, Ghent University, *Winfred van de Put*, Netherlands Institute in Athens, *Cornelis Stal*, Ghent University, *Alain De Wulf*, Ghent University, *Kim Van Liefferinge*, Ghent University, *Thomas Pieters*, Ghent University, *Koen Van Gelder*, Ghent University, *Guy Dierkens*, Ghent University, *Alexandra Alexandridou*, Université Libre de Bruxelles, *Simon Claeys*, Ghent University, and *Lilian Karali*, National and Kapodistrian University of Athens

This paper presents the preliminary results of an intensive survey that took place on the southern half of the Velatouri Hill between 2012 and 2015. As a collaborative endeavor of Ghent and Utrecht Universities, it neatly supplements the Belgian Thorikos Archaeological Project that started in 1963. During the study campaign of 2015, we inventoried all finds from the top of the Velatouri, an area of some 30,000 m² (7.5 acres). This allowed us to detail and partly rewrite the occupational narrative of this part of Thorikos.

The principal aim of the intrasite survey has been to tie together all dispersed excavation zones of the last half-century and to bring them into one occupational narrative. The choice for the southern slopes of the Velatouri was based on the fact that almost all fieldwork had been taking place here and the fact that, like many coastal and insular sites in Greece, this would have offered the best settlement conditions, well protected against the northern winds.

The survey methodology, developed in close collaboration with John Bintliff (Leiden), starts from the existing grid of 50 x 50 m (macro) squares, materialized on the ground with concrete poles. These were further subdivided in 25 x 25 m squares, forming the basic collection units. Each unit was walked for 20 minutes by four students, "hovering" from the corners to the square's center, picking up all artifacts (pottery, lithics, grinding stones, metals, litharge, etc.) as well as seashells and pebbles. No selection was made in the field; all finds were washed, bagged, and studied.

The top of the Velatouri has long been known for the Middle Helladic/Late Helladic and Late Helladic monumental graves on its northern saddle and northeastern edge, first excavated by Valerios Stais. The main hitherto-known periods on the southern summit had been represented by sparse Final Neolithic/Early Helladic finds, Middle Helladic architecture, some Late Helladic pottery, Protogeometric to Early Archaic pottery and architecture, and archaic/classical pottery and evidence of ancestor cults related to the Bronze Age graves.

The study of the survey finds showed a stronger presence of Final Neolithic and Early Helladic finds next to the previously known phases, most likely associated with the earliest settlement. Mycenaean, Daedalic, and archaic terracotta fragments, as well as specific seashells, suggest a multiperiod ritual activity in the area. In Attic perspective, the seventh-century B.C.E. domestic evidence is important. The fourth century B.C.E., otherwise well represented in Thorikos, seems to be absent from the survey finds.

The 2015 Mazi Archaeological Project: A Report on the Second Field Season

Alex R. Knodell, Carleton College, *Sylvian Fachard*, University of Geneva, and *Kalliopi Papangeli*, Ephorate of Antiquities of West Attika, Piraeus, and the Islands

The second field season of the Mazi Archaeological Project (MAP) was a continuation and substantial expansion of regional survey activities that began in 2014 as a collaboration between the Ephorate of Antiquities of West Attika, Piraeus, and the Islands and the Swiss School of Archaeology in Greece. The focus of the project is the Mazi Plain: a small, well-watered agricultural basin in the Kithairon and Pateras mountain ranges. Located in the oft-contested borderlands on the fringes of Attica, Boeotia, and the Megarid, the study area is also situated at a critical crossroads on the main land route between Eleusis and Thebes, which connects Attica and Boeotia directly; it also links central Greece to the Isthmus and the Peloponnese. Stemming from these geographical factors and the rich history of borderlands and border studies, MAP is a diachronic regional survey that aims to address questions of territoriality, regionality, and connectivity in the long term.

In June and July of 2015, an international team carried out intensive and extensive pedestrian archaeological survey, as well as systematic programs of architectural photogrammetry, multispectral satellite imagery analysis and ground-truthing, aerial photography, and geomorphological studies. In contrast to the 2014 season, in which a small team worked primarily in a single area in the vicinity of ancient Oinoe and the Mazi Tower, the 2015 season expanded to focus efforts in three different areas: (1) the Kouloumbi Valley, immediately south of the Mazi Plain proper; (2) the northeast quadrant of the survey area, in the environs of the monastery of Osios Meletios; and (3) at and around the fortress and settlement of ancient Eleutherai. The side-by-side survey in 2015 covered some 6 km^2 of territory in 1,490 survey units, documenting some 216 archaeological features (the coverage in 2014 was just under 2 km^2). Several new discoveries came to light, and various previously known sites received for the first time systematic and thorough documentation. Highlights include the discovery of a large prehistoric site and two substantial settlements of the Byzantine period, the location of Pausanias' "Cave of Antiope," and substantial efforts at Eleutherai to document the fortress and settlement through DGPS mapping, photogrammetry, and cleaning at the Temple of Dionysos Eleuthereus. This paper discusses these aspects of the project in the context of our broader results and provides a set of preliminary interpretations concerning the long-term settlement pattern and history of the Mazi Plain.

The Western Argolid Regional Project: Results of the 2015 Season
Sarah James, University of Colorado, Boulder, *Dimitri Nakassis*, University of Toronto, and *Scott Gallimore*, Wilfrid Laurier University

The summer of 2015 was the second of three planned field seasons for the Western Argolid Regional Project. This interdisciplinary project, carried out under the auspices of the Canadian Institute in Greece, is centered on an intensive diachronic archaeological survey of the upper valleys of the Inachos River to the north and west of Argos. Our survey seeks to investigate the nature of the relationships between the communities in and around the western Argolid. This is a significant issue, since although Argos is a major center in virtually all periods of Greek history, its regional context and its connection to other cities in southern Greece is poorly understood.

In 2015, the survey worked in a broad strip of rugged territory approximately 10 km northwest of Argos, just as the Inachos River valley opens up into the Argive Plain. This region, near the modern villages of Schinochori and Malandreni, is the likeliest location of ancient Lyrkcia, an Argive settlement that Pausanias (2.25.4–5) found abandoned along the northern thoroughfare to Mantineia.

In the course of a six-week field season, the project surveyed an area of 6.8 km² at an extremely high level of intensity: survey units averaged 0.26 ha in size. The survey area is busy with most of the major periods typically identified by pedestrian surveys, with peaks in the Mycenaean, Medieval, early modern, and especially the Classical to Hellenistic periods; in contrast to the usual pattern in the Peloponnese, however, Late Roman is not ubiquitous. It is surprising, given the proximity of the 2015 survey area to Argos, that artifact densities were low (on average, 53 artifacts per hectare), less than half of the densities recorded in the 2014 field season in the vicinity of ancient Orneai (109 artifacts per hectare). This can be considered the result of the combination of two factors: first, extremely low "off-site" densities, and second, the presence of a handful of sites, none of which was very large or high density. Nevertheless, these sites make a significant contribution to our understanding of the ancient to early modern networks connecting the communities of the Argolid, which differ considerably from those in use today.

SESSION 5E
Greek and Latin Epigraphy

CHAIR: *John P. Bodel*, Brown University

Keeping Track of Time on Late Hellenistic Cyprus: A New Parapegma from Yeronisos
Ilaria Bultrighini, University College London, and *Joan Breton Connelly*, New York University

The small island of Yeronisos ("Holy Island") lies just off Cape Drepanon on the western coast of Cyprus, 18 km north of Paphos. Work undertaken by New York University's Yeronisos Island Expedition since 1990 has established the site as an important pilgrimage destination during the first century B.C.E., the final phase of Ptolemaic rule on Cyprus. The sanctuary site comprises a broad complex of rooms and courtyards functioning as a center of food preparation and consumption for those who traveled out to worship Apollo.

In 1992, a small (6.4 x 5.4 cm), fragmentary limestone plaque was unearthed within the main building complex. It is inscribed with the Greek ordinal numerals from third to fifth, listed on three consecutive lines. To the left of each of these three words is a hole. From the same area, an additional limestone fragment, possibly related to the previous one, preserves the Greek cardinal number nine. This paper presents the first comprehensive study of these epigraphic documents from Yeronisos, which we interpret as fragments of ancient calendrical devices known as *parapegmata*. These instruments (attested in different shapes and materials in Greek and Roman contexts) were used to keep track of various cyclical phenomena, including days of the month and week, zodiac signs, and astronomical events. By moving a peg or pegs from one hole to the next each day, the user of the device kept track of the involved cycle of time. All Greek *parapegmata* known so far—both epigraphic and literary—are either astronomical or astrometeorological. They either provide information about astronomical events alone or correlate astronomical phenomena with meteorological conditions—for example, facilitating weather forecasts. Surviving fragments of Greek *parapegmata* are generally large in scale, suggesting that they were displayed in public spaces. By contrast, the small size of the Yeronisos *parapegma* suggests private use by an individual who wished to keep track of the days of the month. Despite its fragmentary state, the Yeronisos *parapegma* is a unique and meaningful discovery that gives an intimate glimpse of life on Hellenistic Yeronisos and that expands our understanding of ancient Greek calendrical devices.

Curse Tablets and Wells in Private Houses in Antioch
Alexander Hollmann, University of Washington

At some point in the third or fourth century C.E., someone slipped a number of lead curse tablets into a well in the House of the Calendar. Depositing curse tablets in wells and cisterns is well known. But the choice of a well in a private house is a phenomenon that does not seem to have received attention and needs explanation. I suggest some reasons for this phenomenon, considering also tablets found in the House of Gê and the Seasons in nearby Daphne. I investigate the way in which some of the tablets refer to their location in the well and harness this in their spell.

Located in a courtyard in the interior of the house, next to the triclinium, the well would have been hard to access for an outsider. The situation is quite different from the wells in the Athenian Agora, for example, which were accessible to everyone and which contained caches of curse tablets directed against private individuals. Antioch had wells and fountains in public places: why go to the trouble of sneaking into a private house or the expense of bribing one of the servants? Deposition of a curse tablet in a well is generally assumed to be effective because the water was believed to act as a conduit to the underworld and the chthonic daimones needed to carry out the wishes of the petitioner. In the case of the tablets from the House of the Calendar and the House of Gê and the Seasons, this practice is combined with placement of the tablet as close as possible to the victim, perhaps in his or her house.

A well or cistern in a courtyard that contains a nymphaeum is a typical feature of Antiochene houses, and Dobbins has pointed out the close relationship between these spaces and the triclinium with its rich mosaic floors. He draws attention to the sightlines that link this area to important parts of the house. Perhaps the interconnectedness of these sightlines is precisely what magical practitioners counted on when they insinuated their tablets into the houses of Antioch and dropped them in the wells. I suggest that the individuals named in the tablets were closely associated with the house in whose wells they were found and in the case of the House of Gê and the Seasons may allow us to identify the owner.

Bilingualism and Monumentalization in Roman Anatolia
Andrea F. Gatzke, State University of New York at New Paltz

Monuments have long played a central role in our understanding of the geographical and ideological topography of ancient cities. Monumentalization allowed cities, groups, and individuals to display their wealth and advertise their generosity to resident and visiting populations. Various scholars have shown that monuments shape the public perception of benefactors and recipients in various ways, including choices in architecture, wording of the inscriptions, placement within the larger urban context, and inclusion of art and statuary on the monuments.

In spite of this, little attention has been paid to the language choice in monumental inscriptions. But as Laurence and Sears wrote (*Written Space in the Latin West, 200 B.C.–A.D. 300* [London 2013] 2), "language is needed and writing is a necessity for public space in the Roman Empire"; it is central to our understanding of monumentality. Some scholars have considered how language contributes to a monument's ideological presence and the city's topography, but there has been little focus on the question of bilingualism as a key tool for expressing one's public image. The choice to include a multilanguage text—whether a perfect or partial translation or even a remarkably different text—reflects an acknowledgement of a diverse audience with unique interests and sympathies. The existence of bilingualism in both monumental and private inscriptions suggests that the inclusion of a second language was not simply a show of the benefactor's status but also a reflection of the benefactor's assumptions about the potential audience.

In this paper, I use bilingual monumental inscriptions from various cities throughout Roman Anatolia to examine what these texts, and the language choices in them, reveal to us about how the benefactors expressed their public and civic identities. I then consider the varying use of Latin and Greek as an indicator of the audiences to whom benefactors wished their monuments to appeal. I begin with a focus on Ephesus, whose bilinguals have dominated the discussion on monumental language in Anatolia, and then examine other cities throughout Anatolia in order to understand monumental bilingualism on a broader scale. My paper argues that language differentiation became a way for emperors and prominent individuals to rewrite the landscape of the older Greek and Anatolian cities in a way that was in line with Roman imperial policy, while simultaneously connecting themselves to the local populations on whose support they relied for their own success.

How to Praise the Emperor: Graffiti Evidence for a Roman Acclamatory Formula
Bryan Brinkman, Brown University

Popular acclamation—the collective vocalization from crowds—was a seemingly widespread phenomenon in the Roman empire. One use of these acclamations was to offer praise to individuals, including the Roman emperor. While certain literary sources comment on the frequency of these praising acclamations (e.g., Tac., *Hist.* 1.32, 1.90), the actual words used in the vocalizations are less certain (especially prior to late antiquity). In this paper, I offer a reading of one graffito from Pompeii (*CIL* 4 1118; *CLE* 952) and suggest how, when placed in its social and epigraphic context, the text illuminates our understanding of a particular acclamatory formula.

CIL 4 1118 reads "I have now taught the stones to speak those pleasing words: 'Well wishes to Claudius Nero'" (Iam docui [si]lices verba [benign]a loqui/Claudio Nero feli[c]it[e]r). I argue that this graffito can be viewed as a commentary on the practice of popular acclamation and provides insight concerning the common use of what I call the "*feliciter* formula" (*feliciter* + name in the dative; "good fortune to . . . "). There are a number of graffiti from Pompeii that contain the *feliciter* formula, including in reference to Nero (e.g., Iudici(i)s Augusti p(atris) p(atriae) et Poppaeae Aug(ustae) feliciter [*CIL* 4 3726]). However, *CIL* 4 1118 makes explicit the use the formula in oral contexts, indicating the connection with popular acclamation. This connection is made clear when I place this graffito alongside a select few literary passages from Petronius (*Sat.* 60.7) and Phaedrus (5.1.4) that together point toward the popular uses of this formula in acclamation. I conclude by discussing the importance of these *feliciter* acclamations within the larger context of the communication of the imperial ideal of *felicitas* ("good fortune")—the core concept at the root of *feliciter*.

SESSION 5F
Eastern Mediterranean Interaction

CHAIR: *Eric H. Cline*, The George Washington University

Political Cuisines: The Aegean-West Anatolian Interface Through the Lens of Late Prehistoric Drinking Practices
Jess Whalen, Cosumnes River College

The iconic two-handled *depas amphikypellon* tankard is an indelible symbol of the elite culture emerging in western Anatolia during the Early Bronze Age (EB) II–III (ca. 2650–2000 B.C.E.). Its circulation in the west, however, does not support widespread and sudden coalescence. A closer look at ware and finishing characteristics reveals that the adoption of the depas and related shapes occurred over a longer period than is typically described. The EB II–III "Complex" exhibits regional variation, and coalescence occurs only only at the end of a long period of adoption. Elite culture, then, is not swift and universal but emerges gradually along lines of existing economic and cultural traditions.

This paper presents key differences in the construction and finishing of EB II–III Complex shapes and proposes a chronological time frame for their adoption in different areas of the west. Shapes includes the *depas amphikypellon* as well as vessels appropriate for displaying and consuming large quantities of food. Regional variation across Complex shapes clarifies the nature of interaction with the neighboring Cyclades as well as the northeast Aegean. This variation may constitute subregions of Aegean and Cycladic culture in western Anatolia or at least areas of longstanding cultural integration.

The different ways that drinking vessels were constructed and handled constitute a visual manifestation of cultural identity through drink. Vessel production mirrors developments in cooking and metallurgy, suggesting that new technology tempered both household commensality and large-scale feasting practices. Clarifying the chronology of drinking vessels in the west allows a tentative reconstruction of cultural identity along the western Anatolian coast. This suggests areas of economic integration and technological exchange. Taken together, these indices outline a new model for the emergence of prestige markers and social complexity during the period.

The Serraglio, Eleona, and Langada Archaeological Project (SELAP): Report on the 2012 to 2015 Study Seasons
Salvatore Vitale, Università degli Studi di Pisa, *Toula Marketou*, 22nd Ephorate of Prehistoric and Classical Antiquities, *Nicholas G. Blackwell*, North Carolina State University, *Ioannis Iliopoulos*, University of Patras, *Calla McNamee*, Wiener Laboratory, American School of Classical Studies at Athens, *Jerolyn Morrison*, University of Leicester, and *Kalliopi-Sofia Passa*, University of Patras

This paper presents the results of the 2012 to 2015 seasons of the Serraglio, Eleona, and Langada Archaeological Project (SELAP), a research endeavor carried out since 2009 on Kos under the auspices of the Italian Archaeological School at Athens in close collaboration with the Greek Archaeological Service. SELAP is based on the study of the materials and the sites discovered by Luigi Morricone on Kos between 1935 and 1946, with the aim of providing new information on the phases from the Final Neolithic to the Late Protogeometric period.

During the 2012 to 2015 seasons, SELAP's research goals were examined through a multidisciplinary approach, which incorporated the contextual study of the archaeological materials, the landscape and spatial analysis of the sites of the Asklupis, the "Serraglio," Eleona, and Langada, and the geological prospection for the identification of ancient clay and stone sources.

The analysis of the landscape contributed to a better understanding of settlement patterns, particularly the shift from protected inland locations to the coastal site of the "Serraglio" during the Early Bronze Age 3. Through collaboration with the Ephorate, the results of recent Greek excavations and Morricone's previous excavations were combined to produce a definitive chronological sequence at the Serraglio from the end of the Early Bronze Age to the Late Protogeometric period. The study of the pottery shed new light on some controversial phases of the Koan prehistory, such as the Late Bronze Age to the Early Iron Age transition. The analysis of the Late Bronze Age finds produced detailed information on cultural developments on the island, refining our understanding of the complex interplay between indigenous, Minoan, and Mycenaean traditions. The investigation of the socioeconomic trajectories of the settlement of the Serraglio indicated that Kos had a prominent role in the political scenario of the southeast Aegean during Late Helladic (LH) IIIB, suggesting that the island may have played an important role in the so-called Ahhijawa kingdom. The uneven distribution of jewelry, weapons, and bronze tools between the Mycenaean cemeteries of Eleona and Langada provided evidence for a status distinction, with the latter cemetery including the wealthier individuals of the community. Finally, the study of the human bones from these two sites revealed that cremation was more common than previously thought and began as early as LH IIIA2–IIIB. Thus Kos may have played a key role in the spread of this particular rite from Anatolia to the western Aegean.

Results of the 2015 Excavation Season at Tel Kabri, Israel

Eric H. Cline, The George Washington University, *Assaf Yasur-Landau*, University of Haifa, and *Andrew J. Koh*, Brandeis University

The 2015 excavations at Tel Kabri, the capital of a Middle Bronze Age Canaanite kingdom located in the western Galilee region of modern Israel, lasted from 14 June to 9 July 2015. Highlights of the season included the discovery of three more storage rooms containing a minimum of 70 jars, connected to the original "wine cellar" (Room 2440) discovered in 2013. Combining these with the discoveries of the 2013 season, we can now confidently report that we have located a storage complex belonging to the palace, with at least 110 large restorable jars still in situ within four storage rooms. Organic residue analysis (ORA) is currently being conducted on each jar to determine the contents.

The discovery of these three additional storerooms filled with a large quantity of storage vessels may prove to be an important cornerstone in our understanding of the Middle Bronze Age palace and its operation at Tel Kabri. The complex was planned and constructed as one unit during phase DW III, the last phase of the palace, dating to the Middle Bronze II period, very likely within the 17th century B.C.E. It was also destroyed during the same period, collapsing on top of the full contingency of storage vessels. The distinct possibility that the storage complex was preceded in time by a series of earlier rooms dating to phase DW IV was also raised this season and should be examined in future seasons.

C-PEPL: Renewed Excavations at Pyla-*Kokkinokremos* (Cyprus). Preliminary Results of the 2014–2015 Campaigns

Simon Jusseret, University of Texas at Austin, *Joachim Bretschneider*, KU Leuven, *Jan Driessen*, Université catholique de Louvain, and *Athanasia Kanta*, Mediterranean Archaeological Society

Since its discovery by P. Dikaios in the early 1950s, the settlement of Pyla-*Kokkinokremos* (southeast Cyprus) has occupied a prominent position in the debates surrounding the "collapse" of eastern Mediterranean societies ca. 1200 B.C.E. Constructed ex nihilo on a low coastal plateau and occupied for no more than a few decades between ca. 1230 and 1180 B.C.E. (Late Cypriot IIC–IIIA), the settlement history of Kokkinokremos contrasts sharply with those of its prestigious neighbors in the Larnaca Bay, Kition and Hala Sultan Tekke. Although the identity of the settlers that once built and occupied Kokkinokremos remains subject to debate, recent explorations by V. Karageorghis and A. Kanta (2010–2011) have increasingly emphasized the inadequacy of earlier diffusionist models (colony of Aegean migrants, Sea Peoples' settlement).

To clarify the settlement structure and elucidate the social and environmental circumstances surrounding the foundation and subsequent planned abandonment of the site, a new collaborative project was initiated in 2014 (C-PEPL—Cyprus-Pyla Excavation Project Louvain) between the universities of Louvain and Leuven (Université catholique de Louvain, KU Leuven) and the Mediterranean Archaeological Society. The first two field campaigns of the project (2014–2015), centered on previously unexplored sectors of Kokkinokremos, provided important new clues as to the organization of the settlement, including the extensive occupation of the plateau (in all probability covering its entire surface of ca. 7 ha), as well as the widespread character of local and foreign material products. Similarly, the casemate architecture identified by V. Karageorghis and A. Kanta on the eastern and western edges of Kokkinokremos appears repeated in the southern and northern sectors of the plateau. However, discovery and excavation of a number of rock-cut shafts previously interpreted as cisterns has shown that at least some of these structures may have served as underground storage systems. Finally, evidence for metalworking activities in the northeastern sector of the plateau could point to a degree of functional specialization between various sectors of Kokkinokremos.

Cypriot Evidence in the Early Iron Age Aegean: An Alternative View from the Cyclades
Giorgos Bourogiannis, Museums of World Culture

The discussion of Cypro-Aegean interaction during the Early Iron Age usually focuses on certain areas of the Aegean where Cypriot evidence is more abundant—namely, Crete, Euboea, and the Dodecanese. However, recent research has considerably enhanced our knowledge of contacts between the Aegean and East. The combination of new fieldwork and publications has shown that the impact of Cyprus during the Early Iron Age was actually greater than initially thought and that it had encompassed a larger part of the Aegean world.

Situated at the center of the Aegean Sea, the Cyclades display some strong, albeit not always direct, evidence of contacts with Cyprus, while Cypriot influence has recently been traced in many groups of material from the Cycladic Islands. This paper investigates the Cypriot and Cypriot-related evidence that was found in the Cyclades during the Geometric period. It also investigates how Cypriot evidence develops after the seventh century B.C.E., during the earliest part of the Archaic period. Recent excavations and publications are considered, while comparisons with other parts of the Aegean world are made, to better assess the Cycladic participation in the Cypro-Aegean interaction. The discussion focuses on the islands of Naxos, Delos, Mykonos, and Thera, where the majority of this evidence was produced.

SESSION 5G
Funerary Iconography

CHAIR: *Aileen Ajootian*, University of Mississippi

A New Insight into the *Dexiosis*: Analysis of Familial Relationships on Athenian Gravestones of the Fifth and Fourth Centuries B.C.E.
Hugh P. Thomas, University of Sydney, Australia

Around the 430s B.C.E., grave stelai were reincorporated into Athenian funerary rituals after a lacuna of 70 years. These sculptures primarily depicted scenes of the family unit interacting. The most common gesture performed was the *dexiosis*, or handshake motif, which was incorporated in well over half of the extant gravestones. The gesture consists of two figures shaking hands, with either both individuals standing or one seated. The frequency of its depiction has led to the *dexiosis* being a subject of great interest and debate, albeit one fraught with difficulty. A gravestone is a monument to the memory of the deceased and as such, their age, status, and relationships are represented in an idealized way. Questions have revolved around the theoretical location of this union and whether the scene represents a mythical meeting of figures both alive and dead, or simply a physical representation of an emotional relationship. One important aspect of the gesture that has frequently been overlooked is familial relationships. Although it is often mentioned that the *dexiosis* was a way of linking family members, even a brief review of current literature on Attic tombstones demonstrates that the identification of familial relationships is based on interpreting the gender and age of the figures taking part.

Through a detailed analysis of the seated version of the gesture, along with a study of the related inscriptional evidence found on the tombstones, this paper demonstrates that the position of family members was not ambiguous but highly structured, with specific iconographic conventions adhered to by Athenian sculptors. This allows for the identification of family members via their position in the scene rather than through other defining features, such as dress and age. The controlled composition of the scene is representative of the internal domestic hierarchy of the Greek family unit. In turn, the steadfast employment of this standard illuminates a small percentage of gravestones that challenge this iconographic trend, highlighting issues such as Athenian funerary practice, the reuse of tombstones, and modern forgeries.

Local History, Lasting Legacy: The "Alexander" Sarcophagus in Context
Rachel Spradley, Southern Methodist University

This paper reinterprets the "Alexander" Sarcophagus within its local context and offers new insight into the aims of its patron, Abdalonymos of Sidon. Named for the portrait of Alexander the Great included in its relief program, the Sarcophagus is often held up among the great monuments of Early Hellenistic Greek art and as an example of the conqueror's spread of Greek culture to the east. This characterization, however, renders several features of the sarcophagus anomalous, particularly the presence of Persian iconography and the ambivalent portrayal of Greek and Persian figures. In this paper, I demonstrate that a close consideration of local history as well as the object's archaeological context—the royal necropolis at Sidon—dissolves these apparent paradoxes. I employ Chris Gosden's theory of the shared cultural milieu, situating Abdalonymos as part of a local elite with a centuries-long tradition of artistic exchange while also addressing his unique political concerns as a king appointed by Alexander (*Archaeology and Colonialism* [Cambridge 2004]).

Though certainly engaged with Greek artistic traditions, this monument also continues a long-standing local tradition in its Phoenician context, as evidenced by the 16 other sarcophagi excavated from the same tomb complex. The reliefs reflect developments in Greek artistic style that occurred outside Greece and began long before Alexander's conquests. Likely portraits of Abdalonymos indicate that he and other Phoenician elites had adopted Persian dress during the centuries of Achaemenid rule that preceded Alexander's rise. Of the four primary relief panels, two battle scenes acknowledge the historic enmity between Greeks and Persians—though both are portrayed here showing valor and strength—while two hunt scenes show them in cooperation. The sarcophagus' placement within the tomb chamber, rarely considered previously, notably privileges the battle scenes. Here Alexander and Abdalonymos are directly paralleled, each bearing down on an opponent in a traditional Late Classical composition. This iconography, however, also conveys the sentiment that there is no true winner in war. Through these reliefs, therefore, I suggest that the king carefully draws power from both sides, now united by Alexander on a grand scale and Abdalonymos on a local one. I argue that through the form and figural program of his sarcophagus, Abdalonymos asserts his legitimacy not only as successor to Alexander but also as heir to a local royal tradition and an equally illustrious heritage from the region's Persian past, thus defining his legacy in distinctly local terms.

The Rape of Persephone and the Death of Soteris: A Case of Two Fresco Fragments and a Funerary Epitaph from a Roman *Columbarium*
Adam Tabeling, Johns Hopkins University

A funerary epitaph, written in elegiac couplet, was dedicated by a grieving mother to her young daughter Soteris, who tragically passed away at the age of five. The epitaph was discovered in a *columbarium* on the Via Salaria in Rome, along with two fresco fragments that decorated Soteris' tomb. One fragment depicts Dis Pater, the god of the underworld, abducting Persephone, while the other depicts Persephone's mother, the goddess Ceres, who stands in an open field with a wild pig at her side. In his version of the Rape of Persephone, the poet Ovid recounts that when Ceres reached the field from which Persephone was abducted, pigs muddled Persephone's footprints and Ceres was unable to trace her path, therefore losing custody of her daughter to Dis Pater. Thus, the two fresco fragments belong together and make up a larger Rape of Persephone scene, one that I argue is the mythological analogue of Soteris' epitaph. Just as Ceres lost her daughter Persephone to Dis Pater, so, too, did Soteris' mother lose her young daughter to the god of death.

The Power of Hands: Decoding Gestures on the Roman Provincial Tombstones in Noricum and Pannonia
Tatiana Ivleva, Newcastle University

The practice of commemoration in Rome and the western Roman provinces, the performance of funerary customs, ritual behavior, and burial remains are well-studied topics. In contrast, depictions of the hands of the deceased have rarely received detailed attention from scholars studying the Roman provinces. Yet in Roman provincial funerary art one can encounter a variety of gestures showing the interactive nature of these acts: the deceased were depicted with a staged gesture proclaiming a certain meaning to viewers, which added emotional color to the written words of an inscription.

This paper presents the analysis of gestural language of approximately 300 funerary tombstones found in the Roman provinces of Noricum and Pannonia and dated to the late first to third centuries C.E. In these provinces, there seems to have been a great choice in how the hands of a deceased and his or her family members were depicted, where one was able to choose between an index- and middle-finger extended gesture, an index and middle finger extended touching a scroll, or an index- and pinkie-finger extended gesture, among many others. The contemporary scholarship often sees these gestures on Norican and Pannonian tombstones as being signs of Roman citizenship, intellectual superiority, or social status and often accredits them with being attention getting. I suggest, in contrast, that some gestures may not have been Roman in nature but a consequence of previously established un-Roman gestures, appropriated into the local set of values and norms. I demonstrate that, for instance, the index- and middle-finger extended gesture yields strong analogies to the bronze hands devoted to the god Sabazios, a first-century B.C.E. to first-century C.E. Thraco-Phrygian mystery cult. While being cultural correspondents, votive hands of Near Eastern origin and funeral gestural symbolism of central European Roman provinces are viewed here not as a direct adoption or imitation but as part of a global gestural communication system, circulating and spreading to the known Roman world.

In sum, the paper analyzes hidden meanings behind particular gestures used within the nonverbal medium of stone monuments and proposes that various gestures on tombstones were applied as a form of narration to project, possibly encoded, messages to the audience. It moreover challenges the complementary role of the hand gestures depicted and exposes their power and impact as meaningful signifiers.

SESSION 5H
Undergraduate Paper Session

CHAIR: *Nancy T. de Grummond*, Florida State University

Formative Period Cylinder Stamps from Tlatilco, Mexico: An Iconographic and Functional Analysis of Proto-Writing
Carly Pope, Princeton University

Pre-Columbian ceramic cylinder stamps, as portable objects that often lack archaeological context, have generally been studied as a single category by scholars, who have written about them solely in surveys of this topic. In this essay, however, only those stamps associated with the site of Tlatilco, Mexico, are examined in order to determine the specific role they played in this particular ancient society. By means of this in-depth, narrow study of the corpus of stamps and the archaeology of the site, in contrast with general deductions about function made by other scholars, the iconography of the stamps can be seen to encode relatively specific messages using culturally puissant signs. These meaning-laden symbols that decorate the stamps with figural designs, and maybe even those bearing geometric patterns as well, can be understood as an important stage in the development of early writing in Mesoamerica.

Princess, Prisoner, Queen: Searching for Identity and Agency in the Life of Kleopatra Selene
Sara Stack, Kalamazoo College

Kleopatra Selene is one of history's forgotten women, mentioned only as a footnote to her infamous parents, the Roman general Marcus Antonius and the last queen of Egypt, Kleopatra VII. Details of her life are scarce, and little is known about her self-identification. Did she identify as a Roman and queen only through her marriage to Juba II? Or did she consider herself a Ptolemy, and perhaps the legitimate queen of Egypt in exile? Recent scholarly attention allows us to view Selene's life as a progression from a childhood and adolescence in which others controlled her image for their own purposes to an adulthood in which she exercised agency over her depictions. G. Capriotti Vittozzi proposed a theory identifying a statue of two child-gods found at the Temple of Dendera as Kleopatra Selene and her twin, Alexander Helios. Selene is also featured in a recent book by Duane Roller, although it focuses on her husband, with Selene relegated to a supporting role. However, Selene has never been explored as a historical figure in her own right. What we know of her suggests that she was an independent and politically active woman who was strongly associated with Egypt and the Ptolemaic dynasty. For the first time, we are able to trace ownership of Selene's representation throughout her life. First, she was an Egyptian princess whose image was carefully crafted by her mother as an embodiment of Ptolemaic power and the unique cultural syncretism of their dynasty, as seen in the Dendera statue. After her parents' defeat, Selene was Augustus' prisoner and political pawn, marched in his Egyptian triumph as a symbol of her fallen dynasty and conquered nation. As queen of Mauretania, she appeared on coins with Juba, wearing the diadem and melon coiffure of Ptolemaic queens. She issued solo coins with politically incendiary symbols, such as the regalia of Isis and a crocodile, a reclamation of the crocodile imagery used by Augustus in his "Egypt captured" coins. Her coins always bore the Greek legend "basilissa Kleopatra," her mother's title. This suggests that Selene exercised agency as queen of Mauretania and chose to express her identity as a Ptolemaic queen in exile. When the scattered corpus of ancient material culture and texts relating to Selene is unified and analyzed through a feminist lens, a new understanding emerges of her increasingly empowered agency and self-identification as a North African queen.

Artemis in Athienou-*Malloura*, Cyprus: Revealing Gendered Relationships Among Cypriot Deities

Caitlyn Ewers, Creighton University

In the mid fifth century B.C.E., the cult of the goddess Artemis spread to Cyprus from Greece and by the Hellenistic period had grown in popularity and spread across the island. Artemis, a *potnia theron* (Mistress of Animals), is closely associated with fauna in terms of hunting as well as animal fertility; in Cypriot votive art, she is often depicted carrying a quiver and accompanied by a fawn or dog to illustrate this fact. Artemis is also thought to have assimilated qualities of an ancient Cypriot mother goddess or "Great Goddess" and therefore has ties to human fertility and procreation.

Despite these characteristically feminine qualities, however, Artemis imagery is almost always found sharing space in Cypriot sanctuaries with male deities, such as the Cypriot incarnations of Apollo, Herakles, Zeus, and Pan. This paper explores the iconography of Artemis and of the gods alongside whom she is often found, drawing comparanda from contemporary sites around the island (e.g., Idalion, Pyla, Salamis, Vouni) but focusing specifically on imagery from the inland rural sanctuary at Athienou-*Malloura*. Malloura's open-air sanctuary, in use from the Geometric through Roman periods, has yielded several thousand fragments of votive sculpture over the past quarter-century of excavation, the vast majority of which depict males, both gods and generic human figures. Most of the comparatively few female votives are thought to depict Artemis and are significant not in spite of but because of their rarity. Through a careful examination of these pieces and the iconography of the male deities represented at Malloura, this paper reveals the parallels between the goddess of the hunt and the gods with whom she shares worship space, with the ultimate goal of elucidating their relationship and explaining the proximity of their dedications. Specifically, I suggest that Artemis' affinity for animals and her faunal attributes compare favorably with all four major male deities known to have been worshiped at Malloura, although the goddess' gender alters how this affinity was perceived, as the combination of feminine identity and young animals emphasizes her role as a fertility goddess. I argue that her perpetual virginal state enables her to fulfill disparate roles as goddess of the hunt, a specifically male activity, and of fertility, a classically female trait, by separating sexuality from gender and establishing her as a figure of individual power unbridled by males such as those alongside whom she was venerated.

The Coroplast's Network: Identifying Stylistic and Cultural Exchange Patterns Through Examination of Sicilian Terracotta Figurines
Sarah Gorman, Old Dominion University

By the Early Hellenistic period, Syracuse had emerged as the leading center of Greek culture on the island of Sicily. Syracuse's increased importance was not limited to economic or political power; the city seems to have also become the creative center on which smaller, hinterland workshops became reliant. Molds and figurines from Syracuse have been discovered at sites across the island and have been identified by the hard buff-brown clay found in the area. Through examination of clay composition, style, and technique, one can identify the workshop in which the figurine was created and in some cases the coroplast who fashioned the mold, as is the case of the Boston Tanagra figurine. Stylistic similarities and the geographic origin of the coroplasts nuance our understanding of networks of cultural exchange on the island of Sicily. This paper explores the relationships between the Syracusan workshops and craftsmen in subsidiary cities around Sicily.

Many of the terracotta figurines found in Sicily can fit into several types, and none is more prevalent than the Tanagra type. The earliest known Sicilian Tanagra figurine has been attributed to the Syracusan workshop and dates to the first quarter of the third century. While the original concept of a Tanagra can be traced to Athens, the workshop in Syracuse has been credited with the creation of multiple Sicilian variants of the Tanagra type. Molds and figurines of the Tanagra variant—in the distinctive Syracusan clay—have been found around the island. To further my claim, I focus on two bodies of evidence—figurines and the molds used to make them. This includes two molds found at Morgantina, one of a pig's head, the other a reclining male figure. There are also numerous images of Artemis discovered in Gela that have been attributed to the Syracusan workshop based solely on style.

Investigation of figurines and molds sheds light on the nature and extent of the culture and artistic network that stretched across Sicily during the Early Hellenistic period. The figurines of Syracusan origin found throughout indicate that an external market existed for terracottas produced in the city. Moreover, the Syracusan molds suggest that a secondary market existed among craftsmen eager to produce Syracusan types. Syracuse emerges from this network of styles as the center of an island-wide coroplast industry, not only supplying other cities with not only figurines but also the means to produce their own.

SESSION 5I
New Perspectives on Urban Life in Pompeii and Ostia

CHAIR: *Steven Ellis*, University of Cincinnati

Navigating Public Space: Pathfinding and Passage Architecture in Roman Pompeii
Benjamin M. Crowther, University of Texas at Austin

The built environment of the Roman city was shaped by issues of traffic and pedestrian movement. Nowhere was this more prevalent than in the public areas of the city, which accommodated and controlled larger numbers of citizens, foreigners, and slaves than any other urban area. For 19th- and 20th-century city planners and architects, the design of Roman forums and other Roman public architecture represented equal access to civic centers and their institutions. A survey of public space in Roman Pompeii, however, indicates that gates and other mechanisms limited access to many of these areas, including the forum. In the course of this paper, I explore the evidence for gates, doors, fences, and other barriers that controlled access to public space in order to determine how such mechanisms shaped and nuanced pedestrian movement.

For a case study, I have chosen the so-called entertainment district of Region VIII, Insula VII in Pompeii, a zone with an interrelated complex of public buildings and spaces, each of which fulfilled particular roles for the urban community. Within this complex, the presence of stone thresholds located at interfaces between buildings offers insight into patterns of pedestrian movement. Thresholds provide evidence for the physical characteristics of the portal, including pivot cuts and locking mechanisms, cuts for doorjambs, and traces of metallic remains that indicate some of the materials used. These sorts of architectural cues provide texture to public space and can aid in the identification of pedestrian routes through this region. I argue that specific routes and paths were significant markers of social status for the pedestrians that traversed them. For instance, architectural changes limiting points of entry into the quadriporticus created a more exclusive space that was better suited to managing crowds of visitors. In the Triangular Forum, the use of marble thresholds with extensive decorative elements along one particular path articulated a route from the Via Abbondanza to the theater, likely associated with processions of the city's leading magistrates and priests. Within the public realm of the city, such patterns of movement created social distinction between different groups in the urban community. This integration of passage architecture into investigations of the built environment offers a preliminary model for considering, on the ground, how the public spaces of the Roman city needed to be navigated and negotiated based on factors such as citizen status or social standing.

The Staircase as a Window into City Life: The Evidence from Ostia Antica
Evan M. Rap, University of Texas at Austin

It has long been customary in evaluating Roman urban architecture to assume that staircases led to upper-floor residential space, even when nothing of the upper floor remains. Recent work has begun to complicate that assumption, but no one has yet taken advantage of the largest contiguous excavated urban area in Italy—Ostia Antica. This paper presents the evidence for the placement and arrangement of staircases at Ostia to argue that they contain a surprising amount of social information. Moreover, it addresses the heretofore unexamined topic of staircase decoration to invite reconsideration of some of the most well-known buildings at Ostia.

Staircases have traditionally been classified as either internal or external—internal staircases being those accessible from within a building and external those approached independently of the interior. Although the rooms reached via internal staircases are often treated as closely connected to the ground floor—especially in houses—Ostian buildings show that this cannot always be the case. For example, the Insula delle Muse (III.ix.22) has long been considered the largest and best-appointed dwelling in Ostia prior to late antiquity. That status rests heavily on treating both floors of the apartment as a single unit. In reality, its sole staircase is situated just inside the main entrance, allowing access to the upper level without penetrating the lower residential areas. It is therefore likely that, like the other apartments of the Case a Giardino complex (III.ix.1–24), this house was designed to allow each floor to be rented separately. Thus, even at the highest levels of Ostian wealth, cohabitation and space sharing were anticipated.

The differences in staircases' decoration also highlight the varied uses they were intended for. Ostian streets frequently see staircases juxtaposed against other doorways and corridors. In almost every case, staircases are visually marked from those other entrances. Sometimes they are decorated with travertine and brick pilasters, perhaps in an attempt to invite traffic to the rooms above. Elsewhere, stairs are the only unadorned entrance along a street, suggesting that their rooms were not intended for the public.

In short, because staircases were necessary for buildings but had to be deployed differently for different kinds of social space on the upper floors, they can give us a more refined picture of Roman urban life than is possible without them.

The Cityscape and Religious Activity: New Insights into Processions in Ostia
Katherine A. Crawford, University of Southampton

Religion was woven into the fabric of Roman daily activity, acting as an integral part of society. Despite its evident importance, its placement within the urban environment and how people interacted with religion on a daily basis remain less fully understood. Using Ostia, Rome's ancient port, as a case study, this paper considers the integration of religion by analyzing the access and visibility of temples within the urban environment in terms of their location along processional routes. Despite an extensive number of studies pertaining to particular temples, there is currently no scholarship that considers Ostian religion on the basis of temple placement and its relationship to the surrounding urban environment. The applied methodology builds on previous studies concerning urban construction, spatial studies, and movement within the city to explore how visibility and perception influenced the construction and placement of temples along processional routes used during religious festivals and processions. As processions were not static events but constantly changing to adapt to different circumstances, temples provided an essential framework for the execution and display of religious rituals. Study of the spatial position of temples within Ostia provides insight into the dynamic relationship that existed between religious spaces and the negotiation of ritual activities.

Acoustics in Archaeological Context: A Case Study of the Baths of Neptune at Ostia

Jeffrey D. Veitch, University of Kent

Until recently, archaeological evidence has not been applied to the field of acoustics or sound studies. The archaeological evidence, however, provides a wealth of data for describing the acoustic character of ancient spaces, even incomplete spaces. Drawing on the archaeological remains, this paper analyzes the acoustic characteristics of the Baths of Neptune in Ostia. The bath complex, built ca. 130 C.E. following brickstamp analysis by DeLaine, was part of an imperial funded project and connected with the surrounding buildings. The remaining archaeological materials provide the basic structure of the complex, such as building materials, decoration, and dimensions, which can be used to measure certain acoustic properties. These basic elements, regularly a part of archaeological reporting, form the foundation for acoustic analysis in built spaces. A mathematical model of the acoustic characteristics can be produced for the Baths of Neptune, which display the variation in aural character from space to space. In the case of the Baths of Neptune, however, certain features remain unknown because of the lack of survival.

These unknown elements can be hypothesized and added to the model with the necessary precaution. Therefore, a comparative analysis was undertaken of the reconstructed bath complex from the Chester Roman fortress. Analysis of the Chester bath complex was performed using the same acoustic analysis as that used for the Baths of Neptune. These analyses were then tested with on-site acoustic analysis and recording at the reconstructed bath complex based on the Chester baths. Applying modern acoustic design software, readings of the various spaces of the bath complex were taken and compared with the mathematically derived measurements from site documentation. By testing the mathematical acoustic models, the veracity of such tools can be understood, as well as their value in reconstructing ancient spaces. In the end, the Baths of Neptune can be reassessed based on the acoustic characteristics of the spaces and potential reconstructions of the space critically examined.

SESSION 5J
Ancient Necropoleis and Cemeteries: New Approaches

CHAIR: To be announced

Finding the Peucetians: Using Burial Practices to Identify a South Italian Culture
Bice Peruzzi, Grand Valley State University

By examining the funerary practices of the inhabitants of Peucetia (central Apulia, Italy), this paper illustrates how such practices can be successfully employed to reconstruct transformations within a society. Apulia was only marginally touched by Greek colonization and was largely inhabited by non-Greek populations. The analysis of pottery types and burial customs demonstrates that at least from the seventh century B.C.E. a distinct archaeological culture occupied the central part of the region. In scholarship, this population is traditionally known as the Peucetians. The Peucetians have left no written records and were largely ignored by ancient sources. Moreover, their settlements have scarcely been excavated. Thus, their tomb culture is our best evidence on their worldview.

As anthropological studies have demonstrated, changes in burial customs usually reflect moments of social reorganization. Thus, the focus of this paper is not the evidence of death per se (tomb architecture, grave goods, and human remains) but rather the actions taken by the ancient agents who chose the elements that created the archaeological record. This approach provides insights into ancient behavior from material culture and permits a reconstruction of the more ephemeral aspects of Peucetian society.

Extensive changes in the material culture produced by funerary practices allow us to recognize three major periods in Peucetia (525–350 B.C.E., 350–300 B.C.E., 300–200 B.C.E.). The first two were bookmarked by moments of social stress, probably caused by a combination of internal and external causes. During this time, we see the emergence of new social groups who used funerals as arenas to negotiate status and consumed artifacts that highlighted their ties to their community and to other, external ones to legitimize their newfound power. The third period, instead, saw the progressive dissolution of the traditional order: urbanization and the disappearance of displays of conspicuous consumption during funerals both point toward the transformation of the social hierarchy and to the emergence of new urban elites who used different ways to show status.

Traditional approaches to artifacts found in Peucetian tombs have been affected by a hellenocentric perspective. As a consequence, archaeological literature on this region has focused on the relationship between the local population and the Greek colonists. Yet by looking at the artifacts in their archaeological and social context we are able to give voice to the "otherwise mute" Peucetians. Thus, we can begin to write the social biography of this population.

Malliotaki: A Roman Cemetery in Southeast Crete

Susan Kirkpatrick Smith, Kennesaw State University, and *Stavroula Apostolakou*, 24th Ephorate of Prehistoric and Classical Antiquities

The Malliotaki site in southern Crete, excavated by the 24th Ephorate of Prehistoric and Classical Antiquities of the Greek Ministry of Culture in 1997, is one of several Roman cemeteries associated with the Roman city Hierapytna (modern Ierapetra). The cemetery was used from the middle first to early third century C.E. Nineteen tombs were recovered; 11 were tile-covered, while the other eight were simple pits or too badly disturbed to determine construction. Ceramic vases and lamps, glass unguentaria, bronze and ivory pins, jewelry, bronze coins, and fragments of terracotta figurines, along with the remains of at least 15 individuals, were recovered from the tombs. Analysis of the tombs, their grave offerings, and the skeletal remains of the individuals buried within them provides the first comprehensive picture of a Roman cemetery from Crete.

Funerary Stelae and Local Expression in Roman Hispania

Scott de Brestian, Central Michigan University

Over the last 15 years, scholars have increasingly looked to funerary stelae to provide a window into the development and expression of local identity in both Italy and the Roman provinces. Although these studies have revealed many regional and local variations in the decoration and epigraphic content of stelae, there remain many questions regarding the ways in which specific patterns of decoration and text develop, as well as how we can move from the material object to broader conclusions about the societies in question.

This paper proposes a variety of methodological approaches to the study of regional and local groupings of Roman funerary stelae based on a series of case studies from northern and central Spain. An analysis of the evidence shows that no single model explains the evolution of Spanish funerary stelae. Only by applying a combination of different models can we explain the observed diversity in the material evidence.

In some cases, we can tie regional styles to artistic traditions that antedate the Roman conquest. However, more often there is little correlation between these styles and attested cultural groupings. Most local funerary expressions appear to develop during a relatively short period of time associated with the appearance of new urban and rural settlement patterns in the course of the first century C.E. This involved the adoption of a "universal" visual language of funerary display that at the same time permitted the emergence of significant local variations that served as visual markers of new identities. Local fashions were thus positioned within a larger peer-to-peer elite network that allowed for clarity in communication and an effective statement of both local and imperial allegiances.

The Late Antique/Early Medieval Cemetery at the Vicus Martis Tudertium

John D. Muccigrosso, Drew University, *Jill Rhodes*, Drew University, and *Sarah Harvey*, Kent State University

During the seven years of excavation at the Umbrian site of the Vicus Martis Tudertium along the Via Flaminia, several mostly partial burials have been discovered. After detailed biophysical examination of the excavated human remains in 2014, radiocarbon dating was performed on bones from three of the individuals this spring. Although this is a small number of samples, it still enables us to draw some conclusions about the history of the site and the region more broadly.

The burials are dated to the Late Antique/Early Medieval period, specifically from the fifth to the seventh century. They therefore postdate the majority of the archaeological material excavated at the *vicus*, which has a range that stops in the fourth century. Given that several of the burials were placed inside already existing structures, apparently right on the floor, it is not surprising that those structures had been long abandoned when turned to secondary use for the burials. This dating of the burials helps complete our understanding of the history of this part of Umbria in this period, when it was severely depopulated and population centers like the *vicus* and the nearby city of Carsulae were apparently completely abandoned . . . by the living.

In addition, the dating helps to relate the *vicus* to the well-known burial spot close by on the Flaminia, the only known set of catacombs in Umbria. First described in the 17th century, these were excavated in several phases during the 20th century. The recovered material dates mainly to the fourth and fifth centuries. Although evidence from lamps preserved at both sites suggests that there is some chronological overlap with the *vicus*, it now seems that the *vicus* came into use as a cemetery near the end of the life of the catacombs, if not after they had ceased to be used entirely. In addition, the later dates for the burials put them close to the foundation of the modern town of Massa Martana, which rose to prominence during the Medieval period when this part of Umbria again increased in population.

We also discuss some results of further research on the skeletal material and what it may suggest about the occupations of the local population, including some comparanda for the unusual burial of two legs.

SESSION 6A
Pottery in Context

CHAIR: *Thomas H. Carpenter*, Ohio University

Tarquinia, the Affecter, and Athenian Vases Abroad
Sheramy D. Bundrick, University of South Florida St. Petersburg

In the 1876 *Bullettino dell'Instituto di Corrispondenza Archeologica*, Wolfgang Helbig discussed excavations undertaken by the Marzi brothers that year on their land at Tarquinia. Among the finds, Helbig described four pit tombs set close to one another: all were stone-lined with stone lids, and inside each was a black-figure amphora serving as a cinerary urn, the deceased's ashes still inside but with no accompanying objects. He speculated that two of the amphoras were locally made; another was badly damaged, but he suggested it may have been Greek; and the best-preserved amphora, he said, was "of the style which the Roman antiquarians call Tyrrhenian." Helbig provided this amphora's measurements and described every figure and object in its two scenes down to the smallest detail.

Despite his specificity, and despite that other Tarquinian vases dispersed onto the 19th-century art market have since been recognized, this particular example has eluded identification. In this paper, I offer a match for the lost pot: an amphora in the Harvard University Art Museums by the potter/painter known to modern scholars as the Affecter (1977.216.2244). It was acquired by Henry W. Haynes and bequeathed to the university's classics department together with other objects in his collection.

The amphora's definitive connection with Tarquinia and knowledge of its find context permit closer examination from two perspectives: first, from the point of view of the Affecter, many of whose vases were exported over his long and prolific career. In her 1975 book, Heide Mommsen placed the Harvard amphora into her Group IB and classified it as one of the Affecter's earliest works; we can now see in this group a definite leaning not only toward Etruria but also toward Tarquinia specifically. This raises questions about the Athenian pottery trade around the mid sixth century B.C.E. and the extent to which it can be described (at least in part) as targeted or directed.

The amphora can also be considered from the perspective of the Etruscan family who selected it for their loved one's cinerary urn. Although inhumation was the primary rite in Tarquinia at this time, cremation had a strong local tradition; stone-lined pit graves, for instance, find parallels as far back as the Early Iron Age. This paper discusses the integration of imported vases into existing customs and how shape and iconography proved appropriate for the amphora's final resting place.

Interactive Imports: Exploring the Relationship of Imported to Local Pottery at Geraki in Laconia
Elizabeth M. Langridge, American College of Greece, DEREE

The ancient acropolis at Geraki (*perioikic Geronthrai*) is one of the few historical-period settlements (as opposed to sanctuaries or graveyards) in Laconia that has been explored systematically. This is particularly true for the well-preserved material from the Hellenistic period, as compared with the scanty material from earlier in the historical period and the almost nonexistent later material that has been revealed over the course of the Dutch excavations. Thus, its carefully excavated stratigraphy gives archaeologists the opportunity to begin to construct meaningful chronological sequences for this period in Laconia as well as to examine critically the interaction of local vs. imported forms and how they may have been used.

This paper explores the interaction of local and imported pottery from the site in the Hellenistic period from a variety of perspectives. First, it outlines the initial scaffolding of a variety of imported and local shapes into a chronological framework that helps form groundwork dating, not just for Geraki but also for the larger area of Laconia. It also considers how imported drinking forms interacted with local ones to supplement or supplant ways in which drinking was carried out at Geraki in this period in the light of what we know of fully enfranchised Spartiate vs. a secondary *perioikic* population. Finally, it uses these same forms to consider differentiation between local, regional, and imported pottery and what further work needs to be done to stabilize these definitions for an area and period that is still little known.

Athenian Moldmade Relief Bowls on Delos
Susan L. Rotroff, Washington University in Saint Louis

The island of Delos is well known as a treasure house of Hellenistic material culture and particularly of the minor arts. In 1977, Alfred Laumonier published the lion's share of the Hellenistic moldmade relief bowls ("Megarian" bowls) unearthed there in the great excavations of the first half of the 20th century. He dedicated the first of two planned volumes to the approximately 6,000 fragments of bowls imported from Ionia, formerly known as "Delian" bowls on the basis of their ubiquity on Delos, and by far the most numerous type on the island (*La céramique hellénistique à reliefs, 1. Ateliers "ioniens." Délos* 31 [Paris 1977]). There the project stalled, however, and a planned second volume on bowls imported from other sites was never published. This paper presents the results of my study of the Athenian moldmade bowls on Delos. Although their numbers are dwarfed by the Ionian bowls, they constitute the second-largest group on Delos and, with more than 400 pieces, the largest assemblage of Athenian moldmade bowls outside of Athens itself.

This material offers a number of insights, both into the production of moldmade bowls and into Athenian-Delian relations. First, although much of the collection arrived after Rome awarded Athens control of the island in 167, a surprisingly large number of fragments date within the first third of the second century, demonstrating close ties between Athens and Delos before control was established. The availability of this new market, however, had a deleterious effect on Athenian production, as potters cut corners to make more products to meet increased demand. The results are visible in the simpler and less delicately designed and produced bowls of the second quarter of the second century. Some of the bowls on Delos provide new evidence for the process of throwing vessels within the mold, suggesting that a wheelmade blank was inserted in the mold and pressed into it as the wheel turned. Finally, the collection preserves a surprisingly high number of bowls attributable to Hausmann's Workshop, a rare group up to now known primarily from 19th-century finds from Megara (the original "Megarian" bowls). The examples on Delos show considerable variation in fabric, suggesting the export of molds and the manufacture of the bowls themselves at various sites, possibly including Delos itself.

Exploring the Beginning of the Kerameikos of Pella in the Hellenistic Period: Evidence from a Deposit East of the Agora

Alexandros Laftsidis, University of Cincinnati

Research on Hellenistic pottery has already argued that pottery production in the Early Hellenistic period (late fourth to early third century B.C.E.) was inextricably connected with Athenian pottery. Pergamon and other cities that later developed into important pottery centers continued to base their early pottery needs to some extent on Athenian imports before starting to produce their own distinct pottery. The same development has been observed, in particular, for Macedonia in cities such as Veroia and Aiani. It has not been, however, so far fully explored in its capital Pella, especially in nonfunerary contexts. Thus, in this paper I argue that Athenian ceramic influence was still strong in residential contexts of Pella in the late fourth and early third century B.C.E.

The paper demonstrates the conditions prevalent in Pella during the last quarter of the fourth century B.C.E. through the presentation of pottery discovered in a road excavation immediately east of the agora. Even though this is not the first assemblage of this period uncovered in an urban context of Pella, it is nevertheless the first showing such a clear Athenian influence. Some of the pottery is Attic in origin, as indicated by the inclusions-free, reddish fabric of many examples. Moreover, typically Athenian shapes, such as bowls, kantharoi, bolsals, and skyphoi, are very frequent. Furthermore, typical Athenian production conventions, such as the multiple grooves, reserved bands, *miltos*, and shiny black glaze, are used, while decorative motives, such as the high-quality stamped palmettes, resemble those employed in Athens in the same period. There are also many vases that, despite being local products, clearly follow Athenian models. For example, Attic-type skyphoi feature characteristic painted circles on the underside. Hence, the higher than usual occurrence in this deposit of true Attic or Atticizing vases demonstrates that the *kerameikos* of Pella, which would develop in the third century B.C.E. onward into an independent robust and influential pottery center, initially went through a phase of Attic imitation. The examination of this material contributes to our knowledge of the local economy and society of Pella in the transition from the fourth to the third century B.C.E. The paper argues that the influx of wealth in Macedonia after the campaign of Alexander III enabled a larger portion of the local population to acquire Attic pottery, which was viewed as a luxury item that elevated one's social status.

Breaking the Silence: Philomela in the Athenian World of Images

Danielle Smotherman, Bryn Mawr College

Speech is readily recognized as one of the most common means of communication, but it is not the only one. There are instances in Greek myth in which individuals were silenced so that they would not be able to communicate a crime and subsequently found an alternative means of communication. One of the best-known examples is the case of Philomela, who was raped by her sister's husband, Tereus, on her journey to visit her sister. To prevent her from telling the tale, Tereus removes her tongue. Philomela outwits Tereus by finding an unconventional means to communicate with her sister through an act of weaving. The two sisters join forces for revenge by murdering Tereus' son and serving him to his father at a banquet. The deed was not left unpunished. During Tereus' pursuit of the women, the gods intervened by transforming all three individuals into birds.

This myth was represented on Attic vases beginning in the Late Archaic and Early Classical periods and continued to gain popularity in later periods. Philomena's nonverbal communication with her sister is a critical part of the story, but this aspect was of little importance to the vase painters. They were far more interested in picturing the consequences of her overcoming the speech impairment, which resulted in the punishment of Tereus. In this paper, I examine in detail three representations of Philomela on vases with the purpose of finding out how the vase painters chose to characterize visually a person who is creative enough to communicate with her sister silently and courageous enough to seek justice.

Using communication theory, I argue that vase painters in Athens and Attica employed visual markers, such as gestures and body language, to visualize silent modes of communication between figures on vases and to transmit the "message" to the viewer. I show that the visual markers of Philomela are quite different than those of Tereus and different from typical female visualizations. Philomela is characterized as a silent but active figure by her visual markers; these visual markers operate on two levels: differentiating her deeds and form of communication, and expressing her silent nature to the viewer. By emphasizing this aspect of the myth, the vase painters express the message to the viewer that Philomela is an unconventional but strong woman who can and does break outside female socio-cultural boundaries, taking justice into her own hands.

Body Hair and the Greek Ideal
Timothy J. McNiven, Ohio State University

Body hair is often a sign of Otherness in Athenian vase painting, with some black-figure satyrs covered with tufts of hair, a feature that becomes the distinguishing feature of the Painter of the Woolly Satyrs in red-figure. In the first decades of the fifth century, however, a number of vase painters, such as Onesimos, the Brygos Painter, and the Foundry Painter, portray men who are members of the citizen class with body hair. A beard, of course, distinguishes a man from a youth, but how does the presence of body hair distinguish these men from their body-groomed companions? Should they be read as Others like the satyrs? Or is this just a realistic detail that marks the products of one school of painters?

The same artists' satyrs lack body hair, like the majority of their male figures, so there must be something special about the hirsute men. A number of the hairy men are shown vomiting or misbehaving in other ways, suggesting that the artists are using body hair as a marker for a degree of Otherness. Since the distinction between Self and Other is ultimately a winner-take-all proposition, showing some men as hirsute indicates that they are "otherish," in their lack of control as much as in their animalian bodies.

As is often the case in iconography, mythological scenes help make the distinction clearer. On a cup in New York attributed to Onesimos, Herakles fights the sons of Eurytos, one of whom has a hairy body. Since the members of the

Oechalian royal family are respectably Greek and noble, they would normally not be seen as Other. Yet, by cheating Herakles, the ultimate Greek male, Eurytos and his sons show their relative unworthiness. The Brygos Painter, in contrast, shows both Ajax and Odysseus with body hair, when they are arguing for the arms of Achilles. These are both great heroes, but in this episode in particular, they exhibit a loss of control, a deficiency of *sophrosyne*. They are less than heroic, as it were.

Read this way, paying attention to such secondary sexual characteristics adds another dimension to the complicated definition of what it meant to be a man in ancient Athens.

The Gates of Hades and the Infernal Waters: Exploring the Significance of the Topography of the Greek Underworld on Attic Vases
Kara K. Burns, University of South Alabama

Homer, in books 10 and 11 of his *Odyssey*, describes in great detail the Greek world of the dead: a region of violent rivers and darkness populated by a forest of black poplars culminating in the dreaded House of Death. Homer continues with his description in book 24, adding a prominent White Rock, the Sun's Western Gates, the Land of Dreams, and the Fields of Asphodel. Following in Homer's footsteps, many other ancient Greek authors, including Hesiod and Aristophanes, enhance our knowledge of the topography of the Greek underworld. Unfortunately, depictions of the topography of Hades in extant Greek art are far less numerous; however, a glimpse of the Greek world of the dead can be found on a small number of archaic and classical Athenian vases. The earliest of these illustrations are typically found on black- and red-figure vases portraying legendary figures, most often Herakles and Sisyphus. On these vases, the most prevalent topographical feature is the Gates of Hades, easily identified by the presence of one or more of its divine inhabitants: Kerberos, Hades, and/or Persephone. In the last half of the fifth century B.C.E., there is a dramatic move away from Hades' gates to the shores of the infernal waters. The most numerous depictions of the Greek underworld during the Greek High Classical period are on Attic white-ground lekythoi that portray Charon awaiting the dead as they make their journey to the afterlife. In this paper, I explore the images of the Greek underworld on Attic vases, comparing the topographical features illustrated on these vases with the extant literary descriptions of the Greek world of the dead in an attempt to understand the significance of this shift in location from the Gates of Hades to the edge of the infernal waters.

The Hunt in Courtship Scenes: A Reevaluation
Andrew Lear, AIA Member at Large

In 1989, and again in 1997, Alain Schnapp declared that in pederastic courtship scenes in Athenian vase painting, "the lover is to the beloved what the hunter is to his prey" ("Eros the Hunter," with Jean-Louis Durand, in Claude Bérard et al., *A City of Images: Iconography and Society in Ancient Greece* [Princeton 1989] 67–83, esp. 79–80; *Le chasseur et la cité* [Paris 1997] 255). More recently, Judith Barringer has written a book-length version of this theory (*The Hunt in Ancient Greece* [Baltimore 2001]), and it is now a commonplace in the scholarly world, where one frequently hears pederastic courtship scenes referred to as "scenes of erotic pursuit." The theory derives largely from the interpretation of courtship scenes involving court-ing gifts of game animals: on its reading, the *erastes'* offer to the *eromenos* of a game animal implies an analogy between the *eromenos* and the game animal. In this paper, I argue that this interpretation is incorrect. Iconographical elements from hunting scenes do appear frequently in these scenes, but their role is the same as that of the elements of athletic iconography that occur in them equally or more often: that of identifying the actors (both *erastes* and *eromenos*) as participants in the valorized elite activities of hunting and athletics. Although, furthermore, it is true that game animals (in particular hares) are common gifts in these scenes, other gifts with different potential implications (fighting cocks, lyres, flowers, etc.) are also common, and a number of scenes imply strongly that game animals and other gifts are analogous. I argue that the central common element of these scenes is not a specific type of gift but rather the act(s) of giving and receiving gifts. Thus the scene type does not assimilate courtship to the hunt but rather to gift exchange, that most valued of archaic Greek customs/institutions. Textual parallels confirm the plausibility of this interpretation: while later authors (e.g., Pl., *Soph.* 222d–e; Callim. 31 Pf.) compare pederastic courtship to the hunt, archaic Greeks (e.g., Thgn. 1263–64) depict it instead as an exchange—the exchange of charis (in the form of nurturing, gifts, and/or political favors) for charis (in the form of beauty and sexual "favors").

SESSION 6B: Workshop
Evidence and Emergency Responses to Cultural Heritage Destruction in the Middle East

MODERATOR: *Katharyn Hanson*, University of Pennsylvania

Workshop Overview Statement

How can the international and academic community respond to the current destruction of cultural heritage occurring in the Middle East? The international regime of heritage protection during conflict rests upon an agreement that actors within the modern system of nation-states will refrain from damaging cultural heritage out of humanitarian concerns. But in the present crisis, one actor, the Is-lamic State, rejects that system. The Syrian Arab Republic government has also been implicated in extensive damage to historic and religious sites. The destruc-tion of cultural heritage accompanying intrastate and ethnonationalist conflict is a well-known but little-studied phenomenon often designed to erase the presence and history of a rival social or ethnic group. Yet despite considerable scholarship directed toward violations of civil and political rights during these and other con-flicts, there is a general tendency to view damage to cultural heritage as an un-fortunate collateral outcome, rather than as a common tactic of intimidation and subjugation. Although prior research suggests that the purposeful destruction of cultural heritage may escalate a conflict, few studies have identified factors leading to such an intensification. Furthermore, even less attention has been given to what measures may protect heritage sites and the people who care about them in conflict situations. Successful interventions are rare, and, in the present crisis, there is an acute need to examine what factors might result in positive outcomes. This panel explores the destruction and protection of cultural heritage in the context of recent events in Syria and Iraq. In looking at the intentional destruction of cultural heritage, panelists will discuss the social dynamics involved, methods employed in documentation, emergency preservation interventions that have occurred or are currently underway, legal implications of damage to cultural heritage, and practical and ethical responsibilities of museums and other heritage professionals in crisis situations.

PANELISTS: *Brian Daniels*, University of Pennsylvania, *Susan Wolfinbarger*, AAAS, *Cori Wegner*, Smithsonian Institution, *Susan Kane*, Oberlin College, *Salam al Kuntar*, University of Pennsylvania, and *Sarah Parcak*, University of Alabama

SESSION 6C: Colloquium
Thoughts for Raiment: Theoretical and Methodological Approaches to Dress and Adornment in Antiquity

ORGANIZER: *Megan Cifarelli*, Manhattanville College

Colloquium Overview Statement

The residues of practices relating to dress and adornment are present in many ways in the archaeological and visual records of the ancient world, from the physical traces of dressed bodies to images depicting them to texts describing textile production and sumptuary customs. Previous scholarship has provided useful typological frameworks but has often viewed these objects as static trappings of status and gender. The goal of this session is to illuminate the dynamic role of dress in the performance and construction of aspects of individual and social identity and to encourage collaborative dialogue within the study of the archaeology of dress and the body in antiquity, from the Neolithic era through the Roman empire.

The first two papers analyze archaeological evidence for the association of dress and adornment with sexed bodies in mortuary contexts, moving away from the use of artifacts to determine the sex of the deceased to the investigation of the material role of these objects within disparate communities. "Deciphering Gender" applies a statistical methodology to detect the gendered patterns by which dress-related artifacts are associated with sexed skeletal remains in the Bay of Naples from the first century C.E. and then probes those patterns to evaluate the role of personal adornment in the creation of gendered identities. "Costly Choices" explores the gendered use of ornaments in the burials of the early first millennium B.C.E. at Hasanlu, Iran, applying costly signaling theory to interpret the manner in which particular articles of dress and adornment participated in the negotiation of local power relations.

The second two papers study examples of particular social and aesthetic contexts in which dress and adornment operate, using context-specific strategies for understanding the interactions between these objects, their wearers, and viewers. "Surface Tensions on Greek and Etruscan Jewelry" applies the theoretical concepts of "visibility" and "enchantment" to the study of gold jewelry with figural details so small as to require intimate social distances for their appreciation, challenging assumptions about the symbolic value of jewelry and its intended audiences. "Theorizing Religious Dress" explores the role of religious dress in ancient Greece, investigating both the potential and the limitations of the application of contemporary dress theory to illuminate the role of dress and adornment in the context of ancient religion.

Finally, "Identifying Halaf" proposes an innovative theoretical framework by which figurines provide evidence for dress and adornment as components in a constellation of lived bodily practices, rather than as simple markers of sex, gender, or social status. Each of these papers, drawing on materials ranging chronologically and geographically, touch on the ways in which dress interacts with power and materiality, highlighting its unique role in the dynamic negotiation of identities in the ancient world.

DISCUSSANT: *Mireille M. Lee*, Vanderbilt University

Deciphering Gender: A New Methodological Approach to Ancient Jewelry
Courtney Ward, Montclair State University

The study of gender and identity through the archaeology of material culture is vital to modern scholars seeking to comprehend the social structures of Roman society. The active use of material culture was integral in both the creation and reinforcement of self-identities based on social distinctions, such as sex, age, and status. Jewelry is more than a beautiful item in a museum display or auction catalogue; these were objects worn by real individuals, and they played a significant role in establishing gender identity. This paper is based on the results of my research into the finds of jewelry and associated skeletal remains from the Bay of Naples. The goal of this research was to see how jewelry was used in the creation of gender identities for men and women during the first century C.E. Key to this analysis was the creation of a new methodology for the evaluation of objects of personal adornment and skeletal remains—a methodology that is the basis of this paper.

For my analysis, I assigned a numerical value or score to individual items of jewelry based on various aspects that would have affected the piece's monetary value and therefore the status of the object, including the materials used, the quality of the material, the object's weight, and the intricacy of design and craftsmanship. I was then able to make a direct comparison between the pathologies of the associated skeletal remains, their perceived socioeconomic background, and their related adornment. This allowed me to make conclusions about how different types and forms of jewelry, and the materials from which they were made, were used to create eight diverse gender identities. It is this methodology that I present in this paper.

Costly Choices: Signaling Theory and the Role of Personal Adornment at Hasanlu, Iran
Megan Cifarelli, Manhattanville College

The study of mortuary goods has long been dominated by the Saxe-Binford approach, which characterizes the durable goods found in burials as representations of the social identity and status of the bodies with whom they are associated. At the same time, a growing body of work has probed more deeply the role of dress and personal adornment, lasting residues of which are present in the archaeological record largely in burial contexts, as active elements in the construction of identity rather than passive reflections. While these approaches to the interpretation of the durable traces of dress found in burials are useful, they are less satisfying when one is seeking explanations for abrupt changes in practice, as evidenced in the material record.

This paper explores the potential of costly signaling theory, a concept developed in the context of evolutionary archaeology, for the interpretation of new and militarized assemblages that appear in the burials of the early first millennium B.C.E. at Hasanlu, Iran. This was a period of external threat and internal upheaval at the site, which was located on the fringes of the expansionist Assyrian empire in the west and in the path of the burgeoning Urartian state from the north. The new patterns of distribution of classes of artifacts associated with dress and adornment are first analyzed for their correlation to the sex and age of the skeletons they adorn. The changes in practice, then, are evaluated according to costly signaling theory, a notion that delves deeper than holistic concepts of site-wide "militarization" to provide an understanding of shifts in mortuary dress as a mutually beneficial form of social communication by which empowered persons negotiate identity and power at the site.

Surface Tensions on Greek and Etruscan Jewelry
Alexis Cantor, Franklin & Marshall University

The gleam of gold is one of its defining features. Research into the visual perception and enchantment of prehistoric European ornaments suggests that such sensory experiences added significantly to the symbolic value of gold. While European jewelry incorporates relief work, twisting, and engraving, it does not typically use the favorite forms of surface decoration found in Mediterranean ornaments: filigree and granulation. These embellishments represent advanced craftsmanship (and certainly that technology carried its own cultural value), but application of texture to earrings, necklaces, and clothing ornaments diminishes one of the key properties of gold: its glitter. The reduction in luminosity also changes the perception of the ornament by onlookers. Various styles of Greek and Etruscan jewelry, such as the *a baule* earrings of Etruria or Hellenistic necklaces and wreaths, embed miniature figures visible only close up. These styles would require smaller, more intimate social distances between wearers and viewers than pieces with little surface decoration. This paper applies theoretical approaches of visibility and enchantment to first-millennium B.C.E. jewelry. For whom did people wear jewelry, and how visible was it expected to be? What changing patterns in jewelry visibility can be identified, and how should scholars incorporate that into studies of costume and dress? How can we think about the intersection of technology/craftsmanship, iconography, the functions of adornment, and the effects of these concepts on social interactions? While many other factors—cost, specific costume requirements, possible amuletic and magical powers—undoubtedly played a role in the choice of jewelry types and styles, visual perception is a necessary component of personal adornment and merits further study.

Theorizing Religious Dress
Laura Gawlinski, Loyola University Chicago

To understand the role of dress in religious experience and belief more fully, theoretical approaches have recently begun to include phenomenology, performativity, and embodiment (e.g., Hume, *The Religious Life of Dress* [London and New York 2013]). Yet "difference" remains the organizing principle behind these approaches: the role of dress in religion is defined by its ability to mark difference between religious groups, difference between religious and secular society, difference by hierarchy, and difference of intensity of devotion. From papal vestments that strengthen authority to controversy over the legal status of veils worn by Muslim women, religious-based power and conflict between religious and nonreligious segments of society are at the forefront. But this underpinning in difference must be negotiated when confronting religions of periods and cultures in which uniformity of belief, cohesion between civic and religious systems, and fluid religious hierarchies are present.

This paper examines the limitations and opportunities of dress theory for Greek religion. In contrast to the modern religious systems to which these theories have been applied, Greek religion is embedded in its culture without definitive separation between civic and religious life. There is relative homogeneity in deities, belief, and practice even across city-states. The religious hierarchy is less strict, and rarely is specialized knowledge or spirituality required for power. What constitutes religious dress in such a context? Should dress in religion be approached differently from dress in other areas of the society? Are some theoretical approaches less suitable? Through an examination of the ramifications of the structural differences in this religious system, a more inclusive view of the intersection of dress and religion can be posited that will be useful to a broader range of religions and periods.

Because religious dress combines the spheres of religion and dress, the variety of approaches to religion must be considered; religion cannot be reified and then dress theory simply applied. A crossover between disciplines and approaches will provide more models and possibilities. For example, modern religious dress is viewed as conservative, but with a longer historical view methodologies can develop increased sensitivity to change; likewise, treatments of ancient religious dress can become more aware of individuals in addition to groups. Opening a dialogue between theoretical approaches to dress and to religion encourages a cross-pollination of ideas beyond the trappings of "difference." Acknowledging the variety of religious systems creates a more nuanced and broadly applicable framework for religious dress.

Identifying Halaf: Embodiment and Adornment in Sixth-Millennium Mesopotamia

Ellen Belcher, John Jay College of Criminal Justice

This paper presents the methodological and theoretical framework developed for a study of a corpus of figurines excavated from sixth-millennium settlements in southeastern Turkey, northern Syria, and northern Iraq from the Halaf tradition (sixth millennium B.C.E.). I present methods of figurine analysis to record the conceiving, making, using, and discarding of figurines and consider how these acts are entangled in social relationships with bodily practices.

Typologies of figurine form, decoration, adornment, and manipulation can be directly related to Halaf lived body practices, most of which do not survive in the archaeological record. The figurines indicate these practices may have included manipulation, adornment, masking, and skin decoration. Documentation of figurine representation supports theoretical ideas about how the lived body was conceptualized and adorned in the Halaf. This paper considers ways that these embodied ideas and imagery were shared across settlements and how they functioned to reinforce an embodied community identity.

SESSION 6D
Fieldwork in Greece

CHAIR: To be announced

Excavations at Azoria, East Crete 2013–2015

Margaret S. Mook, Iowa State University, *Donald C. Haggis*, University of North Carolina at Chapel Hill, *Rodney D. Fitzsimons*, Trent University, *C. Margaret Scarry*, University of North Carolina at Chapel Hill, and *W. Flint Dibble*, University of Cincinnati

This report presents a summary of work conducted during three years of the second campaign of excavation at the archaic site of Azoria in eastern Crete. On the South Acropolis, we explored two houses and several rooms of the Communal Dining Building, a complex of public dining halls, food-processing areas, and storerooms. Stratigraphic excavations on the southwest slope recovered evidence of Late Minoan (LM) IIIC, Late Geometric, and earlier seventh-century occupation underlying the archaic levels.

Current fieldwork demonstrates that the Communal Dining Building consisted of at least 19 rooms covering an area of more than 1,000 m², and forming the uppermost part of a civic complex that dominated the west slope of the hill. In

2013–2015 we exposed three food-processing rooms and five dining rooms of this building. The pattern of intercommunication suggests that two or more dining halls were associated with their own food-processing and storage areas, forming discrete clusters within the building. The functional complexity and replication of storage and food-processing areas suggests separate groups of participants dining together in the same building, but with horizontal distinctions afforded by separate spaces for socially distinct groups, not unlike historically attested *hetairiai* conducting public *syssitia* (common mess) in the *andreion* (dining hall).

Stratigraphic soundings along the southwest slope exposed a deep layer of cobble fill deposited in the late seventh century as a foundation for streets and buildings of the archaic city. Excavation within this deep fill deposit exposed structures of LM IIIC date as well as isolated buildings of eighth- and earlier seventh-century date. One well-preserved structure is the Protoarchaic Building, which consists of several rooms with phases of use spanning the seventh century: a hearth room, a storeroom, food-processing rooms, and a pottery kiln. The building has a LM IIIC to Protogeometric tholos tomb incorporated in its southeast corner and probably functioned for communal meals and sacrifices associated with ancestral cults, probably not unlike the so-called hearth temples or house temples at Dreros, Prinias, and Kommos.

This work provides the most complete archaeological evidence for our understanding of urbanization in the seventh century; the sixth century as a chronological phase and cultural context on the island; the only evidence to date for communal dining in sixth-century Crete; and the organization of households as the principal social and economic units of the Cretan city of the seventh to early fifth century B.C.E.

New Research on the Temple of Ismenion Apollo at Thebes, Boeotia: Thebes Excavation Synergasia Project

David R. Scahill, American School of Classical Studies at Athens, *Stephanie Larson*, Bucknell University, *Kevin Daly*, Bucknell University, *Alexandra Charami*, Ephor of Prehistoric and Classical Antiquities, 9th Ephorate, and *Nikos Kontogiannis*, Epimelitis of Byzantine Antiquity, 9th Ephorate

In this paper, I present the first results of a new full documentation and analysis of the Temple of Apollo on the Ismenion Hill at Thebes, one of the aims of the current Thebes Excavation Synergasia Project.

The documentation consists of new photogrammetric, digital modeling of the preserved remains of the temple, including one of the capitals, several unfinished column drums, newly excavated frieze and geison fragments, and the lower in situ foundations at the west end belonging to the fourth-century B.C.E. phase, as well as other architectural fragments of a different limestone that may belong to its archaic predecessor. I also present detailed documentation and analysis of evidence provided by remains on the site for the process of temple construction, including the inscription "ΕΞΩ" on the underside of one preserved capital, which may have directed the placement of the capital in the course of carrying out column refinements. Based on this documentation and research, I present new reconstruction drawings for the design of the Temple of Apollo, dated on historical and stylistic grounds between 400 and 350 B.C.E., including proportional relationships among architectural elements, length and width of the building, and elevation of the colonnade up to the roof. I conclude by situating the temple in the wider development of temple design regionally in Greece between the end of the fifth century and the beginning of the Hellenistic period.

Ancient Methone Archaeological Project: An Overview of the First Two Seasons of Fieldwork (2014–2015)

Manthos Bessios, Greek Ministry of Culture, Ephorate of Prehistoric & Classical Antiquities of Pieria, *John K. Papadopoulos*, University of California, Los Angeles, and *Sarah P. Morris*, University of California, Los Angeles

The exploration of ancient Methone, conducted as a collaboration between the American School of Classical Studies at Athens and the KZ′ Ephorate of Prehistoric & Classical Antiquities (now Ephorate of Pieria), concluded its second season in 2015. The site controlled the southern approach of the Thermaic Gulf, along with riverine connections to the lucrative inland resources of Macedonia, Thessaly, and the greater Balkans beyond. As a critical node in any network that involved the north Aegean, it became a veritable middle ground for Mycenaean, Phoenician, Euboian, Athenian, and finally Macedonian traders, prospectors, colonists, and conquerors. Although traditionally a colony of Eretria in the eighth century B.C.E., Methone enjoyed a much longer and continuous occupation, extending back to the Final Neolithic era, through various stages of the Bronze Age, and into the Early Iron Age and Archaic and Classical periods, before the city was destroyed by Philip II in 354 B.C.E. The Ancient Methone Archaeological Project explores and synthesizes all phases of this history.

This paper presents the results of the first two seasons of fieldwork (2014–2015) at Methone, beginning with targeted excavations on the West Hill (the so-called Acropolis), especially the Early Iron Age through Classical-period industrial area with a new kiln and related installations, conceivably for metalwork, as well as deposits dating from the siege of Philip II. The paper also provides overviews of the 2014 intensive survey of the site and its surroundings (an area of some 80 ha), as well as preliminary results of both geophysical and geomorphological surveys of the ancient settlement and coastline with its potential harbors. In addition to these three separate surveys, the paper presents an overview of the Terrestrial LIDAR Survey of Methone conducted by colleagues from the University of California, Los Angeles and the U.S. Geological Survey, representing one of the first such surveys of an archaeological site in Greece. Our coordinated scientific investigations aim at a comprehensive urban history of a site occupied for more than three millennia and subject to constant environmental transformations by its riverine and maritime landscape.

Publication plans for the project include the ongoing study of one of the largest corpora of early Greek alphabetic inscriptions, discovered in 2003–2013, preliminary analyses of the prehistoric settlement and Bronze Age tombs, and the conditions and circumstances of the emergence of an Iron Age manufacturing and trading center, Eretrian colony, and ally of Athens.

Olynthos, Greece—2015 Season

Zosia H. Archibald, University of Liverpool, *Lisa Nevett*, University of Michigan, and *Bettina Tsigarida*, Greek Archaeological Service

I present the results of the second of five projected field seasons at Olynthos, Chalkidice, which took place in 2015, involving intensive area survey north and east of the city site, as well as excavation of a house unit. Following an evaluation of six trial trenches, opened in 2014, on the North Hill, in an area previously subjected to a program of resistivity and magnetometry, one house was selected for complete excavation.

The aim of this season's excavation strategy has been to explore all available behavioral aspects of a residential property using a context-based approach and to identify floors using microstratigraphy. Five 5 x 5 m trenches were opened, which extended over the northern and western half of the house, as well as over a *stenopos* (passage) between two houses within a single block. The westernmost trench included parts of several rooms in the adjacent house, on the other side of the passage. These small interiors included a "flue," an area bounded by stone foundations, containing ash, as well as a small deposit of animal bones. The passage contained a large deposit of roof tiles, which included fragments of a beehive.

Within the principal house, three rooms, including a bathroom, were investigated. Considerable quantities of pottery were discovered within each room, much of which appears to have collapsed from an upper story. The bulk of the ceramic evidence consists of local, or regionally produced, table and storage vessels. This offers rich potential for understanding dining and eating habits at Olynthos. From this season's investigations it is clear that Olynthian houses do have some phasing within individual rooms and that the excavation of single residential units can provide new data, which is much fuller and more varied than the original excavations at the site have suggested.

The survey complements the evidence discovered through excavation and shows how a combination of methods can enhance the quality of information we can hope to derive from new field projects.

The Molyvoti, Thrace, Archaeological Project, 2015

Nathan T. Arrington, Princeton University, and *Thomas F. Tartaron*, University of Pennsylvania

The Molyvoti, Thrace, Archaeological Project (MTAP) concluded its third and final field season in 2015. The *synergasia* between the American School of Classical Studies at Athens and the Ephorate of Antiquities of Rhodope (Komotini) explores the ancient settlement inconclusively identified as ancient Stryme in its evolving regional, political, economic, and cultural contexts.

Excavation focused on the fourth-century B.C.E. "House of the Gorgon," fully revealing the 18.5 x 18.5 m structure. Ceramics, organic remains, and a diverse assemblage of finds, including more than 300 coins, attest to the daily life of the inhabitants and to the role of the settlement in trade. A courtyard was identified, and two wells were investigated, with excellent preservation of artifacts and ecofacts.

The earlier and later phases of the structure were also explored. Features that predated the House of the Gorgon were identified underneath the fourth-century B.C.E. floor. In the fourth to early fifth century C.E., the house was repurposed into a farm or villa. Some rooms were destroyed, some were reused, and others were turned into a dumping ground. A long, wide retaining wall was constructed across the width of the classical house, and deep fill was laid against it. In the late fifth to first half of the sixth century C.E., a circular structure possibly associated with a nearby grinding stone feature was built over the first Late Roman remains.

Surface survey explored nearly 6 km^2 of the city's hinterland in 1,329 survey units. The results can be compared with data from the excavation and from the 2014 urban survey. Prehistoric and archaic material was sparse, while classical to Hellenistic material was dense. However, it did not extend continuously or uniformly outward from the city walls. The Early and Middle Roman periods, almost completely absent from the city, were identified on survey, with indications of prosperity. There was an increase in activity during the Late Roman period, followed by a contraction or nucleation in the Byzantine period. In sharp contrast with the 2014 urban survey, in the hinterland coins were almost completely absent, and hopper mills were greatly reduced in number. These patterns may shed light on the unique economic role of the settlement on the Molyvoti Peninsula.

Eight preliminary places of special interest, or POSIs, were identified in the 2015 survey, most of them multiperiod. In addition, 42 tumuli were explored and mapped.

SESSION 6E: Colloquium
The Current State and Future Prospects of the Archaeology of Graeco-Roman Egypt
Sponsored by the Near Eastern Archaeology Interest Group

ORGANIZER: *Sara E. Cole*, Yale University

Colloquium Overview Statement
This colloquium explores recent archaeological work at Graeco-Roman sites in Egypt. In the past, this period has received less archaeological attention than the more popular pharaonic era. In recent years, however, this has begun to change. The papers presented cover a range of current excavations and the ways scholars are using old and new archaeological data to advance research on this dynamic period of Egyptian history.

Scholars are now turning their attention to underinvestigated areas such as settlement patterns, the archaeology of military conflict, domestic archaeology, and mortuary practices. Two sites, Tell Timai and Kom al-Ahmer, provide evidence for settlement and migration patterns in the Graeco-Roman Delta. Tell Timai (Thmuis) in the Eastern Delta is the focus of "More Than Just a Stone: Archaeological Correlates of the Rosetta Stone Text at Tell Timai in the Nile Delta." Archaeological evidence has emerged for the destruction and strategic renewal of this urban area resulting from the Great Rebellion of 206–185 B.C.E. under the Ptolemies. A new expedition in the Western Delta, detailed in "The Kom al-Ahmer/Kom

Wasit Archaeological Project: The Discovery of a Hellenistic-Roman Town in the Western Delta of Egypt," has tentatively identified the Roman nome capital Metelis. At the household level, "The Role of Excavation in the Future of Romano-Egyptian Domestic Archaeology" investigates how data from the Amheida Project (Trimithis) in Egypt's Dakhla Oasis can reconstruct domestic life in the western oases under Roman rule. Traditional Egyptian centers such as Abydos continued to thrive alongside newly founded Graeco-Roman settlements. "Mortuary and Ritual Landscapes at Ptolemaic Abydos" discusses how funerary practices at this site during the Ptolemaic period mapped onto enduring Egyptian ritual.

Scholars are also exploring how best to preserve, use, and disseminate this archaeological data. "Dating Pottery with the Help of Pottery (with Writing)" pairs inscriptions with ceramic analysis to date the pottery assemblage found by the Amheida Project in 2015. "The Karanis Housing Project: Visualizing Legacy Data and Reimagining an Old Excavation" discusses the digitization of early 20th-century finds from Karanis and how this data can engage students with Egyptian archaeology in the classroom. Finally, "Panel Painting from Roman Egypt: Gods and Mortals. Preview of an Exhibition at the Getty Villa, Malibu" details conservation techniques used on the paintings in this exhibition to preserve them for both scholars and the general public.

More Than Just a Stone: Archaeological Correlates of the Rosetta Stone Text at Tell Timal In the Nile Delta

Jay Silverstein, University of Hawaii

The Rosetta Stone's place in history is inextricably linked to the modern European decipherment of Egyptian hieroglyphics in the 19th century C.E., a fame that ironically severs it from its historical context in the remarkable events of the early second century B.C.E. In this paper, we bring the Rosetta Stone back in time to the context of when it was created and when copies were erected across Egypt during the Great Rebellion that threatened to topple the Ptolemaic Dynasty and revive indigenous Egyptian rule.

Tell Timai, the ancient city of Thmuis, sits at the defunct junction of the Mendesian Branch of the Nile and the Butic Canal. In the middle of the Ptolemaic period, Thmuis transformed from a tributary town of the temple city of Mendes, once capital of all Egypt, to become the next capital of the Mendesian nome. The fulcrum for this transition that saw the decline of Mendes and the rise of Thmuis from a suburb to a Greek metropolis was the Great Rebellion that lasted from 206 to 185 B.C.E.

Various historical sources including the Rosetta Stone, the second Memphis Decree, and Polybius discuss sieges, battles, and reforms of the Great Rebellion in some detail. Missing from our knowledge of these events are archaeological correlates. At Thmuis, the University of Hawaii Project has uncovered an extensive destruction event with evidence of violence that corresponds with the timing of the Great Rebellion. Likewise, the Pennsylvania State University project at Mendes has uncovered some synchronous parallels hinting at dramatic economic and political decline at Mendes. The evidence is building rapidly and with considerable weight to propose that Thmuis suffered considerable destruction during the rebellion followed by a deliberate plan of urban renewal very much along the ideals of a Greek polis. Considering the calculated nature of much of Hellenistic imperialism, we propose that the rise of Thmuis was, in the wake of the Great Rebellion, part of a strategic plan to reinforce Ptolemaic authority in the region and undercut the dominance the temple complex of Mendes had enjoyed for more than 2,000 years.

The Kom al-Ahmer/Kom Wasit Archaeological Project: The Discovery of a Hellenistic-Roman Town in the Western Delta of Egypt

Mohamed Kenawi, Alexandria Center for Hellenistic Studies, Bibliotheca Alexandrina, *Cristina Mondin*, Centro Archeologico Italo-Egiziano, and *Giorgia Marchiori*,

Alexandria's hinterland was a nexus for regional and interregional trade systems in the Graeco-Roman era that has been long neglected. As a result of survey investigations in the Egyptian Delta by P. Wilson in 2004 and M. Kenawi in 2008, new research has begun in the ancient Metelite province.

The archaeological mission at Kom al-Ahmer and Kom Wasit, in the modern region of Beheira in the western Delta, started in 2012. This project is directed by M. Kenawi, G. Marchiori, and C. Mondin and takes place under the coordination of the University of Padova, the Italian-Egyptian Archaeological Centre, and Catania University. Excavation has shown the abundant wealth of the region, which is reflected in the second-largest surviving Roman bath complex in Egypt—second in size only to the baths at Kom el-Dikka in Alexandria—found in Kom al-Ahmer. This site appears to have been the nome capital Metelis in the Roman period. The adjoining Kom Wasit was occupied from Late Dynastic times until the Early Roman period (ca. seventh century B.C.E. to first century C.E.). It appears that the occupants of Kom Wasit migrated to Kom al-Ahmer as the Rosetta branch of the Nile shifted. Kom al-Ahmer remained inhabited until at least the 10th century C.E.

The location of these two sites makes them well placed for trade, as they are situated 6 km east of the Rosetta branch of the Nile, 40 km south of Heracleion-Thonis, and 53 km southeast of Alexandria. Excavation and more detailed survey at Kom al-Ahmer in 2012, 2014, and 2015 yielded significant finds, including a building with a paved floor and adjoining redbrick basin and a market area. At Kom Wasit, the remains of a complete Ptolemaic town have been discovered thanks to a magnetometry survey. The plan of the town includes a temple, tower houses, storage area, tens of streets, and two main squares.

New technology used at both sites, including magnetometry, geophysical survey, and aerial photography, in addition to the intensive excavation conducted in 2014, revealed important discoveries that will add valuable historical data for the region. After four years of fieldwork and analysis we have a complete urban plan of a town in the western Delta. Detailed information is being gained from the study of the Roman and Late Roman structures at Kom al-Ahmer, providing new knowledge of daily life in a countryside town.

The Role of Excavation in the Future of Romano-Egyptian Domestic Archaeology
Anna Lucille Boozer, CUNY, Baruch College

Romano-Egyptian domestic archaeology has a long history of study dating back to the late 19th century. In particular, the University of Michigan excavations at Karanis in the early 20th century defined academic understandings of domestic life. Although these excavations revealed a large number of well-preserved structures replete with material culture and texts, we still have much to learn about Romano-Egyptian houses and everyday life. This paper suggests that it is necessary to pursue additional excavations that employ a suite of new theoretical, methodological, and scientific tools. Recent work at Trimithis (Roman Amheida) in the Dakhleh Oasis illustrates the potential of acquiring more refined as well as completely new data through excavation. These novel data do not replace prior excavation results, but they can help us to make new insights into the material, documentary, and photographic archives from prior excavations.

Mortuary and Ritual Landscapes at Ptolemaic Abydos
Thomas Landvatter, Valparaiso University

The study of Ptolemaic Egypt has traditionally focused on areas of major Greek settlement or state interest rather than traditional Egyptian centers. One such center is Abydos, one of the more important mortuary and ritual sites in Egypt. As the burial place of the first pharaohs of a united Egypt, center of the cult of the god of the dead Osiris, and location of cemeteries in near-constant use for more than 3,500 years, Abydos is nearly unparalleled in its utility for the study of diachronic change in both funerary and ritual practice, as well as for examining Egyptians' interactions with preexisting landscapes. Thus, Abydos is an important case study for understanding social change in Egypt over the long term, and in particular during periods of intense cross-cultural interaction, such as the Ptolemaic period. Though research at Abydos has traditionally focused on the earlier ?pharaonic? periods, in particular the Early Dynastic through the New Kingdom, Abydos abounds in material from the period of Ptolemaic rule.

This paper integrates results from recent fieldwork at the site with material from early 20th-century excavations to examine funerary practice at Ptolemaic Abydos, arguing that even during the period of Graeco-Macedonian rule, funerary practice was oriented around a long-standing ritual landscape that had existed since the Middle Kingdom. The tomb of the First Dynasty pharaoh Djer had by 2000 B.C.E. been reinterpreted as the literal tomb of Osiris and was the focus of yearly ritual processions from the main temple. Evidence from early 20th-century excavations, particularly those of Peet and Petrie, demonstrate that the areas closest to this processional route had the highest levels of mortuary activity in the Ptolemaic period. Based on both published and unpublished archival material, the character of funerary activity, particularly with respect to the mortuary assemblage, is similar to elite funerary practice elsewhere in Egypt at this time. Excavations by the University of Michigan's Abydos Middle Cemetery Project revealed a large, Ptolemaic-period elite tomb complex originally occupied by two priests. This tomb complex was also oriented along the processional route, and material found in this complex was comparable to that found in the earlier excavations. The focus on the processional way as marker of elite identity continued through at least the Late Ptolemaic period, when the processional way was blocked by a new cemetery, marking a distinct shift in the funerary and ritual landscape.

Dating Pottery with the Help of Pottery (with Writing)
Roger Bagnall, New York University, and *Irene Soto*, New York University

Ceramic chronology is typically approximate, often very approximate. Even where coins or dated texts are found with pottery in context, it is hard to give beginning or end dates for fabrics and shapes. The 2015 season at Amheida presented us with a rare opportunity to escape these constraints and pin down a transition very closely.

Initial excavations on a building, termed House B10, revealed a collapsed second-story room that was used as a storage facility for the house. Within this unit, more than 70 storage jars were found alongside numerous ostraka. Most of the jars broke when the floor of the second story collapsed, but some of the vessels were complete and still sealed with mud stoppers that contained embedded ostraka in them. These allowed us finally to see just how these stoppers and tags functioned. These tags state the name of the well that watered the field from which the wine came. The tags furthermore list regnal years and names of individuals who produced the wine.

Prior excavation seasons at the site and meticulous ceramic analysis have allowed for a careful chronology of forms and fabrics at Amheida, especially those belonging to the fourth century C.E. The assemblage found in the storage unit of the jars showed typological forms of jars that were common throughout the century, but there was a marked lack of certain specific fabrics and importations that mark the mid fourth century and later in other areas of the site. The absence of Late Roman Amphoras 1 and 7, African Red Slip and its local imitation Oasis Red Slip, imported wine bottles from the nearby Kharga Oasis, and the calcium-rich Christian Brittle Cooking Ware all seemed to indicate a date prior to the 350s.

The series of regnal years in the well tags showed a large chronological span, belonging to Constantine or Constantius II, or both. Closer analysis showed specifically a sequence of years 9–30, apparently of one emperor. Onomastic analysis turned up an individual known from both earlier and later years in the run, which thus can be only the years of Constantine.

The careful study of the more than 80 ostraka accompanied by the ceramic analysis thus safely dates the stratigraphic unit, and its pottery assemblage, to the reign of Constantine, or 314–335 C.E. The precision of the ceramic chronology thus obtained is remarkable.

The Karanis Housing Project: Visualizing Legacy Data and Reimagining an Old Excavation

Andrew Wilburn, Oberlin College, *Ryan Reynolds*, University of California, Berkeley, *Miranda Rutherford*, Oberlin College, *Samantha Mater*, Oberlin College, and *Olivia Fountain*, Oberlin College

Excavated by the University of Michigan between 1924 and 1935, the site of Karanis in the Egyptian Fayum can be used to explore domestic space as well as the interactions between residents of a village. Hundreds of buildings were unearthed, yielding an unparalleled record of life in antiquity and the workings of a colonial settlement documented in papyri and artifacts. A significant amount of the data from the site remains unpublished and understudied. While the Michigan excavations were not as scientific as those undertaken in the 21st century, the methodology used by the excavators was revolutionary for the time. The Karanis Housing Project makes the legacy data from the Michigan excavations readily available to both scholars and the lay public. The end user will be able to perform customized searches and explore a specific building's contents or assess coherence in the distribution of particular objects, all within a digital map of the site. Ideally, this will permit high-level analyses of the data, including neighborhood and network studies, a reassessment of site stratigraphy, and analyses of archaeological distribution patterns and depositional sequences, all of which will complement the ongoing work at the site.

This paper explores the particular challenges and benefits in digitizing and analyzing legacy data related to Graeco-Roman Egypt. Of the more than 35,000 objects found on the site, only about 14,000 were retained, limiting our ability to study all of the finds. Other legacy data from Karanis include hand-drawn maps and plans, records of all the objects—some of dubious accuracy—recovered from each room or building, and a typology of ceramics recently rediscovered in the archives. The digital collation of these data can provide a much-needed reassessment and evaluation of Karanis and its formation processes, ideally rectifying site phasing and chronology. Moving outwards, these data can be associated with preexisting digital resources to expand our understanding of both the site and the larger geographic region. Such digital projects hold significant potential for expanding the visibility of Graeco-Roman Egypt and its multiethnic residents in the college classroom. Moreover, undergraduates can be directly incorporated into the research process, engaging with and producing content that will be useful to other scholars and students, while simultaneously developing transferable technical skills.

Panel Painting from Roman Egypt: Gods and Mortals. Preview of an Exhibition at the Getty Villa, Malibu

Mary Louise Hart, J. Paul Getty Museum, Getty Villa

In 2018, the J. Paul Getty Museum at the Getty Villa, with its important collection of Romano-Egyptian funerary painting, including a rare first-century "red shroud" mummy containing its original portrait panel, will present an international exhibition on Late Antique portraiture and panel painting. The core of this comprehensive exhibition will consist of encaustic and tempera funerary portraits, mummies, and related masks from the first century B.C.E. through the middle of the third century C.E. as well as extraordinary painted shrouds extending into the fourth century. A significant collection of gold-glass portraits and the first comprehensive display of Late Antique "pagan icons" will help shape the aesthetic and iconographic contexts. Interpreted as precursors to Early Christian icon painting and as a link to the lost paintings of the ancient world, the "pagan icons" have been the topic of much scholarly scrutiny. This will be their first exhibition as a group.

Loans from major collections in the United States and Europe (and potentially Cairo) will make this exhibition possible. Many of these institutions are also participants in the APPEAR (Ancient Panel Paintings: Examination, Analysis, and Research) conservation project initiated by the Getty. APPEAR is an online database compiled in collaboration with over 20 major museums, designed to allow specialists to examine these artifacts across collections and thus better comprehend the material makeup, dating, tools, and techniques of the production of ancient mummy portraits. One section of the exhibition will be arranged in pairings and groups of similarly painted funerary portraits to investigate the creative process of the ancient painter. Through technical imaging, such as X-radiography, ultraviolet, infrared, and visible induced luminescence, scholars can now gain new insights into the techniques and practices of the last paintings of antiquity.

In 1997, when the exhibition "Ancient Faces" opened at the British Museum, it was seen as the most up-to-date and comprehensive presentation of this material. Twenty years later, the Getty exhibition will build on that accomplishment by incorporating scientific methodology into a contextual presentation of this compelling imagery.

SESSION 6F: Colloquium
Exploring a Terra Incognita: Recent Research on Bronze Age Habitation in the Southern Ierapetra Isthmus

ORGANIZERS: *Emilia Oddo*, University of Cincinnati, and *Konstantinos Chalikias*, University of Athens

Colloquium Overview Statement

The objective of this colloquium is to bring together scholars who work and study the Bronze Age settlement patterns and material culture of the southern Ierapetra Isthmus, a region that actively participated in coastal and maritime trade networks of east Crete. During the past few decades, a number of archaeological projects have taken place along the northern Ierapetra Isthmus, essential for the reconstruction of the settlement history of the Mirabello Bay, while the Ierapetra area has been widely neglected in archaeological studies until recently. The new excavations at Gaidourophas, Anatoli Stavromenos, Chryssi Island, and Bramiana and the ongoing research at the site of Myrtos Pyrgos have demonstrated that the coastal valley of Ierapetra was a vibrant and thriving settlement landscape during Minoan times. This colloquium has three principal goals: to promote intellectual discourse among scholars who work in the area, to enrich an already extensive archaeological database of the Mirabello Bay and east Crete, and to explore, based on the evidence, the Ierapetra region as a possible large economic and administrative center of Proto- and Neopalatial Crete. The outcomes of this colloquium will represent the first step toward further research in southeast Crete.

The Final Neolithic to Early Minoan I Transition in the Southern Ierapetra Isthmus, Crete

Krzysztof Nowicki, Polish Academy of Sciences

In this paper, I address the problem of settlement changes that took place in the southern part of the Ierapetra Isthmus (and in the neighboring areas to the north and along the southern coast) during the Final Neolithic and the early Early Minoan (EM) I periods (ca. 3700/3600–2900 B.C.E.). The core of my arguments is based on a number of new sites that have been recorded and studied during the last 20 years of fieldwork, following the excavation at Monastiraki Katalimata— the first Final Neolithic defensible site identified in this region. The new research made it possible to differentiate at least three phases of substantial changes in individual settlement locations and settlement organizations, which are more or less chronologically related to three pottery-based periods: Final Neolithic (FN) I, FN II, and early EM I. The newly discovered sites, especially those representing the FN I period (apart from Katalimata, also Pano Chorio, Vainia Stavromenos, Anatoli Pandotinou Koryfi, Chrissi Belegrina Bay, and the excavated site of Azoria in the northern part of the isthmus), complement the picture of the dynamic Late Neolithic–FN I–FN II sequence of settlement changes that was earlier known only in the Mesara.

The first phase is represented by FN I settlements, which (apart from the site on Chrissi) show a retreat of population to defensible locations along the steep western side of the West Siteia Mountains, which bound the Ierapetra Isthmus on its east. The characteristics of FN I sites indicate that their inhabitants were very familiar with the local landscape. They probably moved from the neighboring lowland of the isthmus they inhabited during the Late Neolithic period. The topography of the settlements of the next period (FN II) and especially a completely new settlement pattern, though it was also characterized by defensibility, show a substantially more complex social organization with a well-developed concept of a territorial ownership not seen on Crete before the FN II period. Already in this period we can reconstruct a division of the Ierapetra Isthmus into two territories: the northern one, with the major settlement on the Vasiliki Kefala hill, and the southern one, with the center on the Vainia Stavromenos hill. Although both the hills also yielded some poor evidence of FN I date, there is no doubt that they had became the main settlements in the Ierapetra Isthmus only with the arrival of new people in FN II.

The division of the Ierapetra Isthmus into two territories survived, as in some other regions of Crete, through the early EM I period. One of the best examples of the site that marked and/or defended the border between the northern and southern territories is Afroditi Kefali. Probably it was the southernmost "guard station" of the northern territory centered around Vasiliki Kefala, whereas the site on the northern lower spur of the Profitis Elias ridge may have marked the northern border of the Vainia Stavromenos territory.

By the more advanced EM I period, probably when the initial tension between the FN II to early EM I territories decreased and the right of individual communities to the land they had seized in the FN II period was acknowledged by the neighbors, the "defensive structures" such as that of the Afroditi Kefali were abandoned and the FN II to early EM I territories started to merge into bigger territorial units by intensifying all kinds of interaction, including trade. The same process of territorial division during the FN II period followed by some decrease of can be observed in the East Siteia Peninsula. The abovementioned changes of settlement patterns on Crete must have been related to the processes of expansion and population movement recorded all over the Aegean but are especially well evidenced in the Dodecanese.

The Early Minoan I Fortified Hilltop Site at Aphrodite's Kephali
Philip P. Betancourt, Temple University

Although a number of small fortified sites from Early Minoan (EM) I have been noted in eastern Crete from surface survey, the first one to be excavated is Aphrodite's Kephali. It was excavated in two seasons, one under the direction of Theodore Eliopoulos and one directed by Vili Apostolakou. The site was cleaned and studied by Apostolakou and the author in 2006 and 2007. Aphrodite's Kephali is located on a hill overlooking the north–south trade route across the Isthmus of Ierapetra in eastern Crete. Its fortification wall surrounded a small compound with the entrance to a cave, an open courtyard, and a small building. The EM I pottery included pithoi and smaller storage containers including EM I Hagios Onouphrios Ware from the south coast and calcite-tempered pottery from the north coast. The site may have been a border station between the north and south coasts where people could seek refuge in times of danger. Among the finds are an early class of arrow points, pottery in more than 10 classes, and evidence for wine and olive oil as residues in ceramic containers.

The Minoan Peak Sanctuary at Anatoli Stavromenos: Preliminary Evidence from the Excavation of the Peak Sanctuary of Minoan Hiera
Yiannis Papadatos, University of Athens

This paper deals with the recent discoveries from the excavations carried out by the University of Athens and the Ephorate of Antiquities of Lasithi at the site of Stavromenos, near Anatoli, Hierapetra. The excavations revealed a Neopalatial peak sanctuary at an altitude approximately 900 masl. On the basis of visual control, the sanctuary seems to have served a wide area, covering the entire Hierapetra Plain and the isthmus, the area of Myrtos, the mountain routes, and the inland valleys, as well as the north and south coastlines.

Although Stavromenos is similar to other peak sanctuaries across Crete, some interesting peculiarities may imply differences in the rituals or the history of use. First, there is a high predominance of clay figurines representing young males, suggesting some sort of initiation rituals not attested in other Cretan peak sanctuaries so far. Second, unlike most peak sanctuaries, its main phase of use is the Neopalatial period. The existence of a probable Protopalatial peak sanctuary in the nearby lower peak of Pantotinou Koryfi suggests a spatial shift in the associated rituals, which may be connected to social and political changes in the habitation of the area of Hierapetra. In any case, the presence of a Neopalatial peak sanctuary above Hierapetra reinforces the idea of the presence of an important Minoan urban center in the plain, of which very little is presently known.

A Bronze Age Fishing Village on Chryssi
Thomas M. Brogan, INSTAP, *Vili Apostolakou*, Ephor Emeritus, *Philip P. Betancourt*, Temple University, and *Dimitra Mylona*, INSTAP Study Center for East Crete

Excavations by the 24th Ephorate of the Greek Ministry of Culture on the island of Chryssi, which lies several miles south of Ierapetra, have uncovered remains of a Bronze Age settlement dating to the Late Minoan IB period. The contents of four dwellings indicate that the inhabitants abandoned the island suddenly, leaving behind a rich collection of artifacts and organic materials. Among of the most prominent finds from the settlement are large deposits of crushed purple shells pointing to the settlement's involvement in the purple-dye industry. A workshop for purple-dye production was actually located in Building B.1. Further study of the houses reveals that this industry was part of a larger, intensive effort to exploit the abundant marine resources around the island. These activities included not only the capture of fish and shellfish for food but also fishing for triton shellfish to supply the workshops that transformed them into tools and ritual objects. These activities are clearly documented by the abundance of fish bones and seashells in the houses as well as equipment for fishing.

This paper reviews the new evidence from Chryssi for "harvesting the sea" and explores why and how this remote island was permanently occupied only briefly in the Bronze Age. There are clear indications that the inhabitants of this remote island developed particular strategies to overcome the limitations of local resources while also drawing heavily on connections with settlements on Crete in the Ierapetra region for supplies that were unavailable. The emerging picture gives the impression that life in this remote setting was specialized rather than a marginal component of the regional economy. We expect that physical traces in the form of large settlements, perhaps even with a Minoan palace, still lie buried somewhere beneath the modern landscape of Ierapetra.

Exploring the Marginal Lands: Investigating Minoan Land-Use Patterns and Landscape Transformation in the Mountains of the Ierapetra
Konstantinos Chalikias, University of Athens

Nestled in the Anatoli Mountains west of Ierapetra lies the Neopalatial megalithic building of Gaidourophas. The building is part of a wide and complex network of sites that stretch from the Ierapetra area to the mountains of Kroustas in the Mirabello Bay. Similar settlements have been found in other parts of east

Crete—for example, Lamnoni and Katelionas, Avgo Valley, and Mari Plateau—indicating a trend that has its roots in the Protopalatial period. Settlement activity intensifies during the Neopalatial period, a phenomenon related to the intensive exploitation of marginal habitats for their natural resources. The goal of this paper is to demonstrate that the construction and management of these buildings was an organized and well-planned enterprise that was executed by a nearby palatial authority. The site of Gaidourophas is unique among these buildings because it occupies a strategic location, linking the Anatoli Mountains to the coastal plain of Ierapetra and maybe a possible, yet undiscovered, Minoan center.

Death on the Isthmus: Late Minoan III Tombs of the Mirabello Bay and Ierapetra Areas

R. Angus K. Smith, Brock University

While the Ierapetra area has produced little to no evidence of Late Minoan (LM) III settlements, the realm of the dead presents a different picture. Chance finds, rescue excavations, and a few larger excavations of cemeteries have produced a relatively robust picture of mortuary traditions in this region. This paper considers the LM III mortuary traditions of the Ierapetra area and compares them with traditions in the Mirabello Bay region on the northern side of the Isthmus of Ierapetra. In particular, it looks at the large cemeteries of Episkopi and Arapi Skala in the Ierapetra area and at Mochlos and Myrsini on the eastern side of the Mirabello Bay. Under consideration are the cemeteries and their settings, architecture, chronology, and material remains. Particular attention is paid to the ceramic traditions evidenced by the tombs, since these tend to be the most plentiful and best published of the material remains. By comparing the mortuary traditions of the Ierapetra area to those in the Mirabello Bay on the northern side of the isthmus, it is hoped that a better understanding of the cultural identity and interconnectedness of the larger isthmus region can be achieved.

Myrtos Pyrgos and the Malia-Lasithi State Revisited

Carl Knappett, University of Toronto, and *Gerald Cadogan*, British School of Archaeology

This paper revisits the argument for a "Malia-Lasithi state" based largely on the extensive Middle Minoan (MM) IIB pottery from Myrtos Pyrgos. With considerable progress recently having been made toward the final publication of "Pyrgos III," we are now better placed than ever to present the numerous features of the pottery that have strong parallels with other sites in east Crete. Moreover, important Middle Minoan discoveries in east Crete in the past decade allow for more thorough and wide-ranging comparisons, with newly excavated deposits from Malia, Petras, Chryssi, Papadiakampos, and Pefka, among other sites. It is argued here that particular attention must be paid to the phases within the Protopalatial period—that is, MM IB, MM IIA, and MM IIB—as ceramic developments reveal quite significant changes in the regional connectivity and political structures of east Crete.

Consuming in Style: Patterns of (In-)variability Among Tablewares at Neopalatial Myrtos Pyrgos Cistern 2 and Tomb
Emilia Oddo, University of Cincinnati, and *Eleni Hatzaki*, University of Cincinnati

This paper compares and contrasts the tablewares consumed in two different contexts at the Neopalatial site of Myrtos Pyrgos (southeast Crete). The assemblage from Cistern 2 is the largest concentration of fine patterned tableware from the settlement, whereas the equivalent material from the tomb represents a unique Neopalatial funerary assemblage. By considering their context, we propose a stylistic comparison of the two assemblages, focusing on similarities and differences between shapes and decoration. The aim of our paper is to unravel the reasons behind such similarities and differences and to understand the patterns of consumption adopted in these diametrically different contexts.

SESSION 6G
From Foundation to Decay: Town-Planning and Urban Development in Ancient Italy

CHAIR: To be announced

Vulci 3000 Project: Remote Sensing and Archaeological Prospections for the Interpretation of the Etruscan and Roman City of Vulci
Maurizio Forte, Duke University, and *Nevio Danelon*, Duke University

Vulci (10th–3rd centuries B.C.E.), in the province of Viterbo, Italy, was one of the largest and important cities of ancient Etruria and one of the biggest cities in the first millennium B.C.E. in the Italian peninsula.

The habitation site is a unique stratified and untouched urban context that includes, in the same area, Iron Age, Etruscan, Roman, and medieval settlements. It had an area of approximately 126 ha and an estimated population of thousands of inhabitants in the Classical period (sixth to fifth centuries B.C.E.). Nevertheless, study and knowledge of the Etruscan and Roman city are still very limited because of the lack of extensive archaeological excavations and surveys carried out within the urban area. Pending research questions concern the development and transformation of the site from when it was still a noncity, through its transformation into a city and city-state, and finally its further transformation into a Roman city.

In 2013, Duke University launched the Vulci 3000 Project (Vulci in the third millennium), which is focused on a new multidisciplinary approach to the study of the site by combining nondestructive techniques and archaeological excavations in the area of the Western Forum. In 2014–2015, Duke University started an extensive program of archaeological prospections on the archaeological site involving magnetometry, georadar, laser scanning, image modeling and the use of unmanned aerial vehicles (UAVs) for photogrammetric and remote-sensing applications. The comparative analysis of different prospections and data processing produced several thematic maps and a new predictive model of the site (with a specific focus on the area of the Western Forum). In addition, the UAV photogrammetry was able to generate a very accurate digital terrain model and an orthophotograph of the entire site at 2 cm of resolution. This microtopographic analysis, in conjunction with the geophysical prospections, opens new research perspectives on the interpretation of the Etruscan and Roman city and on its spatial organization.

New Data from the Site of Southwest Campetti in Veii

Ugo Fusco, University of Rome, Sapienza

The Campetti complex lies on a downward slope in the southwest area of the plateau of the city of Veii. The site stretches over two natural terraces, occupying a total space of approximately 10,000 m². In 1996, an extensive and continuous research project by Sapienza University of Rome began under the scientific direction of A. Carandini and myself as field director. The stratigraphic excavation project finished in 2009 and brought to light a structured sequence of occupations of the site that can be summarized into nine periods, which span from the end of the ninth century B.C.E. to the modern age. Following this research, interesting interpretations could be made that consider the site to be one of the most complex and monumental archaeological areas of Veii. Moreover, recent geological research has also led to the discovery of hot springs at the site.

The earliest evidence we have of excavations in the area dates back to 1940, while in the 1950s and 1960s further digs were carried out followed by restoration projects in the 1970s. This research led to the interpretation of the area as a private villa datable to the first century B.C.E., based on building techniques. The new research revealed that the first phase of occupation of the site, which corresponds to the first period, dates back to the Iron Age and was characterized by the presence of huts. During the second period (late seventh to fourth century B.C.E.), the area may be interpreted as an urban sanctuary built near one of the city gates. Among the artifacts attributed to the sanctuary and in addition to votive offerings, a fragment of a polychrome clay statue from a group sculpture depicting Aeneas and Anchises and some fragments of a clay statue of Hercules were found. During the fourth period (late first century B.C.E to first century C.E.) and fifth period (second to third century C.E.), the site situated in the immediate suburbs of the Roman municipium has, on the other hand, buildings and infrastructures (cisterns, pools for bathing, nymphaeum, etc.) that suggest the unequivocal public function of the site in which water plays a major role. Some votive inscriptions dedicated to different deities (Igea, Hercules, Fontes, and Diana) define the area as a thermal, therapeutic site where various cults were practiced. The team who carried out the research and I are in the process of finishing a monograph on the excavation.

Refounding the City: Pompeii's Fourth-Century Master Plan

Eric E. Poehler, University of Massachusetts Amherst

Defining the urban topography of Pompeii has been a perennial concern for archaeologists researching the ancient city. It can be see in the earliest research priorities and strategies: from following the circuit of fortifications to establish the city's edge, to chasing streets (rather than the interior of buildings) to understand its internal organization, to the development of an address system that offered a common nomenclature. By the beginning of the 20th century, more than 50% of Pompeii had been uncovered, and competing theories of its development were advanced based almost entirely on formal analyses of the shape of the peculiar grid plan, or plans, that had been revealed. The most influential of these was Francis Haverfield's thesis that Pompeii developed outward from an original nucleus, an *Altstadt*, in a series of expansions, each creating a different grid of streets. By the end of the century, Haverfield's conception had become the *communis opinio*, and Herman Geertman had bolstered it further with metrological data on streets and the city blocks they defined.

Over the last four decades, however, the pendulum of argument about Pompeii's evolution has swung widely away from and back toward the *Altstadt* theory as a result of the ever-increasing volume of pre-79 C.E. excavation data. While scholars once again see an early urban core surrounding the forum, it is no longer a dense archaic town but instead the collapse of a more diffuse archaic settlement behind fortifications of the fifth century B.C.E. The broader impact of this new understanding is simple and powerful: unilinear models of Pompeii's development can no longer be sustained. This paper therefore takes a critical approach to both the traditional notions derived from formal analysis of the grid plan(s) as well as the current zeal to make each new discovery the linchpin of Pompeii's urban history. Beginning with underexamined theoretical issues, this paper introduces equally underexplored influences on urban design, including both physical exigencies (topography, large-scale quarrying) and contemporary social expectations (defense, aesthetics) to argue for the existence of a "Master Plan" that defined all of Pompeii's urban space outside its fifth-century core. The impact of this new design can hardly be overestimated: ca. 300 B.C.E. Pompeii was refounded with a radical new urban plan that would define its urban shape until its last day in 79 C.E.

Plowing Up the World: Exploring the Use of Plowing Scenes on Roman Coins from the Late Republic and Early Empire

Nicole G. Brown, Princeton University

The imagery of the plow and of plowing is among the most vivid associated with Roman agriculture. Indeed, the act of plowing features among the best-known episodes of early Roman myth-history, from Romulus' plowing of the "first furrow" (*sulcus primigenius*) to receive the foundation of the city wall to the famous call-up of Cincinnatus tilling his fields across the Tiber. In the visual record, the scene of a man plowing behind a yoke of oxen, often with a rod or goad in one hand, is perhaps most familiar from its depiction on Roman coins.

This paper examines the increasing use of plowing scenes on coins during the Late Republic and Early Imperial period. Often occurring on the coinage of new (or newly refounded) Roman colonies, such scenes have usually been interpreted as commemorating the historical event of a city's foundation, represented by the ritual plowing of the *sulcus primigenius* and grouped together as a single coin type. A closer comparison, however, reveals an iconography that is by no means uniform. While in some instances, for example, the male figure is shown appropriately attired with his head covered (*cinctu Gabinio*) for the ritual act of plowing the *sulcus primigenius*, other coins show a man in nonreligious clothing, seeming to represent an ordinary colonist engaged in the quintessential task of Roman farming.

Given these and other variations, are all plowing scenes on coins best understood exclusively or primarily as the commemoration of a single historical event (i.e., a city's foundation)? My paper argues that a more productive and encompassing approach is to view the deployment of this imagery on coinage from regions well beyond Rome as acknowledging a perceived and growing spatial divide between the city of Rome and the productive countryside available for cultivation by Romans. Consequently, these coins are shown to form a progression of the idea of the city's historical and spatial development, beginning with Romulus' small, hilltop pastoral village, expanding to an urban center large enough to require that Cincinnatus' plow fields be located across the river, and finally becoming a world empire.

Sulla, Cicero, and Clodius: A Reexamination of the Dates for Ostia's City Walls
Mary Jane Cuyler, University of Sydney

In the late first century C.E., a pair of identical inscriptions (*CIL* 14 4707) were erected above the Porta Romana commemorating a substantial renovation of the gate as well as the original construction of the Late Republican wall circuit. The gate, stretches of the walls, and fragments of the inscriptions were discovered in 1910 and subsequently excavated. Constructed in rough reticulate and incertum tuff blocks, the walls became known as "le mura Sillane" because they were thought to have been built by Sulla after Marius captured Ostia.

Although the Sullan attribution always remained somewhat tentative, an early first-century date for the walls was generally accepted until the 1990s. In a reexamination of the fragments of the Porta Romana inscriptions, F. Zevi read Cicero's name in a lacuna. He argued that Cicero undertook the initial work arranging the construction of Ostia's walls during his consulship in 63 B.C.E. in response to the Catilinarian conspiracy and that Clodius Pulcher finished the project in 58 as tribune of the plebs. This theory has become the *communis opinio*.

A close inspection of photographs and drawings of the inscriptions confirms that a Clodius Pulcher is almost certainly named, but the ubiquity of this name hinders attempts at identifying which Clodius Pulcher. This study demonstrates that the alleged presence of Cicero's name in the inscription is extremely speculative. I further show that the historical and literary evidence for Cicero's patronage of cities and his relationship to Ostia does not support the theory that he played a role in constructing its walls.

Identifying an accurate date for Ostia's walls has become even more important since the Portus Project's 2014 announcement that geophysical survey north of the Tiber had revealed a new section of Ostia's wall, demonstrating that the Tiber did not represent the northern edge of Ostia as was widely supposed. This raises the question of how early Ostia extended north of the river. If the northern wall is coeval with the wall to the south, the northern expansion could be dated to as early as the Late Republic.

A secure date for the construction of the walls requires further strategic excavation, expanding previous campaigns of the German Academy. The need for such new work becomes all the more pressing once we acknowledge the insecure foundations of the present consensus date for the walls.

Continuity and Change at the Roman Port Town of Salapia: The 2014 and 2015 Field Seasons of the Salapia Exploration Project

Darian Marie Totten, Davidson College, *Roberto Goffredo*, University of Foggia, and *Giovanni De Venuto*, University of Foggia

Over the past 20 years, intensive archaeological research—both survey and excavation—has brought to light diverse rural and urban sites that occupy the interior of the Roman province of Apulia in Italy. Notably absent is evidence from coastal sites that can nuance and explain the economic circumstances of this province, as well as increase our understanding of social and cultural developments. Salapia, whose founding in the first century B.C.E. was recounted by Vitruvius (*De arch.* 1.4.1), was a Roman port whose later development is largely unknown from the study of texts or archaeological evidence. We began the Salapia Exploration Project in 2013, along the Salpi Lagoon on the Adriatic, to fill this gap. Through geophysical prospection, we have reconstructed a near-complete urban plan, including the city walls and a suburban quarter, covering approximately 12 ha. Over two seasons of excavation, funded by an AIA Cotsen Grant, we have explored how changes in the urban fabric of the town of Salapia reveal the overall health of the settlement through time. We have found the remains of a conjectured Roman *domus*, with the earliest features dating to the first century C.E. Starting in the second century C.E., various interventions—including the installation of mosaic pavements—speak to new investment in the space. In late antiquity, the addition of a cesspool and repair of the mosaics point to reworking but also signal continued, engaged habitation. Directly adjacent and connected to the *domus*, by the mid second century C.E., we have evidence of an artisanal quarter, likely a tannery, attesting to economic activity and connection to the rural hinterland. This space persists into the fifth century C.E., when we also see the construction of a shop front nearby, with a deposit of eastern amphoras. So with this archaeological evidence have we begun to track the moments of growth in the Imperial period and the persistence of urban life—and port activity—into late antiquity, making Salapia an active player in regional development in Apulia. Starting in the sixth century C.E. do we see a shift in habitation—marked by huts that reuse remains from the Roman city—signaling a slow deurbanization that becomes more articulated in the seventh century C.E. Only then can we propose a new role for this settlement in the region, likely no longer conditioned by its role as a port.

Decay or Repurposing of a Roman City: Gabii in Late Antiquity

Giulia Peresso, Università degli Studi Roma Tre, and *Arianna Zapelloni Pavia*, University of Michigan

The ancient city of Gabii, east of Rome, provides a unique case study on the development of archaic, republican and imperial Mediterranean urbanism and architecture, as pointed out by the ongoing research on the site carried out from

2009 by the Gabii Project of the University of Michigan. The long lifespan of the urban center represents an overview of its social and physical changes throughout its various historical phases, finalizing during late antiquity. However, a little attention has been paid to the changes that arose out of the area after the Severan Age. Moving from a comprehensive account of the information relating to Gabii from the fourth to the 12th centuries C.E., this paper aims to provide an overview of the main transitions that the city underwent during the Late Antique and Early Medieval Ages and a new perspective to decode it.

Integrating archival data with historical cartography and archaeological record, it becomes clear that starting from the fourth century C.E. the boundaries of the city shrink around the Via Prenestina; monumental architecture turns into temporary dwellings; the whole city sheds its skin, physically, and more durable construction techniques are replaced by a dense network of light structures put on top of the imposing public buildings. Habitation levels change, while the demands of new, smaller-scale systems of production result in the fragmentation and reuse of urban spaces. The core center of the city revolves around the rural *paroecia,* and spatial boundaries become increasingly defined by the Christian rite and cult, such as that of the local martyr San Primitivo. What clearly arises from the long-term analysis is the persistency of two main factors leading the reorganization of urban space: religion and economy. Their swings in the balance of power mark one of the best lenses to look at the late history of this small urban center. The data collected by this study result in a very clear and surprisingly rich picture for a historical period until now almost entirely neglected, allowing us to reassess our understanding of its role within the wider context of the rural centers of central Italy during late antiquity. This research not only illustrates the importance of using an integrated archaeological and documentary approach for the study of an urban center but also provides an overview—a suggestion—about how to initiate and apply it to those sites whose destiny only apparently seems to fade in the "Dark Ages."

SESSION 6H
Cities and Countryside in Roman Anatolia

CHAIR: *Andrea Berlin*, Boston University

Possibly the Largest Roman Monumental Arch (Sardis, Western Anatolia)
Brianna Bricker, University of California, Santa Barbara, and *Bahadır Yıldırım*, Harvard Art Museums

Sardis is an ancient city with a tradition of large-scale works: from the Lydian period, enormous tumuli and a massive mudbrick fortification wall, and from later periods, the fourth-largest Ionic temple in the world. We can now add what may be the largest monumental arch in the Roman world. Recent excavation and research just west of where the Lydian fortification gate once stood has brought to light a triple-arch structure that spanned a major road and marked a significant point of entry to the city. The survival of foundations, pier bases, and huge blocks in their fallen positions creates an evocative image of this now-lost monument.

The discovery of key elements such as springers, an inscribed keystone, sections of cross-vaulting, and voussoirs provides convincing evidence with which to reconstruct the masonry vaulting of the vast central span (13.50 m wide) and flanking complex cross-vaults. This paper presents the preliminary findings from ongoing excavations in the area of the arch, a proposed reconstruction of the structure based on extant material and comparanda, a tentative chronology, and the significance of such a monumental arch to both the city of Sardis and the wider Roman world.

Resting in Place in Paphlagonia: Relationship of the Funerary Landscape to Settlement in the Environs of Pompeiopolis

Peri Johnson, University of Illinois at Chicago

Beginning in 2008, the Pompeiopolis in Paphlagonia Project has been documenting an expansion in settlement density leading up to, and continuing through, the Late Roman period in the environs of the Roman city of Pompeiopolis. Whereas this expansion follows settlement trends experienced elsewhere in the Roman empire that saw the abandonment of fortified settlements and florescence of low-lying agricultural settlements in the early centuries of the empire, around Pompeiopolis where rural prosperity begins in the Hellenistic period, cadastral planning is absent, and farmsteads and villages predominate. The distinctiveness of the Roman rural landscape can seem to be one of merely density and prosperity. However, if we turn away from settlement trends to how places are constructed in the landscape, particularly to the rural funerary landscape, we see a rise in prominent tumuli and rock-cut tombs around settlements and lining passageways across the landscape. This paper first argues through an analysis of settlement and funerary landscapes for the emergence of a distinctive pattern of landholding around Pompeiopolis. In contrast to landownership, landholding embraces numerous rights of use from cultivation, pastoralism, forestry, burial, etc., and is a phenomenon that can be aptly studied through archaeological survey. Through the placing of prominent burial monuments, the inhabitants claimed the land they held as their own: both the land they lived in and that over which they held rights of use. The result is a landscape filled up with the burial monuments of the inhabitants as they negotiated their place in the landscape. The understanding of landholding that emerges from the survey evidence around Pompeiopolis, therefore, is not directly relevant to the urban privilege revealed by epigraphy. Rather, we understand more about the processes through which landscapes come to belong to inhabitants during a period of prosperity. This paper secondly proposes that the landscape became more Roman by becoming more Paphlagonian. Materially, becoming Paphlagonian can be the preference for tumuli, understood as attachment to local strategies of disposing of the dead. By the Roman period tumuli have come to supplant rock-cut tombs as the prominent burial of preference. More abstractly, the saturation of the landscape with monuments implies the planting of roots and the attachment of the inhabitants to the places where they lived and the resting places of their dead.

An Urban-Rural Equilibrium: Settlement Patterns and Urban Density in North-Central Anatolia

Erin M. Pitt, University of California, Berkeley

Decades of archaeological surveys in north-central Anatolia have revealed dramatic fluctuations in settlement throughout the region's long history, documenting a range of sites that span 6,500 years. These data, however, have only recently been examined in terms of urbanism during the Roman period. This paper collates and examines the results of numerous regional projects to create a cohesive body of survey data for the region. It then formulates how these results characterize the Roman urban system of north-central Anatolia. Finally, it identifies factors that contributed to its sustainability and longevity during the third century C.E.

The use of archaeological survey to examine the Roman urban system in Pontus, Bithynia, and Paphlagonia investigates three broad questions. First, do increases in the size and number of settlements stem from Roman intervention? Second, how can these patterns be understood and quantified? Third, can survey data adequately estimate the degree of urbanization of the region? This paper examines the broad settlement history of Pontus, Bithynia, and Paphlagonia and highlights elements that characterize settlement patterns and urbanization. These include statistics of expansion, topographical trends, and site continuity. An exploration of site hierarchies and the typologies of settlement follow. Finally, site density and population extrapolation are discussed to assess how intensively and extensively urban life was experienced in these provinces.

These investigations produce conclusions that greatly nuance the defining characteristics of settlement in this region. First, a universal pattern of settlement expansion and continuity among preexisting sites is present. This expansion is linked to Roman intervention and stimulation in the region, though not necessarily a deliberate agenda undertaken by the Roman administration. Second, this stimulus created a unique settlement hierarchy that never existed previously. This hierarchy was composed of specialized types of settlement designed to exploit the countryside for agricultural produce, natural resources and minerals, and manufactured goods at the maximum degree of efficiency. Despite a distinct population increase, archaeological surveys and estimates of population density suggest that village and rural life continued to play a significant (if not dominant) role in the daily lives of the inhabitants of Pontus, Bithynia, and Paphlagonia. Cities and towns were an important part of provincial life and support for the countryside. Yet the provinces remained a world of villages that became even more prevalent throughout the vast countryside of north-central Anatolia.

Perspectival Effects in the Propylon of the Sebasteion at Aphrodisias

Philip T. Stinson, University of Kansas

Results from fieldwork during the summer of 2015 show that the propylon (ca. 25 C.E.) of the Roman imperial cult complex known as the Sebasteion at Aphrodisias has a surprisingly oblique architectural design. The gate's three staircases and aedicular projecting podia are splayed. They open wider toward the Sebasteion's street-like court and temple beyond. The entablatures of the structure also have tapering sides, edges, and moldings. These features differ from so-called optical refinements in classical architecture, which by tradition consist of the shaping and spacing of columns and of the vertical curvature of continuous horizontal components, such as stylobates and entablatures. Their purpose may have been to counteract certain peculiarities of human vision, but this is a matter of debate today. I posit that the propylon is different and has an innovative built-in perspective, which misrepresents physical depth for the sake of theatricality. The propylon offers a nearly complete and well-documented body of evidence for the study of the practice of architectural theory in the Early Imperial Roman period. The wider outcome of this project is the final documentation and publication of the architecture and archaeological contexts of the entire Sebasteion complex.

Reuse or Misuse: Reappropriating Public Baths in Late Antique Asia Minor
Ryan C. Hughes, University of Michigan

Evidence of industrial reuse of public space in Late Antique Asia Minor has usually been read as a sign of the dissolution of local civic institutions and as part of a general trend of urban abandonment. Sometimes referred to as "squatter industry," this type of reuse has been interpreted as largely opportunistic, with private individuals usurping public space in the absence of civic authorities to stop them. Bath complexes, in particular, were prime targets of reuse, as their large interior spaces, abundance of marble and limestone, and resistance to fire made them suitable for a range of industries and a good source of building materials. Moreover, as bath complexes serve as symbols of the cultural and economic power of the Roman empire, the reuse of baths has signaled for many scholars the collapse of civic life in the cities of Asia Minor. When evidence of reuse is placed within the broader context of urban and regional development, however, structured patterns of reoccupation and reuse become apparent, revealing an often premeditated, organized system of reuse. Though the cities of Late Antique Asia Minor exhibit different trajectories of transformation, there are some similarities in the reuse and recycling of bath complexes in the late sixth and early seventh century. These similarities are part of a larger pattern of urban reconfiguration and point to the continued existence of civic authority in some cities.

This paper presents the reuse of bath complexes at three sites: Sardis, Hierapolis, and Anemourion. At all three sites, there are contemporaneous processes of reuse of bath complexes, with each site exhibiting similar patters of reoccupation and recycling. Reuse of these buildings provided raw material for new construction projects, removed "dangerous ruins" from the urban landscape, and put prime real estate back into use. Inside these structures, new products were being made for local, regional, and long-distance consumption. Therefore, the urban reuse and recycling of buildings points not to urban decay but rather to urban restructuring in the face of dramatic change sanctioned and undertaken by corporate civic entities. In reality, the maintenance of the public buildings of the previous generations was no longer socially advantageous and/or economically viable. Industrial reuse of buildings in Asia Minor during the sixth and seventh centuries points not to the wholesale abandonment of urban life but instead to a transformation in the way people thought about the use of public space.

The So-Called Little Baths of Elaiussa Sebaste (Cilicia, Southeastern Turkey)
Emanuele Casagrande Cicci, "Sapienza" University of Rome

Cilicia, located in the southeastern part of Anatolia, remains one of the less studied ancient Roman provinces. In spite of scant research, the settlements discovered throughout the region and archaeological investigations of some of the region's cities, primarily those situated along the coast, are increasing our knowledge about broader historical, architectural, and social developments in the territory under Roman rule. This paper presents the preliminary results of an ongoing study of a bath complex situated in one of these cities: Elaiussa Sebaste. This structure, called the "Little Baths" for its particular dimensions and layout, is one of the few fully excavated baths in the region.

The results of this excavation include the general layout of the building, the plan of the warm rooms, and the position of the praefurnium of the complex, revealed through three initial archaeological campaigns (2012–2014). In 2013 and 2014, a mosaic pavement that covered the original apodyterium was fully exposed and restored. Planned with at least three different carpets, the polychrome mosaic floor includes both geometric and figurative motifs partially preserved today. These investigations brought to light the main entrance to the baths from the outside, including a Greek inscription that welcomes visitors to the complex. Archaeological evidence suggests that the building was constructed during the first to second century C.E. and was abandoned between the sixth and seventh century C.E.

The study of the Little Baths of Elaiussa Sebaste allows us to reexamine the role of baths throughout Cilicia from a broader perspective. These structures, in some cases very similar in terms of layout and arrangement, show evidence of the architectural influence of Rome while retaining elements that reflect regional conventions. This paper presents the architecture, layout, and chronology of the bath building and discusses its later phases of use (e.g., the Byzantine and Armenian periods). The architectural style and general layout of the Little Baths allow us to draw a number of conclusions about its chronology, intended use, and internal division of the spaces. Comparisons between the Little Baths of Elaiussa Sebaste and other small baths known in the region highlight the peculiarities of this type of structure in Cilicia. This study underlines the differences between the specific techniques and styles of the regional building tradition and the most common Roman designs for baths.

SESSION 6I: Colloquium
Five Decades of Excavations at Poggio Civitate

ORGANIZERS: *Kate Kreindler*, Stanford University, and *Tony Tuck*, University of Massachusetts Amherst

Colloquium Overview Statement

This year marks the 50th year of continuous excavations at Poggio Civitate, an Etruscan settlement dating to the seventh and sixth centuries B.C.E. The site itself is uniquely preserved, providing a glimpse of some of the earliest monumental domestic, sacred, and industrial architecture in Italy. After five decades of research, scholarship about Poggio Civitate is extensive. The site's considerable bibliography, as well as excavation records and archival materials, preserves not only a remarkable archaeological record but also an unparalleled meta-archaeological record; five decades worth of materials, records, and publications allow us to reflect on our current thinking about the site and how that has been informed.

Poggio Civitate is both a research project and a long-running field school. Hundreds of students have passed through the program and dozens have gone on to pursue master's and doctoral degrees in archaeology. Six alumni and current scholars affiliated with the project will present papers in this session. The papers are both reflective and forward-looking, in order to highlight current interpretations of the site and future research goals. They address two major initial research questions, which deal with architecture and iconography. They include a paper on the site's monumental architecture, titled "How to Build an Etruscan Palace: Monumentality in the Archaic Period at Poggio Civitate (Murlo)," and a paper on the site's iconography, titled 'Aristocratic Rulers in the Palace at Poggio Civitate (Murlo)? Ideological Interpretations and Archaeological Reality." A third paper, titled "Poggio Digitate: The History and Future of Data Recording and Presentation at an Etruscan Site," bridges earlier and current work by examining means of data collection and processing. Specifically, it focuses on how the site's archival system is continuously evolving to accommodate former excavation methods while allowing for new techniques, technologies, and research questions. The final two papers focus on current research at the site. One, "Zooarchaeological Evidence for Diet, Ritual, and Economy at Poggio Civitate," details recent faunal analyses. The final paper, "Landscape and Community at Poggio Civitate," explores relationships between Poggio Civitate and subordinate satellite communities.

How to Build an Etruscan Palace: Monumentality in the Archaic Period at Poggio Civitate (Murlo)
Gretchen Meyers, Franklin & Marshall College

The Archaic-period structure at Poggio Civitate (Murlo) is one of the most well-known architectural monuments in Etruria. From the earliest years of excavation at the site, this building's significant size, unique courtyard plan, and elaborate terracotta decorations dominated interpretative discussion of the important settlement at Poggio Civitate. Still the subject of countless discussions about architectural form and function, the archaic monumental complex at Poggio Civitate, commonly referred to as a palace, remains the iconic lens through which many discussions of the site begin.

Nonetheless, recent scholarship suggests that as a concept monumentality in the archaeological record refers to more than just the presence of a significant structure within a larger built environment. Rather, a multitude of individual decisions about siting, spatial arrangement, and availability of resources help determine the nature of a given monument and its impact on an ancient visitor. This paper reconsiders the archaic palace at Poggio Civitate by reconstructing such decisions, particularly in light of newly excavated material on the plateau, including two wells, evidence of settlement activity to the west of the archaic building, and uncovered remnants of a nearby road or approach route. In addition, thanks to recent attention to the preceding orientalizing complex at the site, the role of architectural memory—a key component in the ideological impact of monuments—is considered as a contributing factor in the design and implementation of the archaic building phase.

Aristocratic Rulers in the Palace at Poggio Civitate (Murlo)? Ideological Interpretations and Archaeological Reality

Ingrid Edlund-Berry, University of Texas at Austin

Ever since their discovery in 1966, the acroterial terracotta sculptures from the archaic monumental building at the Etruscan site at Poggio Civitate (Murlo) have caught our attention. First published in the preliminary excavation reports, the statues have been studied and restored to represent more than 20 seated and standing male and female figures as well as standing and striding animals (I. Edlund-Berry, *The Seated and Standing Statue Akroteria from Poggio Civitate (Murlo)* [Rome 1992]; D. Newland, "The Acroterial Sculpture and Architectural Terracottas from the Upper Building at Murlo," Ph.D. diss. [1994]).

In most of the literature on Etruscan art and culture, the group of statues is represented by the upper torso of a male bearded figure crowned by a large floppy hat, known as "il cappellone" or "the Murlo cowboy." Linked with the interpretation of the building as a regal or aristocratic dwelling, he and the other statues are seen as depictions of the living rulers or their ancestors, or possibly divine figures that for the lack of iconographic attributes remain anonymous. To date, parallels from other sites provide examples of deities (from Satricum), groups (such as Athena and Herakles from Sant'Omobono in Rome and other sites), or isolated figures (standing man and a dog, from Veii), but there are no immediate prototypes or successors to the Poggio Civitate acroterial statues.

While the identity of the statues would no doubt have been obvious to the contemporary Etruscans, the archaeological context can be used to suggest to us that they should be viewed as part of the total assembly of terracotta decoration on the archaic monumental building, which included a repetitive sequence of female heads, rosettes, waterspouts, gorgon antefixes, and frieze plaques representing banquet scenes, horse races, processions, and seated figures (N.A. Winter, *Symbols of Wealth and Power* [2009]). Although the exact composition of seated and standing figures cannot be ascertained, their location as acroteria, probably facing the central courtyard of the monumental building rather than the roads leading up to it, suggests that they were intended as spectators of the activities performed there, perhaps including the scenes shown on the frieze plaques. As each component of the architectural terracottas served to protect the construction of the monumental building, the rows of statues provided a focus of attention that gave the building a purpose as a place of action viewed by many.

Poggio Digitate: The History and Future of Data Recording and Presentation at an Etruscan Site

Theresa Huntsman, Harvard University Art Museums, and *Eric Kansa,* University of California, Berkeley

The structure of the documentation system employed for the archaeological excavations at Poggio Civitate has been remarkably consistent from the project's beginning in 1966. However, the nature of the data itself has been intimately tied with changing archaeological methods and theoretical perspectives. The level of detail recorded and priorities for particular types of data has gradually become more formalized and systematic over the past five decades. At the same time, the challenge of incorporating and preserving legacy data in a searchable, electronic database has required negotiation between systemizing the data and still retaining the descriptive terminologies, assertions, and perspectives of the original researchers (even if these now sometimes seem in error). The project data set is not static. Archaeological work at Poggio Civitate continues today, so data is constantly created, while older data is continually curated through error correction, ongoing digitization, and the creation of supplemental data.

The publication of the Poggio Civitate with Open Context shows the continued evolution of the project's data-management strategies. Use of Open Context for data management has led to greater formalism in documenting ongoing changes in the Poggio Civitate project data set, since these changes are now tracked publicly using version-control systems. Changing data structures, new records, fixed errors, and other alterations to publicly accessible data now have systematic documentation, and data can be "rolled back" to prior states. In addition, Open Context publishes archaeological documentation as "Linked Open Data" on the web. Linked Open Data approaches center on the use of stable web addresses (URIs) to identify concepts and other entities. Applying Linked Open Data methods to the Poggio Civitate corpus builds on the long-term trends toward greater formalism. The Poggio Civitate corpus now references ontologies and controlled vocabularies used by multiple projects. This helps further contextualize decades of excavations at Poggio Civitate with larger bodies of knowledge and other online data sources.

Zooarchaeological Evidence for Diet, Ritual, and Economy at Poggio Civitate

Sarah Kansa, Alexandria Archive Institute

Fifty years of excavations at Poggio Civitate have recovered large quantities of animal remains. This paper presents the results of zooarchaeological analysis undertaken on these remains over the past five years. Though only a portion of the total assemblage has been analyzed since 2011, the database contains nearly 10,000 bones—among the largest Etruscan faunal assemblages to date. The remains come primarily from the monumental complexes that dominated the site during the seventh and sixth centuries B.C.E. These include a structure thought to be an elite residence, a possible ritual building with a tripartite layout, and an extensive workshop area. Initial analysis of faunal samples from these three areas sheds light on diet, economy, and society at the settlement in general and also indicates some variation in the use of animals in different contexts. The elite residence contained a preponderance of cattle and deer bones, as well as the remains of wild hunted animals such as red deer, boar, bear, and wolf. These animals would have likely played significant roles in ritual and in signaling elite status to those who hunted them and/or displayed their trophies. The workshop area included debris from butchery and evidence for bone and antler working, as well as other animal-processing activities.

In addition to discussing new evidence from these three areas, this paper presents new results from the most recent excavations at the site. A comparison of the faunal remains collected up to 50 years ago with those collected in more recent years helps us establish better parameters for assessing the reliability of the data gleaned from the materials collected with older excavation techniques. This paper concludes with several examples of the broader uses of the faunal data from Poggio Civitate. Because the data are published in Open Context, they can be integrated with related data sets describing other aspects of the site of Poggio Civitate, as well as other sites in the region.

Landscape and Community at Poggio Civitate
Tony Tuck, University of Massachusetts Amherst

Poggio Civitate, situated at the edge of Tuscany's Maremma region, preserves a considerable body of evidence related to community development during the seventh and sixth centuries B.C.E. The monumental scale of the architecture of Poggio Civitate's Piano del Tesoro plateau remains one of the site's many enigmatic features. The two building phases of this area preserve some of the region's largest known structures of the period, replete with a complex system of ornamentation communicating the interests of the site's political and social elite. Excavation beyond Piano del Tesoro reveals that these architectural complexes were not isolated on the hilltop but rather associated with a contemporaneous subordinate community that extended west of the plateau. In addition, a growing body of evidence indicates that several contemporary settlements were located on hilltops surrounding Poggio Civitate as well.

The Orientalizing and Early Archaic periods in central Italy were witness to significant and dynamic social, political, and economic developments throughout the region, resulting in the emergence of large-scale, urbanized communities. Yet the evidence from Poggio Civitate has never fit neatly into our understanding of Etruscan urbanism. Unlike the Etruscan cities situated atop broad plateaus of the Tuscan coast, the landscape surrounding Poggio Civitate is considerably more varied and did not lend itself to large, concentrated populations. Instead, the evidence of five decades of excavation and research now suggests that Poggio Civitate was the center of an emergent community, albeit one that marshaled demographic energies from population centers clustered around the main settlement yet physically separate from it. This different model of political development not only helps explain Poggio Civitate's role in the social system of the region but also provides insight into the manner in which topography plays a central role in community formation throughout this region.

SESSION 6J: Colloquium
Deserted Villages, II: During and After Abandonment
Sponsored by the Medieval and Post-Medieval Archaeology Interest Group

ORGANIZERS: *Deborah E. Brown Stewart*, Dumbarton Oaks Research Library, and *Kostis Kourelis*, Franklin & Marshall College

Colloquium Overview Statement

The papers in this session explore complex processes at work during the abandonment of settlements and the formation of archaeological sites through case studies of modern deserted villages and temporary rural settlements. Rather than supplying a narrative that ends abruptly with the final abandonment of a site as viewed from a much later point in time, each paper thoughtfully considers abandonment and post-abandonment histories traced through years of documentation and investigation of structures and settlements that were abandoned or partially abandoned in the 19th and 20th centuries. Each case study includes evidence from historical documents, photographs, and oral histories to offer a more nuanced understanding of the reasons for abandonment, behaviors associated with deserted villages and rural structures, and significance of deserted villages in cultural landscapes. The combined papers contribute new material for understanding protracted abandonment and postabandonment processes and have significant implications for archaeologists' interpretation of landscapes, settlements, buildings, and assemblages. The papers focus on case studies from three regions in Greece and one from the American prairies.

The panel is dedicated to the memory of Frederick A. Cooper, who pioneered the study of vernacular architecture in Greece and in the American Midwest.

Life in an Abandoned Village: The Case of Lakka Skoutara
William Caraher, University of North Dakota, and *David Pettegrew*, Messiah College

Since 2001, a small team of archaeologists has documented a partially deserted village in the southeast Corinthia through intensive archaeological survey, oral histories, detailed note-taking, and photography. The settlement in the valley known as Lakka Skoutara consists of a dozen-plus longhouses with outbuildings, agricultural features, and a central church, which collectively date in construction, use, and formation to the 19th and mid 20th centuries. Our work to this point has highlighted the regional and global contingencies that made this semivillage boom and bust over the course of a century and a half: population growth and proximity to the nearby village of Sophiko, where the valley's residents originated; temporary habitation during agricultural seasons; a marked shift in agricultural regimes from grain to olives in the early 20th century; permanent residence during the difficult years of World War II; reorientation to resin production in the 1950s; and a new phase of abandonment in the last quarter of the 20th century. Our record of this dynamic rural landscape has supported recent work by Susan Sutton (ed., *Contingent Countryside* [Stanford 2000]) and Hamish Forbes ("Early Modern

Greece: Liquid Landscapes and Fluid Populations," in Davies and Davis, eds., *Between Venice and Istanbul* [Princeton 2007]), among others, about fluid villages and populations in early modern and modern Greece.

In this paper, we discuss the nature, processes, and meanings of abandonment in this Corinthian semivillage. Through photographs and detailed descriptions of the houses and their assemblages conducted during five separate visits (2001, 2004, 2006, and 2009), I draw attention to the ways that the valley's inhabitants and visitors have abandoned, repurposed, and changed the houses and their assemblages over the last generation, and especially in the 10 years we have been visiting the region. In one respect, I show the wide range of states of abandonment of domestic buildings, from still fully inhabited residences to seasonal dwellings, collapsed buildings, and wall foundations. In another respect, I argue that this seemingly deserted valley has never fully been "abandoned," since agricultural activities, sporadic seasonal habitation, shepherding, and road networks continue to affect the material of the settlement. Documentation through photographs, survey, and notes provides a detailed and visual example of the dynamism and complexities of cultural formation processes best documented in the work of Michael Schiffer (*Formation Processes of the Archaeological Record* [Albuquerque 1987]).

An Abandoned Mudbrick Hamlet at Penteskouphi near Corinth: Its Condition, Educational Potential, and Natural Environment

Guy D. R. Sanders, American School of Classical Studies at Athens, *Isabel E. M. Sanders*, Independent Scholar, and *Miyon Yoo*, Independent Scholar

Penteskouphi is a dispersed hamlet of mudbrick houses on a broad marl terrace to the southwest of Acrocorinth and 3 km from ancient Corinth. It was built by farmers from Athika, 12 km distant, and other villages for use when they tended their olives and especially their vines. During the 1970s, farmers replaced their donkeys with pickup trucks and were able to commute to their fields on a daily basis. As a result, their *exospitia* were no longer required except for storage of farm equipment. Today, after 40 years of neglect, nearly all are in varying states of ruin.

In several, the wooden roof beams have rotted through and broken, dumping piles of broken tile on the earthen floors. The exposed mudbrick walls are eroding, creating a talus of clay at the base of the walls inside and outside. These houses present an excellent field school for archaeologists who want to understand archaeological formation processes and the rate of decomposition. For instance, an unmaintained roof seems to last for less than 40 years. One house abandoned well before the 1970s now appears to be just a tumulus of earth.

Over the past decade, we have been making a photographic record of Penteskouphi's ruination and have been using the site as an educational tool. In time, there will be no mudbrick houses left in these states of decay, and Penteskouphi will have transformed from an archaeological site in the making to an archaeological site. Corinth Excavations is currently working on a heritage-management plan with the Ephoria of Ancient Korinth. The end goal is to create a sustainable archaeological park consisting of Acrocorinth, ancient Corinth, and Lechaeum Harbor. Penteskouphi is one of the destinations and part of longer bicycle and hiking routes we are planning to include in the management plan. We are studying both the houses and their agricultural and natural environment so that written and digital materials will be available to the general public. We will also consider how to slow the rate of ruination of some of the houses so that these can continue to inform both scholars and ecotourists.

Drones and Stones: Mapping Deserted Villages in Lidoriki, Greece

Todd Brenningmeyer, Maryville University, *Miltos Katsaros*, National Polytechnic University of Athens, and *Kostis Kourelis*, Franklin & Marshall College

With the construction of the Mornos Reservoir in 1969–1979, the region of Lidoriki lost its traditional natural networks. Recently, bauxite mining has added new pressures on the mountainous landscape of Phocis. In 2011, an interdisciplinary group of scholars initiated the Lidoriki Project to document networks and places that made up the region's premodern landscape. It combines traditional forms of documentation (drawing buildings, oral histories, archival research) with new digital tools, including aerial drone flights and three-dimensional modeling. In addition to surveying the classical city of Fyskos and the medieval fortress of Kallion, the project focuses on vernacular architecture (villages, mills, bridges, roads, churches, monasteries, and caves).

In 2014–2015, the project targeted the deserted village of Aigition for an intensive survey. An elaborate church dated to 1852 and a large number of stone-built houses testify to the village's prosperity in the 19th century. During the 20th century the village was progressively abandoned. The houses lost their roofs and revealed intermediary stages of collapse. The project is surveying the settlement using aerial photography with kites and a quadcopter drone. Through digital photogrammetry, it reproduced a three-dimensional model of the site. Closer architectural study of the house interiors provides invaluable clues about the architectural integrity of the houses, their system of construction, and the interface of various crafts (stonemasonry, carpentry, ironwork). Studying the architectural bones of the houses has also offered architectural analysis about alternative forms of heating and cooling and maximizing ecological resources.

Lidoriki's local preservation community has succeeded in collecting surviving domestic artifacts from the late 19th and early 20th centuries. Textiles, tools, looms, and other implements are stored in storage space. Our team has been cataloguing those artifacts and producing photogrammetric three-dimensional models. Artifacts such as these would have once populated the interior of the houses in Aigition. Through three-dimensional modeling, we hope to repopulate those reconstructed interiors with their appropriate artifacts and are investigating the potential for representing this period in a digital museum. Although precipitated by the Mornos Dam, the abandonment of Lidoriki had begun in the early 1900s with the collapse of the agrarian economy. Large numbers of villagers emigrated to the United States, many to Milwaukee, Wisconsin. Another component of the Lidoriki Project is reconnecting the deserted villages to the Greek-American diaspora. Through an analysis of immigration records and interviews, we hope to close the loop between buildings, objects, and landscapes and people.

Abandoned Settlements in a Historically Abandoned Environment: The Example of Kythera

Lita Tzortozopoulou-Gregory, The Australian Archaeological Institute at Athens, and *Timothy E. Gregory*, Ohio State University

The island of Kythera, midway between the Greek mainland and Crete, has a historically well-established tradition about the phenomenon of abandonment. Some of this has stretched as far as the early modern prediction that the island has been abandoned six times, and the last time (in the future) will lead to the end of the world! This phenomenon has been connected by some with the abandonment of the most important settlements in antiquity, including the large Minoan "colony" at Kastri (Paliopoli—which was also the main port in the Classical period and apparently the main city in the Roman period) and the main city of Archaic and Classical times, which was at Paliokastro. This phenomenon—the "disappearance" of prehistoric and classical cities (and their "rediscovery" in modern times)—is common throughout Greece and hardly requires comment.

The disappearance of settlements in medieval and modern times, however, is a much more interesting issue, and it deserves more sophisticated analysis, involving the reasons for their disappearance (which can, potentially, be varied and many) and, probably, most importantly, the examination of the reasons for the settlements' earlier existence, including study of the roles that individual settlements played in the economic, political, and military systems of various periods.

For Kythera, this analysis would reasonably start with examination of the medieval "capital" of the island, now known as Paliochora but apparently called Ayios Demetrios in the Middle Ages. The causes of the foundation and the abandonment of this settlement, its size, and its "function" have all been examined in several modern studies, and the conclusions have varied enormously among the scholars who have investigated them. This study proposes yet another series of answers, which the authors argue are more in keeping with the sources at our disposal and current understanding of medieval economies and political organization. In addition, we make significant use of the results of systematic archaeological survey carried out between 1999 and 2003 by the Australian Paliochora-Kythera Archaeological Survey and more recent revisiting of some of these settlements. In addition, this research makes use of the 18th-century census records preserved in the Kythera Historical Archives that provide detailed information about the rise and fall of populations as well as oral information that helps us bring our analysis into the 19th and early 20th century.

Wheelock, North Dakota: Incremental and Cyclic Abandonment on the Northern Plains

Richard Rothaus, North Dakota University System, *William Caraher*, University of North Dakota, and *Bret Weber*, University of North Dakota

Wheelock, North Dakota, is representative of intermittent settlements that blink in and out of existence in the boom and bust cycle of extractive industries that dominate the region. Founded in 1902 by ambitious investors and settlers following the Great Northern Railway, Wheelock was promoted for its cheap and rich agricultural land. For a short time, Wheelock prospered, with a school, a bank, a store, a depot, numerous houses, and the first concrete sidewalk in western North Dakota. The agricultural land was not as promised, however; the Dust Bowl arrived, and the population decline began within a few decades of the town's founding. In 1938, only 115 people were to be found in Wheelock. The town was disincorporated in 1994, and the 20 or so remaining residents drifted away shortly thereafter.

The UND ManCamps Project, which focuses on the material culture of workforce housing of the current shale oil boom, has studied Wheelock through multiple site visits and interviews since 2012. A town on the periphery, Wheelock has been reborn by individuals on the periphery. We have documented a spectrum of use activities: the creation of a small ethnic enclave in travel-trailers at the edge of the town; putative property owners renting out abandoned structures, complete with makeshift water and septic systems; short-term squatting; illicit drug manufacturing; and makeshift rebuilding by challenged individuals. Our archaeological research is matched with a series of oral histories collected by the team. By 2014, the need for Wheelock had diminished, and it was once again (nearly) abandoned.

The study of Wheelock has important interpretive and methodological implications for "abandonment archaeology." Because Wheelock blinked in and out of existence within the course of our study, we have been able to study short-term reuse strategies and the abandonment of that short-term reuse. Wheelock is a palimpsest of abandonment, starting from the day it was founded. We have documented a variety of reoccupation strategies and can link those strategies to the goals and practices of discrete groups and individuals. The ability to parse the abandonment process over two years allows for a resolution quite impossible in most archaeological records. Our work not only identifies significant variations in episodic and intermittent abandonment and the material culture signatures of those variations, it also helps frame our concepts of abandonment and the challenges of understanding a complex process that often happens along seldom-noticed peripheries.

SESSION 7A: Joint AIA/SCS Colloquium
Minting an Empire: Negotiating Roman Hegemony Through Coinage
Sponsored by the American Numismatic Society

ORGANIZERS: *Katheryn Whitcomb*, Rutgers University, *Katie Cupello*, Emory University, and *Dominic Machado*, Brown University

Colloquium Overview Statement
This colloquium explores the impacts of Roman hegemony on the production of coinage in regions under Roman influence between the second century B.C.E. and the second century C.E. Through close analysis of the currency systems used in areas dominated by Rome, we explore new avenues for understanding how the Romans conceived of their power vis-à-vis other states and how that power was perceived and negotiated by those under Roman influence.

The papers in this panel build on recent work on "Romanization," which has shifted the focus away from a top-down process to one of reciprocal dialogues between conqueror and conquered, by continuing to explore the ways in which both Roman and non-Roman monetary systems were transformed by the presence of Roman power. We work under two important premises: first, that currency and its response to change is a rich environment within which to consider this interaction; and, second, that both the Romans and those under their rule had some conception of the potential economic and political impact of monetary decisions.

As the Roman empire grew and extended its influence, there were new considerations for both Roman and non-Roman minting authorities. Roman minting authorities were confronted with such issues as, What factors determined whether Rome became involved with the currency regimes of the states over which it exerted influence? Should Rome's policies toward these states change over time? How did new Roman colonies and settlements in the provinces integrate themselves into the economic systems into which they moved? For those experiencing Roman hegemony, related questions arose: How were they to acknowledge the supremacy of Rome while maintaining a local identity? How would a new type of interconnectedness within the Mediterranean world affect the logistics of coin production? What claims to power might be acceptable for local potentates to use? Using these questions as a basis, the papers of this colloquium explore a number of ways in which local and Roman minting authorities negotiated the changing political and economic climate through the production of coinage.

A series of case studies consider these questions in detail. The first paper looks at the *victoriati* issues distributed in the Po River valley as indications of how Rome's numismatic policies acknowledged the idiosyncracies of regional economies. The second paper examines the production and circulation patterns of three silver currencies in Asia as evidence for the Roman alteration of the province's monetary system. The third paper explores the bronze coinages of Chalkis and the expression of Kleopatra VII's authority in the territories given to her by Mark Antony. The fourth paper analyzes the coinage of Philip, son of Herod, and its use of imperial imagery to reinforce the legitimacy of Philip's regime. The final paper investigates the process of Romanization in the imperial use of Asclepius imagery on coinage in the provinces and at Rome. Five minutes will be allotted after each paper for discussion and questions as well as 15 minutes at the conclusion of the panel for general questions and discussion. The panel chair will direct all questions and discussion.

The papers that we have assembled look at this interaction in both the eastern and western parts of the Mediterranean over a span of nearly 400 years. This diversity allows us to investigate the issue not only from the perspective of the imperial power but also from the viewpoint of the periphery. In addition, the broad chronological span allows us to explore how negotiating Roman power may have evolved as Rome grew from the most powerful city-state on the Italian peninsula to the leader of the "known world."

The Distribution of *Victoriati* in the Po River Valley During the Second Century B.C.E.

Dominic Machado, Brown University

This paper presents the results of my analysis of the chronological and geographic distribution of the five largest issues of *victoriati*, a silver coinage without a mark of value minted alongside the denarius for a period of 40 years at the end of the third and beginning of the second century B.C.E. I argue that the *victoriatus'* appearance in the Po River valley in the early second century B.C.E and its metrological similarities to local coinages represent a conscious economic decision related to the contemporaneous Roman colonization initiative in the region. Further, the connection between the distribution of *victoriati* and colonization in the second-century B.C.E. Po River valley aligns well with new models of Roman colonization and forces us to reconsider the mechanisms by which Roman hegemony operated in the Middle Republic.

My analysis of *victoriati* by issue not only confirms earlier studies of the distribution of *victoriati* over time and place, but also reveals new insights into the history of the coinage in the Po River valley. The circulation pattern of the *victoriatus* in the Po River valley differs markedly from the coinage's distribution in Italy, Magna Graecia, and Sicily. While the *victoriatus* reached its peak in these areas during the Second Punic War (218–201 B.C.E.), it did not appear in the Po River valley in significant numbers until the 170s B.C.E. In fact, I argue that the Romans seem to have specifically resumed the production of *victoriati* at this time for distribution in the Po River valley, as RRC 166/1, the largest of the four issues minted from 179 to 170 B.C.E., circulated nearly exclusively in the area.

The distribution of *victoriati* to the Po River valley during the 170s B.C.E. was a carefully thought-out economic decision. Scholars have long noted that the *victoriatus* shows metrological similarities to the coinages of the region, such as the Padane and Massiliote drachms. Further, the fact that the *victoriatus* lacked a mark of value allowed the coin to be assessed on its precious-metal content in areas that had yet to be monetized. The strongest testament to Roman economic foresight, however, is the epigraphic, literary, and numismatic evidence that shows that the *victoriatus* remained important in the Po River valley until the very end of the second century B.C.E.

The historical context of the Po River valley in the second century B.C.E. helps us understand why the Romans minted a coinage that suited the economy of the Po River valley. Not only had the area been recently conquered, but it simultaneously experienced a large influx of Roman colonists at places such as Placentia, Cremona, and Mutina. The usage of the *victoriatus* in this context provides insight into how Rome interacted with its empire in the Middle Republic. While the setting up of colonies in the Po River valley seems to signify a stronger Roman presence in a recently conquered area, no attempt was made to enforce Roman economic norms in the region. Rather, the Roman colonists used a coinage that was falling out of favor in the rest of Italy because it fit well within the preexisting economic contexts of the Po River valley. This picture accords well with new models of Roman colonization during the republic, which emphasize the importance of continuity rather than change in the immediate aftermath of colonial foundation. The *victoriatus* ultimately proves a suitable analogy for Roman economic hegemony in the Middle Republic—both were adaptable and could be used in a variety of places without the disruption of preexisting monetary systems.

Silver and Power: The Three-Fold Roman Impact on the Monetary System of the Provincia Asia (133 B.C.E.–96 C.E.)

Lucia Carbone, Columbia University

εἰς τὸν Εὔξεινον πόντον, Σύλλας δὲ τὴν Ἀσίαν δισμυρίοις
ταλάντοις ἐζημίωσε, προσταχθὲν αὐτῷ τά τε χρήματα ταῦτα
πρᾶξαι καὶ νόμισμα κόψαι

Peace being presently made, Mithridates sailed off to the Euxine Sea,
but Sulla taxed the inhabitants of Asia twenty thousand talents,
and ordered Lucullus to gather wealth and coin the money.
(Plut., *Vit. Luc.* 4.1)

This excerpt from the *Life of Lucullus* describes the aftermath of the First Mithridatic War, after the hasty conclusion of the Peace of Dardanus in 85 B.C.E., and highlights two elements that are central in this paper—namely, that Lucullus, a Roman magistrate, had to "gather" (πρᾶξαι) money and, even more importantly, that he was asked to "issue" currency (νόμισμα κόψαι). Since denarii were not produced and did not circulate in Asia until 49 B.C.E., the currency Lucullus was required to "gather" and "issue" was the cistophorus, a reduced-standard silver tetradrachm whose origins dated back to the Attalid times and whose iconography remained distinctively non-Roman until 59 B.C.E.

How, then, could Lucullus, a Roman magistrate, issue this apparently "non-Roman" currency? What was the level of involvement of Roman provincial power in Asian silver issues? When did Roman silver currency finally arrive in the province? What was the reason that brought the Romans to change the modality of their involvement in the monetary system of the Provincia Asia, apparently moving from a "conservative" attitude to a more "interventionist" one, introducing their own silver currency, the denarius? The numerous attempts to examine the nature of Roman rule in Asia have not grappled seriously with the ubiquitous presence of coinage, which still needs to be assimilated into an inquiry into the transition in structures of power in the region

This paper therefore aims to shed some light on these topics through the original analysis of the production and circulation patterns of three different silver currencies (silver autonomous coinage, cistophori, and denarii) all present in the Provincia Asia in the considered time span and interacting, at a certain level, with one another. Heuristic tools for this research are provided by two databases, one including the civic coinage issued by Asian cities between 133 B.C.E. and 96 C.E. (11,898 coin types) and the other including inscriptions mentioning Roman silver currency in the same years (273 inscriptions). Our thesis is that the establishment of the Roman province of Asia brought elements of novelty in the monetary system of the region, in terms of both production and circulation. The Romans altered the nature of the monetary system in Asia by making it a "relatively" closed currency system, to the difference with the previous Attalid period. Means for the establishment of this currency system were the gradual disappearance of silver autonomous coinages and the coordination of the output of cistophoric mints. This change was probably caused by the necessity of controlling the flow of silver from and to the province and should be put in correlation with the presence of the *societates publicanorum*. This monetary policy, however, was again modified in the 40s B.C.E. with the introduction of the denarius in the circulation pool and, much more relevantly, as an account unit. This finds precise analogies in other eastern provinces of the empire and brought to an end Asian "isolation."

Kleopatra VII's Empire and the Bronze Coinages of Ituraean Chalkis
Katie Cupello, Emory University

This paper explores the ways in which the bronze coins struck for Kleopatra VII at Ituraean Chalkis (i.e., Chalcis sub Libano in Coele Syria) express the queen's authority both as a monarch in her own right and as a partner to Mark Antony. Kleopatra received Chalkis from Antony, the Roman triumvir with hegemony over the eastern provinces, as part of the territorial grant of 37/6 B.C.E. This grant restored to the queen areas that were once part of the overseas empire of the Ptolemies, including Coele Syria and part of Phoenicia. I consider the design choices made by those in charge of the Chalkis mint to illustrate what these coins communicate about Kleopatra in relation to her newly expanded empire and her relationship with Antony. The discussion focuses primarily on the target weight standard, the size and number of denominations, the images and inscribed legends of the obverse and reverse types, and the dating system used.

The Kleopatra bronzes from Chalkis are not unknown. Study of the Chalkis mint's output, however, has consciously pushed aside the Kleopatra coins in favor of treating as a somewhat cohesive group the bronze coinages of the three native Ituraean tetrarchs who ruled Chalkis before and after Kleopatra: Ptolemaios son of Mennaios (85–40 B.C.E.); Lysanias (40–37/6 B.C.E.); and Zenodoros (30–20 B.C.E.), to whom Octavian restored the tetrarchy. Plugging Kleopatra back into the Chalkis equation is a step toward a better understanding not only of these particular coins but also of the coins issued for Kleopatra by other mints, such as Berytos, Orthosia, and Ptolemais.

I address the Kleopatra coins from Chalkis in two parts. First, I present the results of a metrological analysis comparing the coins of Kleopatra with the coins of the three Ituraean tetrarchs. This kind of analysis uses the weights and diameters of as many surviving examples as possible to determine, if doable, the weight standard and number of denominations that are the basis for a particular coinage. It seems, at this point, that the bronzes struck for Kleopatra fit into the scheme already established at the mint of Chalkis; therefore, there was continuity in this respect. Second, I use other facets of the coins' design to demonstrate that Kleopatra was not simply another tetrarch of Chalkis. For example, the Greek legends boldly label her portrait as "Queen Kleopatra" as opposed to "tetrarch and chief priest." Her position as queen is further reinforced by the absence of an ethnic, used at other mints such as Berytos, asserting the identity of Chalkis and its people. Moreover, one of the three reverse types paired with Kleopatra's image is an unnamed portrait of Antony. We have thus an unequivocal declaration of Kleopatra's authority over Chalkis as queen of her Egyptian and foreign kingdoms, with Antony as the subordinate guarantor of her newly obtained territories. This Kleopatra/Antony type of Chalkis makes for a rather interesting comparison with the familiar double-headed silver tetradrachms and denarii depicting the queen and the triumvir. Recent work has determined that Kleopatra, not Antony, occupies the dominant position on the obverse of both denominations. On these coins, however, the obverse and reverse legends provide names and titles for each of them. Here, Antony is on more equal footing, but we are left to wonder just who was in charge and what the vision of a Romano-Ptolemaic empire might have been. After all, the territorial grants of 37/6 B.C.E. were also the first occasion on which Antony publicly acknowledged his children by Kleopatra. In the words of Shakespeare, "Let Rome in Tiber melt" indeed.

Coinage and the Client Prince: Philip the Tetrarch's Homage to the Roman Emperor
Katheryn Whitcomb, Rutgers University

This paper examines the coinage of Philip (r. 4 B.C.E.–34 C.E.), son of Herod the Great and tetrarch of Batanea, Trachonitis, Paneas, and Auranitis, in the context of the coins of three other groups of minting authorities: contemporary client rulers, defined for the purposes of this paper as independent rulers who achieved their position through Roman support; contemporary municipal coinages of Syria; and other successors to Herod. I argue that the coins of Philip, in comparison with these other coinages, demonstrate a remarkable level of preoccupation with the Roman emperors Augustus and Tiberius. This emphasis on the reigning emperor leads to an almost complete absence of expressions of local identity on Philip's coinage. Further, by emphasizing his connection to the emperor, Philip signals that the legitimacy of his rule comes from the central Roman authority rather than from any connection to Herod's legacy. It has been suggested that Philip minted coins bearing the emperor's likeness simply because he ruled over a territory that was predominantly non-Jewish and therefore was not constricted by the Jewish prohibition against graven images, as other Herodians were. I argue, however, that the non-Jewish character of his tetrarchy not only allowed but even mandated that Philip make such a strong connection between his regime and the Roman authority that established it.

My analysis of the coins of Philip is aided by the work of Horster, which examines the use of imperial portraiture and expressions of local civic identity in the Greek East. In addition, the work of Burnett, which discusses the process of "Romanization" in the coinages of Syria, provides valuable background for this paper. Dahmen provides useful context for assessing the extent to which the coinage of Philip is similar to and different from the coinages of other contemporary client rulers. Finally, the works of Hendin, Meshorer, and Fontanille give valuable insights into the coinage of Philip itself.

Each issue of Philip's coinage, minted throughout his long tenure as tetrarch, displays a portrait of the emperor (Augustus or Tiberius) on at least one denomination. Portraits of Livia also appear, perhaps as early as her designation as Augusta in 14 C.E. The reverses of the coins bearing the emperor universally depict the Augusteum, the temple built by Herod at Paneas and dedicated to Augustus. It is remarkable that even on the reverse of these coins, where we would most expect to see an expression of local identity, another symbol referencing the emperor appears. In contrast, the coinages of contemporary client rulers from Mauretania to Commagene exhibit oblique references to the emperor (such as Antiochus IV of Commagene's use of the Capricorn on the reverse of his bronze coinage), but none does so on both sides of the coins. Issues from municipal mints may or may not include portraits of the emperor, and even those that do display strong expressions of local identity on their reverses. Only the coinage of Agrippa I, Philip's nephew, can rival his in its preoccupation with Rome and the emperor. Even the coins of Agrippa, however, consistently represent local imagery as well as imperial imagery.

Philip's use of imperial imagery on both the obverse and reverse of his coins sets him apart from other client rulers, local mints in Syria, and even his fellow successors to Herod. Further, by naming himself Philip the Tetrarch (ΦΙΛΙΠΠΟΣ ΤΕΤΡΑΡΧΟΣ) on his coins, rather than using the title Herod the Tetrarch (ΗΡΩΔΗC ΤΕΤΡΑΡΧΗC) seen on the coins of his brothers, Antipas and Archelaus, he obscures any legitimacy an association with Herod would give him. Clearly, a connection to Roman power carries more currency, in more ways than one, with the audience Philip is trying to reach through his coinage.

The Romanization of a Thoroughly Greek God: Asclepius Coinage of the Roman Empire
Caroline Wazer, Columbia University

In this paper, I argue that an increase in the frequency and geographic range of Roman imperial Asclepius coins, begun by Domitian and continuing until the Third-Century Crisis, is a rich example of Wallace-Hadrill's "circulation" model of hellenization and romanization, a process that continued in waves long after the Roman subjugation of the Greek world. In particular, I draw connections between the appearance of Asclepius on imperial coins and a resurgence of Roman interest in Greek Asclepius sanctuaries after a lengthy period of neglect. This resurgence of interest is well attested by epigraphic and textual evidence. Further, I argue that by the second century C.E., primarily because of political and cultural developments in Rome, Asclepius was no longer seen as a Greek god of medicine with strong regional ties, relatively unimportant in the pantheon except to the sick. Rather, because of the development of ideas connecting the emperor and health, Asclepius' cult took on a political meaning that was transmitted back to Greek cities through a variety of media, the most consistent of which was coinage.

Although Roman interaction with the medical god Asclepius dates from at least the early third century B.C.E., when the senate formally imported his cult to Rome following an epidemic, the god, like ancient medicine as a discipline, was always considered Greek in nature. While certain Roman gods and goddesses, most prominently Salus, took on some of his characteristics on coinage and in other media, Asclepius himself never appeared on Republican or Julio-Claudian coins. Starting in the late first century C.E., however, Asclepius became a mainstay on Roman coinage. The first emperor to mint an Asclepius coin was Domitian; after him, nearly every emperor until the Third-Century Crisis, 18 in all, minted at least one issue of coins bearing an image of Asclepius.

Many Asclepius issues were provincial. Coinage bearing the image of Asclepius had a long tradition, in some cases dating back to the fifth century B.C.E., in a small number of Greek cities with important sanctuaries of the god, such as Pergamon and Kos. Under the Roman empire, however, the number of provincial cities minting Asclepius coins grew dramatically. The British Museum's collection includes Asclepian coins from 162 different cities across the Mediterranean, most of which had no significant historic ties to the god.

While the dramatic geographic expansion of Asclepius coins suggests a broad cultural shift leading to a popularization of the Asclepian cult, the iconography of certain coins hints at the important role Roman emperors took in the god's empire-wide growth in profile. A striking Pergamene issue from the reign of Commodus, which depicts the emperor in military dress hailing Asclepius, sacrificing to him, and eventually being worshiped alongside him as a *synnaos theos*, reveals an intimate relationship between emperor and god. On other provincial coins, empresses including Faustina and Julia Domna are iconographically associated with female figures closely related to Asclepius—namely, his mother Coronis and his daughter Hygieia. Such coins emphasized the connection between the imperial family and the family of Asclepius.

Asclepius coins minted at Rome are fewer, but are also historically significant. While Marcus Aurelius and Caracalla both minted coins with images of the god in Rome, one example from the capital particularly underlines the importance of Asclepius in imperial ideology. In 195 C.E., shortly before they declared war on each other, Septimius Severus and Clodius Albinus (then coconsuls) each minted a series of coins with his own portrait on the obverse and one of several deities on the reverse. The deities chosen include Roma, Victoria, Minerva, and Felicitas, all of which evoke imperial power and foreshadow the coming civil war. The only apparent outlier is Asclepius, who appears on a denarius and an as of Albinus. I argue that in the context of the previous century of numismatic history, Asclepius, too, must be read as a symbol of the emperor.

SESSION 7B: Workshop
Innovation at the Juncture of Conservation and Archaeology: Collaborative Technical Research

MODERATORS: *Anna Serotta*, Brooklyn Museum, and *Vanessa Muros*, University of California, Los Angeles

This workshop will present a series of short talks highlighting technical research projects in which both archaeologists and conservators played critical roles. Archaeological research is by nature interdisciplinary, and best practice often relies on the coming together of specialists from various disciplines to fully explore the question at hand. The unique background of conservators—at the intersection of science, the humanities, and craft—makes these professionals well suited to engage in multifaceted research projects, particularly those dealing with the physical nature of archaeological data. Collaborations between conservators and archaeologists in the investigation of artifact manufacture, materials characterization, and issues regarding ongoing preservation can produce rich results, as will be demonstrated by speakers in this session. The projects presented will emphasize the benefit of this cross-pollination of ideas in the analysis, interpretation, and display of finds and sites.

During this workshop, a series of 10-15 minute talks will be jointly presented by archaeologists and conservators. Presenters will share their research aims and outline their methodology. A 10-minute moderated discussion session will follow each presentation, so that audience members can have the opportunity to engage with presenters and ask questions about both the technical aspects of the work and the interpretation of results. The projects presented will include topics such as the use of new digital imaging technologies, such as reflectance transformation imaging and photogrammetry, to aid in the interpretation and documentation of artifacts and monuments, and the use of portable analytical tools in the characterization of materials.

The goal of this workshop is to demonstrate insightful research that can occur when archaeologists, conservators, and professionals in other allied disciplines come together to jointly address questions about material culture. It is hoped that the projects presented in this session will spark productive discussion and engender future collaborations of this nature.

PANELISTS: *Renee Stein*, Michael C. Carlos Museum, Emory University, *Robert H. Tykot*, University of South Florida, *Nicholas Cahill*, University of Wisconsin–Madison, *Emily B. Frank*, Institute of Fine Arts, New York University, *David R. Scahill*, American School of Classical Studies at Athens, *Alison Hight*, Emory University, *Jessica Walthew*, Metropolitan Museum of Art, *Eve Mayberger*, New York University, and *Colleen O'Shea*, Historic New England, and *Jacob Bongers*, Cotsen Institute of Archaeology, University of California, Los Angeles

SESSION 7C: Colloquium
Depositions and Depositional Processes in Ancient Greek Cities and Sanctuaries

ORGANIZERS: *Astrid Lindenlauf*, Bryn Mawr College, and *Aileen Ajootian*, University of Mississippi

Colloquium Overview Statement

Ancient artifacts and monuments have one thing in common: we have retrieved them from the archaeological record or, to use Schiffer's terminology, they have become archaeologically traceable refuse. Their life history and transition to the archaeological context may have been different, though. Processes and activities leading to the passing out of the use life could range from natural disasters, such as flood and earthquakes, to breakage, destruction, abandonment, ritual deposition, and discard. In addition, the transition to the archaeological record could be gradual and slow—for instance, when a monument was left to decay or when useless artifacts were collected in a large rubbish pit. They could alternatively be quick and irreversible—for instance, when objects were dumped into the sea or when a monument was covered under a thick layer of ash. The variety and the combination of these factors contribute not only to different biographies of artifacts and monuments but also to depositional histories. In this session, we build on formation theory to explain why specific artifacts or monuments or parts thereof ended up at the place where we discovered them. However, we also go beyond formation theory as we try to put human agents at the forefront of our inquiry. By conceptualizing depositional processes as depositional activities rather than atemporal and aspatial behaviors, we try to place more emphasis on valuations of, and attitudes toward, objects that define the ways in which they were treated at the end of their use life and underlying thought processes that guided the ancient Greeks in dealing with old and useless artifacts and monuments.

The first three presentations of our colloquium deal exclusively with votive deposits with a view to highlighting similarities and differences in the treatment of dedications. Sanctuaries include Olympia, Isthmia, and the Acropolis of Athens. The following two presentations also focus on Athens. The fourth paper traces the different pathways of archaic architecture that once stood on the Acropolis. The fifth paper examines material available for reuse in the Roman and Late Antique periods. One of the case studies, the transportation of the classical Ares temple from Pallene into the middle of the Agora, is a later example of a similar narrative. We conclude the session by tracing the depositional histories of classical votive reliefs found in Byzantine assemblages in the Forum of Corinth and shedding some light on the mechanisms bringing about the shift in the valuation of objects as valuable to valueless.

Reconstructing Depositional Processes in the Sanctuary of Zeus in Olympia: Methods, Problems, Results

Heide Frielinghaus, Johannes Gutenberg-Universität Mainz, Germany

The sanctuary of Zeus in Olympia provides many opportunities to study depositional processes for more than 400 years. The fill of about 300 ephemeral wells, the earthworks of several phases of the stadium, and the preparation of the ground for the construction of new buildings gave ample opportunities to discard rubbish of every sort as well as old votive offerings. In the first part of this paper, I discuss various discarding practices in archaic and classical Olympia by analyzing six exemplary deposits that differ with respect to their dates and their topographical setting. The wells under discussion are situated in the so-called southeast area, in the stadium's northern embankment and in the area of the so-called Prytaneion. They demonstrate that these deposits vary in terms of their composition. They also indicate that people could choose between different features and places for disposal. These examples further demonstrate the necessity of taking into consideration the possible simultaneous availability of "rubbish dumps," the shifting of (parts of) older deposits, and the general structural developments of the sanctuary when interpreting the formation of a deposit. Based on these general observations,

I focus on the second part on the deposition of two groups of bronze objects, armor, and bronze vessels, with a view to comparing and contrasting their findspots and the manner in which they were deposited.

The Archaic Reservoir at the Sanctuary of Poseidon at Isthmia: A Study of Depositional Processes
Martha K. Risser, Trinity College, Connecticut

Measuring 5 m in diameter and nearly 20 m deep, the Archaic Reservoir (also called the "Large Circular Pit" and the "Great Circular Pit" in various publications) in the Sanctuary of Poseidon at Isthmia was filled with sculpture, architectural fragments, metal vessels, arms, armor, and about a ton of pottery. Oscar Broneer identified seven levels of fill but noted that they are not clearly separated strata. It is also evident that the material was not deposited in chronological order. Much of the latest material in the main fill, dating to the second and third quarters of the fifth century, was found near the bottom. Vases from the first half of the sixth century and earlier are more numerous in the upper levels. At the top, Broneer's "Level I" included Roman material and was disturbed in post-classical times.

The archaic reservoir was apparently filled during a single event, a cleaning operation that was part of the preparation for the construction of the Classical Temple of Poseidon and a new water source nearby. My paper is an analysis of evidence for the depositional behaviors and procedures at work in the filling activity. First, I review the compositions of the levels. Next, I discuss criteria for distinguishing between levels related to feasting activity, those consisting primarily of debris from the fire that destroyed the Archaic Temple of Poseidon ca. 460–450 B.C.E., and other aspects of the cleaning process. This segues into a discussion of depositional practices and processes. Finally, the wider picture is addressed. What can we infer about dedicatory behaviors, sacrificial practices, dining, sanctuary management, and landscaping at Isthmia during this period?

A Depositional Analysis of the So-Called Kore Pit on the Acropolis of Athens
Astrid Lindenlauf, Bryn Mawr College

Not one of the costly large-scale anathemata that had been dedicated from the late seventh to the fifth century was found in situ when excavations took place on the Acropolis. Instead, they were found in a variety of deposits dotted across the Acropolis. The majority of the pre-Persian dedications were found during the 19th-century excavations close to the Erechtheion and the Parthenon in artificial pockets, where they had been deposited in the course of the reorganization and reconstruction of the Acropolis. Judging from the excavation documentation, the large-scale stone and bronze votive statues were rarely discovered in individual pits or indeed individually but rather in massive strata together with soil and stones, architectural fragments, public inscriptions, small bronzes, tripods, terracotta figurines, lamps, and fragments of pottery. The majority of the statuary dedications were part of the three largest and best-known deposits on the Acropolis, the northern deposit or kore pit (in front of the North Citadel Wall), the southern deposit (south of the Parthenon), and the southeastern deposit (found southeast of the Parthenon), whose composition and chronology Andrew Stewart revised in 2008, when he affirmed that only the northern assemblage consisted exclusively of pre-Persian material.

In this paper, I revisit the so-called kore pit and study it from a depositional point of view. I start by reconstructing its composition based on reports and publications of the excavator. It is suggested that the Athenians did not exclusively choose to deposit korai here. Then, I try to understand the criteria according to which the Athenians selected the votives that were deposited west of the Erechtheion and to discuss whether any of them were ritually destroyed before their deposition. Finally, I address the question of whether this structured deposit should be interpreted as a careful burial or as sacred rubbish. I propose that the Athenians made a special effort to deposit a representative sample of freestanding votive statues in a respectful manner in the first stage of the rebuilding process of the Acropolis before using them solely as construction fill across the Acropolis.

Reduce, Reuse, and Recycle: Cleaning and Clearing of the Athenian Acropolis
Nancy Klein, Texas A&M University

The architectural identity of ancient Greek sanctuaries was expressed by a variety of structures, including temples, treasuries, stoas, gateways, and altars. While monumental stone buildings have the potential to stand for thousands of years, historical sources describe natural disasters and human actions that damaged or rendered obsolete the sacred structures. On the Acropolis of Athens, the architectural form of the sanctuary was shaped by factors that reflect both the best and the worst of human intentions and interventions: religious devotion, expression of social identity, exploitation of natural resources, economic prosperity, political upheavals, defeat and/or victory in war. Correlates in the built environment include the construction of the first monumental peripteral temples and small limestone buildings in the Archaic and Early Classical periods. In 490 B.C.E., the victory over the Persians at Marathon and the availability of marble from Mount Pentelicon in Attica inspired the Athenians to demolish the older limestone temple and build a marble replacement. The Persian occupation and sack of Athens in 480/79 B.C.E. was followed by cleaning and management of the ruins in the period between the eventual Greek victory and the decision to rebuild the sanctuary in the mid fifth century B.C.E.

This paper assesses patterns of architectural reuse and dates of deposition as a means of understanding the processes that shaped the classical sanctuary on the Acropolis of Athens. The 19th-century excavations uncovered architectural elements that were deposited in secondary fills or reused in foundations and structures. Battered but recognizable fragments of limestone architecture and sculpture were found in fill to the east and south of the Parthenon, while better-preserved architectural blocks were identified in the Acropolis walls and building foundations. Recent studies of the Acropolis stratigraphy offer a better understanding of the chronological framework for the phases of deposition, and the dates of the Periclean buildings provide a terminus ante quem for the demise of earlier buildings whose parts were reused in their construction. The results suggest that the sanctuary renovation included the evaluation of materials from buildings that were damaged or obsolete and the active management of these resources through demolition and disposal or stockpiling for later reuse. These observations not only establish a life history for individual structures—date of construction, functional lifespan, and reuse—but also contribute to a larger understanding of the processes that shaped the sanctuary on the Athenian Acropolis in the fifth century B.C.E.

Stones Jumping Out: An Examination of Upcycling as a Depositional Activity in Ancient Athens
Sarah A. Rous, Harvard University

Reuse is one key factor in explaining how artifacts and materials ended up in the places we have discovered them. Instead of being discarded, ritually deposited, or abandoned, old objects and structures could also be put to new uses or used in new contexts. Sometimes the previous function or identity of the old material is completely obliterated in its reuse, as in Schiffer's model, where recycling and lateral cycling reset the life history of an artifact. But sometimes a particular object is chosen for reuse in a particular new context or function based not simply on its physical suitability but also on some aspect of its previous life history. I use the term "upcycling" to refer to this type of intentionally meaningful reuse, where the secondary context preserves some visibility or knowledge of the past life of the object and of the act of reuse itself. Upcycling is reuse undertaken with some sense of purpose and consequence by the artist/patron/conceiver and meant to have implications for its viewer/reader/audience. It is thus a depositional activity that relies on human agents and their goals and, because it makes reference to the past in the present, often affects and draws on the social memory of a community. Recognizing upcycling at work within the archaeological record and examining questions of agency, visibility, and reception can help us interpret acts of reuse more meaningfully in their cultural context.

In this paper, I demonstrate the efficacy of investigating upcycling as a depositional activity by discussing the reuse of architectural elements in the third-century C.E. Post-Herulian Wall, as well as the wholesale transport of the classical Temple of Ares from Pallene into the Athenian Agora in the Early Roman period. In reexamining the Post-Herulian Wall in light of its physical and cultural context within Athens, I argue that by enhancing the visibility of the elements reused in the wall and highlighting their prior functions, the Athenians encouraged collective remembrance of the sack and the subsequent recovery of their city. In the case of the Temple of Ares, following Steuernagel's recent argument that the Areopagus Council was responsible for its transport and reerection, I show that the choice to upcycle the Pallene temple was designed as a statement of identity and authority and fulfilled long-term goals of memory creation.

Finding Their Way: Late Classical Votive Reliefs at Ancient Corinth
Aileen Ajootian, University of Mississippi

More than 100 years of excavation at ancient Corinth have produced quantities of sculpture, but archaic and classical material is rare. One exception is the group of at least 90 classical votive reliefs, which include whole panels and fragments. One piece dates to the late fifth century B.C.E., but most are probably fourth century or early third. These dedications illuminate a period in Corinth's history that is underrepresented not only by marble sculpture but also by buildings. Types include banquet reliefs, equestrian scenes, cave reliefs, and a few where devotees approach recognizable divinities. The marbles come from all over the site. Typically sculpture at Corinth is not found in situ but in secondary or even tertiary settings. Judging from the spatial distribution patterns, marble votive reliefs were more common in some areas than others. From the Asklepieion, northeast of the forum at Corinth, for example, only three votive reliefs have been recovered. The Sanctuary of Demeter on the north slope of Akrocorinth produced none at all. The deposition of fragmentary Late Classical votive reliefs chiefly in Byzantine contexts in the forum at Corinth suggests that the panels were removed from their original settings and broken up but that the pieces remained available for use in nearby constructions. The later history of some votive reliefs at Corinth may point to their first setting and function.

In this paper, I analyze the deposits in the area of the Forum, because more than 25 fragmentary votive reliefs were recovered from trenches in the center of the site between the 1930s and the 1970s. Depending on the excavator, the findspots bear different names: Agora Southeast, Agora Southwest, Forum Southwest, and South Stoa. A closer look at field notebooks reveals that many of these marbles can be located more precisely in late strata—Middle Byzantine or later—over the South Stoa. The construction of the Stoa in the late fourth century B.C.E. absorbed the east wall of a little sixth-century precinct, the so-called Stele Shrine, immediately to its west. This installation continued in use, with the west wall of the stoa now its eastern boundary, until Late Hellenistic times. It is suggested in this paper that while no votive reliefs come from the Stele Shrine itself, many fragments have turned up nearby. Along with terracotta banqueters, horse figurines, and other material, it is possibly that marble plaques were also dedicated in this area during the Late Classical period.

SESSION 7D: Colloquium
Long-Term Urban Dynamics at Knossos: The Knossos Urban Landscape Project, 2005–2015

ORGANIZER: *Todd Whitelaw*, University College London

Colloquium Overview Statement

Knossos in north-central Crete is one of the most widely known archaeological sites in the world. The community is one of a handful of known Early Neolithic villages in the Aegean, established ca. 7000 B.C.E., and it was continuously occupied as one of the major Aegean communities until the Late Antique period, ca. 700 C.E. About 2000 B.C.E., it became the first urban community in Europe and was central to the development of the earliest European state-level society. Following the political collapse at the end of the Bronze Age, it was one of the first urban centers to develop in the Early Iron Age Aegean. A significant center for nearly eight millennia, Knossos serves as an exceptional barometer for long-term cultural developments in the Aegean and, through its widespread connections in many periods, well beyond.

Knossos was first systematically investigated by Sir Arthur Evans and the British School at Athens in 1900. Evans' interests were firmly focused on the later Bronze Age and the area of the palace. Investigations by members of the School and the Hellenic Archaeological Service, continuing to the present, have broadened that chronological and spatial focus, though the Bronze Age core of the site remains the most thoroughly documented. With major research excavations complemented by many rescue excavations, the site is one of the most intensively investigated in the eastern Mediterranean.

The Knossos Urban Landscape Project is a collaboration between the British School at Athens and the Archaeological Service. Initiated to mark the centenary of the start of Evans' excavations and the involvement of the British School at Knossos, the project aims to synthesize and build on the first century of investigations at the site. It has four principal objectives: to record the archaeological resources to aid their protection and inform the management of development in the valley; to document systematically the archaeological record and contextualize the century of previous investigations; to integrate new systematically collected surface data with existing data to reconstruct long-term urban dynamics at Knossos; and to provide a basis for designing future investigations at the site.

Fieldwork was undertaken in 2005, 2007, and 2008, with study seasons undertaken annually since then. This colloquium is the first detailed presentation of interim project results, integrating the new surface data with reassessments of each major phase of occupation for an overview of the development of this exceptional site over eight millennia.

Knossos and Its Immediate Hinterland from the Neolithic to the End of the Prepalatial Period
Borja Legarra Herrero, University College London

The site of Knossos was a significant community within Crete from the beginning of the Neolithic period in the Aegean. It was founded as a small village ca. 7000 B.C.E., immediately adjacent to one of the few perennial rivers in northern Crete. The community expanded gradually through the period, and by the end of the Neolithic, ca. 3200 B.C.E., it was the largest settlement on the island, probably reaching 500–1000 inhabitants. Knossos continued to be an anomalously large community during the Early Bronze Age, and by the Middle Minoan (MM) IA period the community had grown tenfold to become the earliest urban community in the Aegean. Major current debates center on the pace and nature of this transformation, as well the size of the community during the five millennia of the Neolithic and Prepalatial Bronze Age. Alternative views propose either early, slow evolution or late, rapid revolution, leading to very different explanations for the changes experienced by this community and its inhabitants and their wider implications for our understanding of the emergence of civilization in the southern Aegean.

This paper presents new evidence recovered by the Knossos Urban Landscape Project in relation to the Neolithic and Prepalatial periods, with the aim of understanding the growth and social development of the community. The presentation considers the methodological difficulties involved in interpreting the seventh- to third-millennium material from the deeply stratified multiperiod site. It then explores the potential for combining the surface, survey evidence with the data provided by the long sequence of excavations at the site to synthesize a more detailed and accurate picture of the diachronic trajectory of the site from the Neolithic to the Middle Minoan (MM) IA period. Evidence is presented defining the interactions of the community with its immediate hinterland, exploring the changing relations of the growing population with their environment, and considering the conspicuous absence of known Early Bronze Age cemeteries in the area. Also considered is the potential role of Knossos in the long-term expansion of communities across the rest of Crete during the Neolithic and Early Bronze Age. The presentation concludes with a consideration of the dynamic changes in the community in relation to major debates on the development of social complexity on the island.

Protopalatial Knossos: The Development of a Major Urban Community
Andrew Shapland, The British Museum

The Protopalatial period at Knossos is seen as a time of momentous political change. Its start is defined by the building of the palace on the summit of the low Kephala hill, although substantial structures already existed there in the late Prepalatial period. By the time of the major destructions in the Middle Minoan (MM) IIIA phase that mark the end of the Protopalatial period, Knossos was becoming the preeminent site on Crete. These architectural and political changes, however, are only indirectly reflected in the survey material that this paper principally presents. The diagnostic pottery of the Middle Minoan period consists mostly of fine light-on-dark "Kamares Ware" (although painted decoration needed for close dating rarely survives in surface material) and to a lesser extent the mass-produced MM II–IIIA "crude ware," which can be distinguished from Neopalatial ceramics only in the case of particular shapes. Coarse wares are less specifically diagnostic for this period, although a number of fabrics have been identified that were used in the Protopalatial period, aiding chronological attribution. The distribution of fine wares in particular documents the rapid expansion of the urban center to more than 50 ha by the end of the Protopalatial period, a pattern broadly paralleled at the other major central Cretan palatial centers at Malia and Phaistos. This expansion is consistent with the wider territorial expansion of Knossos during this time, which was necessary to support the growing population of the increasingly differentiated urban community.

This paper also examines the relationship of the survey data to the published archaeological features of the Knossos Valley. The Middle Minoan burial landscape of the hills surrounding Knossos is known through extensive excavation. The survey data augment this picture, but it is often difficult to distinguish cemetery areas from the background scatter of settlement debris, a problem compounded by poor visibility in some of the steeper hill-slope areas favored for rock-cut tombs. For the settlement, the survey material defines the boundaries of the urban core in the Protopalatial period in a more consistent way than the uneven distribution of excavations of Middle Minoan houses, clustered close to the palace, had allowed previously. This paper concludes that a combination of survey and excavation data largely provides an accurate picture of the extent of Protopalatial Knossos, although the emphasis in the survey data on closely datable fine wares and recovery biases mean that the picture is still incomplete.

Neopalatial and Mycenaean Knossos: Urban Expansion and Collapse
Joanne Cutler, Cambridge University

The prehistoric city of Knossos reached its maximum extent during the Neopalatial period. Beyond the palace, the city is known principally through the grand houses excavated near the palace by Evans. A few others, some excavated more recently, are more widely distributed. Extramural cemeteries are distributed across the surrounding hill slopes. The Knossos Urban Landscape Project survey data contextualize the information provided by the excavations, producing a clearer picture of the entire palatial settlement.

The distribution of Neopalatial ceramics indicates that the city was considerably larger than previously estimated, extending more than 100 ha, with a significant suburb on the summit of the Ailias Ridge to the east. Occupation extended well beyond the areas of intensive excavation, particularly to the north and northwest of the palace, but it also expanded into areas of earlier cemeteries to the south and west, on the Gypsadhes and Acropolis Hills.

This paper presents the preliminary results of the analysis of the Neopalatial ceramic material, considered in combination with the available data from previous excavations at the site. It examines the evidence for the development and maximum expansion of the Neopalatial city and explores the implications of the significant urban expansion of Knossos for its potential development into a regional administrative center for the whole of central Crete. This paper also considers the possibility that the exceptionally high consumption demands of such a large palatial center (twice the documented extent of Malia and Phaistos, its peers in the Protopalatial period) may have contributed to the Late Minoan (LM) IB collapse of the Knossian Neopalatial administration.

For the succeeding LM II–III periods, controversy continues to surround the date of the final destruction of the palace, in which the bulk of the clay Linear B administrative tablets were preserved. The survey data are integrated with a reconsideration of evidence from excavations in the city and cemeteries to define a two-stage contraction from the Neopalatial maximum extent of the city, corresponding to LM II–IIIA and LM IIIB–IIIC. That the extensive administrative control over central and western Crete documented by the Linear B archive was accompanied by a significant contraction in city size suggests a significant change in the nature of polity administration.

Finally, even in decline during the final Bronze Age phases Knossos appears to have been the largest community on Crete and may be considered to have maintained some role as a local center for north-central Crete.

Early Iron Age Knossos and the Development of the City of the Historical Period
Antonis Kotsonas, University of Cincinnati

Knossos is widely considered one of the most prosperous Aegean communities in the Early Iron Age, particularly on the basis of finds from its cemeteries. Because of later disturbance, predominantly stone robbing down to Bronze Age levels, it has not been possible to document the accompanying settlement very clearly. This paper revisits the evidence for the size and structure of the community, integrating recent fieldwork with evidence from earlier excavations in the settlement and cemeteries. The Knossos Urban Landscape Project recovered an unusually rich assemblage of ceramics from the Early Iron Age, a period that is typically underrepresented in Aegean surveys. The abundance of data provides an opportunity for revisiting the local ceramic sequence and developing macroscopic fabric groups to supplement the existing body of analytical research on the local ceramics. More importantly, these data promise a relatively strong basis for a detailed understanding of the size and organization of the community and its development for nearly half a millennium.

The surface exploration documented a wide scatter of ceramics, including in areas not previously intensively investigated. The scatter extends from the west bank of the Kairatos River to the west slopes of the acropolis hill, and from the north slopes of the Gypsadhes hill to roughly midway between the Minoan palace and the Kephala hill. This extensive area includes both domestic and burial material, and distinguishing between the two is essential for determining the size of the settlement and understanding the demographic, sociopolitical, and economic development of the community.

The picture that emerges from the surface evidence calls into question previous interpretations of the nature and extent of the settlement during the Early Iron Age. The site is shown to have been considerably larger than previously assumed already in the local Protogeometric period (10th to ninth centuries B.C.E.). The continuous distribution of material also demonstrates the expansion of a large nucleated community from a small core, which almost certainly survived from the Late Bronze Age. Survey in the areas of some of the dispersed cemeteries revealed no evidence for dispersed villages associated with each cemetery, refuting the model of polis formation through synoecism for Knossos.

This new understanding of the settlement corresponds much better with the significance given to the site through its burial evidence, in studies of Crete, the Aegean, and the Mediterranean in the Early Iron Age.

Polis and Colony: Urban Knossos from Archaic to Late Antique Times
Conor Trainor, University College Dublin

The landscape focus of the Knossos Urban Landscape Project (KULP) casts new light on urban archaic, classical, Hellenistic, and Roman Knossos and for the first time affords us a view of the city as a whole during its life as a polis and as a colony. Study of the post–Early Iron Age ceramics has just started but is already modifying our understanding of the development of the settlement.

Concentrations of ceramics dating to the Archaic and Classical periods east of the Minoan palace and south of the modern upper village may provide evidence to counter the traditional interpretation of a sixth-century lacuna at Knossos. Classical finds are more common than archaic ones, with activity increasing significantly during the Late Classical period. By Hellenistic times, the city reached its maximum size of 130 ha. At this time, the city appears to have been producing many of the locally consumed ceramics, as well as importing and exporting goods through Cretan, Aegean, Ionian, and wider eastern Mediterranean exchange networks.

During the Early Roman period, Knossos contracted significantly in size, usually attributed to part of its territory being awarded to Capua as a penalty for its opposition to the Roman conquest of Crete. In contrast, the city appears to have undergone significant economic development: the production of Knossian transport amphoras as well as the range of types produced in the city peaked during this time. Production was centered on the area southwest of the acropolis and included the manufacture of ceramics, wine, and honey. A large concentration of nonlocal amphoras near the northern bounds of the city may represent a commercial rather than production locus.

Imported Late Roman amphora and fine ware ceramics are rare, indicating changes in urban character during the third to fifth centuries C.E. The northwestern distribution of most late material indicates why this period has not been widely recognized in excavations in the south of the city and documents a contracting settlement associated with the extensive excavated cemeteries of the fifth to seventh centuries C.E.

To date, archaic through Late Antique Knossos has been interpreted through limited excavations supplemented by written and epigraphic sources, and scholars have had a very patchy understanding of the city as a whole. The results from KULP are enabling us to view the Greek and Roman city of Knossos as a dynamic, functioning settlement within its wider economic and political contexts.

The Long-Term Urban Dynamics of Knossos in Context
Todd Whitelaw, University College London, *A. Vasilakis*, Hellenic Archaeological Service, and *Bredaki, M.*, Hellenic Archaeological Service

As with all surface surveys, the Knossos Urban Landscape Project data are qualified by the battered condition of the recovered material and variable recovery conditions. But unlike with most surveys, we have collected large samples and have the advantage of a very well documented and published local ceramic sequence.

Surprisingly for a site so intensively investigated, approximately three-fifths of the city site and much of the surrounding mortuary landscape had never been documented. The survey extends our understanding of the site spatially but also fills in many gaps, allowing us to contextualize previous isolated excavations, which can now be integrated into our understanding of site development. In addition, all periods are being investigated, redressing the strong prehistoric bias of most major excavations. An explicitly diachronic perspective is challenging but rewarding, cutting across chronological divisions that prioritize different questions.

No single site has had such a continuous focal role not just in north-central Crete but also more widely in the Aegean. Integration of the survey data with results from previous investigations allows us to rewrite the history of the settlement in every period. Following the long, slow development of the Neolithic community, the Early Bronze Age takeoff is not, as assumed for the past 40 years, in the mid third millennium but at its end, in the centuries just prior to the traditional phase of state formation. Dramatic expansion continues through the Protopalatial period, and, contrasting with the other major palatial centers, growth at Knossos continues unabated through the Neopalatial period. This requires that we reconsider the changing political role of Knossos among the major Cretan polities and provides new support for the long-debated question of Knossian hegemony in central Crete. A new perspective can also be provided on the decline of Mycenaean Knossos, with documentation of two stages in its contraction from its Neopalatial maximum. Following the end of the Bronze Age, we can now document a significant Early Iron Age settlement, which expands rapidly during the Protogeometric. Growth continues through the Archaic, Classical, and Hellenistic periods, when the city reaches its maximum scale, paralleling the expansion of the city's regional role on Crete. Changing status following the Roman conquest is represented by significant contraction but requires reassessment with evidence for expanding economic connections. Following Early and Middle Roman prosperity, a long decline can be documented, with the survey finally locating the Late Roman and Late Antique occupation that accompanied the late flowering of the North Cemetery.

SESSION 7E: Colloquium
Pliny's History of Ancient Art: Toward a Contextual Perspective

ORGANIZERS: *Gianfranco Adornato*, Scuola Normale Superiore, Pisa, and *Kenneth Lapatin*, J. Paul Getty Museum

Colloquium Overview Statement

For centuries, Pliny the Elder's chapters on the history of art in the *Naturalis Historia* (books 33–7) have been considered as a list of *excerpta*: 3,000 pieces of information derived from more than 70 Greek and Roman authors taken out of context in order to reconstruct lost sources, treatises, artists' lives, and works of art and their anecdotes. This session aims to offer a new reading of Pliny's books on art and overcome the limitations of previous approaches by encouraging updated historical, philological, and archaeological discussions by pursuing, principally, two contextual perspectives. First, a topographic and architectural approach to the distribution of and interaction between Greek sculpture and Roman monuments in the urban space explores the settings in which the ancient masterpieces were exhibited and appreciated. Drawing on recent excavations, emerging scholarship is reshaping understandings of the visual appearance, holdings, and typological models of Vespasian's Templum Pacis. "The Templum Pacis and Religion in Flavian Rome" situates the Flavian complex not merely as a reflection or continuation of triumphal architecture and imperial patronage but also as Vespasian's self-legitimizing presentation of Rome's sacred past to solidify his position as the head of Rome's religion. "Statues in Circulation: Mapping Pliny's Rome" investigates the complex visual displays and spatial relationships of objects of art in public and private spaces in Rome, tracing movements between Greece and Italy, and in Rome itself. Second, the literary dimension of Pliny's work is analyzed to explore the birth of anecdotes and to understand how particular artists became canonical and provided ethical models; to investigate why Pliny selected some artists and works and excluded others; and to compare his choices with those of his predecessors and his contemporaries. "Eiko-nomia" takes into account the economic dimension of Greek art: Pliny continuously attacks luxury as the main source of moral decadence in his time, but on the other side he puts great attention on costs and materiality of art. "Pliny's Various Scales of Value" combines a fresh discussion on visual, aesthetic, and verbal language with lost statues and monuments in Rome. "Fragments on Greek Artists, Fragments of Greek Artists: A New Approach" aims at assessing a new approach in studying ancient fragments on art and art history by analyzing the fragmentary information within its literary, historical, philosophical, and cultural context.

Through the multidisciplinary perspective of the session, the organizers hope to revitalize discussion of artistic, architectural, and monumental issues in Rome, mainly during the Flavian period and in Pliny's books on art and thus to illuminate the display and reception of Greek art in Roman contexts.

DISCUSSANT: *Christopher Hallett*, University of California, Berkeley

The Templum Pacis and Religion in Vespasianic Rome
John R. Senseney, University of Illinois at Urbana-Champaign

Drawing on recent excavations, emerging scholarship is reshaping understandings of the visual appearance, holdings, and typological models of Vespasian's Templum Pacis. More than just a continuation of the sequence of Imperial forums, the arrangement of its features is seen to reflect local quadriporticus complexes and the Hellenistic victory monuments that influenced them. This paper situates the Flavian complex not as a mere reflection or continuation of triumphal architecture and imperial patronage but also as Vespasian's self-legitimizing presentation of Rome's sacred past to solidify his position as the head of Rome's religion. Through the connection between the complex's dedication and Vespasian's expansion of the pomerium, the complex's visual displays, and its spatial relationships and formal comparisons with existing monuments, I emphasize the overriding religious experience of the Templum Pacis as founded on Vespasian's role in manifesting the martially conditioned cult of Pax in his capacity as imperator and pontifex maximus.

Statues in Circulation: Mapping Pliny's Rome
Eve D'Ambra, Vassar College

Pliny's chapters on the history of art have long frustrated art historians with their surfeit of information and dearth of meaning. The lists of celebrated artists, inventories of imperial plunder, and anecdotal accounts produce a talismanic effect with the litany of Greek masters' names and the prominence of collections of Greek art in Rome. Book 36 lacks a chronological sequence of the artists or a systematic treatment of sculpture (J. Isager, *Pliny on Art and Society* [Odense 1991] 148). The only organizing principle is the location of Greek art in Rome (S. Carey, *Pliny's Catalogue of Culture* [Oxford 2006] 79). The presence of Greek art and its public display attest to Rome's dominion over the world and possession of its myriad treasures.

In a crowded field, why then focus on specific venues of public display of artworks? The emphasis on collections stands out, as if the aggregate of masterworks compounded the quality and appeal of individual statues. Often called "art galleries," the settings of marble statuary collections vary in architectural form (and public access) as porticoes, temples, imperial forums, and gardens. Located both in adjacent and different regions of the city, the collections seem to form a necklace around the Capitol. With recent advances in topographical studies and digital mapping applications, the displays can be seen to forge links among various collections and their patrons. Furthermore, the collections bear similarities in both sculptural types and the sculptors represented, as if to distribute equivalent aesthetic pleasure and luxury across Rome.

Eiko-nomia: Defining Monetary Values and Aesthetic Canons of Greek Art in Roman Society
Gianfranco Adornato, Scuola Normale Superiore, Pisa

In several passages, Pliny the Elder fiercely attacks the decadent behaviors and attitudes of his contemporaries toward luxurious goods, precious stones, and expensive works of art. The Roman obsession of gathering and showing pieces of art in private contexts is well known, and ancient statues usually traveled with the owners: Gaius Cestius, for instance, used to bring a statue in the middle of the battlefield (*NH* 34.48). Even Roman emperors were inclined to pay a lot of money for sculpture or painting: Tiberius acquired a painting for 6 million sestertii (35.70)! In Pliny's account, the art of painting has become poor in technique and embellished by marbles and gold (35.3). From his point of view, the decadence of artistic practices and techniques proceeds with the moral decadence of the Roman society. In the so-called books of art, however, Pliny seems to be very interested in giving information about the price and weight of the pieces of art, as in the case of a painting by Aristeides: Attalus bid 600,000 denarii for it, but Lucius Mummius withdrew the work and dedicated it in Rome, suspecting good quality of which he himself was ignorant (35.24).

In this paper, I aim at collecting all the information in Pliny's *Naturalis Historia* related to the art market, prices, and value of pieces of art to explore economic and aesthetic perspectives and investigate the notions of "value" and "canon" between arts and artists, in Pliny and other ancient authors.

Pliny's Various Scales of Value

Michael Koortbojian, Princeton University

Books 33–7 are marked by a series of different forms of value judgment. Most famous are the numerous absolute judgments on a variety of artistic productions (the first, the biggest, the best, and so on). Yet there are other articulations of value that emerge—and a sequence of these is examined: comparisons between artists' accomplishments; examples of extraordinary value that know no price; and, less frequently, declarations of what can rightly be designated as purely aesthetic value. The paper concludes with a discussion of the problem of anachronism that, at times, appears to have accompanied the assignment of aesthetic value—as Pliny interprets his sources in the light of much later artistic developments and aesthetic concerns.

Fragments on Greek Artists, Fragments of Greek Artists: A New Approach

Eva Falaschi, Scuola Normale Superiore, Pisa

From J. Overbeck's *Die antiken Schriftquellen zur Geschichte der bildenden Künste bei den Griechen* (Leipzig 1868) onward, studies in ancient art history have produced a significant number of fragmentary corpora dedicated to Greek and Roman artists or art theories and terminology.

The main interest in collecting these materials was to recover information on single artists or on theories of art. In this perspective, ancient texts have been excerpted, and the pieces of information on art have been completely taken out of their historical and literary context of transmission. After the new, updated, and enriched Overbeck's edition (Berlin and Boston 2014), it is now possible to go further with this method and enlarge the research to the study of the contexts in which artistic information is transmitted.

This paper aims at assessing a new approach in studying ancient fragments on art and art history by analyzing the fragmentary information within its literary, philological, historical, philosophical, and cultural context, in order to recognize the filters of the author—and the age—that transmit it and consequently to understand how this information can be really used to reconstruct artists' activity. Apelles' judgment on Protogenes and Megabyzus' visit to Apelles' workshop represent the case study of two different kinds of information—the fragment of an artist's writing and an anecdote about a painter. This paper focuses on Pliny's and Plutarch's perspectives on these matters, in order to understand the different points of view and the meanings of the accounts within the literary and philosophical frame of their writings.

SESSION 7F
Textiles, Dress, and Adornment in Antiquity

CHAIR: *Mireille M. Lee*, Vanderbilt University

The Installation Methodology of Display for Tutankhamun Textiles and Clothes as the First Appearance After Discovery
Nagm El Deen Morshed, Grand Egyptian Museum, *Ahmed Abd Elrade Ibrahim Hassan*, Grand Egyptian Museum, *Maggie Effat Adieb Eshak*, Grand Egyptian Museum, and *Moamen Osman*, Grand Egyptian Museum

The textiles of Tutankhamen are considered one the greatest collections discovered inside the tomb as the only complete royal wardrobe until now, although most of them are fragile and in extremely delicate condition. Carter remarked that "the material from this tomb will be of supreme importance to the history of textile art and it needs very careful study."

The collection of the young king included approximately 740 pieces found distributed inside rooms of the tomb, stored in several boxes comprising shirts more than 100 triangular loincloths, garments, and shawls with belts, scarfs, caps, headdresses, and nearly 30 gloves. In other cases, they form part of elaborate ceremonial robes covered with gold sequins and embroideries. In addition, some linen cloth was used for wrapping the funerary equipment, such as the child's shirt that covered the wooden jackal statue of the god Anubis.

The aim of the philosophy installation is to design and create exhibition mounts for different kinds of textiles and garments, flat textiles, and three-dimensional garments. Display methodology of textiles and garments should be based on a consideration of the condition of the object, the exhibition design, length of exhibition, museum environment, and the preservation methodology. This philosophy focuses on how to exhibit textiles and garments in their historical context with the other objects found with them inside the tomb because they belong to one theme. With this philosophy, we must pay more attention to the composition and quality of materials used for storage, exhibition, and mounting, as well as to the effect of the museum environment and methods of displaying the object.

We need to evaluate and refine aesthetic and historic information conveyed to museum visitors through display techniques and label information. It should be noted that certain display methods, such as using "fashion" mannequins as supports for garments of the king, must be take on consideration it quickly attracted the museum community.

Oddy Test in Assessment of the Materials Used for Textile Conservation
Mohamed Ayad, Grand Egyptian Museum Conservation Center, *Ahmed Khamees*, Grand Egyptian Museum Conservation Center, and *Nagm El-Deen Morshed*, Grand Egyptian Museum Conservation Center

Among King Tutankhamen collections, there are numerous textiles and artifacts that contain different kinds of fibers, most of them in a deteriorating condition; therefore, it is necessary to choose carefully the most suitable materials to use in conservation, ones that will guarantee stability over time for these valuable artifacts, because there are a wide range of materials used in conservation, storage, and display. In this research, the Oddy test will be used, as it is considered one of the best methods to evaluate conservation materials.

An accelerated corrosion test is used to evaluate the suitability and safety of materials in and around the artifacts. However, these materials may be safe for conservation, storage, and display purposes; they may emit trace amounts of chemicals that can harm these artifacts over time. Acids, formaldehyde, and other fumes can damage and even destroy delicate artifacts if placed too close.

The Oddy test will also measure the impact of the dyes used in preparing the object supports and stitching yarns, whether natural or synthetic, with various concentrations, so it could determine the materials either be used permanently, temporarily, or if they were prohibited.

This test requires three individual setups to study the corrosion effects of a given sample on four metals commonly involved—silver, copper, iron, and lead—by testing off-gassing. Each metal detects a different set of corrosive agents. The silver is for detecting reduced sulfur compounds and carbonyl sulfides. The lead is for detecting organic acids, aldehyde, and acidic gases. The copper is for detecting chlorides and sulfur compounds. The iron is for detecting nitrogen oxides. If the metal coupons show no signs of corrosion, then the material is deemed suitable to be placed in and around artifacts.

Dress to Impress: Elite Status and Textile Production at Early Gabii
J. Troy Samuels, University of Michigan, and *Matthew Naglak*, University of Michigan

This paper presents a spatial and functional analysis of textile-making tools from an Early Iron Age (700–500 B.C.E.) complex at ancient Gabii, using these data to argue for the importance of textiles and the textile producers themselves in reifying elite identity during this formative urban period in Latium. Based on a contemporaneous series of rich infant burials surrounding this complex, it is suggested that habitation in this area represents an elite occupation, one of the building blocks of the later republican town. Outside of these burials, we argue that a second significant marker of status can be seen in the dense concentration of textile-making tools. These tools and the lost textiles themselves served a dialectical function, both reinforcing and indicative of the inhabitants' elevated status in the preurban region. This assemblage can be used to reconstruct the formative role played by textile production in perpetuating elite status at early Gabii. The Gabines, long known for their distinctive style of toga, were already using clothes to maintain social hierarchies in the earliest phases of habitation at the site.

Since 2009, the University of Michigan has been excavating at the site of ancient Gabii, a Latin city just east of Rome. These excavations have recovered one of the largest collections of textile-making tools from first-millennium B.C.E. settlement contexts in central Italy. Over the past seven seasons of excavation, more than 300 textile-making artifacts have come to light. The vast majority of these objects were recovered from a sequence of structures occupied from the Early Iron Age through the Archaic period. Two classes of objects constitute the bulk of this assemblage:

spindlewhorls and spools (Italian *rocchetti*). Several important studies on textile production and textile tools have been published in recent years, allowing for a better contextualization of the function of these tools in their Italic setting. The Gabii material adds a detailed examination of the production and use of textiles and textile-making tools in early Latium.

These finds make significant contributions to our understanding of urban development in the Gabii-Castiglione region and supplement the contemporary funerary assemblages of textile-making tools found at the nearby necropolis of Osteria dell'Osa. The role of these as elite markers suggests that the continued exploitation of pastoral resources (namely, sheep and their wool) continued to function as an important marker of social differentiation during this transitional phase of sedentary habitation.

Costs Beyond Manpower: Equipment in Rome's Macedonian Wars
Bret Devereaux, University of North Carolina at Chapel Hill

This paper presents a new method of using archaeologically recovered military equipment to assess the cost of fielding armies in the ancient world. The paper then demonstrates this method by focusing on the wars between Rome and Macedon (214–148 B.C.E.). Current scholarship privileges the role of manpower in determining the outcome of these wars. This paper argues that equipment costs are as important as manpower in constraining the size of ancient armies. However, equipment costs are generally neglected by current scholarship, in part because of the impossibility of obtaining sufficient price data from the ancient world. Progress in the discovery and publication of archaeologically recovered military equipment now invites a more intensive examination of battlefield equipment and relative equipment costs. In particular, the recovery of Macedonian military equipment from the royal tombs at Aigai provides an evidence base with which to compare the steadily growing body of examples from the Middle Republic. The paper examines the equipment of the heavy infantry on both sides of the war, the phalanx of the Macedonian army and Rome's *hastati*, *principes*, and *triarii*, as in both armies the heavy infantry was the primary component of the army. Preserved examples of archaeologically recovered military equipment are used to reconstruct the battlefield equipment of the period. Ancient texts, combined with epigraphic evidence, such as the Military Decree of Amphipolis, are used to establish the elements of each side's heavy infantry panoply. This testimony is then correlated with reconstructions of each piece of equipment. Relative cost can then be gauged quantitatively by using metal content as a proxy for cost. To account for uncertainty, maximum and minimum cases are constructed to test conclusions under a variety of assumptions and possible reconstructions. Both sides' equipment is then compared on a per-soldier basis to assess the relative equipment costs to each side. The results of this study show that Roman heavy infantrymen appear to have been more expensive to equip, contrary to the impression of endlessly expendable Roman manpower given by ancient sources such as Polybius and accepted by current scholarship. In contrast, the modest use of metal and preference for nonmetal substitute equipment like the linothorax in the Macedonian panoply suggest an effort to field an army at lower cost.

Fascinating Fascina: Embodiment and the Social Significance of Roman Phallic Pendants

Alissa M. Whitmore, Independent Researcher

Roman phallic pendants are strongly associated with apotropaic protection in ancient texts, specifically for vulnerable children (Varro, *Ling.* 7.79). The diverse archaeological contexts of these artifacts, which come from virtually every place and time period of Roman occupation, and their association with male soldiers and military forts, seem to suggest, however, that these objects were not just for children. Given other Roman uses of phalli as comedic, aggressive, or fertility symbols, I argue that phallic pendants had similarly diverse functions for ancient Romans, which could be separate from, or entwined with, apotropaism.

This paper examines how the function and meaning of these pendants likely varied with the social identities of wearers (adult/child, civilian/solider, male/female). Given the presence of additional phallic imagery—armor mounts—in military contexts, I pay special attention to the use of these pendants by adult Roman men, for whom the wearing of a phallus would include additional meanings of sexuality, virility, power, and force that would likely have been absent for child wearers. Typological studies and use-wear data shed light on how pendants were worn and appeared on the body, revealing that only some phallic pendants would appear erect, which may have implications for their presumed apotropaic functions. These pendants also offer a window onto Roman gender ideology, as men, children, and women used and wore depictions of only one sex's genitalia (with few exceptions) for magical protection, fertility, and power.

In addition to a close study of Roman phallic pendants and their archaeological contexts, my research incorporates anthropological theory and cross-cultural examples from other cultures with phallic objects (i.e., Phoenician, Greek, Moche, Thai) to reflect on the possible uses, meanings, and significance that these pendants had for different members of Roman society.

Color-Coded: The Relationship Between Color, Iconography, and Theory in Hellenistic and Roman Gemstones

Eric Beckman, Indiana University

This paper explores the relationship between the iconography of engraved Hellenistic and Roman gemstones and the color of those stones. While there has been much work on the importance of certain colors of gemstones and on how select engraved images provided the "magical" gems with their protective and amuletic qualities, I argue that specific combinations of color and iconography were employed to enhance the efficacy of the stone. This paper uses as a case study the class of gems depicting scorpions engraved largely (though not exclusively) on yellow or tawny stones, such as agate or yellow jasper. I demonstrate that this association between the scorpion and yellow gems stems from the applications of Greek medical theories as well as Hellenistic and Roman astronomical practices in order to maximize the prophylactic or healing qualities of the gems.

This link between medicine and astronomy is hardly a new concept; it was established as early as the Hippocratic treatise *Airs, Waters, and Places*. The writings of the Hippocratics and Galen suggest a system in which the healthy body achieves a state of balance and harmony, a concept reflected on the macro level in the astronomical works. The medical writers establish a link between the yellow nature of the stones and the qualities of yellow bile and heat. This relationship provides the main point of contact between the medical and astronomical realms, as the characteristic of heat points toward an association with the planet Mars, which, according to Ptolemy's *Tetrabiblos*, has one of its celestial houses in Scorpio. Further exploration of the writings of Ptolemy and other astronomical writers expands on this connection, crafting a network in which the interplay between the scorpion iconography and the yellow nature of the gemstone capitalizes on a complex system of planetary exaltations and other traits in order to enhance the stone's efficacy. This network is further complicated by references to the myth of Orion and Scorpio as catalogued by Aratus and others. By employing specific color and iconographic combinations, Hellenistic and Roman "magical" gems exploited the interplay between medical and astronomical theory to maximize the protective and healing functions of the stones.

The Costumes and Attributes of Late Antique Honorific Monuments: Conformity and Divergence Within the Public and Political Spheres

Elizabeth A. Wueste, University of California, Berkeley

Although the traditional toga may have been the default costume of civic engagement in High Imperial Rome, the decision to portray oneself in the recognizable style of a civil servant was not a mindless reversion to the normative default. In particular, honorific sculptures of Late Antique magistrates display a large enough range of appropriate garments to demonstrate that the negotiation of costumes and attributes was a potent and indicative choice. A comprehensive data set of the 54 extant body sculptures from late antiquity includes statues that wear the imperial toga, the *toga contabulata*, the Late Antique toga, the Greek himation, the military chlamys, and the triumphal cuirass. These costumes were then complemented with a combination of specific accessories and attributes, such as undertunics, leggings, scrolls, boots, sandals, belts, scroll bundles, benches, *mappae*, scepters, wreaths, and fibulae. Previous studies have attempted to isolate particular components as indicative of specific occupation, status, magisterial office, or even religious affiliation. However, the overwhelmingly public and political connotations of almost all of the costumes and attributes of Late Antique honorific statues, in close consideration with the associated epigraphic evidence, reveal that the point of the sculpted bodies was to glorify the more abstract virtues of civil office. The primary role of the statues' costumes was to indicate high status, general occupation, and the qualities desirable of a civil servant: vigilance, justice, responsibility, and education, for instance. Other aspects of identity, such as religion, ethnicity, ancestry, age, and even specific office, may have been referred to obliquely with attributes and accessories, but they were largely glossed over in favor of the larger political and public message. As confirmed by the associated and adjoining inscribed honorific bases, the Late Antique costumes of honorific monuments signaled the general spheres of the honorand's activities and quality of character. The compilation and consideration of this data set is the first such study of its kind for this time period and suggests that there existed a considerable breadth of choice in costume and attributes available to the recipient of a Late Antique honorific sculpture that was not available in earlier periods. This diversity is potentially a reflection of the changing demographics, prestige, qualifications, and public images of the political and social elite in late antiquity.

SESSION 7G: Colloquium
New Fieldwork and Research at Gordion: 2013–2015

ORGANIZERS: *C. Brian Rose*, University of Pennsylvania, and *Kathryn Morgan*, University of Pennsylvania

Colloquium Overview Statement

Between the fall of the Hittite Kingdom and the creation of the Persian empire, there arose in central and southern Asia Minor a series of powerful states generally referred to as Neo-Hittite, and their excavation has yielded an astonishing series of finds that have significantly altered our understanding of early first-millennium Anatolia.

Some of the most dramatic new discoveries have been made at Gordion, the Phrygian capital that controlled much of central Asia Minor for close to two centuries and interacted with empires and states both east and west. A recently revised analysis of the site's chronology has transformed what had been interpreted as a Cimmerian attack of ca. 700 B.C.E. into a conflagration possibly related to new construction that occurred 100 years earlier. The chronology of Phrygian architecture and ceramics has therefore changed substantially, as has our understanding of the history of central Anatolia during the Iron Age.

This colloquium presents the results of fieldwork and research conducted at Gordion during the last three years. The session begins with an overview of excavation, remote sensing, and conservation at the site between 2013 and 2015 and then moves to an examination of the Early Iron Age ceramics at Gordion, which are combined with evidence from settlements around the Sea of Marmara, especially Troy and Maydos, to clarify the multiple strands of migration from the Balkans to Anatolia.

The third paper examines new evidence from a sounding beneath the Terrace Building to explore the relationship between textile production and state formation in Iron Age Gordion, while a paper on mobility and monumentalization examines the relationship between the site's monumental burial mounds and the roads that led into the citadel, using GIS least-cost path analysis as well as aerial photogrammetry.

The next paper deals with two elite cremation burials at Gordion during the Early Achaemenid period. These burials contained skeletons of horses, the iron fittings of a wheeled vehicle, cauldrons and dinoi, and furniture inlays in ivory and colored glass. This is our best evidence for the life of Gordion's elite shortly after the establishment of Persian control. The final paper provides a broader examination of Phrygian influence within Iron Age Anatolia, concluding that there was a stronger Phrygian presence on the western coast than previously believed.

New Excavations and Conservation at Gordion: 2013–2015

C. Brian Rose, University of Pennsylvania

This talk presents the results of new excavations, remote sensing, and conservation activities at the Phrygian capital of Gordion in central Turkey between 2013 and 2015. New excavations began in 2013 with the objective of clarifying the defensive system and city plan of the Early (950–800 B.C.E.) and Middle Phrygian (800–540 B.C.E.) settlement. Fieldwork has focused on the southern side of the Citadel Mound, at the southern end of a major street that appears to have bisected the mound. Excavation yielded a large Early Phrygian (ninth century B.C.E.) glacis or stepped terrace wall of more than 2.5 m in height that supported a substantial fortification wall nearly 3 m wide. New fortifications dating to the Middle Phrygian (eighth century B.C.E.) and Late Phrygian (sixth century B.C.E.) periods were also uncovered in the same area. Fieldwork here has proven that the western side of the mound was fortified and that those fortifications had already been established in the Early Phrygian period. Neither of these details were known previously.

Geophysical prospection focused on Gordion's two residential districts: the Lower Town, which lies to the north and south of the Citadel Mound, and the Outer Town, at the west of the Lower Town. Magnetic prospection in the Lower Town allowed us to reconstruct the complete circuit of the outer fortification wall and to demonstrate that it was built in tandem with a defensive ditch, probably in the early eighth century B.C.E. Magnetic prospection in the Outer Town revealed that the entire district was also surrounded by a ditch 3.5 m in width and a defensive wall 2.5 m wide. At least during the Middle Phrygian period, then, there were three fortification systems in operation at Gordion: one around the citadel, a second around the Lower Town, and a third around the Outer Town.

One of the focal points of our conservation activities was the Early Phrygian Citadel Gate, the stone walls of which still stand to a height of about 10 m, and the Early Phrygian Terrace Complex or industrial district, both of which were badly damaged in a major conflagration of ca. 800 B.C.E. The walls have been strengthened by the insertion of steel cables, and the tops of the restored walls have been protected by a soft capping system entailing the use of shallow-rooted perennial vegetation.

Gordion, Troy, and Maydos: The Late Bronze Age to Iron Age Transition and The Question of Migration

Carolyn C. Aslan, Koç University, and *Gülşah Günata*, Koç University

This paper compares the Late Bronze Age to Iron Age transition at three sites in central and northwestern Anatolia: Gordion, Troy, and Maydos. At Gordion, excavations by Mary Voigt uncovered a series of houses and courtyard deposits ranging from the Late Bronze Age to the Early Iron Age. The houses were discovered within deep layers on the citadel mound, below Early Phrygian levels. The Late Bronze Age levels contain large quantities of wheelmade buff wares with close similarities to Hittite pottery. Early Iron Age contexts show the introduction of handmade wares, which have comparanda in the area of Thrace, the Balkans, and the lower Danube regions. The handmade ceramics from Gordion also share some similarities with handmade wares at Troy.

The site of Troy, like Gordion, had primarily wheelmade gray and tan wares during the Late Bronze Age, but handmade wares were introduced following a destruction ca. 1180 B.C.E. The handmade ceramics at Troy show a much wider range of shapes and decoration than those at Gordion, and one also sees changes in a wide range of material culture, including architecture. Both the extensive architectural remains and the abundance of ceramics attest to Troy's continuing role as a regional center in the 12th–11th centuries.

Near Troy, new excavations at the mound of Maydos on the Gallipoli Peninsula show that this settlement also experienced many of the same changes in terms of ceramics and architecture during the 12th century. Although theories of a migration from the north into Anatolia during the Early Iron Age have been controversial, increasing evidence from Gordion, Troy, and Maydos, as well as other settlements around the Sea of Marmara, provide support for multiple strands of migration from the area of Thrace, the Balkans, and the lower Danube region into Anatolia in the 12th century B.C.E.

The Emperor's New Clothes: Textile Production and State Formation in Iron Age Phrygia
Kathryn Morgan, University of Pennsylvania

The site of Gordion is best known for its spectacular Iron Age destruction level: ca. 800 B.C.E., a catastrophic fire destroyed a neighborhood of workshops and an adjacent elite zone on the Citadel Mound, preserving the rich contents of those buildings in situ for posterity. The series of transformations undergone by the citadel to reach that point, however, are far less understood. This paper presents the results of a recent sondage into the center of the Citadel Mound, conducted by the author in the summer of 2014, to investigate the means and motivation behind one major innovation in the urban design of ninth-century Gordion—the massive, industrial Terrace Building. In this paper, the evidence for large-scale textile production there at the time of the destruction is placed within an architectural, chronological, and geographical context. What does the prominent placement of the Terrace Building within the fortified city center suggest about the role of this particular industry within the Phrygian state economy? What, if any, was the precedent for this highly organized craft center, both at Gordion and within Anatolia more broadly? This study outlines the evidence for the development of textile production at Gordion over time along with possible social and economic functions of textiles in Anatolia in order to examine changes within the organization of the Phrygian state, whose origins and inner workings remain obscure. It further addresses the vexing methodological question of how the small sondages to which archaeologists are increasingly limited can nonetheless contribute to the broader understanding of a city's industry.

Mobility and Monumentalization at Iron Age Gordion

Lucas Stephens, University of Pennsylvania

Mobility through a cultural landscape is structured both by topography and by human agency manifested in the built environment. The archaeology of movement must therefore confront these dimensions of the landscape to understand the relationship between routes and the societies that used them. In this paper, I present preliminary work on a project to analyze the relationship between the ancient monuments and the routes throughout the landscape of Iron Age Gordion by integrating digital and humanistic perspectives.

The area around the urban center of Gordion is dominated by monumental burial tumuli, many of which have yielded intact burial assemblages mostly dating between 850 and 550 B.C.E. Gordion thus presents a unique opportunity to researchers by providing a diachronic perspective on monumental construction within a cultural landscape. Scholars have hypothesized about the existence of various routes in and around Gordion based on the alignment of tumuli, but this issue has never been systematically investigated. Monumental burial and routine travel are two very different forms of social behavior that are nevertheless closely linked at Gordion. Tumuli symbolize an elite group, a family unit, or even a single individual, while the routes were used by a much larger portion of the population. This paper combines GIS least-cost path analysis, made while actually traveling these paths, with data generated through aerial photogrammetry in an effort to understand communication and mobility between Gordion and other contemporary mounded settlements in the vicinity.

Elite Cremation Burials at Achaemenid Persian Gordion

Elspeth Dusinberre, University of Colorado, Boulder

Around 530 B.C.E. two people died at Gordion; their cremated remains were buried on the ridge to the northeast of the citadel mound under tumuli later excavated as Tumulus A and Tumulus E. The cremation burial of Tumulus E has still not been found, but two pits under the tumulus yielded startling and important finds: one contained 11 skeletons of horses and cattle, carefully arranged in concentric circles, while the other held a large deposit of metal artifacts including a bronze tripod cauldron, a bronze dinos with iron loop handles, the iron fittings of a wheeled vehicle, and numerous horse bits. One of these bits is particularly elaborate, with bronze cheekpieces decorated with palmettes recalling the painted warrior of the tomb at Lycian Kızılbel and bronze rein rings in the form of rams' heads. The deposits find no precise parallels and open our eyes to the variety of ways a vast expenditure of wealth might mark a burial. The horse bits as a group connect the presumed occupant of the tomb to the practices and expressions of elite male authority during the Early Achaemenid period in general. Tumulus A covered the cremated remains of an exceptionally wealthy young woman. She was buried with a dismantled vehicle and a remarkable quantity of precious objects, including ivory boxes and figurines, furniture inlays in ivory and colored glass, an alabaster alabastron, a silver mirror, and gold and electrum jewelry. Among the most striking are a gold bracelet with lion's-head terminals and a gold necklace with acorn pendants, as well as a curious ivory duck box with three small internal compartments and the unusual addition of human arms. These tumuli thus draw on the pre-Achaemenid Phrygian past for their form but through their contents demonstrate the cultural fluidity that characterized the elite in Anatolia at the beginning of the Achaemenid period.

Beyond Gordion: The Phrygian-Ionian Interaction Reevaluated
Kurtis T. Tanaka, University of Pennsylvania

Gordion remains the primary Phrygian type-site in Anatolia and serves also as an important linchpin in Anatolian chronology. Recent work at Gordion, especially the "New Chronology," has, however, dramatically altered our understanding of the rise and decline of the site in the Iron Age. The effects of this redating beyond Gordion itself have yet to be fully explored. Thus, taking the new chronology as its point of departure, this paper reevaluates the nature of Phrygian contact with the Ionian coast in the preclassical period. Previous scholarship has neglected this issue, and the (now outmoded) seventh-century "Cimmerian" destruction of Gordion was understood to have paved the way for the rise of Lydia and Gordion's eventual senescence. As we are now forced to disentangle these phenomena, and as the archaeological evidence for the interaction of western and central Anatolian sites continues to grow in quantity, a much more complex web of interaction between Gordion and its western neighbors begins to emerge.

The historical milieu in which the Phrygians interacted with their Greek neighbors is considered first. A critical eye is taken to the recent historiographical hypothesis of a coordinated Phrygian-Greek resistance to Assyrian expansion in southeastern Anatolia. Important new discoveries of Phrygian-style shrines at Phokaia, Chios, Ephesos, and Miletos are used to contextualize this interaction, as it argues for a stronger Phrygian presence on the coast than previously believed. The New Chronology of Gordion has also brought Phrygian material into better alignment with the Geometric and Orientalizing periods, and though Phrygia is not usually understood as a major influence in these periods, exchange between these two cultural frontiers can now be more effectively traced. Ultimately, I argue that recent work at Gordion requires us to revise our perspective on the relations between the Phrygians and their Ionian neighbors.

SESSION 7H
Villas and Countryside in the Roman Empire

CHAIR: *Marsha B. McCoy*, Southern Methodist University

Excavations at Umbro Flumen (Alberese, Italy): Preliminary Results
Alessandro Sebastiani, University of Sheffield

This paper describes the preliminary results of two archaeological seasons at a Roman villa complex in the area of Alberese (Italy). The settlement is built along the Tyrrhenian seacoast line in the territory of the *ager Rusellanus* (southern

Tuscany). Archaeological excavations have revealed a long sequence of occupation, spanning from the second century B.C.E. to at least the late fifth century C.E.

From the Republican period until the late second century C.E., the villa is used
for both residential and productive purposes. The residential area should be located in the southern and western parts of the complex, as the recovery of a large
number of black-and-white mosaic tesserae testifies. In this phase, the villa has
an atrium and a surrounding portico, with a possible impluvium in the center.
The material culture shows the presence of high-quality glass vessels and pottery,
while the remaining rooms are decorated with marble veneers. The discovery of
an olive or wine press, reused in a later wall, testifies to the use of a portion of the
complex also for agricultural productions.

At the beginning of the third century C.E. and throughout the fourth century,
the situation changes, with a series of new rooms arranged in the area of the impluvium. This reorganization involves the construction of at least two dividing
walls in the central portico. A collective kitchen is built in the previous northern
aisle of the atrium, while a large, oval furnace is built in the eastern one. The latter
is dedicated to the production of Egyptian blue pigment (*caeruleum*), as a large
quantity of it surrounds the kiln. Along the northeast perimeter of the complex, a
room hosts a metal workshop. A forge is built against the eastern wall, producing
bronze rivets to fix boats and ships. A series of lead net weights testifies also a specific production linked to fishing activities in the nearby sea and river Ombrone.

A later occupation during the entire fifth century C.E. can be detected through
the recovery of a distinctive assemblage of pottery and coins in some of the latest
contexts. However, modern agricultural activities have possibly destroyed some
of the structures related to this period, and only further research will be able to
shed a light on the Late Antique phase of the settlement.

The Upper Sabina Tiberina Project: Fourth Excavation Season at Vacone

Gary Farney, Rutgers University, *Tyler Franconi*, Oxford University, *Candace Rice*,
University of Edinburgh, *Matt Notarian*, Hiram College, *Giulia Masci*, Science
Museum, London, and *Dylan Bloy*, AIA East Tennessee Society

The 2015 season of excavation at the so-called Villa di Orazio in Vacone, Italy,
carried out under the Upper Sabina Tiberina Project, produced substantial results,
expanding our knowledge of the site's building phases, productive capabilities,
and finds assemblages.

The villa overlies a terrace probably constructed as a *basis villae* sometime around
100 B.C.E. Further excavation in a sloping passageway linking the residential level
to the lower cryptoporticus revealed a side passage into a small round chamber.
A constructed opening in the floor of one of the villa's front rooms opens into this
chamber, possibly a refuse dump. Masonry discovered below floor level in several
parts of the villa, including another vaulted underground chamber, suggests extensive subterranean construction with more to be investigated in the future.

Excavations also revealed many rooms with multiple building phases, exposed
by intrusive early modern trenches dug through floors. We found a wall separating a republican scutulatum pavement from a cobble floor, the strongest piece of a
growing body of evidence that the earlier villa had a substantially different layout

from that of the later, imperial villa. We have also gained more information regarding the later usage of the site; we located at least three separate *cocciopesto* or *opus spicatum* floors that were laid over earlier, imperial-phase mosaics. In conjunction with the apparently incomplete repairs found in three other mosaic floors, these floors suggest a final phase of activity within the house where decoration was no longer a priority.

Work in the area of the olive-pressing facility revealed that the zone was built over, perhaps to convert it to the production of wine. A later *cocciopesto* treading floor emptying into a settling tank was found nearby substantial remains of a dolium. This change in productive capabilities represents an important economic shift for the villa estate.

Finally, with an assemblage of more than 12,000 ceramic sherds and 80 small finds, we can confidently discuss the site's chronology. The pottery dates from the first century B.C.E. through the end of the second century C.E., though most of the assemblage dates to the final century of this period. Coins, now seven in total, date between Vespasian and Antoninus Pius except for a single republican as. Taken together, the finds suggest that the villa was abandoned sometime around 200 C.E.

The 2014 and 2015 Excavation Campaigns at Oplontis Villa B: A New Window into the Development of the Roman Bay of Naples

Ivo van der Graaff, Center for Advanced Study in the Visual Arts, National Gallery of Art, and *John R. Clarke,* University of Texas at Austin

Since 2012, the Oplontis Project has investigated the site known as Oplontis Villa B in modern Torre Annunziata, Italy; it is located 300 m to the east of its famous neighbor, a luxury villa known as Villa A and often attributed to Poppaea. Far from being a villa as the name implies, Oplontis B actually preserves the remains of a small urban settlement buried by Vesuvius in 79 C.E. The site includes warehouses, streets, townhouses, and a two-story building dedicated to the commerce of wine. Working in the 1980s and early 1990s, excavators uncovered and largely rebuilt the complex, intent on turning it into a tourist attraction for the local town. Unfortunately, the money to publish and preserve the complex ran out, leaving it abandoned ever since. The Oplontis Project has undertaken the task of publishing the site. This paper presents the preliminary results of the 2014 and 2015 seasons of excavation.

The aim of the excavations conducted by the project is twofold: to clean and fully document the 79 C.E. level, and to reconstruct the history of the site. In two short seasons spanning a total of four weeks, our team excavated 10 trenches. The first season yielded remains of a complex water system that included a large cistern and conduits that were abandoned and possibly rerouted in antiquity. In the second season, we uncovered evidence for at least three previous phases of occupation. They include the remains of a deliberately razed portico and buildings spanning the late second century B.C.E. and first century C.E. In particular, the remains of the earliest building recovered on-site lie at a different orientation than the complex buried by the eruption. Along with the partial abandonment of the water system, these results point to drastic architectural alterations that likely represent shifts in habitation and economic activity in the area associated with Oplontis.

New Wine, Old Bottles: The Sources of the Aqua Traiana and Their Afterlife

Rabun Taylor, University of Texas at Austin, *Ted O'Neill*, Independent Scholar, *Mike O'Neill*, Independent Scholar, and *Katherine Rinne*, California College of the Arts

Recent discoveries and investigations in the hills and valleys around Lake Bracciano confirm that the sources of the ancient Aqua Traiana, one of the largest aqueducts supplying Rome, were numerous and dazzlingly comprehensive, prefiguring most if not all of the extent of the Acqua Paola, which was built on its walls, channels, and foundations some 1,500 years later. Several springhouses and numerous bridges, long presumed to have been built in the 17th century, are shown to be Roman at the core. Several springhouses in the Boccalupo Valley feature similar designs with distinctive, multiple intakes, but they differ significantly in design from the Trajanic sources we have documented at Santa Fiora and Carestia to the north. They can be shown, in their own ways, to have Roman imperial origins and are probably to be associated uniformly with the Aqua Traiana; at one of them we have discovered Trajanic brickstamps. Another, smaller source to the north, at Sette Botti near Vicarello, is sheltered inside an umbrella-vaulted chamber built or refurbished in the 19th century, but its outtake channel is lined with ancient *opus signinum*. The variability of building styles and water-collection techniques in what we postulate to be a loosely unitary project is only to be expected, given that numerous construction teams, probably called up from different geographic regions, would have been at work on the project simultaneously. A similar degree of mass mobilization is attested in the *misure e stime*, documents recording work on the Acqua Paola in the early years of the 17th century, some of which give direct evidence of the ancient aqueduct line.

Another likely component of the complex network at the headwaters of the Aqua Traiana is the enormous ruined cistern ("Le Colonacce") situated on the heights between the valleys of Boccalupo and Fiora and well above the known sources associated with each. This cistern, which evidently has both Roman and post-antique phases, has received no systematic study, and its function remains utterly unknown. We hypothesize that it initially served as a supplement for the Aqua Traiana, though its later phases of use are mysterious.

The imperial undertaking to capture the region's waters for Rome was massive and coordinated. Recently discovered evidence of a local disaster—a dramatic rise in the lake, submerging many aristocratic villas at its edge—may have utterly disrupted the local power base, thus softening any potential resistance to the emperor's project.

Time and the Past: Modeling Coin Deposition and Recovery Rates from the Roman Peasant Project (Cinigiano, Grosseto)

Stephen A. Collins-Elliott, University of Tennessee, Knoxville

Quantitative comparisons of finds are an intrinsic part of archaeological research: questions of scale and general trends in social and economic processes cannot be addressed without at least some basic notion of quantity. Yet numerous questions can and have been raised about the reliability of raw quantified data, especially with respect to sampling and representativeness. Whereas these questions have largely been treated within the realm of survey archaeology regarding cross-project comparison, they are nevertheless part of a larger issue about how to deal with recovering the past in a quantifiably secure and balanced manner.

The primary issue that I address in this paper is the correspondence among the intensity of project focus, the length of past site occupation, and the resulting quantity of finds. Common sense after all dictates that greater attention in a certain area will result in a greater yield of finds, bringing about a higher aggregate number of artifacts than less thoroughly explored contexts. Accordingly, any map that illustrates the distribution of artifact types has to account for this imbalance. Where various sampling strategies or other weighting measures may not be feasible or easy to account for, I propose a probabilistic model to assess the intensity of fieldwork as a factor in the production of quantitative results. Rather than using a spatial method involving surface area or volume of earth, I propose a time-based model using the Poisson distribution that estimates the rate of artifact recovery over the course of a project season. I then implement a parallel model to account for the differing periods of past occupation as a factor in the rate of ancient coin deposition.

The result is an effective means to assess the distribution of coinage among ancient rural sites in south-central Tuscany (Cinigiano, Grosseto) recovered by the Roman Peasant Project, 2009–2014. The sites in question were excavated for different periods of time, and were also occupied at different moments from the Augustan age to late antiquity. The initial raw count of coins illustrates a sharp ranking among the sites in terms of frequency. But, taking into consideration the influences of both past occupation and present excavation not only significantly alters the resulting distribution but also provides a more secure and nuanced picture of the way in which the ancient inhabitants of the Tuscan countryside used coins in their economic transactions.

Storing the Future: Negotiating Time and Material Change During the Iron Age-Roman Transition in the Northwest Mediterranean

Astrid Van Oyen, University of Cambridge

Among the many changes introduced by Roman colonization of the western provinces, the effect on the temporal organization of life has only begun to be investigated, most recently by A. Gardner (*JSA* 12 [2012] 145–66). Perceptions of time are predicated on experience of material change along the lines of Elias' *Time: An Essay* (Oxford 1992), and this creates scope for an archaeological inquiry into temporalities. Storage practices are particularly suited to such an inquiry: they manage physical changes (degradation/preservation) while anticipating future needs.

This paper examines changes in storage practices between the late Iron Age and Roman periods in southwest France and northeast Spain and asks how these changes affected notions of the future. The late Iron Age socioeconomic structure was centered on sporadic exchange with Mediterranean traders. The large quantities of grain for this exchange were stored hermetically in large subterranean silos, which could preserve their contents over long periods of time but necessitated rapid release once opened. After Roman conquest, the Italian technique of grain storage in aboveground granaries was introduced. While the grain degraded much faster, it facilitated the direct access and regular turnover of grain needed for imperial taxation and administration. The shift in practices of grain storage thus reveals itself as a radical change in the articulation of the future: from an open-ended future to a regular, controllable future.

Meanwhile, vines replaced cereals as the main cultivated product as cash-cropping wine estates populated the northwest Mediterranean. As in Italy, wine was stored in large ceramic jars (*dolia*), sunken below ground level, to ferment. There was no clear cut-off point at which fermentation was done, but as a rule, the longer the process of fermentation, the higher the quality of the resulting wine. Despite sharp differences in technical knowledge and in socioeconomic structure, wine storage in *dolia* came with a similarly open-ended notion of the future as Iron Age silos.

By linking material change to the temporal organization of life, this paper suggests a more nuanced narrative of the Iron Age to Roman transition in the northwest Mediterranean than one taking material culture at face value.

The Santa Susana Archaeological Project 2013–2015: A Field Report

Emma Ljung, Princeton University, *Joey Williams*, Western Iberia Archaeology, and *Rui Mataloto*, Câmara Municipal de Redondo

Despite recent work at sites such as Caladinho, São Cucufate, and Torre de Palma, the Alentejo region of Iberia remains understudied, especially in terms of diachronic perspectives on landscape use, settlement patterns, and related cultural practices. Yet at the 17th-century Igreja de Santa Susana in Redondo County, ample Roman surface remains, first observed in the 1930s, indicate a long-term occupation beginning in the mid first century C.E. extending well into late antiquity. This suggests that the site represents an excellent opportunity to examine the lengthy transition from a landscape negotiated between marginalized pastoralists and colonial settlers in the Early Roman period to one reorganized to accommodate a Roman model of rural settlement, elite display, and intensive agricultural production. Through targeted excavation, intensive survey of the site itself, and medium-intensive survey in the surrounding territories, the Santa Susana Archaeological Project, under the auspices of Western Iberia Archaeology with permits from the Direção-Geral do Património Cultural, seeks to fill this important lacuna in the archaeology of Roman Iberia.

This paper presents the results of the first seasons of excavation and survey at Santa Susana, 2013–2015. Excavation has revealed a multiroom structure with several polychrome mosaic floors, mortared walls, and painted stucco. An apsidal room, flanked by an octagonal room, occupies a central space within what appears to be a bathhouse. This structure has several phases of construction, with floors dating to the second and late third/early fourth centuries C.E., and a post-construction use that extends beyond the fourth century. Another large structure, whose relationship to the bathhouse is still uncertain, has a significantly earlier date in the first century C.E. Materials from survey and excavation—mosaic floors, column bricks, terra sigillata, agricultural implements—and their dispersal throughout the territory confirm the presence of a sizable Roman villa.

Importantly, the materials provide a diachronic view of the transforming landscape and its uses. Unfortunately, both excavation and survey reveal heavy modern disturbances and recent destruction, in particular through ongoing plowing. This emphasizes the pressing need to study and conserve this Roman villa, whose extensive occupation may serve to illuminate a complicated but vital component of life in the western empire: the changing socioeconomic functions of villas at a local and regional level and their role in navigating the control and access to the landscape itself. Consequently, the project will move into a more intensive phase over the upcoming seasons.

SESSION 7I
Cultural Encounters and Frontier Interactions: Part 2

CHAIR: To be announced

Architectural Coin Types at the *Limes*: Questions of Communication, "Romanization," and Self-Empowerment
Allison B. Kidd, New York University, Institute of Fine Arts

In the mid first century B.C.E., a series of coins were issued under the authority of Juba I of Numidia. Each variant within the series features on the obverse a representation of Juba I, identified by the Latin inscription "REX IVBA," while the reverse features a representation of an octastyle temple accompanied by the Neo-Punic legend "Yubai hammamleket." A seamless blend of Roman, Greek, and Carthaginian details, these coins are the first known numismatic artifacts produced outside of the Italic peninsula in which we find depictions of a real, nonfictive architectural structure. While the series in its appearance parallels the numismatic repertoire of Late Republican Rome, the bilingual inscription, the depiction of a distinctly non-Roman place of worship, and its circulation outside the immediate administrative sphere of Rome is significant, and establishes a striking and unique mode of numismatic representation that is subsequently employed by rulers and communities located on the geographic periphery of the Roman world.

This paper locates the coins of Juba I within a numismatic tradition in which groups of people, identified as non-Romans, choose to represent their centers of worship in relation to a communicative standard set by Rome from the first century B.C.E. to the third century C.E. Because the depiction of nonfictive architecture on pictorial media is a distinctly Roman phenomenon, the sudden and prolific appearance of such artifacts outside of Rome, specifically limited to coins that depict cult spaces, is worth attention. Using as case studies the coins of Juba I, Herod Philip II of Judea, and those from the frontier provinces of Syria Phoenice and Arabia Petraea, I explore the way in which these "outliers" adopted and manipulated this aesthetic, economic, and political mode of communication and used it for their own means. This paper traces the evolution of these pictorial representations along with the established repertoire of both the city of Rome and those of the Roman East, arguing that such peripheral groups actively engaged with the architectonic and imaginative *Statbild* of Rome to promote the significance of their own religious milieu. Though often overlooked, this phenomenon gives primacy to the choices made by the producers of these artifacts. Ultimately, I intend to demonstrate here the need to employ a decentralized model of cultural agency, one that subverts even L. Revell and S.J. Keay's progressive interpretation of the term "Romanization" as a two-way discourse.

The Roman-Nubian Frontier during the Reign of Augustus: Archaeological Evidence from Talmis, Meroë, and Qasr Ibrim
Julia Troche, Missouri State University

Augustus' imperial campaigns were memorialized throughout the empire in his *Res Gestae*. In the *Res Gestae* (26), Augustus boasts that the army he sent into Nubia (Ethiopia) not only captured but crushed the Nubian enemies. The scene described is of a single, crushing Roman victory over Lower Nubia as far as the site of Napata. Some scholars, such as László Török, have aptly taken issue with the validity of Augustus' claims and point out that Augustus condensed multiple years of numerous campaigns into a single event within a monumental, political narrative (e.g., Török, *Between Two Worlds: The Frontier Region Between Ancient Nubia and Egypt 3700 BCE–500 AD* [Leiden 2009]). Though the later accounts of Strabo (17.54) and Pliny the Elder (*HN* 6.35) provide slightly more nuanced narratives—Strabo uniquely including a description of Meroitic retaliation—the accounts remain favorable to the Romans and describe interactions at the frontier as primarily concerned with territorial acquisition. In this paper, I highlight archaeological evidence from the Nubian sites of Talmis, Meroë, and Qasr Ibrim, three of the sites described as being conquered by Augustus, to provide a more refined interpretation of interactions at the frontier.

After a brief introduction to the theoretical discourse surrounding frontiers, I describe evidence for reconstructing Roman and Nubian emic conceptions of frontiers. I then present the Roman frontier narrative and compare this narrative with archaeological evidence from Talmis, Meroë, and Qasr Ibrim. Through this study, I suggest a nuanced reconstruction of the frontier zone between Roman Egypt and Nubia, at the time of its formation during the reign of Augustus. Specifically, I show that the frontier can be best described as a dynamic zone of interaction, which at various times was characterized by militaristic aggression, peaceful negotiations, and productive cultural exchange.

Mapping Herod's Harbor with the Pladypos ASV: New Discoveries at Caesarea Maritima, Israel
Bridget Buxton, University of Rhode Island, *Jacob Sharvit*, Israel Antiquities Authority, *Nikola Miskovic*, University of Zagreb, *John R. Hale*, University of Louisville, and *Dror Planer*, Israel Antiquities Authority

We present the results of the 2014 and 2015 Pladypos Project field seasons at Herod the Great's harbor in Caesarea Maritima, Israel, and report on the preliminary investigation of several new shipwrecks discovered in the area. The Pladypos Project is a collaboration between the University of Rhode Island, the Israel

Antiquities Authority Maritime Unit, the Center for Underwater Systems and Technologies at the University of Zagreb, and the University of Louisville. The Pladypos autonomous surface vehicle (ASV) is a robotic platform capable of a variety of site-recording and diver-support functions on shallow-water archaeological sites. It is designed to work in collaboration with scuba divers, who communicate and navigate with the robot's assistance via a custom-designed underwater tablet, creating a fully paperless (or "slate free") underwater survey and site-recording workflow. We demonstrate how the ASV produces fast and precise georeferenced photomosaics and bathymetric maps of underwater landscapes. The need for faster technology-assisted archaeological site mapping and rescue strategies in Israel was highlighted in the winter of 2010/2011, when unusually violent storms caused great devastation at Caesarea both above and below the water and exposed many previously buried artifacts and features. The frequent occurrence of powerful storms in recent years has also created opportunities for archaeologists—for example, by revealing new details about the construction and destruction of Caesarea's Herodian breakwaters and exposing several new shipwrecks. The chance discovery of an 11th-century C.E. hoard of almost 3,000 gold coins from a Fatimid-era shipwreck at Caesarea in February 2015 represents a typical scenario faced by Israel's maritime archaeological unit: a historically significant site that requires urgent salvage by a small dive team working with very limited time and resources. Over the course of two days in the summer of 2015, the Pladypos ASV surveyed a football-field sized area around the site of the discovery, recording the seafloor bathymetry to centimeter accuracy and taking approximately half a million high-resolution photographs. Divers were then able to remove the surface rubble covering the site and recover additional pockets of gold coins without being slowed down by time-consuming manual recording. We conclude with a consideration of future applications of this technology for underwater archaeological exploration, excavation, and conservation and plans for a 2016 expedition in which the Pladypos collaborates with autonomous aerial and underwater robots.

Excavations of an Aksumite Town, Baita Semati (Tigray, Northern Ethiopia)
Cinzia Perlingieri, Center for Digital Archaeology, and *Michael J. Harrower*, Johns Hopkins University

Throughout human history, the Tigray region of northern Ethiopia has been an important crossroads where people of the Mediterranean Basin, the Levant, Egypt, and South Arabia converged. Since the early 1900s, archaeological research in Ethiopia demonstrated that powerful local polities grew from ca. 1000 B.C.E. to achieve international prominence by the first century C.E. with the empire of Aksum existing until ca. 800 C.E. The Aksumites allied with Ptolemaic Egypt first and later with Romans and played an intermediary role in the commercial network between the Mediterranean and India. Between 200 and 400 C.E., Aksum emerged as the capital city of a powerful kingdom dominating the southern Red Sea trade. This paper summarizes the results of the excavations at the Aksumite town of Baita Semati in the Yeha region of northern Tigray and highlights the importance of this site in understanding political and religious change in ancient Ethiopia. Excavations at Baita Semati in 2011, 2012, and 2015 revealed residential and monumental architecture. Until recently, no Middle/Late Aksumite settlements beyond the vicinity of the capital of Aksum had ever been excavated. Baita Semati is of particular importance, as it spans two major historical turning points: (1) the apex of Aksum's control in Yemen between 500 and 600 C.E.; and (2) the Arab conquest of Egypt and the Muslim expansion along the Red Sea, which, combined with internal environmental and economic issues, contributed to the collapse of Aksum at some time between 800 and 900 C.E. Excavations at Baita Semati concentrated in two areas, Area A and Area B. Area A revealed a complex of rectangular buildings delimited by stone masonry walls, of a residential nature, with evidence of activities including food preparation and metal/glass working. Excavations in Area B brought to light a sixth- to seventh-century C.E. monumental palace with rooms and courtyards built with sandstone blocks and masonry walls. The finds associated with this structure, such as a gold signet ring, numerous imported amphoras, cow/bull figurines, and incense burners, suggest an administrative and/or religious character of this palace and likely its ancillary role to the capital of Aksum. The paper offers also an overview of our methodological approach, which integrates stratigraphic excavation and leading-edge digital technologies to facilitate data integration and analysis. These include GPS, GIS, photogrammetric, and three-dimensional representations of the site and an integrated database that allowed an advanced digital research process from data collection to post-excavation processing to reporting and analysis.

Miners or Pilgrims? A New Interpretation of the Faynan Region (Southern Jordan) in Late Antiquity

Ian W.N. Jones, University of California, San Diego

The Faynan region of southern Jordan is noteworthy primarily as the largest source of copper in the southern Levant, and this fact has structured much of the archaeological research conducted in the region. This is certainly true of the Roman period, when Faynan housed a state-controlled copper mine (or *metallum*) at the town of Phaino, known now as Khirbat Faynan. While much productive research has been conducted on the Roman mining industry in Faynan, the metallurgical bias of most projects, including environmental studies, has also biased the identification and explanation of nonmining sites.

This is especially true of Late Antique settlement in Faynan. As copper production at Phaino is attested only in historical sources of the third to fourth centuries C.E., our understanding of fifth- to eighth-century settlement relies heavily on archaeology. Scholars who have attempted to explain Late Antique settlement in Faynan have generally argued for continuity of the copper industry into the seventh century, based on evidence for continuity of sites interpreted as mining-related infrastructure. They assume that copper production ceased with the Islamic conquest, though this contradicts the consensus established by Islamicist archaeologists and historians that the conquest did not immediately cause major change. Some scholars instead place the decline of the copper industry in the fifth century but have little to say about the sixth to eighth centuries.

In this paper, I present an updated view of Late Antique settlement in Faynan. I present evidence for settlement continuity into the eighth century and demonstrate that this settlement was nonmetallurgical. This then requires a new explanatory model. My argument is based first on analysis of new material—primarily ceramics—from the recent University of California, San Diego Edom Lowlands Regional Archaeology Project (ELRAP) excavations at Khirbat Faynan, and second on reanalysis of data from earlier ELRAP surveys and excavations.

Faynan changed substantially between the third and eighth centuries, and I argue that the key transition—the demise of the state-controlled copper industry—occurred in the late fourth or fifth century. Faynan subsequently became a minor center of religious pilgrimage, commemorating Christian martyrs who were sent to the mines, as mentioned in third- to fourth-century historical sources. While this required that some infrastructure facilitating movement through the western valleys of Faynan remained in place through the eighth century, I demonstrate in this paper that there is no compelling reason to view this as evidence for the continuity of the copper industry beyond the fifth century.

SESSION 7J: Colloquium
New Developments in Cultural Property Protection in Conflict Zones

ORGANIZERS: *Laura Childs*, Cultural Heritage by Archaeology and Military Panel, *Nancy Wilkie*, Carleton College, and *Laurie Rush*, Ft. Drum Cultural Resource Manager

Colloquium Overview Statement

This symposium explores some of the new programs and processes developed to protect cultural property in conflict zones. The program scope is multinational and multidisciplinary in policy, methodology, and techniques. The U.S. Committee of the Blue Shield (USCBS) is broadening its initiatives to aid military missions, including collaboration with the AIA, CHAMP, and other organizations. The many, various international programs and processes to protect cultural property are explored for their scope, impact, and lessons learned. There are significant efforts to provide cultural property protection support to military commanders in the Middle East and Africa. The initiative to train college ROTC cadets about the importance of protecting cultural property is expanding significantly. The FBI Art Crimes Division is working with international organizations to counter the extensive illegal trafficking in looted antiquities. The Italian Army is collaborating with host nations to protect their national heritage. CyArk is collaborating with host nations to digitize their cultural heritage sites as part of the USAID's Ambassadors Fund for Cultural Preservation.

The Role of the U.S. Committee of the Blue Shield (USCBS) in the Protection of Cultural Property
Nancy Wilkie, Carleton College

The U.S. Committee of the Blue Shield (USCBS) was founded in 2006 to support the implementation of the 1954 Hague Convention for the Protection of Cultural Property in the Event of Armed Conflict. In addition to raising public awareness about the necessity to protect cultural property, USCBS has worked to train members of the military in all aspects of cultural property protection, whether in war or peacetime. More recently, USCBS has begun to create cultural heritage inventories of archaeological sites, museums, libraries, archives, and religious buildings in areas threatened by armed conflict so that they can be avoided in the event of military action by the U.S. military and its allies. To further this goal, USCBS has entered into Memoranda of Understanding with the Archaeological Institute of America (2015) and the Smithsonian Institution (2014), and it is currently in discussion with other cultural heritage organizations in the United States to form similar alliances.

International Military Cooperation for Cultural Property Protection
Laurie Rush, Ft. Drum Cultural Resource Manager

Sometimes the most important progress in the world of cultural property protection takes place behind the scenes. Over the past three years, a small group of academic and military experts have been working together to establish cultural property protection policy, doctrine, and guidance that can be applied to military coalitions and alliances as well as coordinated peacekeeping efforts. Beginning with the principles and signatories of the 1954 Hague Convention, these efforts include drafting of complex documents and diplomatic efforts to have the commitments these documents represent institutionalized and implemented by ministries of defense across the world. This paper discusses the importance of this type of work and implications for the future if these efforts are successful.

Current Cultural Property Protection Support for U.S. Combatant Commanders
James Zeidler, Colorado State University

The Combatant Command Cultural Heritage Action Group (CCHAG) was established in 2009 as an ad hoc organization of academic professionals, NGOs, DoD civilians, and other interested parties to promote Cultural Property Protection (CPP) awareness within the various DoD Combatant Commands (COCOMs) deployed around the world. This effort has taken the form of CPP training curricula and related educational products as well as technical support in areas such as geospatial data gathering on important cultural heritage sites in conflict areas to ensure that U.S. military forces do not unwittingly damage these resources. This paper addresses two current areas of technical support (1) to U.S. Southern Command (SOUTHCOM) in the development of advanced CPP training modules for military legal staff, military engineers, and military intelligence staff, and (2) to

U.S. Africa Command (AFRICOM) and U.S. Army Africa in the development of geospatial quality-assurance protocols for cultural heritage data collection. Emphasis is placed on the need for this kind of support in full-spectrum operations, not just instances of conflict.

Antiquities Trafficking as Organized Crime: Model and Implementation
Bonni Magness-Gardiner, FBI Art Crimes Division

The FBI Art Crime Team was established in 2004 and launched in 2005 with eight Special Agents, a program manager, and an analyst in response to the looting of the Baghdad Museum. Designed to address an immediate and severe problem, the team evolved over the years to investigate interstate transportation of stolen property, museum theft, and wire fraud/mail fraud involving works of art. In addition, we have investigated trafficking in Native American artifacts under Archaeological Resource Protection Act and Native American Graves Protection and Repatriation Act jurisdiction. Working with law-enforcement partners in the U.S. and overseas, in recent years the FBI has developed a model that looks at antiquities trafficking as organized crime. Identification of nodes of activities within the overall movement of archaeological items from the ground to the market allows us to focus our efforts strategically in pursuing specific investigations.

Cultural Communications, Identity, and Peacekeeping: How to Engage Cultural Heritage in Conflict Zones
Elena Croci, Italian Army Consultant

Monuments stand as memory of human history, especially in those regions that saw the origin of our civilization: Iraq, Syria, Libya, Afghanistan. In these places conflict originates also in the fragility of identities. As a consequence, monuments represent our millenary history, reminding us that the deep roots of our DNA are incessantly destroyed.

From Afghanistan to Libya, often with the collaboration of the Italian Army, a number of projects of cultural communication were set in motion to address these issues. Starting with the preservation of cultural heritage, these projects have sent messages to the local population and have fostered concrete actions dedicated to the creation of a renewed sense of belonging for the remote historical past.

This paper illustrates how, starting from a first phase of observation and study of the area, the primary goal of each project has always been the restoration of the awareness of the artistic ability of humanity throughout our millenary history. It also describes the communication strategies and techniques that, focusing on educational programs, that have the ability to promote a sense of pride and belonging in terms of regional identity, as well as to stimulate individual and collective confidence, all crucial elements for successful peacekeeping operations.

Three-Dimensional Recording for Inventory and Archive of At-Risk Cultural Heritage Sites

Elizabeth Lee, CyArk, Inc.

Three-dimensional digital recording has an important role to play in the inventory and archiving of at-risk cultural heritage sites. CyArk is a nonprofit with the mission of digitally preserving, by way of three-dimensional digital documentation and archiving, at-risk cultural heritage sites for the purposes of conservation, education, and public awareness. In 2013, CyArk launched the 500 Challenge—an initiative to digitally preserve 500 at-risk and culturally significant sites in five years' time. To achieve this goal and scale digital preservation, CyArk partners with universities and governments around the world to build capacity and engage the local stakeholders in the digital documentation of their own cultural heritage. Attendees can learn about this initiative through CyArk's discussion of a recent project in Pakistan, supported by USAID's Ambassadors Fund for Cultural Preservation.